D1606173

# Adulthood and Aging

**Vern L. Bengtson, PhD,** is AARP/University Chair in Gerontology and Professor of Sociology at the University of Southern California. He received his B.A. in 1959 at North Park College and his Ph.D. from the University of Chicago in 1963. He directs the Longitudinal Study of Generations, which he began at U.S.C. in 1970, and continues to be involved in research on the sociology of the life course, socialization, ethnicity,and aging. His publications include *The Social Psychology of Aging* (1973), *Youth, Generations, and Social Change* (with Robert Laufer, 1974), *Grandparenthood* (with Joan Robertson, 1985), *The Measurement of Intergenerational Relations* (with David Mangen and Pierre Landry, 1987) as well as two volumes recently published by Springer Publishing Company: *Intergenerational Linkages: Hidden Connections in American Society* (edited with Robert Harootyan, 1994) and *Adult Intergenerational Relations: Effects of Societal Change* (edited with Linda M. Burton and K. Warner Schaie). He has published over 170 papers in professional journals and books on aging, the life course, and families. He has been a member of review panels for the National Institute of Mental Health and the National Institute on Aging; he has twice won the Reuben Hill Award for outstanding research and theory on the family, presented by the National Council on Family Relations; and most recently he has been honored by the American Sociological Association's Distinguished Scholar Award from the Section on Aging.

# Adulthood AND Aging

## Research on Continuities and Discontinuities

**Vern L. Bengtson, PhD**

*Editor*

*A Tribute to Bernice Neugarten*

**SPRINGER PUBLISHING COMPANY**

Springer Publishing Company, Inc.
536 Broadway
New York, NY 10012-3955

*Cover design by Tom Yabut*
*Production Editor: Pam Lankas*

96 97 98 99 00 / 5 4 3 2 1

**Library of Congress Cataloging-in-Publication Data**

Adulthood and aging : research on continuities and discontinuities /
    Vern L. Bengtson, editor.
        p.   cm.
    Includes bibliographical references and index.
    ISBN 0-8261-9270-X
    1. Adulthood—Psychological aspects.   2. Aging—Psychological
aspects.   3. Adulthood.   4. Aging.   I. Bengtson, Vern L.
BF724.5.A36   1996
305.24—dc20                                                    96-519
                                                                CIP

Printed in the United States of America

*This volume is dedicated to
   Bernice L. Neugarten:*

*Scholar, pioneer in gerontology,
and intellectual mentor
to all of the scholars
whose contributions are represented
in this volume.*

# Contents

*Foreword* by James E. Birren      *xi*

*Preface*      *xv*

*Contributors*      *xvii*

**1   Psychological Immunity and the Late Onset Disorders**      **1**
    *David Gutmann*

    Comments by Bertram J. Cohler      13

**2   Conceptual and Empirical Advances in Understanding
     Aging Well Through Proactive Adaptation**      **18**
    *Eva Kahana and Boaz Kahana*

    Comments by David A. Chiriboga      41

**3   Continuities and Discontinuities in Very Late Life**      **46**
    *Steven H. Zarit*

    Comments by Fay Lomax Cook      66

**4   Life Course and Persistent Psychiatric Illness:
     Social Timing, Cohort, and Intervention**      **69**
    *Bertram J. Cohler, Susan A. Pickett, and Judith A. Cook*

    Comments by Morton A. Lieberman      96

**5   Continuities and Discontinuities in Gender Identity**      **98**
    *Margaret Hellie Huyck*

    Comments by Deborah T. Gold      122

 6  **A Non-Normative Old Age Contrast: Elderly Parents
     Caring for Offspring with Mental Retardation**       **124**
     *Sheldon S. Tobin*

     Comments by Boaz Kahana and Eva Kahana            143

 7  **Perspective on Adult Life Crises**                    **146**
     *Morton A. Lieberman*

     Comments by David Gutmann                         169

 8  **In Search of Continuities and Discontinuities Across
     Time and Culture**                                   **173**
     *David A. Chiriboga*

     Comments by Steven H. Zarit                       200

 9  **On-Time, Off-Time, Out of Time? Reflections on
     Continuity and Discontinuity from an Illness
     Process**                                            **204**
     *Gunhild O. Hagestad*

     Comments by Vern L. Bengtson                      223

10  **Continuities and Discontinuities in Sibling
     Relationships Across the Life Span**                 **228**
     *Deborah T. Gold*

     Comments by Lillian E. Troll                      244

11  **Modified-Extended Families Over Time: Discontinuity
     in Parts, Continuity in Wholes**                     **246**
     *Lillian E. Troll*

     Comments by Margaret H. Huyck                     269

12  **Continuities and Discontinuities in Intergenerational
     Relationships Over Time**                            **271**
     *Vern L. Bengtson*

     Comments by Gunhild O. Hagestad                   304

13  **Continuities and Discontinuities in Public Policy
    on Aging**                                          **308**
    *Robert H. Binstock*

    Comments by W. Andrew Achenbaum              325

14  **Public Support for Programs for Older Americans:
    Continuities Amidst Threats of Discontinuities**    **327**
    *Fay Lomax Cook*

    Comments by Robert H. Binstock               347

15  **Looking at Our Future Selves: Neugarten as
    Gerontology's Seer**                                **350**
    *W. Andrew Achenbaum and Celia Berdes*

    Comments by Sheldon S. Tobin                 368

16  **Profile of Bernice L. Neugarten**                 **371**

*Index*                                                 *377*

# Foreword

This book contains new data, theory, concepts, and ideas about human development in the adult years. Each of the contributors is a recognized researcher and scholar who has actively contributed to our knowledge of aging and human development and of the place of individuals in family and society.

This volume also honors Bernice Neugarten for her many contributions to the field of aging and human development. She has contributed ideas and research, but she has also contributed to the development of graduate students who have now emerged as senior scholars in the field. It is not just the things she has said that have stayed in our minds—the questions she has asked also remain. Never underestimate the power of a well-phrased question, of which Bernice is a master. Sometimes we need to let go of an earlier answer in place of a later one. But as we fumble with the answers we should return to the questions that Bernice is famed for asking.

Not only has she served as a formal mentor, as chair of doctoral dissertation committees of many of the authors who are represented in this volume, but she has also been the informal mentor of many persons outside the immediate family of scholars served by the Committee on Human Development of the University of Chicago.

It seems worthwhile to attempt to describe what *human development* stands for these days, and how it contrasts with other academic disciplines. It is my impression that human development as a field of study has some strengths that are different from the strengths of other fields, such as psychology, sociology, anthropology, or biology. I think of these disciplines as making strong contributions to methodology and as heavily deductive in character. They also engage in dissection of topics and often show drifts toward micro-problem orientation, reflecting categorical divisions of subject matter.

By contrast, when I reflect on human development, I conclude that its orientation is macro and that it is inductive and organismic in character, taking into account large and complex features of human beings. This approach results in a tendency toward integration of knowledge rather than the collection of information about isolated aspects of a topic. Also, I identify human development with a centripetal force in bringing together information, in contrast to the disciplines that seem to result in centrifugal particles of knowledge.

In human development the emphasis is on the individual developing in a social context. This also implies contributions of the genetic background, although that particular emphasis is not in the foreground of human development concerns.

The chapters in this volume were originally presented at a conference in honor of Bernice Neugarten's 79th Birthday. I was struck by the tone of the exchanges, which encouraged not only the expression of new and challenging ideas, but also replies from the other participants. I thought it was like sitting at a family dinner table under the instruction that we don't argue at dinner, but that "we discuss." I felt that the disagreements were expressed in a way that said "I like you, I love you, but in this instance I think you are wrong." Certainly that is a sign of a strong relationship in a strong family. This influence on the scholarly exchange represented in this volume arises from Bernice Neugarten, and it accounts for how she has contributed to human development scholarship as well as to the socialization of individual scholars.

Within scientific disciplines, activity often leads to strong career building but weak institution building. The academic institutions we pass through have strong effects on our lives. In this regard the human development tradition has obviously led to an atmosphere of support, criticism, and the encouragement of curiosity.

The chapters in this volume show that many aspects of human development in the adult years are problematic; crisis is not restricted to childhood and early adult life, but extends into the later years. A shared question about human development is this: What makes the difference between those persons who succumb to crises and suffer disordered lives, and those who differentiate further and come out with a sense of control and mastery and a high quality of life?

There are many facets of human development reported here that provide suggestions about creating conditions that encourage mastery of lives. As individuals, we can draw inferences from these chapters that are useful to us personally, but also we can adapt the information to helping individuals in a changing society. How this information can be translated into strategies for changing institutions and making them more constructive is by no means clear. Individuals are not alone in being inert to behavior change for greater adaptivity, institutions also suffer from this inertia, perhaps to an even greater extent.

Knowledge about human development has great relevance to how our society can help individuals maximize their lives as they undergo rapid change in many facets of daily life. This century has brought with it a gift of longer life greater than in any other period in history. Although there have been roles for smaller numbers of older persons in earlier society, never before have we been faced with a subnation of persons who have left the work force and face decades of further life. From the research presented in these chapters, we can learn how better to prepare individuals and society to optimize the outcomes of change.

The chapters in this volume have provided us a splendid opportunity. We can explore changes at the individual level and the societal level, going beyond what the disciplinary-focused scientists tell us about life, and integrate our discoveries at the dinner table of ideas provided by human development. This is what we have learned to do from Bernice Neugarten, from human development, and from ourselves.

Vern Bengtson, as organizer of the Conference and editor of this volume, is to be singled out for arranging this celebration of the potentials of human development in honor of Bernice, who cultivated them, and where mentorship helped launch Vern's towering career in the social psychology of aging.

JAMES E. BIRREN

# Preface

Throughout five decades of a brilliant scholarly career, Bernice Neugarten has added an incredible wealth of insight to the developing science of gerontology. From my perspective there is a consistent theoretical issue underlying most of her contributions, which in turn reflects one of the central themes in the study of human development and aging: continuities and discontinuities as individuals negotiate the psychological, interpersonal, and sociohistorical changes that occur over their adult life course. This helps to explain the title I have chosen to reflect her many contributions: *Adulthood and Aging—Research on Continuities and Discontinuities.*

In this volume, 19 of Bernice Neugarten's former students and colleagues explore models of continuity and contrast in adult development and apply them to their own current studies. The questions they examine reflect contemporary issues in psychiatry, psychology, policy analysis, social psychology, and sociology related to aging. Within their different topics, each of the authors address ways in which continuity over time is threatened by change over the life course, and also ways in which—paradoxically—some crucial continuities are maintained by adaptive change.

Several individuals should be thanked for their contributions to this volume. First and foremost is Pauline Robinson, until recently UPS Research Professor of Gerontology at the University of Southern California, who has served as managing editor of the volume and whose contributions are reflected in each chapter. Just after this volume went into production she was diagnosed with leukemia, and we wish her our best.

Special thanks go to Linda Hall, Administrative Coordinator in the Andrus Gerontology Center of the University of Southern California, who planned the conference on which this volume is based, assisted in manuscript preparation, and saw to the many exchanges between authors, managing editor, and editor that resulted in this volume.

Acknowledgments are due to Bertram Cohler, of the Committee on Human Development, University of Chicago; and Fay Lomax Cook, Northwestern University, who served as cohosts for the conference. Thanks also are due to Betty Cawelti, Administrative Coordinator of the Committee on Human Development; and Celia Berdes, Associate Director of Northwestern's Buehler Center on Aging, for their many hours of labor to make the conference a success.

On behalf of the contributors to this volume, I want to acknowledge our debt to the Retirement Research Foundation and to its Director, Marilyn Hennessey, for providing the funds to support the conference and the publication of its proceedings. The Retirement Research Foundation has benefited many important projects in gerontology over the years, and we appreciate the support of its Board of Directors, particularly Dr. John Santos, Professor Emeritus of Psychology at the University of Notre Dame, in this volume's commemoration of Bernice Neugarten's 50 years of scholarly contributions.

Support was also provided by the Robert J. Havighurst Memorial Funds at the University of Chicago, administered through the Committee on Human Development. Because Dr. Havighurst was Bernice Neugarten's mentor at the University of Chicago, as well as the founder of the "Human Development" tradition there, this support reflects a most appropriate example of scholarly continuity across several generations—and cohorts—of individual scholars, beginning in the 1930s and continuing into the 21st century of research on the psychological process of aging.

Finally, I want to acknowledge my own profound debt to my teacher, friend, and mentor, Bernice L. Neugarten. She has provided insightful criticism and unstinting support to me since my graduate studies at the University of Chicago and through the years since then. My personal experience of her support is echoed by the other contributors to this volume. Thus: to you, Bea, this book is dedicated.

VERN L. BENGTSON, Editor

# Contributors

**W. Andrew Achenbaum, PhD,** teaches history at the University of Michigan, Ann Arbor, where he serves as Deputy Director of the Institute of Gerontology. His research focuses on the history of the elderly in the United States, and has recently completed a book on the history of gerontology.

**Vern L. Bengtson, PhD,** is AARP/University Chair in Gerontology and Professor of Sociology at the University of Southern California. He is Past President of the Gerontological Society of America and directs the 25-year Longitudinal Study of Generations at USC.

**Celia Berdes** is Associate Director of the Buehler Center on Aging, McGaw Medical Center of Northwestern University, and Assistant Professor of Medicine at Northwestern University Medical School, Chicago, Illinois.

**Robert H. Binstock, PhD,** is Professor of Aging, Health, and Society, at Case Western Reserve University. He is a former President of the Gerontological Society of America and has published 17 books on public policy and aging.

**James E. Birren, PhD, DSc,** is Associate Director of the UCLA Center on Aging at the Multicampus Program of Geriatric Medicine and Gerontology, and Adjunct Professor of Medicine/Gerontology, University of California, Los Angeles. He is also founding Executive Director and Dean Emeritus of the Ethel Percy Andrus Gerontology Center at the University of Southern California. He is Series Editor of the internationally renowned *Handbooks on Aging* and has over 250 publications in academic journals and books.

**David A. Chiriboga, PhD,** is Professor and Chair, Department of Graduate Studies, School of Allied Health Sciences, University of Texas Medical

Branch, Galveston, Texas. He also serves on the faculties of Preventive Medicine and Internal Medicine and is Associate Director of the Center on Aging for his campus.

**Bertram J. Cohler, PhD,** is William Rainey Harper Professor of Social Sciences, The College and Departments of Psychology (and The Committee on Human Development), Psychiatry, and Education, The University of Chicago. Dr. Cohler has served on the faculty of The University of Chicago since 1969.

**Fay Lomax Cook, PhD,** is Professor of Education and Social Policy at Northwestern University and is currently Associate Director of the Center for Urban Affairs and Policy Research at Northwestern University.

**Judith A. Cook, PhD,** is Professor of Psychology and Psychiatry and Director of Mental Health Services Research, The University of Illinois at Chicago.

**Deborah T. Gold, PhD,** is Assistant Professor of Medical Sociology in the Departments of Psychiatry and Sociology and Senior Fellow in the Center for the Study of Aging and Human Development at Duke University Medical Center. She is currently principal investigator of an intervention study with older osteoporotic women living in life-care communities.

**David Gutmann, PhD,** is Professor of Psychiatry and Education at Northwestern University, where he directs doctoral studies in the clinical psychology of later life. He has taught developmental and clinical psychology at Harvard, the University of Michigan and, most recently, at Northwestern.

**Gunhild O. Hagestad, PhD,** is Professor of Sociology at the University of Oslo and Associate Professor of Human Development and Social Policy at Northwestern University. Her research and writing have focused on intergenerational relations and life-course analysis, with a special emphasis on how demographic change has affected lives and relationships.

**Margaret Hellie Huyck, PhD,** is Professor of Psychology at the Illinois Institute of Technology in Chicago. Her research and teaching have focused on adult development and aging, with particular emphasis on the ways gender differences develop over the life course.

**Boaz Kahana, PhD,** is Professor and Director of the Center for Applied Gerontological Research at Cleveland State University. He is currently President of the Ohio Network of Gerontological Consultants and Member at Large on the executive committee of the Association of Gerontological Higher Education and the Behavioral and Social Science Section of the Gerontological Society of America.

**Eva Kahana, PhD,** is Pierce T. and Elizabeth D. Robson Professor of Humanities, Chair of the Department of Sociology, and Director of the Elderly Care Research Center at Case Western Reserve University. She has received the Gerontological Society of America Distinguished Mentorship Award.

**Morton A. Lieberman, PhD,** is Professor of Psychology at the University of California, San Francisco, and Director of both The Aging and Mental Health Program and the Alzheimer Center. Throughout his career he has focused on two central areas of research: the study of adult development and the investigation of change-induction groups.

**Susan A. Pickett, PhD,** is Research Assistant Professor, Department of Psychiatry, Northwestern University Medical School, and Project Director, Thresholds National Research and Training Center on Rehabilitation and Mental Illness in Chicago. Her present research interests focus on social processes and life-course study within families that include a member hospitalized for psychiatric illness.

**Sheldon S. Tobin, PhD,** is Professor in the School of Social Welfare at the University at Albany of the State University of New York. After receiving his doctorate in 1963 from the University of Chicago, he remained on the faculty until coming to Albany in 1982. From 1985 through 1988, he served as Editor-in-Chief of *The Gerontologist.*

**Lillian E. Troll, PhD,** is Professor Emerita, Rutgers University (Psychology Department) and Adjunct Professor, Human Development and Aging and Medical Anthropology, University of California, San Francisco. She has written or edited 12 books on human development and aging.

**Steven H. Zarit, PhD,** is a researcher, educator, and clinician whose work has focused on the mental health problems of older people and their families. He is currently Professor of Human Development and Assistant Director of the Gerontology Center at The Pennsylvania State University; he also holds the appointment as Adjunct Professor, University College of Health Science, Jönköping, Sweden.

# CHAPTER 1

# Psychological Immunity and the Late Onset Disorders

## David Gutmann

### QUANTITATIVE MODELS OF
### LATE ONSET DISORDER

Constancy and change—the themes of our *festschrift* for Bernice Neugarten—are the warp and the woof of all mental processes, normal as well as pathological. In this chapter I will try to clarify their contributions to the late onset mental illnesses of later life.

These special disorders have, over the years, posed a very interesting question to the faculty and students of the Older Adult Program at Northwestern University: namely, why do the afflicted elders, up to now reasonably intact, decompensate—usually for the first time—in this particular season of life? For the most part, our late onset patients are survivors: After a troubled childhood, often involving the loss of one or both parents, they have persevered, they have lived long lives, sometimes marked by trouble, but also by reasonable degrees of love and work. These survivors have not succumbed to the thronging insults of the earlier years; why then do they translate the troubles of the later years into pathogens of clinical scale?

To such questions, the rather dismissive reply from conventional geropsychiatry comes in the quantitative idiom of "science." By this calculus, the increased rate of loss and insult in later life equals greater stress; and more stress presumably equals increased probability of breakdown. This is the "camel's back" model of pathogenesis: The laden beast will endure until a critical mass of burden is reached, at which point any additional straw will cause a decisive rupture of its back. This model does not specify the destructive agents; given a critical mass of fodder, any additional straw can bring about the sudden cracking of the dromedary's back.

## A QUALITATIVE APPROACH TO STRESS

But the camel's back model does not jibe with findings from our clinical investigations of the older patient. In the course of these we do find specificity of stressor, including some paradoxes—a crippling arthritis or a hip fracture can have a more pathogenic effect than a potentially lethal cancer, or deaths of family and friends. Thus, for specially predisposed individuals, threats to mobility can be more crippling, in the psychological as well as the physical sense, than a barrage of potentially lethal but nondisabling diseases. Then too, we find that the great majority of elders—those who do not end up on our treatment services—tote their often considerable bales of straw with resignation, even good humor, and without succumbing to late onset disorder.

Burden, it seems, is subjectively rather than objectively weighted: One man's meat is another man's poison. This being the case, no standard catalogue of later life losses and insults—whether "on time" or "off time"—can steer our diagnostic studies. Meeting a new patient, we still have to ask, "Why does this particular insult provoke in this person and at this time a pathogenic response?" Reaching for answers, we have to deconstruct the halo of idiosyncratic and often catastrophic meanings that can surround a pathogenic stressor—such as a severe arthritis—that might otherwise rank rather low on any objective scale of burden. In this manner, relying on the naturalistic, clinical interview, we open up the patient's unique history of trauma, of victories and defeats; how were victories gained (or undone); how were defeats avoided, reversed—or invited?

In short, the investigation of the immediate disease precipitant leads us into the crucial but usually overlooked self system. The predisposed, historic individual mediates between precipitants and symptoms, and can overburden seemingly minor stresses with destructive meanings. Pursuing this line, we usually find that the last straw breaks the camel's back not because of its added weight, but because the camel is already giving up the fight. But at the same time, we gain new leverage for useful interventions.

## THE PSYCHO-IMMUNE SYSTEM

Going beyond the level of individual pathology and adaptation, I look at the entire psychological system of later life as a kind of beleaguered organism, acting in continuously shifting ways to preserve, in the face of internal and external change, certain vital regularities and consistencies. More to the point, I find it clinically useful to look at the psyche as a kind of immune system, one that—like the body's immune system—is prone to degenerate in later life.

There may be more than a metaphor here: Accumulating evidence from psychoimmunology (see Hammond, 1991; Schindler, 1985; Schleifer, Keller, Siris, Davis, & Stein, 1985) points to a relationship between depressive illness and T-cell attrition[1] suggesting that the psychic and the physical immune systems are extensions of each other, and that both may be components of an overarching, meta-immune system. Like many seeming banalities, "A sound mind in a sound body" is turning out to be scientific truth.

In the course of normal development, we construct, in tandem, the psychic and the physical immune systems. Developing together, these two crucial institutions appear to be co-active: Losses of physical health put heavy burdens on the psyche, and losses of emotional balance lay stresses on the body that the somatic immune system is not well organized to withstand.

Although they mobilize different agents and mechanisms, these two immune systems work toward equivalent ends—the preservation of a continuously benign and self-consistent internal environment (see Staines, Brostoff, & James, 1993, p. 8). Thus, the physical immune system preserves, through a variety of agents and functions, the internal bodily environment in a relatively pristine state: free of toxic agents that are external in origin (viruses, bacteria, poisons, etc.) and could bring about infections or degenerative change. The somatic immune system also cleanses the body of internally generated "alien" elements by removing the debris of dead cells so as to speed the healing of wounds and repair the compromised boundaries of the skin and internal organs. The psychological immune system in its turn acts to preserve the inner environment of the self in a relatively benign state. While the physical immune system monitors the boundaries of the body for potentially noxious elements, the psycho-immune system monitors and maintains the boundary between self and other, or between the familiar, daily self and its unconscious hinterland. Thus, it acts through its various functions to moderate extreme mood swings; to separate fantasy, recognized as such, from the picture of external reality; to keep intruding thoughts out of consciousness and intruding impulses out of behavior; and finally, to temper emotional reactions to any dangerous excitements.[2]

Effective psycho-immunity is a by-product of realistic self-esteem and realistic trust—including a realistic trust in the self, its persistence, its predictability, and its seasoned, tested resources. Trust and self-esteem[3] are the T-cell lymphocytes of the psycho-immune system; the individual furnished with these protections can tolerate the strange, the stranger, and the ever-changing, unfamiliar aspects of the outside world.

Thus, when the psycho-immune system and its boundaries are safely in place, when the "inside" will not be infected by exogenous toxins, then attention and action can safely shift to the exciting world, and to the openings it presents for productive, masterful action. As a consequence, the development of all the organs, senses, and muscles that serve external mastery, communion, and exploration can freely go forward. The appetites for exploration and change are underwritten by a relatively constant, stable inner life.

Trust and self-esteem are in part based on "communities" of good internal presences that have become, in the course of psychosocial development, the essential architectures of self. As infants, human beings live at the center of *transitional space,* a domain peopled with *transitional objects*—others who are known only insofar as they relate to us, and through whom we experience, in external guise, the emotions that they arouse in us. At that early point in development, the self–other distinctions (ego boundaries) are porous—the other is known as an extension of the self, the self is experienced as an extension of the other: "I am my Mommy's little boy." But as we grow and individuate, we separate; forming personal boundaries, we firm up the distinctions between ourselves and those who sponsored the earlier stanzas of development. Trusting them to be on hand when needed, we allow them to have their own unique, distinguishing qualities, different from our own, and to go their own ways.

# DEVELOPMENT AND TRANSITIONAL SPACE

As psychological development advances, the transitional space recedes, away from our primary caretakers, who are left in their own space, in "otherness," beyond our self-boundaries. But the transitional space is never completely abandoned. Receding toward the center, it carries with it, in the form of identifications, the desirable qualities of the other that are conserved as trusted qualities of the self. Thus, in psychologically mature individuals, the transitional space is retained within the self-boundaries; it becomes the arena of dreams, and of fantasies; and it is the inner ground on which developing parts of the psyche meet and bond with valued aspects of the formative other. In later development this blending of other with self is no longer an automatic side effect of porous self-boundaries; in maturity the union is reality-based, founded on imitation, on learning from the other, on the mobilization of self-potentials that bring about structural changes toward mastery. The bonding of the self to selected and valued parts of the other still takes place within transitional space, but is now a consequence of realistic mastery gained in the "apprentice" role. The physical immune system accepts donations of blood and tissue only from compatible donors; by the same token, the psyche becomes more selective, taking in from the space of the other only what it requires, only what conforms to the growing designs of self. As it takes control of inner space, the psychic immune system is strengthened, and made secure; it should last as long as the psychic structures themselves, and the brain in which they are housed.

In short, by becoming internally what we have relinquished externally, we can move ahead, now more trusting of ourselves, into the next developmental passage. Having at the same time strengthened our psycho-immune systems we can tolerate contact with alien agents: the toxic possibilities, both within the self and outside of it, that new development and new ventures may bring into play.

## IMMUNE SYSTEM BREAKDOWN:
## THE LATE ONSET DISORDERS

At-risk individuals do not assemble protective and protected internal assemblages. Early on, our at-risk older patients had been forcibly shunted to an alternate developmental track. From the beginning, they were precocious survivors—of early parent loss, family disruption, and major physical trauma. Their formative tragedies did not—and could not—leave them with an internal residue of good presences. Although they survived their early years, they did not exit them with the internal bases of self-esteem secured and intact. In their cases, the transitional space has never shrunken within the self-boundaries; instead, much as in the early years, it still extends outward to embrace an external community composed of transitional objects: real persons who are experienced—much as in childhood—not as truly separate individuals, but in terms of their usefulness, their service to the self (see Giovacchini, 1993; Winnicott, 1953, pp. 1–26). The immune process of at-risk survivors is not formed on secured structures of the psyche; instead, it uses real persons "out there," who are experienced as if they were figments and extensions of the self. The potential discrepancy between reality and fantasy, between the true qualities of the transitional persons and the virtual reality that has been imposed on them, puts the externally based psycho-immune system chronically at risk.

From the beginning, our late onset patients divide along two major developmental trajectories, each of which leads to a psycho-immune system of distinct character and special vulnerabilities. Some survive their early, formative trauma via an extroverted solution, based on fantasies of providers and rescuers to be sought in the outer world; by contrast, the introversive, autoplastic types seek their redemption internally, in grandiose and narcissistic fantasies about themselves. We will first consider the alloplastic, extroverted individuals.[4]

### The Alloplastic Extroverts

Trusting children, convinced that new caretakers and sponsors will always be there for them, can begin to let go, can individuate from their primary caretakers. But the troubled early experience of the at-risk extroverts does not lead to a condition of trust. Lacking reliable others, they continue looking, even into later life, for the good mothers and good fathers that they never had—or that they had known too briefly. Not having relinquished and mourned their lost caretakers, they have not gone through basic maturational processes: internalizing, letting go, and moving on. Striving for pseudo-independence, some at-risk extroverts may give up on people, while holding on to their need for outside sources of help; these candidates for addiction comb their worlds for the intoxicant substances that are—in their eyes—more trustworthy than inconstant people.

Yearnings for primary relationships are expressed as transferences: that is, in enduring fantasies, shaped as expectations that the lost but unrelinquished primary relationships of the family of orientation will be discovered (or rediscovered) in new situations (for example, in their families of procreation). Via such transferences, they will turn wives into mothers, husbands into fathers, and—in later life—their own children into parents.

In another sense, transferences represent an extension of subjective transitional space into objective social space—the "space of the other." Carrying transitional space beyond the physical boundaries of the self, transferences provide continual grounding, as in early childhood, for the linkage of self and other. Accordingly, when they find others who confirm their transferences—who are, that is, like good parents—then the at-risk extroverts will be comforted and stabilized: The lost condition of care has been restored. Thus, so long as the transference partners conform to the unchanging expectations that are mapped onto them, psycho-immunity (albeit externally located) is maintained, and the at-risk extroverts can endure all the buffets of change and loss without too much distress and without recourse to psychosomatic illness. The straws may pile up, but the camel's back does not break.

But in later life the continuing reliance on transitional objects nested in transitional space carries phase-specific risks. In early life, the transitional space is peopled with nurturing personnel, usually parents who stand ready to meet the child's demands for unstinting care. The subjective demands of the child are not overruled but confirmed by the surrounding, objective realities. But the older at-risk person is much less likely to meet a sponsoring, reciprocal social world. Internalized presences are generated by the self, and conform by definition to its expectations; but real people, "out there," are not compelled to meet and satisfy transference-based expectations. Accordingly, the niche of the vulnerable person is always at risk; particularly in later life (when "cuteness" is no longer an attribute), transferences are more likely to be refuted than accredited by the significant social world.

## The Autoplastic Introverts

In contrast to the extroverts, who continue to hunt through the world for the lost parent, the introverted types concede their trust to themselves: to a narcissistic legend of their own omnipotentiality, or to an illusory conception of their own complete self-sufficiency. Like the disappointed baby who, in Erikson's terms, "finds its thumb and damns the world," the essential, narcissistic legend of introverts is that they need nobody but themselves—that they have, in their own mind and in their own body, all the resources that they and their dependents might require (E. Erikson, personal communication, September, 1962). Their founding myth is that they are their own parents; they feed from the bottles that they alone have made and filled.

In the case of introverts, then, transference is to themselves—to a legend of all-inclusiveness and self-sufficiency. When they were very young, primitive fantasies of omnipotence may have been sufficient to soothe and sustain at-risk introverts, but as they mature, the boundaries between fantasy and reality are tightened, and flagrant illusions, now recognized as such, no longer suffice to maintain psycho-immunity. The myth of the self must be confirmed out there, by significant representatives of external reality.

In response, the introversive fantasist creates psychosocial niches out of the raw material of the social habitat. The subjective community is populated by special individuals willing to take special roles in their psychodrama. While the extroverts comb the world for appropriate vessels for their transferences, the introversive mythicists recruit those who will direct their transferences to them. Some adherents believe in the special legend, agreeing that the fantasist is indeed great. Others of their niche enact parts in the contra-legend: The mythicists proclaim their complete self-sufficiency; it is these OTHERS of their niche who are needy—and, preferably, dependent on them. Where the mythicists are whole, these OTHERS are damaged—and need them to be made whole; and where the mythicists are brave, these OTHERS are cowardly, and need their courage. In short, the myth-makers use selected others as self-objects, to extract the dangerous, contra-legendary aspects out of themselves. Via selected members of the niche, and to sustain the virtual reality of the founding myth, they export these dangerous contents into the ambient niche, into the convoy that has been assembled to receive them.

In short, so long as the founding myth is maintained in its pristine form, albeit by an external bodyguard, the psycho-immune system retains its integrity, and the introversive mythicist can endure, without significant pathology, the escalating insults of later life.

## Losing the Niche

For both the extroverts and the introversive mythicists, the conditions of security are not contained internally, where constancy is assured, but are maintained externally, in congregations that are subject to all the shifting social weathers. In later life, aging at-risk individuals become like wartime convoy commodores, trying to hold their ships in coherent formations despite all the vagaries of weather, ship speeds, and enemy action.

In the autumn of life, the forces that attack niches are stronger than those that bind them together. Older individuals lose access to the special habitats—the family of procreation, the workplace, the playing field—out of which new psychosocial niches can be formed, or established ones regenerated. The nest empties, kinfolk and friends die, workers retire. Older individuals, in any event, get tired and lack the energy to continually monitor, patch, and reassemble their raveling networks.

Losing their special niches, at-risk elders also lose the supply lines to and from the special continuities and constancies that they require. The extroverts lose the ratified transferences that provide continuity and linkage between their families of orientation and, for example, their families of procreation. Thus, when women assert themselves after child raising tasks have been accomplished, concentrate on their own development, and refuse to mother their aging husbands, the result for the man can be a significant depression, or, more commonly, a chronic psychosomatic disorder (Gutmann, 1994, chap. 11). The hospital inpatient unit, with its corps of concerned, TLC-giving nurses, is richly furnished with potential "mothers." As a special habitat the hospital can offer the last repository for maternal transferences; as such, it can easily become the last niche of the dependent older man.

In their turn, when the introversive mythicists lose touch with their admirers and dependents, they lose a vital illusion: that their founding legend is continuous with and co-extensive with shared, consensual reality. But the unsupported personal legend is not abandoned; instead it is recognized for what it is and always has been: a fantasy, and a persecutory one at that. As an older patient put it, "I'm not the man I used to be—and I never was."

Deprived of their believable legend, the introversive mythicists are at risk to become psychotic. In order to restore faith in the myth (and to counter depression) they will often distort their awareness, and spin a paranoid caricature of their actual circumstances: Others have plotted their downfall. The myth is indeed conserved, but at the price of reality and sanity.

In sum, as they lose their certainties, whether found in the world or in themselves, the at-risk individuals—extroverts as well as introversive mythicists—lose their long-maintained psycho-immune system. Without it, they are rendered catastrophically vulnerable to change and loss. It is only at this relatively late point in pathogenesis, after the psychic immune system has been degraded, that the camel's back model becomes relevant. Then and only then will the at-risk individual be undone by the last straw, by the psychological equivalent of opportunistic infections.

Conventional geropsychiatrists confound effects with causes, the incidental symptoms with the full disease process. We begin to bring AIDS under control not by treating Kaposi's sarcoma—by then it is already too late—but by studying the prior attack of the HIV virus on the somatic immune system and learning how to strengthen that system in its own right, so that it will never allow the virus to gain entry. Similarly, if geropsychiatrists troubled to study the historically predisposed patient, they would discern the qualitative roots of disorder, and recognize that the late-blooming pathology begins (as in AIDS) with the degradation of the psycho-immune system, and not with exposure to the latest insult—the psychological equivalent of the latest virus.

It is not enough to treat the incidental symptoms of late onset depression, anxiety, or paranoia; we have to study—so that we can eventually either restore or render unnecessary—the protective structures and functions of the psycho-immune system. To this end, we have to place the historic rather than the symptomatic patient at the forefront of our study and treatment.

# NOTES

[1] There is also a marked possibility—one still awaiting full empirical testing—that certain phase-specific mental disorders of later life actually *protect* the somatic immune system. Thus, paraphrenia (a late-blooming form of paranoia) is, psychologically speaking, the antagonist of the late life depressions: Paraphrenic manifestations suppress depressive symptoms, and also predict—again, by contrast to the late depressions—to longevity (see Hammond, 1991). Possibly then, by suppressing depressive symptoms, the paraphrenias may also counter the immunosuppressive effects of late depressions.

[2] For a somatic analogy we think of the homeostatic mechanisms involved in the regulation of body temperature—a crucial constant. A few degrees variation either up or down is a sign of somatic crisis—fever, or hypothermia. In its response to ever-changing internal and external circumstances, the body calls on constantly changing means to maintain a constant body temperature.

[3] For this insight, regarding the "immunizing" role of self-esteem, I am grateful to Peter L. Giovacchini, M.D.

[4] As the growing individual increases in mastery, it learns also to recognize its own limitations and the limits of parental figures—the early prototypes of the now internal panel of good presences. But the increasing split between the internal ideals and the "corrupted" external reality does not lead to complete disillusion, to an abandonment of the good internal presences. In the natural course of events, we should come to see our parents realistically; but the inner sense of the ideal, omnicompetent parent is not erased; rather, it finds its reciprocal in (and preserves) religion and the public life. Heroes, unordinary beings are still sought in the space of the other; but now that space is located very far from the ordinary precincts of the home. It is in the heavens, or in the society's legendary past.

# REFERENCES

Giovacchini, P. (1993). *Borderline patients, the psychosomatic focus and the therapeutic process.* Northvale, NJ: Aronson.

Gutmann, D. (1994). *Reclaimed powers: Men and women in later life.* Evanston, IL: Northwestern University Press.

Hammond, J. (1991). *A case study of the relocated: A detailed examination of residents and their family caretakers during a radical change.* Unpublished doctoral dissertation, Northwestern University, Evanston, IL.

Schindler, B. (1985). Stress, affective disorders, and immune function. *Medical Clinics of North America, 69*(3), 81–87.

Schleifer, S., Keller, S., Siris, S., Davis, K., & Stein, M. (1985). Depression and immunity. *Archives of General Psychiatry, 42,* 129–133.

Staines, N., Brostoff, J., & James, K. (1993). *Introducing Immunology.* London: Mosby.

Winnicott, D. (1953). *Playing and reality.* London: Tavistock.

# Comments

## Bertram J. Cohler

S tudy of psychopathology across the course of adult life has important implications for understanding more general questions regarding continuity and change over time in adult personality. It also provides an opportunity for study of the interplay of genetic, social, and personal factors and their impact on personality change over time. Conversely, concepts and methods drawn from normative life course social science play an important role in understanding the origin and course of psychopathology. Placing the study of psychopathology within the context of life course social science further informs our understanding of factors associated with both first and later episodes of distress across the adult years. This mutual contribution of normative life course social science and developmental psychopathology is well exemplified in the work of David Gutmann and his colleagues in their continuing study of late onset disorders (Gutmann, Griffin, & Grunes, 1982).

Gutmann has observed that there is a group of middle-aged and older adults who perhaps showed some problems in adjustment earlier in life, but who are able to remain psychologically resilient over the course of several decades and first succumb to an episode of major psychiatric illness (generally affective disorder) somewhat later in life. However, in contrast with conventional explanations in geropsychiatry, which posit that burdens accumulate until they trigger episodes of distress profound enough to require intervention, Gutmann argues that quite specific life changes result in episodes of personal distress. Further, he asserts that reported burdens are specific to particular persons and are not easily represented in normative scales of the magnitude of life changes, such as the Holmes and Rahe Social Readjustment Scale (1967).

*13*

One of the most puzzling questions in the life course study of major psychopathology is the timing of first and subsequent episodes over the course of life (Clausen, 1985; Cohler & Ferrono, 1987; Pogue-Geile, 1991). Most forms of major psychopathology make a first appearance in early adult life; it is assumed that the increased pressure of adjustment to the major roles of the adult years (such as work, partnership, and generativity) lead to enhanced risk for psychopathology among young adults otherwise more predisposed or vulnerable as a consequence of such innate factors as enhanced genetic loading or sequelae of pregnancy and birth complications (Walker, Davis, & Gottlieb, 1991). However, there is a group of patients who only succumb to a first episode of disorder in midlife. Appearance of symptoms among these patients with "late onset disorder" (generally affective disorders) most often takes place within a changing configuration of perceived burden and physical health. Intervention must address those factors that are able to restore a sense of personal vitality. Gutmann and his colleagues have proposed at least two routes through the life course that lead to quite different experiences of illness and predict quite different changes. There are, on one hand, those persons focused primarily upon the external world, who rely upon alloplastic adaptation, are oriented primarily toward the external world, and are able to take advantage of personal resources and social support. On the other hand are those persons focused primarily upon the internal world, who prefer an autoplastic solution relying upon complex constructions of sources of comfort and support. Those older adults more oriented to the external world rely upon external support at times of increased distress while those more oriented to the internal world focus to a greater extent upon imagined constructions that involve others. Different factors are associated with first episodes of mental illness among these two types of older adults, and quite different factors may be important in fostering rehabilitation.

Gutmann's portrayal of two types of pathways through the adult years, which rely upon quite different sources of support, and quite different interventions leading to enhanced functioning, presents an important opportunity for systematic study. Using the manner in which others are experienced, as formulated through detailed interview, it should be possible to develop an empirical typology which could be applied in prospective study of adult lives over time. At least to some extent, his distinction is consistent with findings both from personality study (such as that inspired by Jung's complex formulation of personality, represented by the Myers-Briggs inventory of psychological types based on Jung's formulations; (Myers Briggs & Myers Briggs, 1980; Thorne & Gough, 1991), and also from work on temperament (Kagan 1980, 1994; Kagan & Moss, 1963; Thomas & Chess, 1977; Thomas, Chess, Birch, Hertzig, & Korn, 1963). The studies of shy children grown up by Kagan and his colleagues and by Caspi, Elder, and their colleagues (Caspi, Elder, & Bem, 1988; Caspi, Elder, & Herbener, 1990), in their studies of shy children grown up, provide important first insights in the study of persons taking quite different routes to continued adjustment across the course of life.

The typology portrayed by Gutmann has implications both for the study of the life course and also for the study of both resilience and recovery from episodes of disturbance. Gutmann's emphasis on discrete life changes, experientially meaningful to the prospective patient, rather than a view of onset focusing on accumulated burden and role strain, is consistent with both the view on vulnerability and episode proposed by Beck and Worthen (1972) and the formulation of vulnerability and episode portrayed by Zubin and his colleagues (Zubin, Magaziner, & Steinhauer, 1983; Zubin & Spring, 1977). This approach suggests that episodes of disturbance may be the outcome of a multifactor process including both increased genetic loading for particular modes of major psychiatric disorder and particular life changes, idiosyncratically experienced by prospective patients as particularly disruptive or upsetting.

Comparison of the life course of those patients experiencing a first episode of disorder only in midlife with those patients succumbing to a first episode of disorder across the years of early adulthood raises important questions for life course social science. While it is possible that late onset patients are more disposed or vulnerable to major psychopathology, encountering particular, idiosyncratic, and possibly disruptive life changes by chance only later in life, it is more likely that these are persons who may have a somewhat lower genetic loading for disorder, or for whom pregnancy and birth insults were somewhat reduced. It is important to study the meanings which adults provide for changes taking place in their life in order to understand the significance of particular life changes to continued adjustment. Gutmann's report shows the importance of understanding the subjective experience of both expectable and unexpected, generally adverse changes for oneself and other family members in order to understand the significance of the timing of particular episodes of disorder taking place across the second half of life.

While recognizing the problems with present diagnostic schemes, it is still important to provide at least some phenomenological detail regarding the nature of symptoms and course, and response to intervention. The distinction between autoplastic and alloplastic adaptation across the course of life must be understood within the nature and severity of disturbance. Gutmann's discussion highlights the importance of studying major psychopathology from a life course perspective; a focus on persons succumbing to a first episode of distress only in middle and later life represents a particularly important group of patients to study over relatively long periods of time in order to better understand the determinants of resilience across the course of life. Findings from this group of patients may provide important additional information regarding the determinants of adjustment and psychopathology from childhood to oldest age.

# REFERENCES

Beck, J., & Worthen, K. (1972). Precipitating stress, crisis theory, and hospitalization in schizophrenia and depression. *Archives of General Psychiatry, 26,* 123–129.

Caspi, A., Elder, G., & Bem, D. (1988). Moving away from the world: Life-course patterns of shy children. *Child Development, 24,* 824–831.

Caspi, A., Elder, G., & Herbener, E. (1990). Childhood personality and the prediction of life-course patterns. In L. Robins & M. Rutter (Eds.), *Straight and devious pathways from childhood to adulthood* (pp. 13–35). New York: Cambridge University Press.

Clausen, J. (1985). Mental illness and the life course. In P. Baltes & O. G. Brim, Jr. (Eds.), *Life-span development and behavior* (Vol. 6, pp. 204–242). New York: Academic Press.

Cohler, B., & Ferrono, C. (1987). Schizophrenia and the life course. In N. Miller & G. Cohen (Eds.), *Schizophrenia and aging* (pp. 189–199). New York: Guilford.

Gutmann, D., Griffin, B., & Grunes, J. (1982). Developmental contributions to late-onset affective disorders. In P. B. Baltes & O. G. Brim, Jr. (Eds.), *Life-span development and behavior* (Vol. 4, pp. 244–263). New York: Academic Press.

Holmes, T., & Rahe, R. (1967). The social readjustment rating scale. *Journal of Psychosomatic Research, 11,* 213–218.

Kagan, J. (1980). Perspectives on continuity. In O. G. Brim, Jr., & J. Kagan (Eds.), *Continuity and change in human development* (pp. 26–74). Cambridge: Harvard University Press.

Kagan, J. (1994). *Galen's prophecy: Temperament in human nature.* New York: BasicBooks.

Kagan, J., & Moss, H. (1963). *From birth to maturity.* New York: Wiley.

Myers Briggs, I., & Myers Briggs, P. (1980). *Gifts differing* (10th anniversary edition). Palo Alto, CA: Consulting Psychologists Press.

Pogue-Geile, M. (1991). The development of liability to schizophrenia: Early and late developmental models. In E. Walker (Ed.), *Schizophrenia: A life-course developmental perspective* (pp. 277–299). San Diego: Academic Press.

Thomas, A., & Chess, S. (1977). *Temperament and development.* New York: Brunner/Mazel.

Thomas, A., Chess, S., Birch, H., Hertzig, M., & Korn, S. (1963). *Behavioral individuality in early childhood.* New York: New York University Press.

Thorne, A., & Gough, H. (1991). *Portraits of type: An MBTI research compendium.* Palo Alto, CA: Consulting Psychologists Press.

Walker, E., Davis, A., & Gottlieb, L. (1991). Charting the developmental trajectories to schizophrenia. In D. Cicchetti & Sheree L. Toth (Eds.), *Modes and integrations: Rochester symposium on developmental psychopathology* (Vol. 3, pp. 185–206). Rochester: University of Rochester Press.

Zubin, J., Magaziner, J., & Steinhauer, S. (1983). The metamorphosis of schizophrenia. *Psychological Medicine, 13,* 551–571.

Zubin, J., & Spring, B. (1977). Vulnerability—A new view of schizophrenia. *Journal of Abnormal Psychology, 86,* 103–126.

# CHAPTER 2

# Conceptual and Empirical Advances in Understanding Aging Well Through Proactive Adaptation

Eva Kahana and Boaz Kahana

## DEVELOPING A COMPREHENSIVE MODEL OF AGING

Although there has been a major increase in emphasis on "aging well" in recent gerontological literature, there are few testable conceptual frameworks that address the nature and antecedents of successful or robust aging among the "old-old" (Baltes & Baltes, 1990). Dependency models of aging have emphasized the propensity of older adults to be passive respondents to environmental influences (E. Kahana, B. Kahana, & Kinney, 1990). However, there has been a small but growing group of gerontological researchers who have recognized that older persons can play significant proactive roles and behave in ways that draw upon and can generate resources in their environment (Lawton, 1989). This orientation parallels theoretical developments in the broader field of sociology (Giddens, 1983) that increasingly recognize the role of agency, reflecting progress, intentionality, and responsibility in the actions of human beings.

The proposed model is anchored in our observations of lifestyles and adaptations of old-old residents of three retirement communities. Earlier work by gerontologists cautioned us about the liabilities of relocation among the aged (Schulz & Brenner, 1977). Our early work on adventuresome older persons, who sought discontinuity in their lives by relocating to the Sunbelt (E. Kahana & B. Kahana, 1983), found that self-initiated environmental change may enhance personal control, person–environment fit, and life satisfaction in late life. Thus, studying healthy older adults who sought discontinuity in late life has provided unique insights into both social processes and outcomes of aging well.

The long-term follow-up (total 8 years) of a healthy old-old cohort of 1,000 retirement community residents through our ongoing MERIT Award study will yield longitudinal data on the full range of adaptation to old age. Thus we will be able to identify characteristics of those who succumb to frailty, those who maintain function in spite of ill health, and those who remain in robust good health well into late life. Based on preliminary data from our ongoing longitudinal study as well as our prior research on retirement migration (E. Kahana, B. Kahana, Segall, Riley, & Vosmik, 1986) and our prior work on adaptation of older adults to a wide variety of stresses (B. Kahana, E. Kahana, & Harel, 1989; E. Kahana, B. Kahana, & Young, 1985), we have taken a step toward developing a comprehensive model of successful aging termed *preventive and corrective proactivity* (PCP).

Our model is proposed as a broad formulation, which may be readily tested in a wide variety of settings. It is offered to expand and further elaborate the more traditional stress paradigm, by consideration of preventive as well as corrective adaptations. It explores ways in which older adults shape their armamentarium of resources and enhance their late-life well-being as they prepare to confront and actually face normative stresses of aging. This approach is consistent with Neugarten's (1976) view that normal and expectable life events are precipitants of new adaptations rather than threats to the continuity of the self.

Perhaps the most fundamental question implicit in gerontological research is: "What is successful aging?" Much of gerontological research during the past thirty years has actually focused on the opposite side of this question, identifying problems of aging. But is success just the absence of problems? One could respond to this question affirmatively based on a medical model that considers health to be simply the absence of disease. However, such a response would be considered simplistic based on more comprehensive multidimensional models of health and wellness in later life.

Biopsychosocial models (Engel, 1962) have been increasingly advocated in the literature concerned with aging and health. Treatises on the quality of life (Birren & Dieckmann, 1991; George & Bearon, 1980) represent another leading approach in defining successful aging in multidimensional ways. One of the early multidimensional models of successful aging is Havighurst's (1961) and Neugarten's (1974) life satisfaction model. However, components of such broad models or their interrelationships are insufficiently specified in existing conceptual frameworks or in relevant operational approaches.

Approaches to defining successful aging in the social sciences focus on subjective well-being (George, 1979). Psychological feeling states, broadly descriptive of morale, life satisfaction, happiness, and positive affect, have served as proxies for successful aging (Larson, 1978). However, an orientation to subjective well-being does not have unique relevance to aging (George & Clipp, 1991). Indications that education, income, social supports, or other antecedents contribute to successful aging may simply reflect their contributions to successful living at any age.

In considering factors that differentiate successful aging from "successful living" we found it necessary to consider unique challenges to aging. From a psychosocial vantage point we could best define them in terms of a modified stress paradigm. The first principle of our model is that normative stresses of late life serve as major challenges to successful aging.

Our model recognizes that both genetic and social structural factors, reflected in ascribed status, play critical roles in shaping both stressors and resources available to older persons to combat stressors. Chronic illnesses, for example, may have strong genetic underpinnings. Similarly, limited opportunity structures of women and minority groups may place constraints on their coping resources.

The role of society in defining successful aging has been explored in the work of Featherman, Smith, and Peterson (1990). The social context is also built into the present model in the form of external resources and stressors each of which may be minimized or maximized by society. Thus, societies that provide few roles for elders create stressors through role loss. Societies may also limit or maximize social supports and financial resources available to older adults.

## Conceptual Underpinnings

Our model is predicated on a proactive view of aging, which is consistent with Neugarten's (1974) comments about purposive aspects of human adaptation and Reker, Peacock, and Wong's (1987) view of the older individual as an active, self-constructing, self-reflecting agent embedded in social, cultural, and historical contexts. The major exposition of this orientation within an ecological framework has been offered in Lawton's (1989) work on environmental proactivity. This work is also consistent with George's (1979) analysis of the self as protagonist rather than reactor. Juxtaposed against his well-known concept of environmental docility, in his more recent work, Lawton (1989) has argued for recognizing environmental proactivity among older people, wherein the older person becomes a shaper of his or her environment rather than a mere responder to environmental circumstances. Our model of successful aging views older persons as playing key roles in shaping the external resources that render them less vulnerable to normative stresses of aging and in shaping personal outcomes in the face of stress (Figure 2.1).

Proactivity is seen as playing an important role in preventive as well as corrective actions in response to stress. According to this model, even physically frail or impaired older persons have the potential for successfully responding to stresses by modifying their activities or environment. On the surface, the concept of proactive response to stress may appear paradoxical. The stress is, in fact, the stimulus that activates adaptive responses. Nevertheless, these adaptations may reflect creative problem solving when the older person proactively shapes the environment. This contrasts with a passive reaction where the older person is buffeted by circumstances and exhibits little proactivity. Thus, *proactivity* as used in our model is based on Webster's definition of "pro" as "in favor" of activity rather than presupposing that it is "prior" to or temporally precedes stress (*Webster's New Collegiate Dictionary,* 1958).

Ryff (1982) provides a useful overview of personal characteristics attributed by developmental theorists to those who age successfully. Relevant attributes reviewed by Ryff include self-acceptance, positive

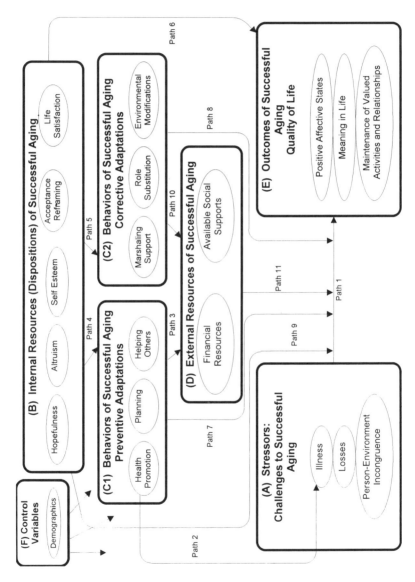

Figure 2.1. Successful aging: Model of preventive–corrective proactivity.

relations with others, autonomy, environmental mastery, purpose in life, and personal growth. These conceptual categories appear both intuitively meaningful and anchored in prior theoretical exposition. However, their interrelationships or relation to other key antecedents or outcomes considered in gerontological research are not specified. The concepts of *hardiness* (Kobasa & Puccetti, 1983) and *coherence* (Antonovsky, 1989) have been proposed as important resistance resources in contributing to invulnerability to stress in late life.

Health promotion models (Pender, 1987), anchored in health belief models (Becker, 1974), have also acknowledged the importance of pursuing wellness and self-actualization among the elderly. Problems in operationalizing these models exist, however, because resistance resources incorporate elements of psychological well-being outcomes. Broad conceptualizations of health promotion also include physical health, personality, subjective well-being, and socioenvironmental resources in their framework of health without specifying how these variables are related to one another. The goal of the proposed model is to provide some guidelines for understanding not only predispositions, resistance resources, or outcomes but also processes by which successful aging might come about. By building testable causal models the proposed formulation may be empirically supported or falsified.

The proposed conceptual framework is also consistent with earlier formulations of E. Kahana (1982) regarding person–environment congruence. Lack of person–environment fit is presented in this framework as a normative stressor, and corrective efforts to cope with stress include both attempts at changing one's environment and activities. Although the model does not posit direct links between stresses and corrective adaptations it may be noted that marshaling support is particularly well-suited to illness-related stresses; role substitution is a useful response to role losses; and environmental or activity modifications are particularly pertinent to lack of person–environment fit.

Working in the area of cognitive aging, Baltes and Baltes (1990) developed a model of successful aging based on selective optimization with compensation to deal with a reduced plasticity. The compensatory component of Baltes's model invokes proactive effort and a search for alternative routes. It does so in a corrective tradition, as it is predicated on responsiveness to limitations in reserve. In our PCP model, proactive preventive adaptations are considered even prior to the onset of any stresses or loss of resources.

The myth of passivity and dependency of the aged has been largely debunked in the field of gerontology (Midlarsky & Kahana, 1994). It is now recognized that even membership in the oldest-old cohort does not preclude someone from aging robustly and maintaining high levels of productivity (Glass, Seeman, Herzog, Kahn, & Berkman, 1995). There is also evidence of positive psychological adaptations by the aged. Blazer (1982) argues that neuroticism diminishes with aging and that decline in defenses frees up energy, which can be directed into helping and advocacy by elders. Birren and Dieckmann (1991) suggest that wise older persons may transcend limitations through divergent thinking. The model proposed here represents an effort to organize some of this convergent evidence regarding aging well.

Although we build our framework on a stress paradigm, our focus on proactivity, seen as the individual's propensity to create resources, also holds a more teleological view of self-actualization. Implicit in our notion of preventive proactivity are adient behaviors such as helping others, based on altruistic motives; these activities are undertaken as forms of meaningful self-expression. They result in the creation of resources, which may be activated in times of stress but have functional autonomy. They are linked to the stress paradigm through their resource-building qualities.

# A DESCRIPTION OF THE PREVENTIVE AND CORRECTIVE PROACTIVITY MODEL

## Model Components

Elements of the proposed PCP model are outlined in Figure 2.1. Due to the complexity of the model, it may be helpful to focus first on stressors (Component A) and outcomes (Component B) in the model. These represent the independent and dependent variables, respectively, that are generally considered in traditional stress paradigms. External resources (Component D) represent traditional buffers in the stress paradigm. Unique elements in the model are next introduced in the form of preventive and corrective adaptations (Components C1 and C2), which constitute behaviors associated with successful aging. Next, we focus on the psychological dispositions (Component B) that serve as antecedents of preventive and proactive adaptations and comprise the internal resources associated with successful aging. Social structural influences are depicted as demographic control variables in Component F in the model. Their influence on every element of the model is acknowledged. Because of our focus on proactivity and volitional aspects of successful aging, we do not attempt to specify the complex influences of social or cultural context in our model.

The conceptual framework of successful aging is based on the assumption that the aged face unique stresses and challenges. Successful aging requires preventive actions that help delay or minimize normative stresses of aging prior to their occurrence. It also calls for effective corrective actions after older adults encounter normative stresses. Dispositional characteristics serve as antecedents of behaviors constituting preventive and corrective adaptations.

## Principles of the Model

The model of preventive and corrective proactivity (PCP) (Figure 2.1) is based on 10 principles:

1. Normative stressors of late life serve as major challenges to outcomes of successful aging.
2. In the absence of proactive adaptations and external resources, stressors lead to negative outcomes (Figure 2.1, Path 1).
3. Older people can engage in proactive behavioral adaptations to ensure that normative challenges of aging are met.
4. Proactive adaptations occur even prior to the onset of stress and serve preventive functions.
5. Preventive functions are accomplished (a) by delaying or minimizing stress (Path 2), or (b) by enhancing external resources (Path 3).
6. Proactive corrective behaviors are activated to solve problems in response to stressors.
7. Dispositions of successful aging are enduring personality and cognitive orientations that lead to behaviors of successful aging both in terms of proactive preventive adaptation (Path 4) and proactive corrective adaptation (Path 5).
8. Dispositions of successful aging have an impact on successful

aging outcomes both directly (Path 6) and indirectly through behaviors of successful aging (Paths 7 and 8), and through external resources of successful aging (Path 11).

9. Preventive proactive behaviors develop external resources (Path 3) and corrective proactive behaviors activate external resources (Path 10), which in turn buffer the effects of stress on outcome (Path 11).

10. Psychological dispositions, proactive behaviors, and external resources all serve as conceptually and operationally distinct but related factors that reduce or buffer the impact of stress on outcomes of successful aging.

## Interrelationships of Elements of the Model

Those who age well are expected to engage in proactive behaviors that serve preventive functions to reduce stress and enhance external resources, which may then be called upon in times of stress. Successful agers are also expected to establish corrective or ameliorative adaptations to deal with normative stresses once they have arisen. Preventive adaptations are seen as buffers or moderators of stress whereas corrective adaptations are seen as mediators because they are responsive to normative stresses. Successful aging outcomes and processes are predicted or enhanced by dispositional factors that have trait-like qualities. Dispositions themselves can be enhanced by learning, modeling, therapy, and developmental change.

Dispositional qualities may serve as antecedents of preventive and corrective adaptations and of successful aging outcomes, or they may buffer the adverse effects of stress on outcomes. Dispositional qualities may be subdivided within a temporal framework, relating older persons to future (hopefulness), present (altruism and self-esteem), or past (reframing and cognitive life satisfaction). Internal dispositional and behavioral domains are considered to be distinct from external resources. The domain traditionally referred to as coping (Lazarus & Folkman, 1984) is subdivided in our model into a cognitive component, which is considered dispositional (e.g., cognitive reframing), and a behavioral component (e.g., health promotion). The behavioral component represents instrumental acts that may be classified as preventive or corrective adaptations. Affective dimensions of coping are not explicitly included in our model, since they cannot be readily distinguished from affective outcome states.

## Elements of the Model and Their Rationale

### *Outcomes of Successful Aging (Component E)*

Three outcome criteria have been selected as broadly salient, if not universal, goals of success for elderly individuals. They include (1) positive affective states, (2) meaning in life, and (3) maintenance of valued activities and relationships.

POSITIVE AFFECTIVE STATES.   Positive affective states represent indications of psychological well-being that have served as measures of positive outcomes in gerontological research. Life satisfaction, which has been proposed by Neugarten, Havighurst, and Tobin (1961) as a multidimensional indicator of psychological well-being, is subdivided in our model into dispositional (trait-like) and outcome (state-like) components. Several elements of the original broad life satisfaction construct, including self-esteem, optimism, and (cognitive) life satisfaction, are treated as dispositional characteristics in our model, based on research evidence that they are stable over time (George & Clipp, 1991) and not readily responsive to environmental influences (Kozma, Stones, & McNeil, 1991).

MEANING IN LIFE.   The inclusion of meaning in life as a salient outcome of successful aging recognizes that success embodies self-actualization and other higher order needs (Maslow, 1970). It is also consistent with Neugarten's view (1969) that a common task of later adulthood is a search for coherence or meaning. By including this outcome variable, the model also recognizes that positive psychological outcomes are possible even in the absence of positive feeling states. Accordingly, a frail older person who is in pain or a survivor of great psychological trauma such as the Holocaust (B. Kahana, E. Kahana, Harel, Kelly, Monaghan, & Holland, in press) may still achieve success by maintaining meaning in his or her life.

MAINTENANCE OF VALUED SOCIAL ACTIVITIES AND RELATIONSHIPS.   This outcome comprises a social rather than psychological aspect of continued meaningfulness in late life. This variable also renders our model cross-culturally applicable to societies (such as China) that do not uphold criteria of subjective well-being as a social ideal (Bond, 1992).

### Stressors: Challenges to Successful Aging (Component A)

Major normative stressors include (1) illness, (2) losses, and (3) person–environment (P–E) incongruence. These are broad classes of stressors, each of which may be further elaborated. Physical illness and frailty are conceptualized as normative stressors in the successful aging model rather than as outcomes of stress. It is recognized that physical illness may also be a consequence of life stress (E. Kahana, 1992). However, many of the chronic illnesses that create increasing frailty in late life (such as arthritis or cancer) are associated with the aging process rather than with specific stressors. For the elderly, chronic illness may best be viewed as a normative challenge to psychological and social well-being outcomes. An innovative feature of our conceptualization is the recognition that preventive adaptations such as health promotion can forestall or delay the onset of certain types of illnesses. Lack of P–E fit represents a salient normative stress of late life that has served as the cornerstone of our earlier formulations (E. Kahana, 1982). Accordingly, elders living in neighborhoods with high crime rates or in housing that no longer fits with their personal needs are viewed as confronting stresses due to lack of P–E fit. Positive life events or life changes that are within the older person's control (such as voluntary relocation) are not expected to pose challenges to successful aging. Such life change is seen as potentially consistent with patterns of successful aging.

### Internal Resources (Dispositions) of Successful Aging (Component B)

Stable personality or cognitive orientations are included here, representing personal coping resources. They serve as the antecedents of the behaviors or lifestyles of successful aging. Dispositions of successful aging include hopefulness, altruism, self-esteem, cognitive coping styles of acceptance/reframing, and cognitive life satisfaction.

HOPEFULNESS OR OPTIMISM.    Birren and Renner (1980) have identified optimistic orientations to the future as important hallmarks of successful aging. The value of optimistic appraisals as coping strategies has also been underscored in recent studies of coping that follow from Seligman's (1975) work. Hopeful or optimistic orientations are likely to enhance proactive preventive adaptation, such as planning for the future.

ALTRUISM.   Maslow (1970) describes self-actualizing individuals as those who have empathy for others. Older adults value an altruistic orientation in both themselves and others (Midlarsky & Kahana, 1994). Altruistic orientations as dispositions are seen as providing a major motivational basis for helping behaviors and productivity in late life (Garfein & Herzog, 1995).

SELF-ESTEEM.   The rationale for this variable was discussed previously in the section on outcomes.

COGNITIVE COPING—ACCEPTANCE/REFRAMING.   There have been reports of age-related increases in "accommodative" coping strategies, such as acceptance, that are likely to reflect older people's understanding that they may be facing uncontrollable events (Brandtstadter & Renner, 1990). In addition, both longitudinal changes and age-related differences in threat minimization or reframing have been demonstrated, with older respondents using more of these strategies than younger ones (Filipp, 1992). The value of acceptance as a coping strategy has also been promulgated in the medical sociological literature in considering coping with chronic illness (Felton & Revenson, 1987).

Cognitive coping styles are built into our model as dispositional variables that generally serve as responses to stressful situations. As such they may be viewed as direct buffers of stress rather than dispositional antecedents of preventive or corrective adaptations. Reframing the situation may also result in corrective adaptations by helping the individual focus on correctable aspects of the problems he or she faces. Older adults may thus cope with limitations posed by illness by refocusing on opportunities for restructuring their environment and make environmental adaptations in response to physical impairment. Alternatively, reframing can help reduce psychological distress in response to social losses.

LIFE SATISFACTION.   The rationale for this variable was discussed previously in the section on outcomes.

## Behaviors of Successful Aging (Component C): Proactive Preventive Adaptations

The model proposes that specific proactive behaviors regularly engaged in by the elderly will serve to delay the onset of physical frailty and will enhance social resources even before the occurrence of illness and other stressors. In our ongoing Florida retirement study we identified three major constellations of preventive behaviors engaged in by respondents: (1) health promotion, (2) planning for the future, and (3) helping others. These orientations have been incorporated in our model of successful aging as representing proactive preventive adaptations.

HEALTH PROMOTION.   Health promotion plays a potentially important role in reducing the risk or postponing the onset of illness and frailty. Physical activity in the elderly is associated with a host of health and rehabilitative benefits (Sallis, Haskell, & Fortmann, 1986; Surgeon General's Workshop on Health Promotion and Aging, 1987). Health promotion practices such as regular exercise, healthful diets, and substance avoidance have been shown to reduce the risks of disease and impairment (Guralnik & Kaplan, 1989).

PLANNING.   The value of planning for late-life adaptations has only begun to be systematically investigated in gerontological research. The use of planning strategies has been associated both with better cognitive responses (Salthouse, 1987) and with increased levels of efficiency and life satisfaction (Lachman & Burack, 1993). Planning for the future, through learning about options and resources in one's environment, can help older persons familiarize themselves with services and program options available to them should the need arise (Lawton, 1989). In addition, lifelong planning is likely to enhance both financial and social resources available to the elderly individual.

HELPING OTHERS.   Helping others and social participation are likely to increase the range of informal social resources available, especially from friends and neighbors (Midlarsky & Kahana, 1994). Helping behavior is consistent with value orientations of retirement-community living (Litwak, 1985) and is likely to result in enhanced social provisions after losses or when frailty occurs.

### Proactive Corrective Adaptations (Component C)

Corrective adaptations are instrumental problem-solving behaviors used to cope with stressful life situations. Three adaptations have been selected based on their relevance to the normative stresses of aging we posited. They include (1) marshaling support, (2) role substitution, and (3) environmental modifications.

MARSHALING SUPPORT. The critical role of social supports in buffering adverse stress effects has been extensively documented in gerontological literature. Such supports are generally studied as environmental provisions that represent external resources to the older person. Only recently has the critical role played by individual initiatives to marshal support been recognized (Gottlieb, 1988). Corrective behaviors of marshaling support are thus represented in our model as distinct from external resources of available social supports. When stresses arise older persons will marshal those supports that are available. Often such supports have been developed through preventive adaptations. Social supports may be marshaled in response to all three normative stresses in our model. They may serve as buffers between stresses related to illness, losses, or lack of P–E fit, and their negative psychosocial sequelae.

ROLE SUBSTITUTION. Social role losses may result in loneliness, loss of valued social activities and relationships, and even loss of a sense of meaning in life (Wortman & Silver, 1990). The compensability of loss in the framework of the stress paradigm has been considered by Pearlin, Menaghan, Lieberman, and Mullan (1981). Role substitution has been invoked as an active effort at counterbalancing role losses; it can help avert the negative sequelae of involuntary role losses (E. Kahana & Riley, 1987).

ENVIRONMENTAL MODIFICATIONS. In his environmental proactivity hypothesis, Lawton (1990) has utilized the environmental mastery concept to describe the efforts by which older persons change their environments to meet demands (French, Rodgers, & Cobb, 1974). Lawton suggests that proactive elders engage in "highly goal directed behavior designed to shape their environment for personal congruent need satisfaction" (p. 639). Our PCP model incorporates environmental modifications as the third aspect of proactivity. The environmental modification literature has concentrated primarily on architectural modifications

(Regnier & Pynoos, 1987) and prosthetic devices (Mann, Hurren, & Tomita 1993). In addition to these two factors, our model incorporates broader notions of relocation and activity modification (E. Kahana et al., 1994).

### External Resources of Successful Aging (Component D)

FINANCIAL RESOURCES AND AVAILABLE SOCIAL SUPPORTS.   We have selected these two of the key external resources generally considered in the gerontological literature and depicted them as distinct from the internal resources or proactive adaptations that helped generate them. Informal and formal social supports, as well as financial and environmental resources, are among the most widely studied predictors of late-life well-being (Kozma et al., 1991; Larson, 1978). It has been documented that friends and family (Krause, 1986), income and assets (O'Bryant & Morgan, 1989), and desirable neighborhoods and housing options (Lawton & Cohen, 1974) facilitate successful aging. Thus far, however, these factors may have been considered primarily as indicators of lucky or privileged aging without much attention to proactive adaptations in which older adults engaged to enhance these resources.

## EVALUATING THE PREVENTIVE AND CORRECTIVE PROACTIVITY MODEL

### Some Empirical Evidence Relative to the Model

Preliminary data from our ongoing Florida retirement study illustrate the prevalence of proactive adaptations among study respondents and point to the potential value of these adaptations for reducing the likelihood of illness and functional limitations and for enhancing social resources (B. Kahana, E. Kahana, Namazi, Kercher, & Stange, 1995).

Perhaps the most striking evidence of the pervasive nature of proactive behaviors among the old-old residing in retirement communities comes from our data on health promotion. Many of our respondents originally moved to a retirement community so that they could live in an environment that supported a health-promoting and active lifestyle.

Our results with regard to health promotion during the second wave of the study support conclusions that "the elderly are extremely health-conscious and very willing to adopt habits that will maintain good health" (Heckler, 1985, p. 225). Thus, 72% of the total sample reported that they currently exercise at least 3 times a week, with 57% of those age 85 or older doing so. Two thirds eat a healthy diet by limiting their intake of salt, sugar, and cholesterol. Only 10% reported having more than one alcoholic drink per day. Ninety-three percent state that they wear seat belts, and nearly half take precautions to protect their skin from the sun. While 6% of residents stated that they currently smoke, 48% of the sample had quit smoking after having smoked for an average of 20 years.

We were also interested in learning about plans respondents had made for their future. During the second wave of the study, 55% reported that they had made plans that included buying special insurance (19%), looking into other communities/facilities (15%), visiting with family members (11%), or arranging for home health care (11%). Four percent of the respondents had made definite plans to relocate to institutional or sheltered care settings that provide additional health care services.

Respondents provided a great deal of assistance to friends and family, with 72% reporting that they provide help to friends, and 42% reporting that they provide help to family. In terms of types of help provided, 61% reported assisting friends with transportation, 53% assisted friends with shopping, and 34% helped friends in times of illness. In assisting family, financial help was most often cited (28%). These preliminary findings provide indications that preventive, proactive adaptation are salient to old-old individuals. The causal relationships proposed in our model will be tested later using longitudinal data. Because of the high level of health maintenance in our sample, the impact of increasing frailty is just now beginning to be manifest.

## Contributions and Limitations of the Model

The PCP model presented here is viewed by us as a step in the direction of linking conceptualization and empirical research relevant to successful aging. The model is still evolving, but steps are being taken to specify some of the important elements of successful aging and place them in a testable causal order. Recognizing the complexity of relationships depicted, we also refrained from specifying the many feedback loops (reverse causal order) that may be anticipated and that can be tested with our longitudinal design and statistical techniques of causal modeling. The proposed model aims to clarify the presentation of commonly interrelated constructs by separating cognitive and attitudinal elements from behavioral elements and from external or environmental constructs.

Although we attempt to address many unanswered questions about processes as well as components of successful aging, our model leaves a number of major questions unanswered. We deliberately stopped short of taking a stance in some debated areas because of several considerations. First, we worked to build flexibility into the PCP model, allowing the choice of specific subcomponents to be altered by other investigators using the model without affecting the integrity of the basic postulates of the model. Second, we recognize that our model is in an early stage in development and empirical data are needed to guide our stances in some debated areas. Third, we view a certain level of flexibility as providing an opportunity for testing the model using alternative assumptions.

The following questions address key areas of flexibility with the hope of generating discussion about difficult issues that are often sidestepped in the gerontological literature:

*Is successful aging ultimately based on achieving positive outcomes or can it be defined in terms of process variables?* Does a person exhibiting proactive preventive adaptations exemplify successful aging even if these adaptations do not succeed in enhancing his or her health (due to genetic factors) or in building social supports (due to structural barriers)? The model can, in our view, be adopted using either assumption. Testing these assumptions would require ability to operationalize biological and structural factors that are not explicitly specified in the model. Accordingly, successful aging can be defined in terms of exhibiting elements of proactive adaptation or in terms of successful outcomes. The model may be employed using either proactivity or achieved outcomes as criteria for success. Value judgments of researchers will ultimately shape which of these assumptions is adopted.

*Which group of variables in the PCP model represent continuities and discontinuities?* The continuing aspects of the self are represented by the trait-like dispositions (e.g., hopefulness) in the model. Normative stresses of aging represent the environmental impetus for change.

These may also be viewed as akin to developmentally mandated adaptive tasks (Havighurst, 1961). The proactive behaviors represent individual adaptations, which reflect personal opportunities for change. Accordingly, the model allows for changing and evolving responses propelled by personal motivation or by change.

*In what fundamental ways do dispositions and outcomes differ?* Dispositional variables are defined as independent variables in our model, referring to trait-like and enduring personality orientations that provide the attitudinal and cognitive context of proactive behaviors. Outcomes, on the other hand, are described as states of being that result from successfully meeting challenges and stresses posed in the course of the aging process. The interrelationship and potential overlap between such states and traits represents a continuing area of challenge to the social and behavioral sciences.

*Is the model applicable to diverse cultural, socioeconomic status, racial, or ethnic groups?* We believe that the basic processes of our model are universal. The fundamental challenges to successful aging in the form of illness or increasing frailty, interpersonal and social loss, and lack of P–E fit occur in all cultures and ethnic groups. The human potential for engaging in preventive and proactive adaptation is also seen as universal, as are the fundamental dispositional characteristics of hopefulness, altruism, self-esteem, and life satisfaction. However, we anticipate that social and cultural factors may facilitate or place constraints on the expression and effectiveness of proactive adaptations for reducing stress and for enhancing external resources. Social structural variables and cultural influences may also modify the impact of stresses on diverse outcomes and affect the role that buffers play. Demographic influences and other social structural features are built into the model indirectly, as they are likely to affect every element of the model but represent relatively immutable influences in a successful aging paradigm. Their role is operationally acknowledged in our consideration of external resources of successful aging.

*Is the model limited to understanding late-life success?* The model can be readily adapted to understanding success at other life stages such as adolescence or midlife. In the present model, age specificity is defined primarily on the basis of the stress component of the paradigm, which includes age-related losses, illness, or level of P–E fit. However, researchers may focus on age-specific aspects of resources and outcome variables as well.

## CONCLUDING NOTE

The impetus for seeking models of successful aging was initiated in the work of the pioneers of social gerontology, Bernice Neugarten and her mentor, Robert Havighurst. As early as her 1964 treatise on personality in middle and late life, Neugarten argued that older people "can and do continue to adapt to new ideas and new behaviors" (p. 42).

It has taken thirty years for successful aging to come of age as a central concern for gerontological researchers (Baltes & Baltes, 1990; Rowe & Kahn, 1987). We are hopeful that the model presented here takes a step toward promoting empirical studies that can provide us with data on the dynamics as well as the structure of the successful aging paradigm.

## REFERENCES

Antonovsky, A. (1989). *Health, stress, and coping: New perspectives on mental and physical well-being.* San Francisco: Jossey-Bass.

Baltes, P. B., & Baltes, M. M. (1990). Psychological perspectives on successful aging: The model of selective optimization with compensation. In P. B. Baltes & M. M. Baltes (Eds.), *Successful aging: Perspectives from the behavioral sciences* (pp. 1–34). New York: Cambridge University Press.

Becker, M. (1974). The health belief model and personal health behavior. *Health Education Monographs, 2,* 236.

Birren, J. E., & Dieckmann, L. (1991). Concepts and content of quality of life in the later years: An overview. In J. E. Birren, J. E. Lubben, J. C. Rowe, & D. E. Deutchman (Eds.), *The concept and measurement of quality of life in the frail elderly* (pp. 344–359). San Diego: Academic Press.

Birren, J. E., & Renner, V. J. (1980). Concepts and issues of mental health and aging. In J. E. Birren & R. B. Sloane (Eds.), *Handbook of mental health and aging* (pp. 3–33). Englewood Cliffs, NJ: Prentice Hall.

Blazer, D. C. (1982). *Depression in late life.* St. Louis: Mosby.

Bond, M. H. (1992). *Beyond the Chinese face: Insights from psychology.* New York: Oxford University Press.

Brandtstadter, J., & Renner, G. (1990). Tenacious goal pursuit and flexible goal adjustment, explication and age-related analysis of assimilative and accommodative strategies of coping. *Psychology and Aging, 5,* 58–67.

Engel, G. (1962). *Psychological development in health and disease.* Philadelphia: Saunders.

Featherman, D., Smith, J., & Peterson, J. (1990). Successful aging in a post-retired society. In P. Baltes & M. Baltes (Eds.), *Successful aging: Perspectives from the behavioral sciences* (pp. 50–93). Cambridge, England: University Press Cambridge.

Felton, B. J., & Revenson, T. A. (1987). Age differences in coping with chronic illness. *Psychology in Aging, 2*(2), 164–170.

Filipp, S. (1992). Could it be worse? The diagnosis of cancer as a prototype of traumatic life events. In L. Montada, S. Filipp, & M. Lerner (Eds.), *Life crises and experiences of loss in adulthood* (pp. 23–56). Hillsdale, NJ: Erlbaum.

French, J. P., Rodgers, W., & Cobb, S. (1974). Adjustment as person–environment fit. In G. V Coelho, D. A. Hamburg, & J. E. Adams (Eds.), *Coping and adaptation* (pp. 316–333). New York: BasicBooks.

Garfein, A., & Herzog, A. (1995). Robust aging among the young-old, old-old and oldest-old. *Journal of Gerontology: Social Sciences, 50B,* S77–S87.

George, L. (1979). The happiness syndrome: Methodological and substantive issues in the study of social-psychological well-being in adulthood. *The Gerontologist, 19,* 210–216.

George, L., & Bearon, L. (1980). *Quality of life in older persons: Meaning and measurement.* New York: Human Science Press.

George, L. K., & Clipp, E. C. (1991). Subjective components of aging well. *Generations, 15*(1), 57–60.

Giddens, A. (1983). *Profiles and critiques in social theory.* Berkeley, CA: University of California Press.

Glass, T., Seeman, T., Herzog, A., Kahn, R., & Berkman, L. (1995). Change in productive activity in late adulthood: MacArthur studies of successful aging. *Journal of Gerontology: Social Sciences, 50B,* S65–S76.

Gottlieb, B. H. (1988). *Marshaling social support: Formats, processes, and effects.* Newbury Park, CA: Sage.

Guralnik, J. M., & Kaplan, G. A. (1989). Predictors of healthy aging: Prospective evidence from the Alameda County study. *American Journal of Public Health, 79*(6), 703–708.

Havighurst, R. (1961). Successful aging. *Gerontologist, 1,* 4–7.

Heckler, M. (1985). Health promotion for older Americans. *Public Health Reports, 100*(2), 225–230.

Kahana, B., Kahana, E., & Harel, Z. (1989). Clinical and gerontological issues facing survivors of the Nazi Holocaust. In P. Marcus & L. Rosenberg (Eds.), *The Holocaust survivor and the family* (pp. 197–210). New York: Prager.

Kahana, B., Kahana, E., Harel, Z., Kelly, K., Monaghan, P., & Holland, L. (in press). Coping with chronic stress among survivors of the Holocaust. In M. Gottlieb (Ed.), *Chronic stress of trauma.* New York: Plenum.

Kahana, B., Kahana, E., Namazi, K., Kercher, K., & Stange, K. (1995). The role of pain in the cascade from chronic illness to social disability and psychological distress in late life. In J. Lomrantz & D. Mostofsky (Eds.), *Pain in the elderly.* New York: Plenum.

Kahana, E. (1982). A congruence model of person–environment interaction. In M. P. Lawton, P. G. Windley, & T. O. Byerts (Eds.), *Aging and the environment—Theoretical approaches* (pp. 97–120). New York: Springer Publishing Co.

Kahana, E. (1992). Stress, research, and aging: Complexities, ambiguities, and paradoxes and promise. In M. Wykle, E. Kahana, & J. Kowal (Eds.), *Stress and health among the elderly* (pp. 239–256). New York: Springer Publishing Co.

Kahana, E., & Kahana, B. (1983). Continuity, discontinuity, futurity, and adaptation of the aged. In G. Rowles & R. Ohta (Eds.), *Aging and milieu: Environmental perspectives on growing old* (pp. 205–228). New York: Academic Press.

Kahana, E., Kahana, B., & Kinney, J. (1990). Coping among vulnerable elders. In Z. Harel, P. Ehrlich, & R. Hubbard (Eds.), *The vulnerable aged: People, services and policies* (pp. 64–85). New York: Springer Publishing Co.

Kahana, E., Kahana, B., Segall, M., Riley, K., & Vosmik, J. (1986). Motivators, resources and barriers in voluntary international migration of the elderly: The case of Israel-bound aged. *Cross-Cultural Gerontology, 1,* 191–208.

Kahana, E., Kahana, B., & Young, R. (1985). Social factors in institutional living. In W. Peterson & J. Quadagno (Eds.), *Social bonds in later life: Aging and interdependence* (pp. 389–419). Newbury Park, CA: Sage.

Kahana, E., Kahana, B., King, C., Brown, J., DeCrane, P., Mackey, D., Monaghan, P., Raff, L., Wu, T., Kercher, K., & Stange, K. (1994). Environmental modifications and disabled elders. In J. C. Rey & C. Tilquin (Eds.), *SYSTED 94: Proceedings of the 5th International Conference on Systems Sciences in Health-Social Services for the Elderly and the Disabled* (pp. 145–150). Lausanne, Switzerland: Swiss Institute for Public Health.

Kahana, E., & Riley, K. (1987). Loss. In G. Maddox (Ed.), *Encyclopedia of aging* (pp. 416–417). New York: Springer Publishing Co.

Kobasa, S. C., & Puccetti, M. C. (1983). Personality and social resources in stress resistance. *Journal of Personality and Social Psychology, 45,* 839–855.

Kozma, A., Stones, M. J., & McNeil, J. K. (1991). *Psychological well-being in later life.* Toronto: Butterworths.

Krause, N. (1986). Social support, stress, and well-being among older adults. *Journal of Gerontology, 41,* 512–519.

Lachman, M., & Burack, O. (1993). Planning and control processes across the life span: An overview. *International Journal of Behavioral Development, 16,* 131–143.

Larson, R. (1978). Thirty years of research on the subjective well-being of older Americans. *Journal of Gerontology, 40,* 375–381.

Lawton, M. P. (1989). Environmental proactivity and affect in older people. In S. Spacapan & S. Oskamp (Eds.), *The social psychology of aging* (pp. 135–163). Newbury Park, CA: Sage.

Lawton, M. P. (1990). Residential environment and self-directedness among older people. *American Psychologist, 45,* 638–640.

Lawton, M. P., & Cohen, J. (1974). The generality of housing impact on the well-being of older people. *Journal of Gerontology, 29,* 194–204.

Lazarus, R., & Folkman, S. (1984). *Stress appraisal and coping.* New York: Springer Publishing Co.

Litwak, E. (1985). *Helping the elderly: The complementarity of informal networks and formal systems.* New York: Guilford.

Mann, W., Hurren, D., & Tomita, M. (1993). Comparison of assistive device use and needs of home-based older persons with different impairments. *American Journal of Occupational Therapy, 47,* 980–986.

Maslow, A. (1970). *The farther reaches of human nature.* New York: Viking.

Midlarsky, E., & Kahana, E. (1994). *Altruism in later life.* Newbury Park, CA: Sage.

Neugarten, B. L. (1969). Continuities and discontinuities of psychological issues into adult life. *Human Development, 12,* 121–130.

Neugarten, B. L. (1974). Successful aging in 1970 and 1990. In E. Pfeiffer (Ed.), *Successful aging: A conference report* (pp. 12–18). Durham, NC: Center for the Study of Aging and Human Development, Duke University.

Neugarten, B. L. (1976). Adaptation and the life cycle. *The Counseling Psychologist, 6*(1), 16–20.

Neugarten, B. L., in collaboration with Berkowitz, H., Crotty, W. J., Cruen, W., Gutman, D. L., Lubin, M. I., Miller, D. I., Peck, R. F., Rosen, J. L., Shukin, A., & Tobin, S. (1964). *Personality in middle and late life.* New York: Atherton.

Neugarten, B. L., Havighurst, R. J., & Tobin, S. S. (1961). The measurement of life satisfaction. *Journal of Gerontology, 16,* 134–143.

O'Bryant, S. L., & Morgan, L. A. (1989). Financial experience and well-being among mature widowed women. *The Gerontologist, 29,* 245–251.

Pearlin, L. I., Menaghan, E. G., Lieberman, M. A., & Mullan, J. T. (1981). The stress process. *Journal of Health and Social Behavior, 22,* 337–356.

Pender, N. (1987). *Health promotion in nursing practice.* Norwalk, CT: Appleton and Lange.

Regnier, V., & Pynoos, J. (Eds.). (1987). *Housing the aged: Design directives and policy considerations.* New York: Elsevier.

Reker, G. T., Peacock, E. J., & Wong, P. T. (1987). Meaning and purpose in life and well-being: A life-span perspective. *Journal of Gerontology, 42*(1), 44–49.

Rowe, J., & Kahn, R. (1987). Human aging: Usual and successful. *Science, 237,* 143–149.

Ryff, C. D. (1982). Successful aging: A developmental approach. *Gerontologist, 22*(2), 209–214.

Sallis, J. F., Haskell, W. L., & Fortmann, S. P. (1986). Moderate-intensity physical activity and cardiovascular risk factors: The Stanford five-city project. *Preventive Medicine, 15,* 561–568.

Salthouse, T. A. (1987). Age, experience, and compensation. In C. Schooler & K. W. Schaie (Eds.), *Cognitive functioning and social structure over the life course* (pp. 142–157). Norwood, NJ: Ablex.

Schulz, R., & Brenner, G. (1977). Relocation of the aged: A review and theoretical analysis. *Journal of Gerontology, 27,* 323–333.

Seligman, M. E. P. (1975). *Helplessness: On depression, development and death.* San Francisco: Freeman.

Surgeon General's Workshop on Health Promotion and Aging. (1987). Summary recommendations of Physical Fitness and Exercise Working Group. *Journal of the American Medical Association, 262,* 2507–2510.

*Webster's New Collegiate Dictionary.* (1958). Springfield, MA: Merriam.

Wortman, C. B., & Silver, R. C. (1990). Successful mastery of bereavement and widowhood: A life-course perspective. In P. B. Baltes & M. M. Baltes (Eds.), *Successful aging: Perspectives from the behavioral sciences* (pp. 225–264). Cambridge, England: Cambridge University Press.

# Comments

## David A. Chiriboga

In the preceding chapter the Kahanas have taken a major step towards a reformulation of how we view issues pertaining to the health and well-being of older people. Rather than focusing on the presence or absence of problems, they focus on a broad continuum of well-being that encompasses successful aging as a legitimate goal and outcome. In these comments, I would like to discuss the Kahana model as it compares to the traditional model of prevention, provide a brief historical perspective on the evolution of their model, and then discuss the complexity of prevention as a topic.

## COMPARISON WITH THE TRADITIONAL MODEL

The traditional model of prevention has three components: (1) primary prevention, which subsumes activities designed to actually prevent health problems from occurring; (2) secondary prevention, which subsumes activities designed to stop or limit, as quickly and effectively as possible, health problems that have occurred; and (3) tertiary prevention, which subsumes efforts at rehabilitation. A defining component of the traditional model is its reliance on the so-called "medical model" of health, which focuses primarily on the negative side of health. This model, it should be pointed out, is not in itself a simplistic one, and has evolved substantially over the past few decades. It was recently interpreted by Wallace (1994, p. 452):

> Individual health has been largely defined in terms of abnormal signs, symptoms, behaviors, and functions as well as overt diseases, conditions, and anatomic and physiologic disruptions. It may be useful

from preventive and policy perspectives to also define health status at least in part as a state of enhanced risk of disease, dysfunction, and death, irrespective of current health status and function.

The limitations of a problem-based model of health and well-being, of course, has long been recognized (e.g., Ng, Davis, Manderscheid, & Elkes, 1981), and in the 1940s this recognition formed the basis for a redefinition of health by the World Health Organization that emphasizes physical, mental, and social well-being. Unfortunately, research on prevention has lagged far behind. However, in the Kahana model we find a promising redefinition.

In this redefinition, we can see that what the Kahanas refer to as *preventive acts* are, at the level of the individual, equivalent to primary prevention. I say at the level of the individual because, in contrast to preventive medicine's traditional focus on community as the level of intervention, the Kahanas have developed a model that puts the focus on individual responsibility and activity.

*Corrective adaptations,* in turn, are equivalent to secondary and tertiary prevention. Here the concern is with behaviors that deal with problems in the most life-enhancing way. Combined with preventive acts, we also see that a critical ingredient of this new model is a proactive perspective in which the individual is not only taking responsibility but is viewed as having the capacity to self-actualize in both the Goldsteinian and Maslovian senses.

What is possibly missing from the model, although actually implicit at both the preventive and adaptive levels, is a third level of activity: acts that take a proactive, life-enhancing stance in the absence of present or anticipated future problems. This level, logically, would precede preventive acts, in that it truly goes deeper than prevention, into domains once reserved for theorists such as Abraham Maslow (1968) and perhaps Kurt Goldstein (1963), as well as the humanists.

## A BRIEF HISTORICAL PERSPECTIVE

As is true for most innovations, the Kahana model has roots in the past. From a historical perspective, these roots would seem to draw from the completely medicalized model of stress first presented by researchers such as Holmes and Rahe (1967), which itself represented traditional public health perspectives on the pathogen/disease relationship. The model of wellness evident in these early stress studies was as follows:

$$STRESS \rightarrow DISEASE$$

This basic model is found, in somewhat altered form, in Path 1 of the Kahana model.

Of interest is that the completely medicalized model ignored the earlier contributions of Selye (1956), who presents what might be called a mediated medical model:

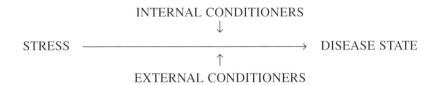

In elaborated form, the Selye model is contained within the Kahana model as the pathways for elements B and D that exist as mediators of the primary pathway (Path 1) between Components A and E. That is, we find internal (B) and external (D) resources described as influencing the relationship between stressors (A) and outcomes (E).

Unusual in a classic stress model is the inclusion, by the Kahanas, of behaviors associated with preventive and corrective acts. The behaviors, moreover, are seen as affecting not only outcomes but also the external resources available to the individual. While this is an important addition, from a model development standpoint, the pathways seem to ignore the possibility that external resources might affect behaviors. For example, having a multitude of social supports available, perhaps because one comes from a large extended family, might affect one's ability to marshal support or substitute roles.

## THE INHERENT COMPLEXITIES OF PREVENTION

When one first encounters the full model of successful aging presented by the Kahanas, it is probably impossible to avoid thinking that it is incredibly complex and perhaps overly detailed, as well as being a rich framework for research. At one level, this complexity in unavoidable: when one considers the multiple forces affecting the life of each individual, it becomes obvious that simple models, such as ones proposed by the early stress researchers, simply fail to capture the essential elements.

However, while the need for complexity is perhaps a necessity, especially at an early stage of model development, I remind the Kahanas of the vital need to keep the endpoint in mind—an end that, one would hope, is more generalized and less focused on specific elements. I recall a recent address by Robert Kaplan, as outgoing president of the Health Psychology Division of the American Psychological Association. Kaplan (1994) recounted his experience reading a cartoon in which the main character, Ziggy, seeks the meaning of life. Encountering a guru, he is advised that the meaning of life is "doin' stuff." At Ziggy's rather shocked response, the guru draws a distinction between the meaning of life and the meaning of death—death means "not doin' stuff." The basic point is that while there may be an inherent complexity to an issue, it is still possible to refine it down to some pretty basic conclusions.

Obviously, one does not reach some profound yet simple statement such as "doin' stuff" without considerable contemplation and experience. Like the Kahanas, one must first appreciate the full complexities of life. However, like the guru, one hopes to distill the critical ingredients.

Overall, then, we find in the Kahana model a person-oriented, proactive model of health. This is a welcome change from the traditional model of prevention, which focuses on how society (i.e., the health professions) can help individuals and communities better run their lives. The emphasis on the positive side of aging also serves to counterbalance the prevailing focus on deviations from asymptomatic (but probably unrewarding) life. At the same time, a cautionary note is perhaps worth introducing: In the quest for the neglected positive side of health, we should be careful not to de-emphasize the reality of the negative side. We should also perhaps recognize the role of fate, or accident: the chance slip that turns into a fall that turns into . . . In all our lives, I would suggest, no matter how successful, there is an element of luck.

# REFERENCES

Goldstein, K. (1963). *Human nature.* New York: Schocken.

Holmes, T., & Rahe, R. (1967). The Social Readjustment Rating Scale. *Journal of Psychosomatic Research, 11,* 213–218.

Kaplan, R. M. (1994). The Ziggy theorem: Toward an outcomes-focused health psychology. *Health Psychology, 13,* 451–460.

Maslow, A. H. (1968). *Toward a psychology of being.* New York: Van Nostrand Reinhold.

Ng, L. K. Y., Davis, D. L., Manderscheid, R. W., & Elkes, J. (1981). Toward a conceptual formulation of health and well-being. In L. K. Y. Ng & D. L. Davis (Eds.), *Strategies for public health: Promoting health and preventing disease* (p. 44). New York: Van Nostrand Reinhold.

Selye, H. (1956). *The stress of life.* New York: McGraw-Hill.

Wallace, R. B. (1994). Assessing the health of individuals and populations in surveys of the elderly: Some concepts and approaches. *The Gerontologist, 34,* 449–453.

# CHAPTER 3

# Continuities and Discontinuities in Very Late Life

## Steven H. Zarit

One of the remarkable characteristics of Bernice Neugarten's distinguished career is her prescience for emerging issues in life span development. Throughout her career, she has led the field into new areas, and defined the framework for their investigation. Her 1974 paper, which differentiated the older population into "young-old" and "old-old" is a contribution of the greatest magnitude; it has had enormous impact on our understanding of the changing nature of the population. As she described in that paper, *young-old* applies to unprecedented numbers of healthy, active older people, who are energetically engaged in leisure and social activities. *Old-old,* in turn, refers to rapidly increasing numbers of people over 75 with significant disabilities, whose health and social needs require an ever growing number of resources (Neugarten, 1974, 1982). Although these terms are frequently used to indicate specific chronological ages (55 to 74 for young-old; 75 and over for old-old), Neugarten's original formulation emphasized patterns of functioning and involvement that are correlated but not isomorphic with age.

As with many of Neugarten's contributions, this distinction ran against the tide of optimism about aging that became the predominant ideology among academics during the 1970s and 1980s. Most observers noted the increased health and well-being of new cohorts of elderly, and expected that it would be only a matter of time until most elderly were fit and vigorous. A particularly influential expression of this optimism is Fries's (1980) proposal, concerning compression of morbidity, that improved health and healthy behaviors at earlier ages delays the incidence of chronic illnesses in later life and results in a briefer period of decline at the end of life. But against the illusory prediction that we would remain forever young, Neugarten identified correctly that we are witnessing two complementary trends: that people are, indeed, living healthy and full lives for longer periods of time, *and* that duration of life with disabilities has been extended (e.g., Guralnik, 1991; Olshansky, Rudberg, Carnes, Cassel, & Brody, 1991).

Neugarten (1982) also took the lead in recognizing the public policy implications of these demographic trends. She posed complex questions about appropriate and equitable distribution of resources in society. Citing how rates of poverty among the elderly have declined while those among children have increased, she speculated that some redirection of resources may be necessary, particularly from those groups of elderly who are financially well-off and do not need entitlements. She challenged the research and policy communities to consider whether age or need should be the basis for benefits. This question of how best to arrange and pay for appropriate health and long-term care services for the old-old while balancing other social needs is likely to be a defining issue in public policy discussions in the United States and many other countries for a long time to come (e.g., Thorslund, 1991).

The distinction between young-old and old-old has been widely adopted by the gerontological field and further elaborated. As the number of people past age 85 has grown dramatically, some demographers have suggested a further differentiation based on chronological age, "oldest-old," to represent this group (Rosenwaike, 1985; Suzman & Riley, 1985). Interest in very late life has carried forward the dynamic interplay originally described by Neugarten between healthy, active life, and the growing probability of decline with advancing age. In a series of insightful papers, Tobin has focused on preservation of the self as a critical task in very late life (Tobin, 1991, 1994, Chapter 6 in this volume; also, Lieberman & Tobin, 1983). He suggests that actively asserting control over one's environment and resisting passivity is related to persistence of the self in the face of age-associated losses. Johnson and Troll (1992) have examined changes in the social world of older women. Of particular note is their characterization of the social networks of the oldest-old as "attenuated," that is, depleted through the death or disability of their friends and relatives, and, in some cases, their children. Combined with changes in functional abilities, attenuation of their social network results in older persons' focusing more on themselves and their immediate surroundings.

As these examples indicate, an engaging body of research on very late life is emerging. Conducting research on people at very advanced ages, however, is difficult, given their frailty and small number in the total population. As a result, relatively few in-depth studies have been conducted on representative samples past age 85.

The present investigation examined people at age 90, an age group not extensively studied to date. Data were drawn from the Octogenarian (OCTO) study, an ongoing longitudinal study of competencies in everyday functioning of the oldest-old in Sweden (Johansson & Zarit, 1995; Johansson, Zarit, & Berg, 1992; Zarit & Johansson, 1993; Zarit, Johansson, & Malmberg, 1995). The OCTO study was designed to assess rates and patterns of everyday competency over time in order to estimate the need for services and other assistance in this age group. Consistent with Neugarten's concerns about the policy implications of an aging population, the focus is on the patterns of functioning and disability at this outermost frontier of the human life span. Function in three domains will be explored: (1) functional health, including activities of daily living (ADL); (2) cognitive competency; and (3) psychological functioning. Tobin's (1991, 1994) proposition of the adaptive advantage of maintaining active control of one's environment is also examined.

# METHODS

## Sample and Design

A stratified random sample of 400 people living in the city of Jönköping and surrounding area in south central Sweden were identified in 1987 from census records and contacted about participating in the study. The names drawn from census data included 100 people from each of four birth cohorts (1897, 1899, 1901, 1903). At that time (1987), respondents were 90, 88, 86, and 84 years old. From the original 400 people identified from census data, 21 had died before they were contacted, one person had moved from the area, and 54 refused to participate.

Excluding people who were deceased or had moved from the area, the participation rate was 86%. The resulting sample consists of 324 people. There were no differences in demographic indicators between those who refused and those who agreed to participate.

Participants have been interviewed at 2-year intervals: 1987, 1989, 1991, and again in 1993 (see Table 3.1). Attrition was high across the waves of interviews. The main reason for attrition was death. The refusal rate was quite low (5% in 1989, 4% in 1991, and 1% in 1993).

Taking advantage of this cohort sequential design, I have assembled a synthetic cohort of people at age 90 for the present study. That is, data on functioning for the 1897 cohort are drawn from the 1987 interview, data for the 1899 cohort are provided by the 1989 interview, and so on. The sample of 90-year-olds consists of 191 people, 83 from the 1897 cohort, 51 from the 1899 cohort, 26 from the 1901 cohort, and 31 from the 1903 cohort (Table 3.2). The size of the sample from later cohorts is necessarily smaller, because of mortality from the original sample and other sources of attrition. Because of the possibility that attrition resulted in a selectively different sample, analyses were conducted to see if birth cohorts differ from one another.

## Procedures and Measures

A comprehensive biomedical, behavioral and social assessment was conducted by licensed nurses in respondents' places of residence. This assessment included tests of health and health behaviors, social networks, cognitive functioning, self-report inventories, and functional health (ADL). Demographic and socioeconomic information was also

**TABLE 3.1** **Selection of a Sample of 90-Year-Olds from the Cohort Sequential OCTO Study**

| Year of birth | Year of interview | | | |
|---|---|---|---|---|
| | 1987 | 1989 | 1991 | 1993 |
| 1897 | **90** | 92 | 94 | 96 |
| 1899 | 88 | **90** | 92 | 94 |
| 1901 | 86 | 88 | **90** | 92 |
| 1903 | 84 | 86 | 88 | **90** |

TABLE 3.2    90-Year-Old Men and Women from Each Birth Cohort

|       |     | \multicolumn{5}{c}{Birth cohort} | | | | |
|-------|-----|------|------|------|------|-------|
|       |     | 1897 | 1899 | 1901 | 1903 | Total |
| Men   | *N* | 27   | 12   | 7    | 8    | 54    |
|       | %   | (32) | (24) | (27) | (26) | (28)  |
| Women | *N* | 56   | 39   | 19   | 23   | 137   |
|       | %   | (68) | (76) | (73) | (74) | (72)  |
| Total *N* |  | 83   | 51   | 26   | 31   | 191   |

obtained. The interviews averaged 3.5 hours in length, with frequent breaks if a respondent became fatigued. A reliable informant was used if participants were unable to provide some information themselves (except for cognitive functioning). The present investigation focuses on the domains of functional health, cognitive performance, and psychological functioning.

### *Functional Health*

Information has been obtained for four areas of functional health: (1) mobility, (2) personal activities of daily living (PADL), (3) instrumental activities of daily living (IADL), and (4) sensory functioning.

MOBILITY.    Participants were assessed for their ability to perform eight mobility tasks: (1) getting around indoors; (2) getting around outdoors; (3) using stairs; (4) bending, crouching, and kneeling; (5) picking an item up off the floor; (6) moving from bed to a chair; (7) reaching an item at shoulder height; and (8) handling small objects or writing. Respondents indicated whether they could perform each activity without difficulty, with a small amount of difficulty, with a great deal of difficulty, or were unable to perform the activity. To indicate overall mobility, the number of tasks that respondents could perform with no or a little difficulty were summed. Alpha for the mobility scale is .96.

PERSONAL ACTIVITIES OF DAILY LIVING (PADL).    Six PADL tasks were selected from similar scales (e.g., Katz, Ford, Moskowitz, Jackson, &

Jaffe, 1963; Lawton, 1971). The items were: (1) bathing or showering, (2) washing oneself, (3) grooming, (4) dressing, (5) using the toilet, and (6) feeding oneself. Items were rated in the same manner as for mobility tasks. Alpha for the PADL scale is .95.

INSTRUMENTAL ACTIVITIES OF DAILY LIVING (IADL).   Eight IADL tasks were selected from standard scales (e.g., Lawton, 1971). The items were: (1) heavy housework, (2) laundry, (3) making the bed, (4) meal preparation, (5) shopping for food, (6) moving and lifting things, (7) banking and post office, and (8) using the telephone. Items were rated in the same manner as for mobility tasks. Alpha for the IADL scale is .96.

SENSORY FUNCTIONING.   Although not typically included in functional health, sensory decline can have a major impact on competency and well-being, contributing in a variety of direct and indirect ways to difficulties in performing activities of daily living, and in communications with other people. In the present study, sensory functioning was assessed using a protocol for rating hearing and vision. Participants' hearing was evaluated by the nurse interviewers for ability to hear normal conversations, radio, television, and the degree to which adjustments had to be made in order to facilitate hearing. Vision was assessed for the ability to see and respond to normal visual stimuli encountered in daily life, such as newspapers, familiar objects, and faces. Summary ratings of the degree of difficulty with visual and hearing tasks were made by the interviewers based on these assessments.

### Cognitive Functioning

Cognitive functioning was assessed with a battery of five tests. The battery included one widely used test for screening cognitive impairment, the Mini-Mental State Examination (MMSE; Folstein, Folstein, & McHugh, 1975). The other four tests were developed specifically for assessing older people, and use everyday stimuli in familiar tasks. This ecological approach was adopted to assess competency in everyday functioning and to minimize deficits in performance due to unfamiliarity with a task or a lack of interest. In addition to the tests, ratings were made using *Diagnostic and Statistical Manual of Mental Disorders (DSM-III-R)* criteria to identify the presence of dementia (American Psychiatric Association, 1987).

MMSE.   The MMSE is a 21-item scale (total score=30 points) designed to screen for deficits associated with dementia and other cognitive disorders. Items assess orientation, attention, memory, verbal abilities, and constructional performance.

PROSE RECALL.   Subjects are asked to recall a 100-word story that is presented orally to them. The story has a humorous point in order to engage their interest. Scoring is similar to the familiar story recall task on the Wechsler Memory Scale (Wechsler, 1945).

MEMORY-IN-REALITY (MIR).   This test varies traditional list-learning tasks by presenting subjects with 10 common objects and asking them to place each item in a three-dimensional model of an apartment. After a 30-minute delay, subjects are asked to recall the items and where they had been placed (Johansson, 1988/1989). Scores for free recall are reported in this chapter.

CLOCK TEST.   Similar to commonly used neuropsychological assessment techniques, the clock test is comprised of three time-telling tasks: (1) drawing a clock and setting the hands to a specified time, (2) setting the hands of a wooden clock to a specific time, and (3) telling what time it is. A large wooden clock face with movable hands has been specifically constructed for this task to minimize problems due to poor vision.

COUNT MONEY.   Subjects are given four denominations of coins and asked to make certain predetermined sums of money, using the fewest numbers of coins possible.

These tests are described in more detail in Johansson and Zarit (1991) and in Goodman and Zarit (1995).

*DSM-III-R* DIAGNOSIS.   Criteria for dementia taken from *DSM-III-R* were operationalized using the available data on cognitive functioning and performance on complex instrumental activities of daily living. Information on vision and hearing loss was also considered as a possible contributing factor to poor cognitive performance. Two clinical psychologists evaluated each case independently and had an inter-rater agreement of 94% ($\kappa$ coefficient = .88) (Johansson & Zarit, 1995). In cases where there was disagreement, a third rater was brought in to make an independent assessment and a case conference was held to resolve the disagreement. No attempt was made to identify type of dementia. For more information on the rating procedure, see Johansson and Zarit (1995).

### *Psychological Functioning*

Two main domains of psychological functioning were assessed: (1) mastery and (2) depression. In addition, participants were asked to assess their global subjective health and subjective memory.

MASTERY. Mastery is measured by an 8-item scale developed by Pearlin (e.g., Pearlin & Schooler, 1978), which has been widely used in a variety of research contexts. The scale assesses the degree to which people feel they have control or influence over the events in their lives. As such, the Mastery scale is similar to measures of personal control. Alpha for the scale using the present sample is .70. Positive scores indicate higher degrees of mastery.

DEPRESSION. A short, 11-item version of the familiar Center for Epidemiological Studies Depression Scale (CES-D) was used (Kohout, Berkman, Evans, & Cornoni-Huntley, 1993; Radloff, 1977). Items include both positive and negative emotions. Subjects indicate the extent to which they have felt a certain way during the past week. Alpha for the scale using the present sample is .86. Higher scores indicate more depression.

SUBJECTIVE RATINGS OF HEALTH AND MEMORY. Participants were asked to rate their health and memory on 7-point scales, with choices ranging from extremely poor to extremely good. In addition, they were asked to compare their current health and memory to their condition 2 years ago. These types of subjective ratings have frequently been used in the gerontological literature.

## Analyses

The main objective of this paper is to describe functioning at age 90, particularly, the balance between independence and disability. Performance on each of the measures is presented in detail. In addition, to test Tobin's hypothesis about the importance in late life of exerting control over one's environment, mastery is correlated with the other psychological and functional health measures.

The number of respondents with usable data varied somewhat from measure to measure. In cases of more demanding tests or more sophisticated questions, it was not possible to obtain information from people with significant cognitive deficits. Analyses utilized the maximum number of people available for any particular measure.

# RESULTS

The sample of 90-year-olds consists of 54 men (28%) and 137 women (72%) (Table 3.2). Respondents had, on average, 6.4 years of schooling, which is typical of older Swedish cohorts. Only 27 people were currently married (14%), 32 were divorced, separated, or never married (17%), and the remaining 132 were widowed (69%). Ninety-six respondents, or just over 50% of the sample, lived in ordinary housing. Another 29 (15%) lived in service apartments in which supportive services such as meals and housekeeping were available. The remaining 66 respondents (35%) resided in nursing homes, old age homes, or similar care institutions. Three quarters of the people living in ordinary housing lived alone.

Tables 3.3 through 3.6 present information on functional health, including mobility, personal activities of daily living, instrumental activities of daily living, and sensory abilities. For mobility, participants were able to perform with no or little difficulty an average of 5.21 ($SD$=2.99) of the 8 tasks. The activities on which they had the greatest difficulty were getting around outdoors and climbing stairs. Respondents were able to perform an average of 4.38 ($SD$=2.15) of the 6 PADLs with little or no difficulty. Bathing posed problems for the greatest number of respondents, with 36% unable to bathe and another 16% able to do so only with great difficulty.

Respondents had considerably more difficulty with instrumental activities of daily living, performing an average of 3.42 ($SD$=3.19) out of 8 activities with little or no difficulty. Nearly one half of the sample was unable to perform each IADL, with most disability reported for

**TABLE 3.3  Performance on Mobility Tasks (*N* = 188)**

|  | No difficulty | Small amount of difficulty | Much difficulty | Unable to perform |
|---|---|---|---|---|
| Get around indoors | 39% | 31% | 9% | 21% |
| Get around outdoors | 22 | 27 | 22 | 29 |
| Use stairs | 28 | 22 | 16 | 34 |
| Bend, crouch, and kneel | 33 | 25 | 16 | 26 |
| Pick up an item from the floor | 58 | 17 | 5 | 20 |
| Move from bed to a chair | 59 | 17 | 4 | 19 |
| Reach an item at shoulder height | 51 | 27 | 7 | 15 |
| Handle small items or write | 52 | 13 | 19 | 16 |

Mean number of independent activities* 5.21
*SD* 2.99

*No difficulty or a small amount of difficulty.

**TABLE 3.4  Performance of Personal Activities of Daily Living (*N* = 191)**

|  | No difficulty | Small amount of difficulty | Much difficulty | Unable to perform |
|---|---|---|---|---|
| Bathe or shower | 27% | 21% | 16% | 36% |
| Wash oneself | 63 | 13 | 6 | 18 |
| Grooming | 62 | 14 | 6 | 18 |
| Dress | 55 | 20 | 5 | 20 |
| Use the toilet | 67 | 7 | 4 | 23 |
| Feed oneself | 80 | 8 | 3 | 9 |

Mean number of independent activities* 4.37
*SD* 2.15

*No difficulty or a small amount of difficulty.

**TABLE 3.5   Performance of Instrumental Activities of Daily Living**
**(*N* = 187)**

|  | No difficulty | Small amount of difficulty | Much difficulty | Unable to perform |
|---|---|---|---|---|
| Heavy housework | 7% | 18% | 12% | 63% |
| Laundry | 30 | 14 | 4 | 51 |
| Make the bed | 38 | 11 | 8 | 43 |
| Meal preparation | 31 | 13 | 9 | 46 |
| Shop for food | 18 | 11 | 10 | 61 |
| Move and lift things | 26 | 19 | 11 | 44 |
| Post and banking | 29 | 10 | 10 | 51 |
| Use the telephone | 55 | 11 | 5 | 28 |

Mean number of independent activities* 3.42
*SD* 3.19

*No difficulty or a small amount of difficulty.

**TABLE 3.6   Nurses' Ratings of Vision and Hearing**

| Vision (*N* = 177) | |
|---|---|
| No Problem | 36% |
| Small Problem | 39 |
| Large Problem | 23 |
| Blind | 2 |
| Hearing (*N* = 181) | |
| No Problem | 44% |
| Small Problem | 41 |
| Large Problem | 14 |
| Deaf | 1 |

heavy housework (63% unable to perform at all) and shopping (61% unable to perform at all).

By contrast, sensory functioning was surprisingly good in this sample. Seventy five percent of participants had no or only small difficulties with vision, and 85% had no or only small difficulties with hearing.

**TABLE 3.7  Cognitive Performance**

|  | Mean | *SD* |
|---|---|---|
| MMSE (*N* = 176) (range 0–30) | 20.10 | 9.15 |
| MIR (*N* = 133) (range 0–10) | 4.94 | 3.43 |
| Story recall (*N* = 170) (range 0–16) | 7.64 | 5.30 |
| Clock test (*N* = 165) (range 0–15) | 9.39 | 6.15 |
| Count money (*N* = 162) (range 0–8) | 5.70 | 3.26 |

Turning to cognitive functioning, Table 3.7 shows mean performance on the 5 cognitive measures; Table 3.8 shows the rate of diagnosis of dementia, using *DSM-III-R* criteria. Performance on each measure was quite varied, with some respondents scoring at the top levels of every scale, and others able to give only minimal responses. As an example, the mean on the MMSE was 20.10 (*SD*=9.12). Scores of 10 or less were reported for 19% of subjects, indicating severe cognitive impairment. By comparison, one half the sample had scores of 23 and above, including 14% with scores of 29 or 30 (the top score). Not surprisingly, larger proportions of respondents were able to perform at very high levels on the more familiar tasks (clock test, count money).

It was possible to assess 185 respondents for dementia, using *DSM-III-R* criteria. Information available on the remaining 6 people was insufficient for making a rating. As shown in Table 3.8, 73 people, or 40% of the sample, met the criteria for diagnosis of dementia.

**TABLE 3.8  Proportion of Respondents Meeting Criteria for Dementia**

|  | *N* | *%* |
|---|---|---|
| *DSM-III-R* criteria for dementia |  |  |
| No dementia | 112 | 60 |
| Dementia | 73 | 40 |

*Note.* Six subjects had insufficient information to be rated.

Mean scores on the four psychological measures are shown in Table 3.9. There were considerably more missing data on these measures, because many cognitively impaired participants could not respond to the questions. The people responding on these scales generally gave a very positive assessment of themselves. Mastery scores were high, with respondents on average endorsing items as somewhat true of them, while rejecting negative items. The strongest response was to the item, "feeling helpless when facing problems and difficulties," with subjects indicating they rarely or never felt that way. On the 11-item version of the depression scale (CES-D), participants' average response was that they experienced depressive feelings on occasion, but not often. The items most commonly endorsed were "feeling lonely" and "not feeling confident about the future." Respondents rated both subjective health and subjective memory positively, with the average ratings as "somewhat good." Interestingly, when asked to compare current functioning in these domains to how they felt 2 years ago, a majority of respondents indicated they had declined.

To examine Tobin's hypothesis about the adaptive function of taking control of the environment in later life, correlations were made between Mastery and the other psychological and functional health measures. Because only 120 subjects completed the Mastery scale, these results reflect a truncated sample comprised mainly of better functioning individuals. As shown in Table 3.10, Mastery was associated with better functioning in mobility and activities of daily living, better ratings of subjective health and memory, and less depression.

Finally, the relation of birth year to the various measures used in this study was considered. In general, year of birth was not related to func-

**TABLE 3.9  Psychological Functioning**

|  | Mean | SD |
|---|---|---|
| Mastery ($N = 120$) (range 8–32) | 22.15 | 3.40 |
| Depression ($N = 139$) (range 0–33) | 9.19 | 5.60 |
| Subjective health ($N = 155$) (range 1–7) | 5.39 | 1.05 |
| Subjective memory ($N = 155$) (range 1–7) | 4.99 | 1.36 |

**TABLE 3.10  Correlations of Mastery and Other Psychological and Functional Health Measures**

| | Mastery | Depression | Perceived health | Perceived memory | Mobility | PADL | IADL |
|---|---|---|---|---|---|---|---|
| Mastery | — | | | | | | |
| Depression | -.60** | — | | | | | |
| Perceived health | .38** | -.34** | — | | | | |
| Perceived memory | .32** | -.33** | .30** | — | | | |
| Mobility | .53** | -.40** | .37** | .12 | — | | |
| PADL | .51** | -.37** | .34** | .21* | .85** | — | |
| IADL | .62** | -.35** | .32** | .30** | .72** | .72** | — |

*Note. N* varied, depending on the comparison.
\* *p* < .01
\*\* *p* < .001

59

tioning, but there were some exceptions. The variables on which there were significant differences among the birth cohorts, as indicated by analysis of variances, were: MIR, $F=2.99$, 3, 184, $p<.05$; PADL, $F=2.87$, 3, 184, $p<.05$; Mastery, $F=4.61$, 3, 116, $p<.01$; and years of education, $F=4.45$, 3, 163, $p<.01$. In all instances except education, later cohorts (1901, 1903) had a greater advantage, reflecting the likelihood that attrition produced a small, positive bias. For education, however, the 1899 cohort had slightly more years of schooling than other cohorts (mean=7.07 years, compared to 6.15 for 1897, 6.32 for 1901, and 6.10 for 1903). This finding was probably due to chance. Overall, the number of variables on which there were cohort differences was relatively small.

## DISCUSSION

This examination of 90-year-olds has generated paradoxical findings of relatively high rates of disability, as well as continued independence among a surprisingly large proportion of the sample. Disabilities are most likely to be present in IADLs, which are more complex and taxing activities than PADLs. Highest rates of disabilities are found for heavy housework, shopping, and banking. Mobility is limited, particularly in movement outside one's place of residence. This pattern of disabilities suggests a closing in of one's world, as independent activity outside one's house or place of residence becomes increasingly rare. Rates of cognitive impairment and dementia are also considerable. As a consequence, we can expect that support and care of 90-year-olds will be complicated and expensive.

It is perhaps more remarkable that so many 90-year-olds continue to function competently in the domains which were assessed. Indeed, the vast majority remain completely independent or nearly so in PADLs. Despite their limitations in IADLs, one half of the sample reside in independent housing, a large majority of whom live alone. This pattern undoubtedly is related to the availability of home services and other supportive help in Sweden, but it also suggests a preference for independence in very late life that warrants further study.

One factor contributing to this relatively high level of competency among 90-year-olds is selective survival. As my colleagues and I have shown in previous work using longitudinal data from this sample (Johansson & Zarit, 1995; Zarit et al., 1995), people with ADL and cognitive disabilities have higher rates of mortality than people who remain functionally competent. As a consequence of this selective mortality, new cases of disability do not add to the total of disabled in the population; instead, they take the place of old cases who have died. Under these circumstances, the overall prevalence of disability in the population does not increase rapidly in these advanced age groups. These findings indicate a high risk that significant ADL and cognitive disabilities will develop some time before death, but that survivors to age 90 are a select and hardy group, a majority of whom remain competent in most activities.

The results support and extend Neugarten's original conceptualization of young-old and old-old. The transition from independence to disability, which is encompassed by this dichotomy, is, perhaps, the most central event of later life. This transition becomes increasingly likely with advancing age, but can occur at any time, including before 65. Ironically, some of the participants in this study are chronologically among the oldest old, but functionally similar to the young-old, remaining relatively active, independent, and competent despite advancing age. Ninety year olds are a select and advantaged group for whom morbidity may indeed be compressed to a short period of time.

Tobin's notion about adaptation in very late life, that is, the importance of taking an active role in controlling one's environment, is worth examining in this light. In the present sample, it was possible to examine the relation of mastery, a construct similar to control, to competency. The sample for these analyses, however, was restricted to better functioning individuals, who were able to complete the Mastery Scale. For that group, a strong relation was found between having a greater sense of mastery and better health and psychological functioning. Since the data for mastery and functioning were obtained simultaneously, it was not possible to test the direction of effects. Using longitudinal data from the original OCTO sample, however, we found evidence that higher levels of mastery at baseline were related to better functional outcomes 2 years later (Kwee, Zarit, & Johansson, 1994). Measures of health and vitality did not account for changes in functioning over time. Thus, mastery, control, and related constructs may tap processes of adaptation that reduce the likelihood of decline.

From a policy perspective, there are two immediate implications of these findings. First, as has been widely observed, the oldest-old have considerable need for services. The combination of ADL disabilities and cognitive problems at these advanced ages poses special challenges for the organization and delivery of services and other kinds of assistance, and probably also increases the cost of care. The projected growth in numbers of people in these age groups will continue to strain society's resources, making it critical that we examine questions such as whether public funding should be available based on age or need. The considerable need of dependent elderly, the high rates of poverty among the young, and other contemporary social problems mean that we must make difficult decisions on allocating scarce resources.

Paradoxically, however, increasing the amount of help to an older person may decrease feelings of mastery or control over the environment. How to provide services in ways that promote rather than limit autonomy is a long-standing concern in the field that perhaps should be revisited (Kahn, 1975). In a sense, the key issue for many older people may be the knowledge that help would actually be available if needed. That assurance is available in Sweden, despite some recent cutbacks in services. Our more fragmented system of social and health services may inadvertently increase anxiety and decrease feelings of control (e.g., MaloneBeach, Zarit, & Spore, 1992).

In conclusion, life at age 90 appears as a more dramatic example of the young-old and old-old distinction. With advancing age, the transition to functional dependency becomes more likely, but even at 90 a significant proportion of people function independently in many areas of their lives. As the number of very old people continues to increase, Neugarten's distinction between young-old and old-old and her concern about the equitable distribution of resources in society provide an insightful framework for examining how best to support and, ultimately, to understand people in very late life.

# ACKNOWLEDGMENTS

This research has been supported by a grant from the Swedish Social Research Council. I would like to acknowledge the contributions of Bo Malmberg, Boo Johansson, and Stig Berg, of the Institute of Gerontology,

University College of Health Science, Jönköping, Sweden, who provided the overall direction to the OCTO study. I would also like to thank Elia Kwee and Shelly Tobin for their critical reading of earlier drafts of this manuscript.

## REFERENCES

American Psychiatric Association. (1987). *Diagnostic and statistical manual of mental disorders* (3rd ed., rev.). Washington, DC: Author.

Folstein, M. F., Folstein, S. E., & McHugh, P. R. (1975). "Mini-mental state." A practical method for grading the cognitive status of patients for the clinician. *Journal of Psychiatric Research, 17,* 189–198.

Fries, J. F. (1980). Aging, natural death and the compression of morbidity. *New England Journal of Medicine, 303,* 130–135.

Goodman, C. R., & Zarit, S. H. (1995). Ecological measures of cognitive functioning: A validation study. *International Psychogeriatrics, 7,* 1–12.

Guralnik, J. M. (1991). Prospects for the compression of morbidity: The challenge posed by increasing disability in the years prior to death. *Journal of Aging and Health, 3*(2), 138–154.

Johansson, B. (1988/89). *Minnestestet MIR* [The MIR Memory Test]. Stockholm: Psykologiforlaget.

Johansson, B., & Zarit, S. H. (1991). Dementia and cognitive impairment in the oldest old: A comparison of two rating methods. *International Psychogeriatrics, 3*(1), 29–38.

Johansson, B., & Zarit, S. H. (1995). Prevalence and incidence of dementia in the oldest old: A longitudinal study of a population-based sample of 84-90-year olds in Sweden. *International Journal of Geriatric Psychiatry.*

Johansson, B., Zarit, S. H., & Berg, S. (1992). Changes in cognitive functioning of the oldest old. *Journal of Gerontology: Psychological Sciences, 47,* P75–P80.

Johnson, C. L., & Troll, L. (1992). Family functioning in late late life. *Journal of Gerontology: Social Sciences, 47,* S66–S72.

Kahn, R. L. (1975). Mental health and the future aged. *The Gerontologist, 15*(1, Part 2), 24–31.

Katz, S., Ford, A. B., Moskowitz, R. W., Jackson, B. S., & Jaffe, M. W. (1963). Studies of illness in the aged. The index of ADL: A standardized measure of biological and psychosocial function. *Journal of the American Medical Association, 185,* 914–919.

Kohout, F. J., Berkman, L. F., Evans, D. A., & Cornoni-Huntley, J. (1993). Two shorter forms of the CES-D depression symptoms index. *Journal of Aging and Health, 5,* 179–193.

Kwee, E., Zarit, S. H., & Johansson, B. (1994, November). *Stability and decline in activities of daily living in the oldest old: A longitudinal study.* Paper presented at the meeting of the Gerontological Society of America, Atlanta.

Lawton, M. P. (1971). The functional assessment of elderly people. *Journal of the American Geriatrics Society, 19,* 465–481.

Lieberman, M. A., & Tobin, S. S. (1983). *The experience of old age: Stress, coping and survival.* New York: BasicBooks.

MaloneBeach, E. E., Zarit, S. H., & Spore, D. L. (1992). Caregivers' perceptions of case management and community-based services: Barriers to service use. *Journal of Applied Gerontology, 11,* 146–159.

Neugarten, B. L. (1974). Age groups in American society and the rise of the young-old. *Annals of the American Academy of Political and Social Science, 415,* 187–198.

Neugarten, B. L. (1982). Policy for the 1980s: Age or need entitlement. In B. L. Neugarten (Ed.), *Age or need? Public policies for older people* (pp. 19–32). Beverly Hills: Sage.

Olshansky, S. J., Rudberg, M. A., Carnes, B. A., Cassel, C. K., & Brody, J. A. (1991). Trading off longer life for worsening health: The expansion of morbidity hypothesis. *Journal of Aging and Health, 3,* 194–216.

Pearlin, L. I., & Schooler, C. (1978). The structure of coping. *Journal of Health and Social Behavior, 19,* 2–21.

Radloff, L. S. (1977). The CES-D scale: A self-report depression scale for research in the general population. *Applied Psychological Measurement, 1,* 385–401.

Rosenwaike, I. (1985). A demographic portrait of the oldest old. *Milbank Memorial Fund Quarterly/Health and Society, 63*(2), 187–205.

Suzman, R., & Riley, M. W. (1985). Introducing the "oldest old." *Milbank Memorial Fund Quarterly/Health and Society, 63*(2), 177–186.

Thorslund, M. (1991). The increasing number of very old people will change the Swedish model of the welfare state. *Social Science Medicine, 32,* 455–464.

Tobin, S. S. (1991). *Personhood in advanced old age: Implications for practice.* New York: Springer Publishing Co.

Tobin, S. S. (1994, November). *Continuities and discontinuities in advanced aging.* Paper presented at the meeting of the Gerontological Society of America, Atlanta.

Wechsler, D. (1945). A standardized memory scale for clinical use. *Journal of Psychology, 19,* 87–95.

Zarit, S. H., & Johansson, B. (1993). Functional impairment and co-disability in the oldest old: A multidimensional approach. *Journal of Aging and Health, 5,* 291–305.

Zarit, S. H., Johansson, B., & Malmberg, B. (1995). Changes in functional competency in the oldest old: A longitudinal study. *Journal of Aging and Health, 7,* 3–23.

# Comments

## Fay Lomax Cook

In describing functioning among adults at age 90, Steven Zarit's research illustrates the continuing truth of points that Bernice Neugarten first helped draw to gerontologists' attention a number of years ago. First, older adults are a very heterogeneous group. As Neugarten noted,

> It is important to recognize that people grow old in very different ways, and they become increasingly different from one another with the passage of time, at least until the very terminal stage of life when biological decrement may level out individual differences. (1982, p. 36)

Zarit shows that, even at age 90, the adults whom he studied were a very diverse group. They were homogeneous in only one way—their age.

Second, among older adults, there exist the young-old and the old-old. Although Neugarten first described the distinction between the young-old and the old-old as based on chronological age (1974, p. 187; 1975, p. 7), she later elaborated on that distinction and argued that it should be seen not as one of chronological age but rather as one of frailty and ill health (1982, p. 21). She noted that "The young-old are those men and women who are healthy and vigorous retirees. . . . The old-old, by contrast, are persons who have suffered major physical or mental deterioration" (p. 22).

Zarit's research illuminates Neugarten's analysis further by showing that although chronological age clearly increases the likelihood of functional losses, there remain the young-old among the oldest old. A significant proportion of the adults in Zarit's sample—even at age 90—function independently in many areas of their lives.

In illuminating our understanding of the different ways in which adults at age 90 function, Zarit shows that mastery is particularly important—the degree to which people feel they have control or influence over the events in their lives. Specifically, he found that adults aged 90 with a greater sense of mastery have better health and psychological functioning. Further, the association between mastery and better health and psychological functioning was confirmed in longitudinal analysis: Feelings of mastery at one point in time predict better functioning at a later point in time. This finding clarifies the causal direction of the relationship.

Sense of mastery is important not only to older people. It is important throughout the life course—as the kindergartner makes the transition to school for the first time, as the pubescent adolescent makes the transition to high school, as the more mature adolescent makes the transition from high school to either work or college, as the adult makes transitions to job, to marriage, to retirement, and to coping with ill health of self or family member. This is the notion that National Institute on Aging officials had in mind when they requested proposals for research on sense of control through the life course in the late 1980s. Zarit has helped us learn much more about the importance of one aspect of sense of control—mastery—in this chapter.

Those of us interested in human development and social policy must think in greater detail about how we can build into social programs experiences that will facilitate not only feelings of mastery, but also experiences of mastery. As policy advisers or policy makers, it is important that we help to translate social science findings into practice when such translation appears both possible and useful.

As scholars, we have delineated differences between sense of control and self-efficacy. We now need more carefully to delineate the differences, if any, between mastery and sense of control. If there is no difference, we should probably try to be consistent and use only one term to describe what we mean. Finally, given the great heterogeneity throughout the life course that Bernice Neugarten's research and writings have shown there to be and that Steven Zarit has shown there to be even among adults age 90, I think it may be useful to learn more about the ways in which mastery may mean different things for different people at different points in the life course and at any one point in the life course.

# REFERENCES

Neugarten, B. L. (1974). Age groups in American society and the rise of the young-old. *The Annals of the American Academy of Political and Social Science, 415,* 187–198.

Neugarten, B. L. (1975). The future and the young-old. *The Gerontologist, 15,* 4–9.

Neugarten, B. L. (1982). *Age or need? Public policies for older people.* Beverly Hills: Sage.

# CHAPTER 4

# Life Course and Persistent Psychiatric Illness: Social Timing, Cohort, and Intervention

## Bertram J. Cohler, Susan A. Pickett, and Judith A. Cook

The life course perspective has proven significant both in understanding social change, as in studies of intergenerational relations (Bengtson & Allen, 1993; Bengtson & Black, 1973; Elder, 1984; Flacks, 1971), and also in the study of particular lives over time (Elder, 1992; Elder & Caspi, 1990). Circumstances of individual lives, including unexpected life changes, are experienced within the context of a unique configuration of social and historical events that determine the timing of expectable role transitions. These social and historical factors (such as war, natural disasters, and economic dislocation) shape the very structure and extent of the convoy of consociates (Antonucci, 1990; Kahn & Antonucci, 1980; Plath, 1980) so important as the source of those socially constructed meanings of particular life events (Bengtson & Allen, 1993; Durkheim, 1915; Mannheim, 1923/1952; Neugarten, Moore, & Lowe, 1965; Sorokin & Merton, 1937). Indeed, little can be said about particular lives without recognizing the impact upon them of social and historical context. The life course perspective calls into question any predefined assumptions regarding personality change and age; there is little reason to assume constancy in personality or world view and particular ages outside of location within a particular point in time.

This chapter uses concepts founded in life course social science in the study of persistent psychiatric illness, which has an impact not only on the life of the afflicted patient, but also on the larger family unit. Formerly viewed as a disturbance particularly relevant for the lives of young adults, it is now recognized that first episodes of psychiatric illness such as schizophrenia may take place in later life (Cohler & Ferrono, 1987; Jeste, 1991, 1993; Yassa, 1991), and that the best way to understand the life course of those challenged by persistent distress over the course of adult life is as alternation between periods in which symptoms are relatively quiescent and periods when life changes, often idiosyncratic, trigger complex psychobiological systems, leading to changes in brain chemistry and such behavioral symptoms as hallucinations, delusions, and marked mood fluctuations. The behavioral changes, in turn, require intervention, which most often leads to a period of psychiatric hospitalization, stabilization of symptoms through medication and psychotherapy, and then return to the community for an indefinite period of time.

These unpredictable episodes occur across the course of adult life, and often appear to be triggered by particular life changes posing what is perceived as an insuperable obstacle, such as a college examination or job change. Successive episodes often lead to significant impairment in functioning in major adult roles and problems in effectively managing the developmental tasks of adult life. Psychiatric illness occurs among people functioning at both high and low levels of attainment prior to the onset of the disturbance. In all cases, the catastrophe presents challenges to both personal and familial coping ability (Tobin, Chapter 6, this volume), and creates particular challenges for continuing family or community care (Sheehan, 1982).

While the life course following the first episode shows marked variation (some adults remain symptom free in the community for many years between episodes), subsequent episodes pose the threat of continual disruption for the lives of both patient and family. Further, both across the course of life and across cohorts of patients and their families, the meaning of disturbance and intervention shifts dramatically. Among persons with schizophrenia, there are significant cohort differences in terms of age at first onset, treatments available at age of onset, history of intervention using psychosocial and psychoactive treatment, duration of time between episodes, and changing attitudes within both the professional and lay community regarding the origins of the illness. Experiences with both initial and subsequent hospitalizations, including the period of crisis prior to hospitalization and the impact of dealing with the hospital, take their toll on the family's capacity to deal with the challenge (Cohler, Pickett, & Cook, 1991; Costell & Reiss, 1982; Costell, Reiss, Berkman, & Jones, 1981). Moreover, particular issues are posed when parents are dealing with the first hospitalization of young adult offspring and when much older parents are dealing with persistently troubled middle-aged and older offspring still requiring continuing care or even periodic rehospitalization (Cook, Lefley, Pickett, & Cohler, 1994).

There has been relatively little effort to understand schizophrenia in terms of concepts and methods pioneered by life course social science (Harding, 1991; Strauss & Harding, 1990). The very complexity of life history and treatment patterns among schizophrenic adults and their families suggests the value of a life course perspective in understanding this disturbance as an eruptive, adverse life change for both patient and family. The scholarly framework for this reconsideration is founded in Neugarten's (1979) overview on psychiatry and the course of life, which calls for a reconsideration of continuity and change across the course of adult lives, and which shows the significance of social timing and cohort as essential in understanding both personal and social change.

## LIFE COURSE AND SOCIAL CHANGE

Explaining social change remains a challenge for the social sciences. Maintenance of social life might be explained through analysis of the function of particular social institutions, but the manner in which social life changes over time has been much more difficult to understand. For example, it is clear that relations between men and women are understood in quite different ways now than even three decades ago. The period from 1965–1975 represented a "watershed" in American social life; both values and actions showed dramatic change over that 10-year period. The capacity to understand this change may be tied to recognition of the significance of the linked concepts of *cohort* and *generation* in social life.

## Life Span and Life Course: Social Time and Expectable Transitions

Across the past three decades there has been a dramatic shift in the study of lives over time from a life span or life cycle perspective to a life course perspective (Hagestad, 1990; Hagestad & Neugarten, 1985). Although the concept of life cycle focuses upon particular persons understood as transformed from a predefined period to another period in an ordered, cyclical sequence, the concept of the life course presumes an open system, recognizing social and historical process, and understanding lives over time within the context of both expectable and eruptive life changes (Elder, 1992; Neugarten & Hagestad, 1976). The life course perspective portrays persons within a much larger context of socially constructed transitions, which are reflected in the conceptions of self and other within particular societies at particular times. Particular lives reflect these shared conceptions as modified through uniquely ordered yet unpredictable life circumstances.

Central to the life course perspective is the concept of *generation,* which, as Troll (1970) and Bengtson, Furlong, and Laufer (1974) have discussed, refers to three age-linked characteristics: place in society within a cluster of four or five groups alive at the same time; period or point in the course of life such as youth or middle age; and cohort, or persons of a given birth year who have experienced similar social and historical events in common. The very age distribution in society leads to groups of persons with understandings of self, others, and experience largely shaped by particular historical events, which, together with the timing of expectable and eruptive life changes, determine individual life circumstances and morale (Cohler & Boxer, 1984; Pearlin, 1980; Pearlin, Menaghan, Lieberman, & Mullan, 1981). The concept of *point* or *period* in the course of life suggests that persons in similar social circumstances represent a convoy of consociates who interpret expectable role transitions associated with particular transition points in predictable ways. From school leaving to advent of parenthood, retirement, or widowhood, response to transitions cannot be understood apart from a life history of particular events taking place over time.

Finally, the concept of *generation* includes the concept of *cohort* or group of persons of a given birth year who are of a particular age when they experience these social and historical events. A preschool child will have a quite different response to such catastrophes as war or natural disaster than a teenager or middle-aged adult (Tuttle, 1993). Being of a particular age at the time of the experience leads to some shared understanding of the subsequent course of life; this understanding is different for those who were either younger or older at the time these events took place. The life course perspective suggests that it is difficult to talk about expectable timetables for life transitions—just as it is difficult to portray modal personality patterns for persons of particular ages, or particular points in the course of life such as adolescence or midlife—except as qualified in terms of generation, understood in terms of particular sociohistorical changes taking place for persons born at about the same time and traveling through the course of life as a cohort. However, it is also important to heed Rosow's (1978) caution that it is difficult to determine the boundaries of a cohort or to know how many years constitute a significant cohort difference.

These aspects of generation determine how persons understand the sequence and timing of both expectable and eruptive events across the course of life. Neugarten and her colleagues (1965) have shown that, among generations alive at any point in time, there is shared agreement regarding the definition of age. Although older adults are somewhat more tolerant than younger adults of variation in the time for the occurrence of particular role transitions, there is broad agreement on what constitutes childhood, adolescence, adulthood, and later life. Following Durkheim's (1915/1965) discussion of time and the ritual life of the community, Sorokin and Merton (1937), Roth (1963), Neugarten and Hagestad (1976), Hazan (1980), and Hagestad and Neugarten (1985) have suggested that persons carry an internal timetable for expectable role transitions and associated life changes.

Across the course of life, persons continually compare their own place with that shared definition of being "on-time," or of being "off-time"—early or late. Even very young children learn the sequence of expectable events taking place across the course of life, from first entrance into school through school leaving, first job, marriage or partnership, advent of parenthood, retirement, widowhood, and death (Farnham-Diggory, 1966). These expectable life changes are the background of personal experience. Particular, generally unpredictable, life circumstances, both adverse and positive, take place in the context of these expectable life changes (Pearlin, Menaghan, Lieberman, & Mullan, 1981). Eruptive life changes, such as widowhood in the fourth decade of a woman's life rather than in the eighth decade, pose particular problems, both because there are few consociates with whom to share burdens and to provide assistance, and also because there has been little time to rehearse these life changes through observation of others who have confronted and managed such adversity (Neugarten & Hagestad, 1976).

Seltzer (1976) and Cohler and Boxer (1984) have suggested that the experience of positive morale or life satisfaction is largely determined by the sense of being on-time for expectable role transitions or life changes. The sense that life changes and role transitions are taking place as expected, and that one is on-time for these events consistent with other members of a cohort or generation, is associated with enhanced personal congruence. At the same time, it is important to recognize that there may be cohort differences in definition of timing of role transitions. Within the generation of young adults who were born roughly in the late 1960s and early 1970s, the so-called "Generation X-ers," problems in finding employment in an economy experiencing serious dislocation have led to the realization that their first job may not take place until their late 20s, leading to postponement of marriage and parenthood. Comparing their own place in the course of life with preceding generations, these young adults experience lowered morale and frustration from being late off-time for these particular role transitions. However, compared to the lives of other members of their generation, the displacement appears much less bleak and morale improves.

Being early off-time poses particular disadvantages because of lack of preparation for the change, together with lack of others experiencing similar changes with whom to share the experience and realize enhanced support. Although, as Furstenberg, Brooks-Gunn, and Morgan (1987) have suggested, persons may in later life overcome the problems associated with such early off-time transitions as advent of parenthood, at least at the time this transition poses significant burdens. On the other hand, being late off-time in terms of the shared timetable for life changes has certain advantages. As Nydegger (1980, 1981) and Daniels and Weingarten (1982) have observed, men who make the transition to parenthood late are more settled in their career and more comfortable with themselves than men who make this transition on time, when they are involved with establishing a career and other early adult concerns.

## Cohort and Social Change

Schaie's (1984) summary of his work on the Seattle Longitudinal Study highlights the significance of generation (understood as cohort) for psychometric test findings. The work of Glen Elder and his colleagues, summarized in Elder and Caspi (1990), has provided an understanding of the manner in which these events shape the course of lives over time. Using data collected at the Institute of Human Development at the University of California, Berkeley, Elder (1974) was able to show the differential impact of the Great Depression on the adjustment of groups of preschool and adolescent boys and girls. Elder's work has provided an opportunity to understand how persons born at about the same time, experiencing particular events in common, are similarly affected in the subsequent course of life. As Elder and Caspi (1990) observe, year of birth serves to locate persons in history, and provides an index of the range of events likely to have an impact upon particular lives.

Elder and Caspi further suggest that the pile-up of historical events may have a particular impact upon lives. For example, for those persons born after World War II—who arrived at mid-adolescence during the turbulent years of the 1960s following the assassinations of John F. Kennedy, Martin Luther King, Jr., and Robert Kennedy—the urban riots of the time, the Vietnam conflict, and the totality of this tumultuous era shaped their lives. The experiences of the decade of the 1960s led subsequently to a number of different outcomes, depending upon circumstances of "birth and fortune" of this very large birth cohort (Easterlin, 1987), such as becoming social radicals or conservatives, and remaining social activists or becoming yuppies. The very size of this cohort has inspired lifelong competition for resources ranging from college entrance to jobs and access to health care, and is likely to influence the lives of its members through oldest age.

The concept of *cohort,* understood as an index of particular social and historical events shaping the lives of all those of a particular age experiencing these events in common, becomes a major factor in understanding social change. There is some evidence that events taking place during adolescence are particularly likely to have an impact upon later experience of self and others (Clausen, 1993; Schuman & Scott, 1989). The adolescent experiences of the "60s Generation," those coming of age across the turbulent era of the 1960s, was vastly different from those who were adolescents ten years earlier, during the Eisenhower years, when American society was particularly prosperous and peaceful, or ten years later, when the impact of the social unrest of the 1960s had led to a conservative backlash and enhanced emphasis on individual choice and rational decision making as the determinants of life chances.

Considering that at any one time there may be several age cohorts alive when a series of linked social and historical events occurs, the dynamics of response by these cohorts to both particular events and succeeding events becomes a major factor in understanding social change and intergenerational (cohort) conflicts at particular points in time. Recognizing that socialization processes refer both to "forward" socialization of younger by older persons and also "backward" social-ization of older by younger persons, the complex dynamics of social change become ever more difficult to study (Cook & Cohler, 1986). For example, the social values of the cohort of persons who were in their mid-teens during the era of the turbulent 1960s affected the values of the larger society. Increased personal freedom and tolerance for varia-tion in lifestyle, together with increased recognition of the importance of social equality, all stem from the effect of "reverse" socialization by articulate members of this cohort on social institutions ranging from higher education to the federal government. Indeed, there may be no modern period in which social attitudes changed as rapidly as during the decade from about 1965–1975.

## LIVING "OUTSIDE OF TIME": SCHIZOPHRENIC ADULTS AND THEIR FAMILIES

If persons continually evaluate their own lives in terms of a definition of the course of life that is shared within and across generations alive at any one time, morale will be largely a function of remaining within the range of life transitions expected for the members of a cohort or generation. Further, morale extends beyond particular persons to the larger family. As Cohler (1983) and Pruchno, Blow, and Smyer (1984) have observed, families consist of interlinked lives; the problems and attainments of one generation within the family have an impact on that of other generations. For example, in the study of women hospitalized for psychiatric illness during the years when there are young children at home, this generally unexpected, adverse life change affects husband, parents of both husband and wife, and even the larger kin group, who may be called in to assist the husband and father to manage home, family, and work (Grunebaum, Gamer, & Cohler, 1983). In a similar manner, when an older adult develops Alzheimer's disease, this adversity affects not only offspring, but also the patient's own brothers and sisters and other members of the family as well (Cohler, Groves, Borden, & Lazarus, 1989; Horwitz, Tessler, Fisher, & Gamache, 1992). Particularly when the older patient is single, brothers and sisters play major roles in assisting with finances, housekeeping, and other aspects of the patient's life (Cohler et al., 1991).

## SCHIZOPHRENIA, AGING, AND THE LIFE COURSE

Psychiatric illness represents an important area in which to apply the significance of the social timetable across the life course. Formerly seen simply as non-normative actions and personal disorganization resulting in episodes of hospitalization and return to the community, psychiatric illness, when viewed from a life course perspective, results in off-time life transitions that affect the morale of both patient and family over periods of decades. Consistent with Hogan's (1981) discussion of disrupted careers, the very pattern of hospitalization and discharge leads to discontinuous careers, which affect future earning power in the labor market and capacity to perform effectively in such other adult roles as spouse or parent. In the main, persons with persistent psychiatric illness live "outside of social time." The very sense of living outside of time (unable to fully participate in expectable transitions across the life course), the very sense of such a non-normative life course, assumes implicitly the capacity for comparing one's own career with that more generally expected in society. Lowered morale and the negative symptoms characteristic of schizophrenia (Andreasen, 1985) may be seen, at least in part, as a consequence of this recognition of living outside of time.

To date, there has been very little study of social timing among persons with persistent psychiatric illness. Little recognition has been given to the significance of changing treatment regimes (e.g., the move away from extended hospitalizations to the use of psychotropic medication and return to community care) as sociohistorical events likely to determine the experience of self, other, and illness in quite different ways across successive cohorts of persons with schizophrenia at particular points in the course of life. However, available findings contrasting first episodes of schizophrenic illness in early adulthood with those in middle age suggest a course of illness in which the first episode appears after midlife may be less virulent, presenting with fewer symptoms of the illness (Bridge, Cannon, & Wyatt, 1978; Jeste, 1993).

Further, there is some evidence that, even among persons persistently hospitalized over long periods of time, middle age leads to enhanced awareness of the finitude of life (Marshall, 1975, 1986; Munnichs, 1966), including awareness that more time has been lived already than remains to be lived (Lawton, 1972). This very awareness of finitude requires some shared understanding of the expectable duration of life, and the ability to compare present situation with this shared timetable of the duration of life itself. It may well be that aging fosters enhanced concern with reminiscence and life review among older psychiatrically ill persons just as it does among nondisabled older counterparts; to date there has been little study of this issue (Seeman, 1976).

It is still not clear what the impact has been of the experience of being outside of time on more recent cohorts of persons who have been persistently psychiatrically ill since early adulthood and who now spend increasing amounts of time in the community. Community residence has been assumed to foster enhanced performance of expectable adult norms through more frequent contact with prevailing expectations for adults within the community, and to make possible the resumption of work and more frequent contact with family members (Simmons & Freeman, 1959). This contact, however, may only enhance the sense of poor morale by burdening these adults with expectations they are unable to realize (Angrist, Lefton, Dinitz, & Pasamanick, 1968), and with being off-time, that is, no longer within the framework of expectable transitions that define adulthood (Hagestad, Chapter 9, this volume). Comparison between their own attainments and those of brothers and sisters, former friends, and associates may further exacerbate the gulf these adults experience between their present life and the accomplishments of others.

Similarly, interruptions in the career of life by successive episodes of exacerbation of symptoms, rehospitalization, and discharge may be so disruptive for maintenance of a sense of personal integrity that the experience of social time may be affected. The person may continue to experience himself or herself as outside of time, in spite of community dwelling. Hagestad's (this volume) moving portrayal of the impact of physical illness on personal career across the course of life would support this view of intervention as inherently disruptive, even though enhanced contact with the community is possible when persons are not continually hospitalized across the course of adult life. The questions these issues raise must be pursued recognizing the great variation that exists within the life world of persistently psychiatrically ill adults, from those who are nearly continuously hospitalized over time to those fortunate adults who are able to remain in the community for longer periods of time between episodes and who are better able to resume at least some of the expectable tasks of adult life (Clausen, 1984a, 1984b; Cohler & Ferrono, 1987).

Recognizing the significant cohort changes that have taken place in the past four decades in the course of schizophrenia and means of intervention in this disturbance, it is striking that there has been so little effort to understand this illness in terms of life course social science. The most systematic study of this issue has been reported by Clausen (1984b) in a review of work begun in the mid-1950s at the National Institute of Mental Health (NIMH) intramural program, following persons with schizophrenia and their families over a period of several years. Nearly two decades following the original study, a group of these former patients, together with similar patients studied elsewhere, were called in for an additional round of interviews. Clausen's surprising findings were that most of the ill individuals in the NIMH study had been able to return home, resume former jobs, continue life within their family, and make a satisfactory community adjustment. A second, additional cohort of persons hospitalized during the 1970s, when hospital stays were shorter, also reported reasonably effective adjustment upon returning home to family and community. While more than a third reported additional episodes of illness, hospitalization, and return to the community, most former patients were able to make an effective adjustment. Significantly, more than half of men initially hospitalized for schizophrenia in the 1950s remained symptom free, functioned effectively in the community, and reported continuity in their relationships with wives and other family members.

While, as Clausen observes, questions may be posed regarding the reliability of the diagnosis (e.g., many persons diagnosed with schizophrenia in the 1950s would today be given a diagnosis of bipolar disorder), these findings illustrate the variety of life outcomes possible with-in a group of adults hospitalized with major mental illness. Further, similar conclusions were reached by a number of European investiga-tors (summarized in Cohler & Ferrono, 1987). Clausen (1984b) also supports the variety of outcomes based on the follow-through study of families of persons hospitalized as a part of the NIMH schizophrenia program. Three reports based on a group of persons hospitalized in the only state hospital in Vermont (Harding, 1991; Harding, Brooks, & Strauss, 1984; Harding, Brooks, Ashikaga, Strauss, & Landerl, 1987). The majority of the former patients studied by Harding and her colleagues were able to maintain an effective community adjustment and were not rehospitalized. Critics of the Vermont study have argued that individuals functioning so well within the community could not have been "really" schizophrenic. However, there maybe fewer pressures exerted on adults living in largely rural Vermont than on adults living urban lifestyles.

Findings reported by Clausen (1984a, 1984b) and by Strauss and his colleagues (Strauss, 1989; Strauss, Hafez, Lieberman, & Harding, 1985; Strauss & Harding, 1990), suggest quite different life paths and wide variation in the adult life course of persons hospitalized for psychiatric illness. Indeed, only about a fifth of persons with schizophrenia, prin-cipally defined by Bleuler (1911/1950) and Kraepelin (1902, 1913/1919) as *dementia praecox* or the group of schizophrenias, might be charac-terized as maintaining continuous or nearly continuous residence apart from the community. Most adults with persistent psychiatric disorder spend periods of some duration in the community, interrupted by episodes of acute distress and exacerbation of symptoms leading to rehospitalization. This expectable course of life among adults first showing psychiatric distress in young to mid-adulthood has been por-trayed by Zubin and his colleagues (Zubin, Magaziner, & Steinhauer, 1983; Zubin & Spring, 1977; Zubin & Steinhauer, 1981), using the con-cept of *vulnerability.*

Consistent with Beck and Worthen's (1972) discussion of the idio-syncratic nature of the life changes identified by these patients as responsible for episodes of enhanced distress, and Gottesman and Shields' (1982) discussion of the genetics of schizophrenia, Zubin and his colleagues suggest that differential genetic loading for major men-tal disorders is associated with differences in vulnerability to episodes of disorders. Among those adults with a higher genetic loading, experi-ence of particular life changes with particular meanings may trigger a first episode, which then enhances the probability of later episodes. Implicit in Zubin's discussion is the assumption that a first episode is disruptive to the shared timetable for expectable role transitions. Hospitalized for varying lengths of time, these adults are excused from expectable adult role performance because of illness and soon find themselves outside of time. Remaining apart from the community and vulnerable, they become successively more isolated and outside of time to the point where they have little connection with the expectable course of adult lives.

For these troubled adults, life goes on without them; they exist outside of time, which passes around them as family and friends continue on the expectable course of life (Hagestad, this volume). Even if remaining in care for a brief duration, these adults are unable to resume prior life upon discharge from care. Their idiosyncratic approach to others, together with cognitive changes, often leave even highly functioning adults unable to resume successful careers and close family ties following episodes of illness (Clausen, 1984a). Although, as Freeman and Simmons (1963) note, reduced expectations foster lowered role performance, enhanced expectations for resuming roles assumed prior to illness may lead to greater posthospital distress, as Angrist et al. (1968) have shown.

## Life Course and Care: Family and Patient Together

Over the past few years, there has been dramatic reconsideration of the place of the family in major mental illness. While, formerly, family interactional or communication processes were considered responsible for the onset of illness through "forward" socialization of offspring into irrationality by parents unable to effectively negotiate reality (Dinitz, Lefton, Angrist, & Pasamanick, 1961a, 1961b; Lidz, 1973; Lidz et al., 1965; Singer & Wynne, 1963; Wynne, Singer, Bartko, & Toohey, 1977), contemporary perspectives regarding the family of persons with persistent psychiatric illness focus on the nature of the individual's relationship with parents and brothers and sisters. Methods of studying relations between the adult generations parallel those used more generally in the study of parent-offspring ties. Indeed, even the tradition of "expressed emotion" (Leff & Vaughn, 1985), stressing the impact of parental hostility and criticism as a factor presumed to be associated with early return to the hospital, is regarded as problematic (Hatfield, Spaniol, & Zipple, 1987).

Following Lefley's (1987) call to reconsider intergenerational relations between distressed offspring and their parents in terms of lifetime caregiving, this intergenerational caregiving perspective has informed the work of groups studying psychiatrically ill adults and their parents at several sites: Boston University (Jung & Spaniol, 1983; Jung, Spaniol, & Anthony, 1983; Spaniol, 1987; Spaniol & Jung, 1983), the University of Massachusetts at Amherst (Gubman & Tessler, 1987; Horwitz et al., 1992; Tessler, Fisher, & Gamache, 1990; Tessler, Killian, & Gubman, 1987), the University of Wisconsin-Madison (Greenley, 1972, 1979; Greenberg, Greenley, McKee, Brown, & Griffin-Francell, 1993; Greenberg, Seltzer, & Greenley, 1993; Pickett, Greenley, & Greenberg, in press; Seltzer, Greenberg, & Wyngaarden-Krauss, 1995), and the University of Chicago and the Thresholds National Research and Training Center on Rehabilitation and Mental Illness (Cohler et al., 1991; Cook & Cohler, 1986; Cook, Hoffschmidt, Cohler, & Pickett, 1992; Cook et al., 1994; Cook & Pickett, 1988; Pickett, Cook, & Cohler, 1994; Pickett, Cook, & Solomon, in press; Pickett, Vraniak, Cook, & Cohler, 1994). The Boston University group has been concerned principally with the relationship of family process to intervention, and the Amherst group to survey studies of patients and their families. The Madison and Chicago investigators have focused particularly on the family of later adulthood, including both middle-aged and older ill offspring and their much older parents, and on frustrations and satisfactions founded in providing care for older, persistently troubled offspring.

As these researchers have shown, issues of cohort and social timing are essential in understanding the lives of adults with persistent psychiatric illness and the reciprocal impact of parents' disappointments and resumption of caregiving for their ill adult offspring (Cook & Cohler, 1986; Cook et al., 1994; Pickett et al., 1994). Studies of intergenerational relations show that a first episode of psychiatric illness in young adulthood—later marked by a life course of difficulty in maintaining pre-illness levels of functioning, failure to realize expectable role attainments, and uncertainty about the future—takes a toll on the family. Parental disappointment is often evident (Pickett et al., 1994; Pickett et al., in press). For example, one parental couple told of their son's breakdown, which occurred while he was attending an elite Ivy League college. He was formerly a promising student and active in college life, but disappointment about the end of a relationship triggered an initial episode of schizophrenia. Following a stay in an outstanding psychiatric hospital, this young man was unable to resume studies and dropped out of college. Returning home, he drifted around the community, became involved in substance abuse, experienced increased symptoms, and was hospitalized again near his home. A brief hospital stay was followed by a decision to leave home; residence in a closely monitored, hospital-related halfway house permitted the young man to begin work at a local fast-food chain. He has maintained himself precariously in this work, but his adjustment continues to be tenuous and his social relations remain impoverished. His parents want to maintain contact yet are embarrassed by their son's inability to engage in appropriate conversation.

Just as more generally in contemporary society, both persons with persistent psychiatric illness and their family caregivers are living longer. Particular problems are faced by much older parents caring for their middle-aged ill offspring. While the burden most likely reported by younger parents concerns the antisocial behavior so often characteristic of persons experiencing episodes of disturbance, the burden most often reported by older parents concerns provision for the future and increased cognitive preoccupation with the ill child's problems (Cook et al., 1994). There is concern for the support of the troubled offspring in the event of the parent's own death, and continuing parental disappointment that the ill offspring has failed to reach his or her own potential.

Among the most frequently requested services of the National Alliance for the Mentally Ill (NAMI) is legal assistance, both in order to provide care for an offspring limited in coping ability in the event of parental death and in order to ensure that the ill offspring's care will not burden nondisabled siblings. However, as Cicirelli (1980, 1985) and Horwitz et al. (1992) have shown, brothers and sisters continue to support each other across the course of life, regardless of illness and infirmity. A pilot study underway by the group of investigators at Thresholds and the University of Chicago show that among older adults residing in intermediate care facilities (board and care), brothers and sisters maintain contact even after parents are deceased, providing both quality control for the kind of care their afflicted siblings receive, and helping out with small financial donations and birthday and holiday gifts. Many of these brothers and sisters invite their ill siblings home for holidays or for brief visits. Not only do they believe that this support is consistent with what their own parents would have expected of them but also they gain an enhanced sense of personal integrity and satisfaction based on doing what they believe to be right for their afflicted siblings. Cohler et al. (1989) report similar findings from the study of brothers and sisters of older adults afflicted with Alzheimer's disease.

These findings suggest that parental preoccupation with brothers and sisters being burdened by demands of caregiving may reflect more the concerns of parents themselves than the reality of caregiving. Indeed, the primary concern parents face is their own disappointment and frustration with their offspring's limitations in being able to realize expectable developmental tasks and role transitions of the adult years. Parental disappointments regarding the failure of troubled offspring to resume the expected course of adult life are most marked among older parents, particularly when the offspring's first episode has been later in the course of life (Cook & Pickett, 1988). Winkler (1986) has suggested further that older parents may be more involved than younger parents in the process of life review (Butler, 1963). Review of the past may reactivate awareness of aspirations for their offspring's success earlier in life. Older parents also may grieve both the loss of the offspring's ability to provide caregiving for them and the fact that there may not be grandchildren. Obviously, if the ill offspring is an only child, these problems will be further highlighted.

Other factors, such as ethnicity and gender, also influence parental expectations and caregiving burden. Significantly, African American families who report strong intergenerational ties and a variety of kindred to assist with support and direct caregiving, through contribution of time and other "in-kind" resources, are likely to fare better than European American counterparts (Pickett et al., 1994). European American parents are more likely to continue to hold out expectations for significant performance within expectable adult roles and are thus particularly likely to be disappointed. African American parents appear to more accurately estimate their offspring's personal strengths and weaknesses than European-American parents and to be most troubled by illness-related factors such as inappropriate social contact, while European-American parents appear most troubled by limitations in the offspring's ability to attain expected success within the adult world. Reported feelings of burden are similar but the characteristics of the burden and of the disappointment appear to be different.

Mothers are particularly burdened, since they continue to be the primary care providers within the family of adulthood (Cook, 1988). As one 85-year-old mother of a 60-year-old ill adult offspring observed, "We have lived together most of his life and he still won't take out the garbage." The Wisconsin group (Greenberg, Greenley, et al., 1993) report that mothers are particularly affected by offspring with persistent psychiatric illness, but that mothers living apart from their afflicted offspring may experience even greater role strain and a greater number of health-related problems than co-residing generations, because of increased financial burdens of supporting two households.

Older mothers of adults with psychiatric illness experience a greater degree of both burden and frustration than is reported among mothers of developmentally disabled offspring (Greenberg, Greeley, et al., 1993). Consistent with discussion of comparative burden posed by persistent psychiatric illness and developmental disability (Cohler et al., 1991), Greenberg, Seltzer, and Greenley (1993) suggest that it is the sudden onset of psychiatric illness that is particularly disruptive for parents of psychiatrically ill adults; parents of developmentally challenged adults have dealt with limitations in offspring coping ability for many years, sometimes stemming from prenatal life.

In part as a consequence of disappointments first encountered in adulthood, and in part as a consequence of the inherently greater disruption evoked by psychiatric illness, mothers find it difficult to manage their feelings of burden and frustration, which are expressed as emotion-centered rather than problem-centered coping (Lazarus & Folkman, 1984). They deal with their offspring in ways that reflect the feelings of hostility and criticism reported in the studies of Leff and Vaughn (1985), Falloon, Boyd, and McGill (1984), and others studying psychiatric illness within the family of the adult years (Cohler et al., 1991). These mothers in middle and later life caring for middle-aged and older repeatedly rehospitalized offspring lack the perspective on offspring illness and family response more characteristic of mothers of developmentally disabled offspring, who rely to a greater extent on problem-centered coping, such as planning for the future, and on a more positive reinterpretation of present family relations.

Just as with family caregivers for patients with Alzheimer's disease, feelings of frustration and burden are enhanced by several factors related to the sense of control. Caregivers lack control over the psychiatrically ill offspring's expression of distress; they cannot predict times when symptoms are likely to become exacerbated; and they feel help-less before the offspring's behavior and expression of feelings.

# CONCLUSION

A life course perspective, focusing on socially constructed determinants of continuity and change over time, widens the range of study possible of adult lives within the context of both family and community. Rather than considering the course of development in terms of pre-defined tasks, stages, or presumably irreversible sequences, the life course perspective provides an "open systems" approach to understanding meaning for persons as they negotiate both expectable transitions and unexpected, generally adverse, life changes that disrupt the expectable course of adult lives. In the first place, the concept of a social timetable highlights the extent to which present understanding of self, others, and experience are constructed within a world of shared meanings. Those life changes which are early off-time in terms of expectable course of life, such as adolescent pregnancy or unexpected illness and loss of spouse or partner, are particularly adverse because of a lack of others experiencing similar disruption and available to offer support and understanding, together with lack of preparation for such change. Preparation and support missing from such early off-time transitions are two characteristics of on-time transitions.

Concepts of social time and shared timetable are limited by participation within a particular generation or cohort, defined in terms of both birth year and shared experience of particular sociohistorical events. The very definition of expectable transitions into and out of adult social roles, together with the sequence of these transitions and the impact of adverse, off-time changes, must be viewed within the context of particular generations or cohorts. The presence within a society at any given time of successive cohorts defining events in somewhat different terms lends variety and complexity to social life, and represents a source of social change. A recognition that older adults attempt to socialize younger adults into new roles across the course of life, and also that younger adults attempt *reciprocal socialization* of older adults into new definitions of these roles, fosters new understanding of the dynamics of intergenerational relations.

To date, there has been little application of life course concepts to the study of non-normative life changes. Psychiatric illness represents a particularly important avenue for the extension of these life course concepts. For both the ill individual and family alike, a first episode of psychiatric illness at any point in the course of life is a disruptive, non-normative event. There is no "best" time for persons to succumb to an episode of personal distress. This adverse life change disrupts family life and takes both the ill person and the family outside of expectable time for adult role transitions. Adjustment to feelings of disappointment, resolution of feelings of grief over unrealized offspring attainment, and recognition of feelings of disappointment, anger, frustration, and burden must take place among parents and other family members as a requisite for providing care for the afflicted offspring or support and assistance for the primary caregivers.

The feelings are particularly intense among families with parents no longer young at the time of the offspring's illness. Older parents expect to be cared for, rather than having to provide additional care into oldest age. In addition, older parents worry particularly about care for their afflicted offspring in the event of their own death. These findings from systematic study of adult families with psychiatrically ill offspring must further be qualified both in terms of cohort membership, since treatment opportunities have changed over time, and also in terms of ethnicity, social status, and other elements of social life. Within prior generations, when afflicted offspring remained within institutional settings for longer periods of time, family life may have been less disrupted than at the present time, when the family is increasingly expected to be the primary caregiver. The expectation that persistently psychiatrically ill family members will remain at home with parents through the parents' own oldest age appears more a source of strain than of comfort and satisfaction. The present cohort of persistently ill offspring and their parents will be confronted with caregiving conflicts without parallel across recent generations of patients and their families. To date, little is known about either the dimensions of the problem or the course of relations between parents and their afflicted offspring across the second half of life. Available findings suggest only that parents of psychiatrically ill offspring experience greater burden and lowered morale than parents of older developmentally challenged adults.

The sudden and off-time adversity characterized by a first episode of major mental illness, particularly schizophrenia, among otherwise well-functioning adults, presents parents with stress similar in many respects to life-threatening physical illness among offspring. Further, at least within the present cohort of middle-aged and older parents caring for their offspring, the parents' preparation for the future following their own death appears to present the greatest caregiving burden. However, across both middle age and later life, the particularly disruptive impact of the socially inappropriate actions of persistently troubled offspring, together with lack of effective community-based programs other than relocation into long-term care, impose continuing stress on the lives and marriages of parents (Sheehan, 1982).

Important problems remain to be studied regarding, persistently psychiatrically ill men or women as they age and their much older parents and their siblings. To date, while it is assumed that concerns regarding burdens are shared by both much older parents and nondisabled siblings, findings from the study of brothers and sisters of elders with Alzheimer's disease suggest that siblings are willing to accept responsibility for an ill brother or sister and that they derive some sense of personal satisfaction and enhanced personal integrity from fulfilling an obligation they believe to be proper within their family. The problem of caregiving for middle-aged and older persistently psychiatrically ill offspring and their families, understood in terms of age, cohort, and timing across the course of life, promises to shape future study of family caregiving and to inform our very understanding of variation in the life course and social timing, when viewed within the context of cohort membership.

# REFERENCES

Andreasen, N. (1985). Positive vs. negative schizophrenia: A critical evaluation. *Schizophrenia Bulletin, 11*, 380–389.

Angrist, S., Lefton, M., Dinitz, S., & Pasamanick, B. (1968). *Women after treatment.* New York: Appleton-Century.

Antonucci, T. (1990). Social supports and social relationships. In R. H. Binstock & L. K. George (Eds.), *Handbook of aging and the social sciences* (3rd ed., pp. 205–227). New York: Academic Press.

Beck, J., & Worthen, K. (1972). Precipitating stress, crisis, theory and hospitalization in schizophrenia and depression. *Archives of General Psychiatry, 26*, 123–129.

Bengtson, V., & Allen, K. (1993). The life course perspective applied to families over time. In P. Boss, W. Doherty, R. LaRossa, W. Schumm, & S. Steinmetz (Eds.), *Sourcebook of family theories and methods: A contextual approach* (pp. 469–498). New York: Plenum.

Bengtson, V., & Black, K. (1973). Intergenerational relations and continuities in socialization. In P. Baltes & K. W. Schaie (Eds.), *Life-span developmental psychology: Personality and socialization* (pp. 207–234). New York: Academic Press.

Bengtson, V., Furlong, M., & Laufer, R. (1974). Time, aging, and the continuity of social structure: Themes and issues in generational analysis. *Journal of Social Issues, 30,* 1–30.

Bleuler, E. (1950). *Dementia praecox or the group of schizophrenias* (H. Zinkin, Trans.). New York: International Universities Press. (Original work published 1911)

Bridge, T., Cannon, E., & Wyatt, R. (1978). Burned out schizophrenia: Evidence for age-effects on schizophrenic symptomatology. *Journal of Gerontology, 33,* 835–839.

Butler, R. (1963). The "life review": An interpretation of reminiscence in the aged. *Psychiatry, 26,* 65–76.

Cicirelli, V. (1980). Sibling relations in adulthood. In L. W. Poon (Ed.), *Aging in the 1980s* (pp. 455–462). Washington, DC: The American Psychological Association.

Cicirelli, V. (1985). The role of siblings as family caretakers. In W. Sauer & R. Coward (Eds.), *Social support networks and the care of the elderly: Theory, research, and practice* (pp. 93–107). New York: Springer Publishing Co.

Clausen, J. (1984a). A fifteen to twenty year follow-up of married adult psychiatric patients. In L. Erlenmeyer-Kimling, N. Miller, & B. Dohrenwend (Eds.), *Life-span research on the prediction of psychopathology* (pp. 175–194). New York: Academic Press.

Clausen, J. (1984b). Mental illness and the life course. In P. B. Baltes & O. G. Brim, Jr. (Eds.), *Life-span development and behavior* (Vol. 6, pp. 204–242). New York: Academic Press.

Clausen, J. (1993). *American lives: Looking back at the children of the great depression.* New York: Free Press/Macmillan.

Cohler, B. (1983). Autonomy and interdependence in the family of adulthood: A psychological perspective. *The Gerontologist, 23,* 33–39.

Cohler, B., & Boxer, A. (1984). Middle adulthood: Settling into the world-person, time, and context. In D. Offer & M. Sabshin (Eds.), *Normality and the life-cycle: A critical integration* (pp. 145–203). New York: BasicBooks.

Cohler, B., & Ferrono, C. (1987). Schizophrenia and the adult life-course. In N. E. Miller & G. Cohen (Eds.), *Schizophrenia and aging* (pp. 189–200). New York: Guilford.

Cohler, B., Groves, L., Borden, W., & Lazarus, L. (1989). Caring for family members with Alzheimer's disease. In E. Light & B. Lebowitz (Eds.), *Alzheimer's disease, treatment and family stress: Directions for research* (pp. 50–105). Washington, DC: U.S. Government Printing Office.

Cohler, B., Pickett, S., & Cook, J. (1991). The psychiatric patient grows older: Issues in family care. In E. Light & B. Lebowitz (Eds.), *The elderly with chronic mental illness* (pp. 82–110). New York: Springer Publishing Co.

Cook, J. (1988). Who "mothers" the chronically mentally ill? *Family Relations, 37,* 42–49.

Cook, J., & Cohler, B. (1986). Reciprocal socialization and the care of offspring with cancer and with schizophrenia. *Lifespan Developmental Psychology, 9,* 101–129.

Cook, J., Hoffschmidt, S., Cohler, B., & Pickett, S. (1992). Marital satisfaction among parents of the severely mentally ill living in the community. *American Journal of Orthopsychiatry, 62,* 552–563.

Cook, J., Lefley, H., Pickett, S., & Cohler, B. (1994). Parental aging and family burden in major mental illness. *American Journal of Orthopsychiatry, 64,* 435–447.

Cook, J., & Pickett, S. (1988). Feelings of burden among parents residing with chronically mentally ill offspring. *The Journal of Applied Social Sciences, 12,* 79–107.

Costell, R., & Reiss, D. (1982). The family meets the hospital: Clinical presentation of a laboratory-based family typology. *Archives of General Psychiatry, 39,* 433–438.

Costell, R., Reiss, D., Berkman, H., & Jones, C. (1981). The family meets the hospital: Predicting the family's perception of the treatment program from its problem solving style. *Archives of General Psychiatry, 38,* 569–577.

Daniels, P., & Weingarten, K. (1982). S*ooner or later: The timing of parenthood in adult lives.* New York: Norton.

Dinitz, S., Angrist, S., Lefton, M., & Pasamanick, B. (1961a). The posthospital functioning of former mental hospital patients. *Mental Hygiene, 45,* 579–588.

Dinitz, S., Lefton, M., Angrist, S., & Pasamanick, B. (1961b). Psychiatric and social attributes as predictors of case outcome in mental hospitalization. *Social Problems, 8.*

Durkheim, E. (1965). *The elementary forms of the religious life* (J. W. Swain, Trans.). New York: Free Press/Macmillan. (Original work published 1915)

Easterlin, R. (1987). *Birth and fortune: The impact of numbers on personal welfare,* 2nd ed. Chicago: The University of Chicago Press.

Elder, G., Jr. (1974). *Children of the Great Depression.* Chicago: University of Chicago Press.

Elder, G. (1984). Families, kin, and the life course: A sociological perspective.

In R. D. Parke (Ed.), *Review of child development research: Vol. 7. The family* (pp. 80–136). Chicago: University of Chicago Press.

Elder, G. (1992). Life course. In E. Borgatta & M. Borgatta (Eds.), *Encyclopedia of sociology* (Vol. 3, pp. 1120–1130). New York: Macmillan.

Elder, G., & Caspi, A. (1990). Studying lives in a changing society: Sociological and personological explorations (Henry A. Murray Lecture Series). In A. Rabin, R. A. Zucker, R. Emmons, & S. Frank (Eds.), *Studying persons and lives* (pp. 201–247). New York: Springer Publishing Co.

Falloon, I., Boyd, J., & McGill, C. (1984). *Family care of schizophrenia.* New York: Guilford.

Farnham-Diggory, S. (1966). Self, future, and time: A developmental study of the concepts of psychotic, brain injured, and normal children. *Monographs of the Society for Research in Child Development, 33* (Monograph 103).

Flacks, R. (1971). *Youth and social change.* Chicago: Markham.

Freeman, H., & Simmons, O. (1963). *The mental patient comes home.* New York: Wiley.

Furstenberg, F., Brooks-Gunn, J., & Morgan, S. (1987). *Adolescent mothers in later life.* New York: Cambridge University Press.

Gottesman, I., & Shields, J. (1982). *Schizophrenia: The epigenetic puzzle.* New York: Cambridge University Press.

Greenberg, J., Greenley, J., McKee, D., Brown, R., & Griffin-Francell, C. (1993). Mothers caring for an adult child with schizophrenia: The effects of subjective burden on maternal health. *Family Relations, 42,* 205–211.

Greenberg, J., Seltzer, M., & Greenley, J. (1993). Aging parents of adults with disabilities: The gratification and frustrations of later-life caregiving. *The Gerontologist, 33,* 542–550.

Greenley, J. (1972). The psychiatric patient's family and length of hospitalization. *Journal of Health and Social Behavior, 13,* 25–37.

Greenley, J. (1979). Family symptom tolerance and rehospitalization experiences of psychiatric patients. In R. Simmons (Ed.), *Research in community and mental health* (pp. 357–386). Greenwich, CT: JAI.

Grunebaum H., Gamer, E., & Cohler, B. (1983). The spouse in depressed families. In H. Morrison (Ed.), *Children of depressed parents: Risk, identification, and intervention* (pp. 139–158). New York: Grune & Stratton.

Gubman, G., & Tessler, R. (1987). The impact of mental illness on families: Concepts and priorities. *Journal of Family Issues, 8,* 226–245.

Hagestad, G. (1990). Social perspectives on the life course. In R. Binstock & L. K. George (Eds.), *Handbook of aging and the social sciences* (3rd ed., pp. 151–168). New York: Academic Press.

Hagestad, G., & Neugarten, B. (1985). Age and the life-course. In R. Binstock & E. Shanas (Eds.), *Handbook of aging and society* (2nd ed., pp. 35–61). New York: Van Nostrand Reinhold.

Harding, C. (1991). Aging and schizophrenia: Plasticity, reversibility, and/or compensation. In E. Walker (Ed.), *Schizophrenia: A life-course developmental perspective* (pp. 256–273). New York: Academic Press.

Harding, C., Brooks, G., Ashikaga, T., Strauss, J., & Landerl, P. (1987). Aging and social functioning in once-chronic schizophrenic patients 22–62 years after first admission: The Vermont story. In N. E. Miller & G. Cohen (Eds.), *Schizophrenia and aging* (pp. 74–82). New York: Guilford.

Harding, C., Brooks, G., & Strauss, J. (1984). Life assessment of a cohort of chronic schizophrenics discharged 20 years ago. In S. Mednick, M. Harway, & K. Finello (Eds.), *Handbook of longitudinal research* (Vol. 2, pp. 375–393). New York: Prager.

Hatfield, A., Spaniol, L., & Zipple, A. (1987). Expressed emotion: A family perspective. *Schizophrenia Bulletin, 13,* 221–226.

Hazan, H. (1980). *The limbo people: A study of the constitution of the time universey among the aged.* London: Routledge and Kegan Paul.

Hogan, D. (1981). *Transitions and social change: The early lives of American men.* New York: Academic Press.

Horwitz, A., Tessler, R., Fisher, G., & Gamache, G. (1992). The role of adult siblings in providing social support to the severely mentally ill. *Journal of Marriage and the Family, 54,* 233–241.

Jeste, D. (1991). Neuroleptic treatment of chronically mentally ill elderly: Suggestions of future research. In E. Light & B. Lebowitz (Eds.), *The elderly with chronic mental illness* (pp. 133–145). New York: Springer Publishing Co.

Jeste, D. (1993). Late-life schizophrenia: Editor's introduction. *Schizophrenia Bulletin, 19,* 687–689.

Jung, H., & Spaniol, L. (1983). *Families as a central resource in the rehabilitation of the severely psychiatrically disabled: Preliminary results of the needs and coping skills of families.* Unpublished manuscript.

Jung, H., Spaniol, L., & Anthony, W. (1983). *Family coping and schizophrenia.* Unpublished manuscript.

Kahn, R., & Antonucci, T. (1980). Convoys over the life course: Attachment, roles, and social support. In P. B. Baltes & O. G. Brim, Jr. (Eds.), *Life-span development and behavior* (Vol. 3, pp. 254–286). New York: Academic Press.

Kraepelin, E. (1902). *Clinical psychiatry: A textbook for students and physicians* (6th ed., A. Diefendorf, Trans.). New York: Macmillan.

Kraepelin, E. (1919). *Textbook of psychiatry: Vol. III: Endogenous dementias* (R. Barclay, Trans.). Edinburgh: E. S. Livingstone. (Original work published 1913)

Lawton, P. (1972). Schizophrenia forty-five years later. *The Journal of Genetic Psychology, 121,* 133–145.

Lazarus, R., & Folkman, S. (1984). *Stress, appraisal, and coping.* New York: Springer Publishing Co.

Leff, J., & Vaughn, C. (1985). *Expressed emotion in families.* New York: Guilford.

Lefley, H. (1987). Aging parents as caregivers of mentally ill adult children: An emerging social problem. *Hospital and Community Psychiatry, 10,* 1063–1070.

Lidz, T. (1973). *The origin and treatment of schizophrenic disorders.* New York: BasicBooks.

Lidz, T., Fleck, S., Cornelison, A., & Associates (1965). *Schizophrenia and the family.* New York: International Universities Press.

Mannheim, K. (1952). The problem of generations. In K. Mannheim, *Essays on the sociology of knowledge* (pp. 276–322). London: Routledge & Kegan Paul. (Original work published in 1923)

Marshall, V. (1975). Age and awareness of finitude in developmental gerontology. *Omega, 6,* 113–129.

Marshall, V. (1986). A sociological perspective on aging and dying. In V. Marshall (Ed.), *Later life: The social psychology of aging* (pp. 125–146). Thousand Oaks, CA: Sage.

Munnichs, J. (1966). *Old age and finitude: A contribution to psychogerontology.* New York: Karger.

Neugarten, B. (1979). Time, age, and the life-cycle. *American Journal of Psychiatry, 136,* 887–894.

Neugarten, B., & Hagestad, G. (1976). Age and the life course. In R. Binstock & E. Shanas (Eds.), *Handbook of aging and the social sciences* (pp. 35–55). New York: Van Nostrand Reinhold.

Neugarten, B., Moore, J., & Lowe, J. (1965). Age norms, age constraints, and adult socialization. *The American Journal of Sociology, 70,* 710–717.

Nydegger, C. (1980). Role and age transitions: A potpourri of issues. In C. Fry & J. Keith (Eds.), *New methods of old age research: Anthropological alternatives* (pp. 127–145). Loyola University of Chicago: Center for Urban Studies.

Nydegger, C. (1981). On being caught up in time. *Human Development, 24,* 1–12.

Pearlin, L. (1980). Life strains and psychological distress among adults. In E. Erikson & N. Smelser (Eds.), *Themes of love and work in adulthood* (pp. 174–192). Cambridge: Harvard University Press.

Pearlin, L., Menaghan, B., Lieberman, M., & Mullan, J. (1981). The stress process. *Journal of Health and Social Behavior, 22,* 337–356.

Pickett, S., Cook, J., & Cohler, B. (1994). Caregiving burden experienced by parents of offspring with severe mental illness: The impact of off-timedness. *The Journal of Applied Social Sciences, 18,* 199–207.

Pickett, S., Cook, J., & Solomon, M. (in press). Dealing with daughters' difficulties: Caregiving burdens by parents of female offspring with severe mental illness. In J. R. Greenley (Ed.), *Research in community mental health*. Greenwich, CT: JAI.

Pickett, S., Greenley, J., & Greenberg, J. (in press). Off-timedness as a contributor to subjective burdens of parents of offspring with severe mental illness. *Family Relations*.

Pickett, S., Vraniak, D., Cook, J., & Cohler, B. (1994). Strength in adversity: Blacks bear burden better than whites. *Professional Psychology: Research and Practice, 24,* 460–467.

Plath, D. (1980). Contours of consociation: Lessons from a Japanese narrative. In P. B. Baltes & O. G. Brim, Jr. (Eds.), *Life-span development and behavior* (Vol. 3, pp. 287–307). New York: Academic Press.

Pruchno, R., Blow, F., & Smyer, M. (1984). Life-events and interdependent lives. *The Gerontologist, 27,* 31–41.

Rosow, I. (1978). What is a cohort and why? *Human Development, 21,* 65–75.

Roth, J. (1963). *Timetables: Structuring the passage of time in hospital treatment and other careers.* Indianapolis: Bobbs-Merrill.

Schaie, K. W. (1984). The Seattle longitudinal study: A 2-year exploration of the psychometric intelligence of adulthood. In K. W. Schaie (Ed.), *Longitudinal studies of personality* (pp. 64–135). New York: Guilford.

Schuman, H., & Scott, J. (1989). Generations and collective memories. *American Sociological Review, 54,* 359–381.

Seeman, M. (1976). Time and schizophrenia. *Psychiatry, 39,* 189–195.

Seltzer, M. (1976). Suggestions for examination in time-disordered relationships. In J. Gubrium (Ed.), *Time, roles and self in old age* (pp. 111–125). New York: Human Sciences.

Seltzer, M. M., Greenberg, J., & Wyngaarden-Krauss, M. (1995). A comparison of coping strategies of aging mothers of adults with mental illness or mental retardation. *Psychology and Aging, 10,* 64–75.

Sheehan, S. (1982). *Is there no place on earth for me?* Boston: Houghton-Mifflin.

Simmons, O., & Freeman, H. (1959). Familial expectations and posthospital performance of mental patients. *Human Relations, 12,* 233–241.

Singer, M., & Wynne, L. (1963). Thought disorder and family relations of schizophrenics: IV. Results and implications. *Archives of General Psychiatry, 12,* 201–212.

Sorokin, P., & Merton, R. (1937). Social time: A methodological and functional analysis. *The American Journal of Sociology, 42,* 615–629.

Spaniol, L. (1987). Coping strategies of family caregivers. In A. Hatfield & H. P. Lefley (Eds.), *Families of the mentally ill: Coping and adaptation* (pp. 208–224). New York: Guilford.

Spaniol, L., & Jung, H. (1983). *Issues and concerns of families that include a person with severe mental illness.* Unpublished manuscript.

Strauss, J. (1989). Mediating processes in schizophrenia: Toward a new dynamic psychiatry. *British Journal of Psychiatry, 155* (Suppl.), 22–28.

Strauss, J., Hafez, H., Lieberman, P., & Harding, C. (1985). The course of psychiatric disorder: III. Longitudinal principles. *American Journal of Psychiatry, 142,* 289–296.

Strauss, J., & Harding, C. (1990). Relationships between adult development and the course of mental disorder. In J. Rolf, A. Masten, D. Cicchetti, K. Nuechterlein, & S. Weintraub (Eds.), *Risk and protective factors in the development of psychopathology* (pp. 514–535). New York: Cambridge University Press.

Tessler, R., Fisher, C., & Gamache, G. (1990). *Dilemmas of kinship: Mental illness and the modern American family.* Amherst, MA: Amherst Social and Demographic Research Institute and the University of Massachusetts.

Tessler, R., Killian, L., & Gubman, G. (1987). Stages in family response to mental illness: An ideal type. *Psychosocial Rehabilitation Journal, 10,* 3–16.

Troll, L. (1970). Issues in the study of generations. *International Journal of Aging and Human Development, 1,* 199–218.

Tuttle, W., Jr. (1993). America's home front children in World War II. In G. Elder, J. Modell, & R. D. Parke (Eds.), *Children in time and place: Developmental and historical insights* (pp. 27–46). New York: Cambridge University Press.

Winkler, L. (1986). Periodic stresses in families of children with mental retardation. *American Journal of Mental Deficiency, 90,* 703–706.

Wynne, L., Singer, M., Bartko, K., & Toohey, M. (1977). Schizophrenics and their families: Recent research on parental communication. In J. M. Tanner (Ed.), *Developments in psychiatric research* (pp. 254–286). London: Hodder & Stoughton.

Yassa, R. (1991). Late-onset schizophrenia. In E. Walker (Ed.), *Schizophrenia: A life-course developmental perspective* (pp. 243–256). New York: Academic Press.

Zubin, J., Magaziner, J., & Steinhauer, S. (1983). The metamorphosis of schizophrenia. *Psychological Medicine, 13,* 551–571.

Zubin, J., & Spring, B. (1977). Vulnerability—A new view of schizophrenia. *Journal of Abnormal Psychology, 86,* 103–126.

Zubin, J., & Steinhauer, S. (1981). How to break the logjam in schizophrenia: A look beyond genetics. *Journal of Nervous and Mental Disease, 169,* 477–492.

# Comments

## Morton A. Lieberman

C ohler and his colleagues raise a stimulating challenge to the conventional views of serious mental illness. By bringing together a wide diversity of intellectual disciplines and their attendant research, they make a strong case for reexamining how we think about mental disorders. The concepts they draw upon are familiar and cherished for an audience steeped in the traditions of the adult life span. They are likely to be seen as either radical or refreshing by the majority of mental health scholars. Those who favor simplistic explanations (based currently on the gene) or the rapidly disappearing few who cling to early family dynamics as the etiological culprit will probably turn away from the authors' message. However, it is to be hoped that the bulk of mental health experts, whose views of serious disorders are more complex, will attend to this important call for reconceptualization.

Understanding mental illness in a life course perspective can lead to significant enhancement of both the research design and, above all, the questions that need to be addressed in developing a fuller understanding of such disorders as schizophrenia. We are not long past the early version of the *Diagnostic and Statistical Manual of Mental Disorders (DSM)* that did not permit a diagnosis of schizophrenia if the first occurrence was noted after age 40. Such idiocies serve to alert us that the messages that Cohler, Pickett, and Cook present in their chapter are required.

Examining the life course of schizophrenia in the light of concepts of adult development, particularly timing and social history changes, offers considerable promise. The authors have provided us with a broad brush stroke of convincing arguments that the field needs to paint a directional sign to future research. How such research will be done and the difficult definition of complex ideas, such as social history and context, still await us.

# CHAPTER 5

# Continuities and Discontinuities in Gender Identity

## Margaret Hellie Huyck

In this chapter I address six questions about continuity and change in gender:

1. How should we define and measure gender?
2. Does gender become less salient in later life?
3. Is there a generation gap in gender?
4. Are shifts in parental responsibility linked to gender styles in midlife?
5. Are early experiences related to midlife gender styles?
6. So what?

What are the implications for clinical practice and further research?

I will argue that gender remains important for most people throughout life. Some aspects of gender endure because they are rooted in biological realities and early frameworks of understanding, and are maintained by later experiences. Other aspects change, for a variety of complex reasons. I will draw largely on what young adults and their middle-aged and aging parents from a midwestern city called Parkville have revealed about the ways gender shapes their life experiences. The Parkville families represent one important variety of experience, but I will not presume to generalize to other sociological categories.

# DEFINING AND MEASURING GENDER

## Conceptualizing Gender

Over the past two decades social scientists have refined the ways we think about males and females, especially in adulthood (Huyck, 1989a, 1989b). We now distinguish sex from gender. *Sex* includes the biological differentiation, genetically coded, which leads to reproductive specialization, prototypic body configurations, and—perhaps—differential vulnerabilities in health. It is not very clear whether genetic sex also codes for differential cognitive and emotional response patterns (Plomin, 1990). *Gender* refers to all the social and psychological consequences of sexual differentiation.

There is a great deal of continuing debate about how to conceptualize gender (Turner, 1994), and much of the debate refers back to the classic nature-nurture question: Is gender part of biological destiny or a social construction? I find Erik Erikson's (1963) general conceptualization useful: Behaviors are shaped by the interacting influences of soma, psyche, and culture. We can look for the sources of continuity and change in any or all of these processes. In Erikson's model, the body is the bedrock; psychic processes and cultural constraints must operate within the parameters set by sex-linked genetic differentiation. Beyond this general framework, several other models of gender development help clarify the parameters.

Both object relations theory and some cognitive theories are developing models that focus on explaining psychic processes (Huyck, 1994). Object relations models argue that the primary motivation is toward emotional intimacy, that unconscious desires and fantasies may shape behavior at least as much as conscious, rational thought does, and that psychological defense mechanisms are used to keep unacceptable thoughts and impulses out of conscious awareness. Because of the primacy of emotional intimacy, all babies initially identify with the feminine, at least if their primary caregiver is a woman. Girls can retain this early identification, although they are faced with the need to create their own version of feminine identity in order to establish enough separation from the mother to act as an autonomous adult. The challenge for separation comes earlier for boys, since they are treated differently from infancy on, and are typically given many messages that they will not grow up to be like the mother. In this model, an important psychic challenge for men throughout life is how to experience emotional intimacy without feeling feminized or even infantilized.

Cognitive theories about gender explain how the general cognitive processes operate to use sex as one of the earliest categorizing variables; once persons are sorted into a category of male or female, all other processing about characteristics is done within existing frameworks of understanding about that category (Cross & Markus, 1993). These basic cognitive processes lead persons not only to stereotype on the basis of minimal cues, but to act in ways that evoke the expected behaviors (Geis, 1993). Cognitive schemas do change as a result of repeated instances of poor fit between expectations and reality. Change is difficult, however, because new experiences are selectively perceived and interpreted from the perspective of the initial frameworks. The early cognitive frameworks or schemas begin to be established in the second year, as part of the acquisition of language and categorizing competencies. The cognitive models do not postulate any inherent content of the schemas, beyond stating that schemas acquired reflect the experiences available to the child.

## Research on Gender

I have been particularly interested in two related issues: variability in gender identity and developmental contributions to gender identity. The focus of my concern lies in the ways in which individuals understand their own gender, that is, in the psychic processes. Most of the research has assumed that individuals think of themselves as masculine (M) or feminine (F), in rather global ways, and most of the scales designed to measure gender identity are global M/F scales. During the 1970s and 1980s, especially, other paradigms emerged. Individuals could be androgynous or unisex—combining "masculine" and "feminine" characteristics equally. They could be "transcendent"—in the belief that sex has limited consequences and characteristics and behaviors should not be linked to gender either by oneself or by others (Rebecca, Hefner, & Olesanky, 1976). Or, individuals could even experience "crossover" (Gutmann, 1975), whereby they show strong evidence of characteristics associated with the other sex; men, for example, may come to experience themselves as feminine rather than masculine.

I felt all these conceptualizations oversimplified the diverse ways in which women and men described themselves as gendered and underestimated the extent to which feeling "appropriately gendered" is important to persons themselves and to all who interact with them. Thus, I wanted to explore the varieties of femininity and masculinity used by adults to think about themselves and others, and to explore how they dealt with personal qualities they could not fit into their own conceptualization of gender.

The second major question has to do with understanding how sociocultural and major normative developmental events modify such interpretations. It seemed plausible to expect that the women's movement's efforts to redefine gender would have some impact, which could be interpreted as cohort effects. More specifically, I wanted to test some of the hypotheses advanced by David Gutmann in his explorations of how transitions in parental responsibility transform gender-related qualities. Gutmann (1977) used cross-cultural and clinical evidence to show that men move their stance from one of what he called active to passive mastery, and women move from more passive to more active mastery. In 1974 he hypothesized that these midlife shifts were linked to the phasing out of parental responsibility, allowing parents to reclaim repressed aspects of the self (Gutmann, 1975). Although the descriptions of behaviors were compelling, I was not comfortable with the conceptualization of the shift as one into androgyny or unisex, and I was absolutely opposed to conceptualizing these patterns as reflecting a crossover.

Exploring these questions is not easy. Knowing that culture also shapes gender, I decided to explore developmental shifts in gender identity within a restricted cultural group, preferably one that was similar to the relatively traditional cultures used by Gutmann to develop his hypothesis. The "parental imperative" model (Gutmann, 1975; Gutmann & Huyck, 1994) applies specifically to heterosexual couples engaged in long-term parenting relationships, in cultures that validate the social and psychological sacrifices made by both genders in order to parent effectively. Such couples were included in my Parkville sample.

### The Parkville Project

The Parkville sample was recruited from a sample of graduates from the public high school in Parkville, an established community outside a major metropolis in the Midwest. Parkville began as an independent village with strong settlement from Western European immigrants; until the past two decades, the community was almost entirely white, and the sample are all white. Among the parent generation, half of the sample are Catholic; most of the rest are Protestant. They are broadly middle-class. The sample was selected to represent the most geographically and maritally stable families; the parents of the high school graduates selected randomly had to be still alive, married to each other, and the young adult child had to be living within two hours' driving distance of the parental home.

Data collection included three phases. An initial interview was used to gather demographic data and assess appropriateness for inclusion. Those who were selected were asked to complete a packet of self-report questionnaires, including standardized measures for gender and mental health. Following this, personal interviews were conducted; one explored the parent–young adult relationship, and the other explored the individual's life structure. The final sample included members from approximately 140 families; the number available for specific analyses varies. Most of the data were collected in the early 1980s. Sample characteristics are shown in Table 5.1.

A summary of some of the research questions and findings about gender in Parkville provides some clues about the structure, continuity, and change of gender identity.

ARE MASCULINITY AND FEMININITY UNITARY SCALES?    A standardized self-report scale designed to yield global masculinity and femininity scales (the PRF-Andro Scale; see Berzins, Welling, & Wetter, 1978) was completed by most of the participants. In order to assess whether the summary scale scores were useful indexes of gender, we did factor analyses on the scales for 149 middle-aged women and 127 middle-aged men (Huyck, 1990). Three meaningful scales emerged for masculinity (dominance, rigid autonomy, and counterphobic adventure seeking), and three for femininity (active nurturing, externalized security, and denial of self-indulgence). Correlations between the factors indicate that this self-report measure does, indeed, tap quite different subdimensions of the general constructs of masculinity and femininity. It argues against any simplistic model of androgyny. Rather, one may be classified as androgynous on measures such as these by scoring relatively high on a variety of factors; different combinations may have quite different consequences.

**TABLE 5.1  Sample Characteristics**

|  | Fathers | Mothers | Sons | Daughters |
|---|---|---|---|---|
| Number | (115) | (115) | (57) | (58) |
| Age (*M/SD/*Range) | 57.8/6.7/44–78 | 53.9/5.6/43–68 | 25.6/2.7/22–31 | 25.7/2.7/21–30 |
| *Education* |  |  |  |  |
| Graduate work | 25.7% | 10.4% | 10.5% | 8.6% |
| College graduate | 26.5 | 26.1 | 36.8 | 56.9 |
| Some college | 20.4 | 34.8 | 47.4 | 24.1 |
| High school graduate | 20.4 | 34.8 | 5.3 | 6.9 |
| Some high school, less | 6.2 | 4.3 | 0.0 | 3.4 |
| *Occupational status* |  |  |  |  |
| Executive, professional, manager | 43.0 | 16.5 | 26.3 | 17.2 |
| Administrative | 32.5 | 24.3 | 29.8 | 27.6 |
| Clerical | 7.9 | 16.5 | 14.0 | 12.1 |
| Skilled | 9.6 | 2.6 | 10.5 | 1.7 |
| Homemaker, unskilled labor | 2.6 | 39.1 | 8.8 | 25.8 |
| Unemployed, seeking work | 3.5 | 0.9 | 10.5 | 15.5 |
| *Present work status* |  |  |  |  |
| Full-time employed | 80.5 | 41.7 | 84.2 | 57.4 |
| Part-time employed | 0.9 | 17.4 | 0.0 | 1.9 |
| Homemaker | 0.0 | 34.8 | 0.0 | 22.2 |
| Retired | 15.0 | 4.3 | 0.0 | 0.0 |
| School, full- or part-time | 0.9 | 0.9 | 10.6 | 11.1 |
| Unemployed | 2.7 | 0.9 | 5.3 | 7.4 |

**TABLE 5.1** *(Continued)*

|  | Fathers | Mothers | Sons | Daughters |
|---|---|---|---|---|
| *Religious affiliation* |  |  |  |  |
| Catholic | 49.1% | 52.6% | 40.0% | 35.8% |
| Protestant | 39.5 | 40.4 | 30.9 | 32.1 |
| Jewish | 3.5 | 2.6 | 1.8 | 3.8 |
| Other | 2.7 | 4.4 | 3.6 | 1.9 |
| None | 5.3 | 0.0 | 23.6 | 26.4 |
| *Marital status* |  |  |  |  |
| Married | 100.0 | 100.0 | 36.8 | 54.4 |
| Divorced | 0.0 | 0.0 | 1.8 | 1.8 |
| Single | 0.0 | 0.0 | 61.4 | 43.9 |
| *Residence* |  |  |  |  |
| With parents | 0.0 | 0.0 | 35.1 | 26.3 |
| Own home | 100.0 | 100.0 | 56.1 | 66.7 |
| Other | 0.0 | 0.0 | 8.9 | 7.0 |
| *Children* |  |  |  |  |
| With children | 100.0 | 100.0 | 24.6 | 34.5 |
| Number (Mean/Range) | 4.3/1–11 | 4.3/1–11 | 0.35/0–3 | 0.53/0–4 |

HOW DO INDIVIDUALS DESCRIBE THEMSELVES IN GENDER TERMS?   Another assessment of gender styles utilized interview responses to questions about personal definitions of gender. Respondents were asked about the characteristics they associated with masculinity and femininity, how they thought men and women differ psychologically, whether they think of themselves as feminine (if female) or masculine (if male) and how that self-perception influenced the things they did or did not do, and whether there were any ways in which they were not so feminine (if female) or masculine (if male). Two ratings of the gender interview materials were obtained. First, discrete, gender-relevant self-attributions were identified by listing every one of the 91 different ways in which respondents described their gender. Second, more global styles were drawn from previous research and a general familiarity with the interviews from this sample. Because the results of the second measure were confirmed by the self-attributions, the findings reported here are in terms of the gender styles. Zucker (1988) developed an initial set of styles for 134 middle-aged mothers and 105 middle-aged fathers; Angelaccio (1990) found that, with minor modifications, the styles could also describe the 66 young adult sons and 67 young adult daughters in Zuker's sample.

Men were classified as experiencing a specific masculine style on the basis of their descriptions of how they were masculine, and women were classified on the basis of their descriptions of how they were feminine. Three gender-congruent styles were evident for men—*macho, leader,* and *family man,* and three parallel gender-congruent styles for women—*femme, nurturer,* and *family woman.* While most indicated one of these dominant styles, some indicated that they perceived themselves in two or even all three of the styles.

In addition, we were interested in how respondents experienced themselves, in terms of having qualities which they themselves felt were "gender incongruent" or "gender expanded." These ratings reflect our desire to go beyond a global concept of androgyny to explore more precisely how individuals are experiencing aspects that they associate with the other gender. Some individuals denied that there was any way in which they were not masculine/feminine. We identified two gender expansion options, which we labeled *inner androgyny* and *activity* (initially called *task*) *androgyny.* Finally, we identified two options which reflected diminished or compromised gender congruency (rather than an expansion into the modalities associated with the "other" gender):

persons who indicated they felt "less of" a man or woman than they had been or than they wished they were in terms of their own internalized standards of masculinity or femininity *(diminished)*; and those who said that while they could "pass" as socially masculine or feminine, it was largely a charade and a facade which they preferred to drop *(facade)*. The distribution of responses for each of the gender style measures is shown in Table 5.2.

We examined patterns of gender styles. Although men could be classified into several concurrent *congruent* masculine styles and several *expanded* or *compromised* styles, most were classified as having one congruent and one expanded style. No gender-congruent style was exclusively associated with another style. For example, 36.7% of the 49 men who were classified as family men were also classified as experiencing inner androgyny; another 30.6% of the family men denied any gender-expanded styles. Similarly, most women were classified as having one congruent and one expanded style, and no gender-congruent style was exclusively associated with a particular expanded style. The implication is that adult men and women develop complex and individualized schemas in which they experience themselves as acceptably

**TABLE 5.2   Gender Styles by Sex and Generation: Percentage Endorsing Various Styles, as Coded from Interviews**

|  | Middle-aged | | Young adult | |
|---|---|---|---|---|
|  | Men | Women | Men | Women |
| Number | (105) | (134) | (66) | (67) |
| *Gender-congruent styles* | | | | |
| Macho/Femme | 27.6% | 52.2% | 30.3% | 44.8% |
| Leader/Nurturer | 25.7 | 29.9 | 27.3 | 31.3 |
| Family roles | 46.7 | 23.1 | 33.3 | 19.4 |
| Denial of androgyny | 35.2 | 32.8 | 34.8 | 16.4 |
| *Gender-expanded styles* | | | | |
| Activity androgyny | 17.1 | 26.1 | 9.1 | 9.0 |
| Inner androgyny | 29.5 | 28.4 | 31.8 | 23.9 |
| *Gender-compromised styles* | | | | |
| Nonstereotypic; diminished | 19.1 | 14.9 | 36.4 | 59.7 |
| Facade | 4.8 | 3.7 | 15.2 | 16.4 |

feminine or masculine in ways congruent with their sex. The women seem to rely substantially on controlling their appearance and demeanor; having secured their femininity, as it were, by these means, they are comfortable with actions and stances that they regard as more masculine. Behaving in such masculine ways, however, does not make them feel unfeminine as long as they have a secure sense of gender-congruent style. Similarly, even when men lose muscular strength (which nearly all the men associated with masculinity), or occupational power, they anchor their sense of masculinity in their willingness to be there for their families, to provide as best they can, to keep concerns to themselves that might worry their wife or children, and to serve as head of family to the best of their ability. As long as they can feel they have done this reasonably well, they can feel secure in their gender-congruent identity. From that stance, they can expand into other arenas without feeling unmanned.

These analyses confirmed our expectation that gender must be conceptualized as complex and diverse. Global conceptualizations of masculinity, femininity, or, particularly, androgyny are not likely to be very informative. We need more precise constructs of gender styles, and ways of measuring such styles.

## GENDER IN LATER LIFE

The problems of measuring life course change are well known, as are the challenges of understanding the possible reasons for observed changes or continuities (Schaie, Campbell, Meredith, & Rawlings, 1992). We do not, alas, have the ideal data set of time-sequential measures. However, the data taken from family members of different generations within one community can provide interesting ways of examining possible developmental and cohort effects, although they provide no sure way of deciding either how much change is evident or why we might observe such changes. We have used a number of strategies to explore the issues: estimating the salience of gender by relating gender measures to mental health measures, assessing similarity within same-sex parent–child dyads, relating marital interaction styles to measures of parental responsibility and health, and relating resistance to change in gender style to recollections of early experience.

The view that gender becomes less relevant as one moves into middle and later life is captured in the notion of the *normal androgyny* of later life (Gutmann, 1987) and in the concept of *gender transcendence* as a positive developmental achievement (Pleck, 1975). In order to explore the concept of gender transcendence, I examined patterns of relationships between the gender-linked self-attribution factor scores to three measures of psychological well-being: self-esteem, sense of mastery, and psychosomatic distress (Huyck, 1991). These relationships were assessed within groups homogeneous on sex, occupational status, and age. One index of gender transcendence would be the independence of gender measures from other important feelings about the self.

We can describe as gender transcendent persons for whom none of the gender factors predicted any of the mental health measures; this profile is evident among the older, upper status women. It is also clear that the older, upper status men are gender sensitive: In one third of the analyses gender was a significant predictor of mental health. They seem to be confronted with the particular challenge of avoiding a passive feminine stance, since admitting to the desire for protection is associated with negative self-evaluations. Men can protect their self evaluation by managing or controlling others or by managing their own fears. Unfortunately, this set of analyses has not yet been repeated with the young adult sample, so that our adult life perspective is limited. The findings do suggest, however, that gender remains very salient for the adult men.

## THE GENERATION GAP IN GENDER

The second strategy for examining continuity and change was to examine parent-child dyad congruence (Huyck, Zucker, Angelaccio, & deGrange, 1991). For these analyses each young adult child was compared with his or her own same-sex parent on the ways in which gender style was expressed. The sample for these analyses included only pairs where gender style ratings were available for both generations; we had 66 father–son and 67 mother–daughter dyad pairs. We used three measures of the child's age: chronological age (21–25 and 26–31); marital status (single vs. married); and parental status (no children vs. one or more children). The results are shown in Table 5.3.

**TABLE 5.3   Development of Gender Congruence: Parent–Young Adult Similarity by Young Adult Age**

|  | Younger | | | Older | | |
|---|---|---|---|---|---|---|
|  | Age | Single | No kids | Age | Married | Parent |
| **Father/son** | | | | | | |
| Number of parent–child dyads | (22) | (33) | (38) | (34) | (21) | (14) |
| PRF-Masculinity | — | s | S | S | S | — |
| PRF-Femininity | — | — | — | — | — | — |
| *Gender-congruent styles* | | | | | | |
| Macho | — | s | — | S | — | — |
| Leader | — | — | — | — | — | — |
| Family | F | — | — | — | — | — |
| Denial of androgyny | — | — | — | s | — | — |
| *Gender-expanded options* | | | | | | |
| Activity androgyny | — | — | — | — | — | — |
| Inner androgyny | — | — | — | F | — | — |
| *Gender-compromised styles* | | | | | | |
| Non-stereotypic; diminished | s | s | s | s | — | — |
| Facade | s | s | s | s | — | — |
| **Mother/daughter** | | | | | | |
| Number of parent–child dyads | (25) | (27) | (38) | (33) | (31) | (20) |
| PRF-Masculinity | D | D | D | — | — | — |
| PRF-Femininity | — | — | — | — | — | — |
| *Gender-congruent styles* | | | | | | |
| Femme | — | D | — | — | — | — |
| Nurturer | D | D | — | — | — | — |
| Family | d | — | — | — | — | — |
| Denial of androgyny | — | d | — | — | — | — |

**TABLE 5.3**   *(Continued)*

|  | Younger | | | Older | | |
|---|---|---|---|---|---|---|
|  | Age | Single | No kids | Age | Married | Parent |
| *Gender-expanded options* | | | | | | |
| Activity androgyny | — | d | — | — | — | — |
| Inner androgyny | — | d | — | — | — | — |
| *Gender-compromised options* | | | | | | |
| Nonstereotypical; | | | | | | |
| diminished | D | D | — | — | — | — |
| Facade | d | D | — | — | — | — |

*Note.* Single = not married, not a parent; No kids = Married, no kids; Married = no kids;
Parent = married, kids.
Younger = 21–25/ Older = 26–31.
S,D,F = Son, Daughter, or Father more likely to have high score or style at $p > .05$.
s,d = son or daughter more likely to have high score or style at $p > .10$.

Dissimilarity from the mother was evident only in the younger women, primarily when the daughter was unmarried. The young adult women (under 25) showed what we might expect from a social change or cohort model: They had higher self-report masculinity scale scores, and they were more likely to describe themselves as not very feminine or consciously playing a feminine role when it seemed necessary or useful. However, a cohort model is challenged because the more mature young women do not differ from their own mothers on any of the gender measures. This suggests that some of the apparent generational differences evident, particularly in studies utilizing college students, may be linked to developmental rather than social change issues.

The pattern of similarity to one's own mother, I believe (on the basis of familiarity with the interviews and personal experiences), reflect three processes. First, and probably the most fundamental process, is the daughter's movement into the social-psychological role of wife/partner, by which she links her life structure to a chosen man's. Most of these young women also hope, and intend, to become mothers. The patterns of behavior which she perceives to have worked for her parents in realizing these desires are evoked when she herself assumes responsibilities as a wife and mother. Having focused on developing autonomy from the mother during their adolescent and younger adult years, young women in a slightly later stage, can become like their mother's without feeling absorbed or merged. Many of the older young adult women described this transition in relation to their mother, indicating how they had felt they had to be, or act, deliberately differently from their mother in order to gain a sense of their own identity; but that having done so, they could see the merits of their mother's position, and recognize their own similarity to their mother without feeling threatened. (See Frank, Avery, & Laman, 1988, for a discussion of autonomy and relatedness between young adults and their parents in this sample.)

The second process reflects the mother's own developmental changes. As has been well documented in other research, many women become more self-confident and assertive in midlife. Among the midlife mothers in Parkville, this greater assertiveness was largely evident when they described their marriage relationship as children left home. (This transition is discussed below.)

The third process involves the ways in which both generations are socializing each other, and both are being influenced by larger social changes. The middle-aged mothers described ways in which they had modified their assumptions about what was necessary or even desirable for feminine behavior, on the basis of discussions with daughters and daughters-in-law and by observing how these younger women managed their lives. It is also important to point out that some mothers are watching their daughters and are intensely uncomfortable with what they regard as "unfeminine" behavior, because they fear it will threaten the stability of the marriage or jeopardize the emotional security of their grandchildren. Both generations talked about their awareness of the women's movement; exhortations from the media were filtered through the family culture, which probably helps account for the high mother-daughter congruence.

When we examine the pattern for the father-son dyads, several differences are evident. As expected from much other research, the young adult men generally score higher on the self-report masculinity scale than do their own fathers; however, it is notable that this is not true for the sons who have become fathers themselves. Some of the younger sons seem to be differentiating themselves from their own fathers by psychologically distancing from gender issues generally. This is most evident in the relatively small group of young adult men (15%) who report a gender-compromised style of facade. These are young men who seem to be saying that the responsibilities of masculinity are too great for them. Their interviews make it clear that they do not feel capable of assuming what they regard as the burdens of being a good provider and protector. Many of them have fathers whom they regard as abusive; masculine strength is seen as more brutalizing and intrusive than supportive, and they seem to lack alternative, more positive images of masculinity. On the other hand, the young adult men who have married are very similar to their own fathers. Interestingly, the more masculine (higher M score) middle-aged fathers are more likely to have sons who have married in their 20s, indicating another family influence on these patterns of movement into adulthood.

Overall, the results suggest that both younger sons and daughters differentiate from their own same-sex parent partly by redefining aspects of gender. These kinds of differentiation might suggest a "generation gap," or strong evidence of social change. However, the fact that the gap within family dyads is no longer evident as the young person moves into adult family roles (of marriage and parenthood) strongly supports a family developmental model of gender style.

## THE MIDLIFE LINK BETWEEN PARENTAL RESPONSIBILITY AND GENDER STYLE

A third research strategy was to construct a more systematic test of the parental imperative model. The primary transformations that Gutmann describes relate to aspects of the self that are linked to gender identity. He describes a process of repressing aspects of the self that might interfere with effective parenting, on the assumption that mothers and fathers are responsible in distinctive ways. As the needs to protect vulnerable children diminish, the imperative for repression also diminishes.

A key challenge to testing the hypothesis is to measure the complex construct of parental responsibility; in spite of several attempts (e.g., Huyck, 1989a) I do not feel confident we have yet developed a good measurement instrument. The analyses here take the presence or absence of children in the home as one (crude) measure of the extent to which parental responsibility is likely to exist. Because it was not clear when the sense of parental responsibility phases out among this largely middle-class sample, we assessed the impact of having children under 18 living at home, or having children under 24 at home. Data for these analyses were drawn from the 134 middle-aged women and 105 of their husbands who participated in all phases of the study.

On the self-report PRF-Andro Scale (Berzins et al., 1978), whether or not there were children at home did not affect how masculine the fathers said they felt. However, in line with the model, fathers with no children under 24 at home were more likely to describe themselves in the feminine terms of the scale. In addition, coded responses for the ways they felt about their own gender style were congruent with the model. Men with children under 18 at home were more likely to say there were no ways in which they were not masculine. The results suggest, then, that men's sense of themselves as masculine is affected by having younger children at home, and that they will become more open to admitting feminine aspects of the self as children leave the home. In contrast, the women's sense of themselves as feminine seems to be minimally affected by the maturing of their children. Neither the femininity scores on the PRF-Andro self-report scale nor any of the interview descriptions of gender varied with parental phase for women.

Another key assertion of Gutmann's model is that mothers need to repress their own competitive, self-assertive, or even aggressive potentials in order to tend to the needs of their vulnerable children and to keep the husband/provider near. While aggression directed at children is generally considered harmful, most mothers would probably argue that good mothering requires substantial assertiveness, particularly as children become older and require direction. However, given the vulnerabilities of many men, the key issue may be of containing assertion in the marriage relationship.

In order to assess whether the marriage relationship is renegotiated as the children leave the parental home, David Gutmann and I coded the interviews for the ways in which each person dealt with conflicts in the marriage (Huyck & Gutmann, 1992). The personal life structure interviews included a section on the marriage, inquiring about gratifications, strains, and ways of dealing with conflicts. These responses were coded separately for husbands and wives, with categories developed to reflect the kinds of responses found in the data. Five kinds of responses were identified for the wives: "Patriarchal" (the wife concedes influence to her husband and feels he is entitled), "covert assertion" (she has complaints about the relationship but does not feel free to express them), "ambivalent assertion" (she makes some complaints but feels ambivalent about doing so), "overt unambivalent assertion" (she is clearly and openly critical and pressing for change), and "matriarchal" (she describes herself as comfortably in control of the relationship). Nine different styles were identified for the husbands: "patriarchal," "resisting wife's assertiveness," "crisis," "separate peace," "conceding generally to wife," "conceding to domineering wife," "conceding because ill," "egalitarian," and "union." These reflect different strategies for dealing with perceived conflicts within the marriage.

Women showed a clear pattern of increased assertiveness within the marriage as the nest emptied. Women with children under 24 still at home were more likely to fall into the categories of patriarchal, covertly assertive, or ambivalently assertive. As college-age children grow up and/or move on, the women become more openly assertive in the relationship, leading to open conflict in some of the relationships. Some of the wives describe themselves as comfortably in charge. The shift, then, is from patriarchy to something more like partnership or matriarchy. Although these shifts are also correlated with chronological age, only the measure of parental phase is an independent predictor of renegotiating the marriage. This finding is clearly in accord with the model.

The men's descriptions of the ways in which they deal with marital conflict also varied with parenting phase. Men who have no children under 24 at home are more likely to say they share power or concede to their wives.

In order to test the parental imperative model, we need to take account of competing explanations for the variability observed in gender-linked self concepts and in marital behaviors. As one step toward this goal, regression analyses were done predicting the gender measures and the marital styles from chronological age, health, and occupational status. Chronological age and social status do not make independent contributions to these patterns, nor are women's patterns affected by their own or their husband's health. However, it appears that a husband's marital behavior is linked to his health: Men who described more serious health problems were also more likely to describe themselves as conceding power to their wife.

These data suggest a complex model of how the parental imperative may affect fathers and mothers. As children mature and leave home, women seem to become more assertive in the marriage relationship. The women seem to be able to assimilate their increased assertiveness to their general sense of themselves as feminine and nurturing; they do not describe themselves as more masculine or less feminine even though they acknowledge that their behavior within the marriage has changed. However, their husbands seem to feel challenged and even threatened by the increased assertiveness, and the husbands are likely to feel unmanned and to describe themselves as less masculine.

# EARLY EXPERIENCES AND MIDLIFE GENDER STYLES

A fourth strategy for examining developmental contributions to gender-linked schemas involved intensive analyses of a randomly selected subset of cases in order to relate recollections of early relationships with parents to contemporary gender styles. One section of the interview with the middle-aged parents included questions about what each parent was like when they were growing up and how they got along during that time; another section inquired about images of themselves as young adults. Individual case studies illustrated the ways in which memories of early gender models can influence the ways in which middle-aged women deal with the potentials for revising (especially expanding) their gender identities when children were launched. The case histories illustrated the subtle ways in which past and present combined to shape the ways women feel about themselves as women and the ways they deal with potentials for change in gendered behaviors (Huyck, 1994).

A more systematic case analysis was carried out by David Gutmann with the middle-aged men, building on his and colleagues' extensive work in the study of late onset psychopathology (Gutmann & Huyck, 1994). The analyses of clinical cases suggested that many of the persons who appeared as "clinical casualties" in midlife were really responding catastrophically to the normal transitions in gender-linked expectations and self conceptions (Gutmann, Griffin, & Grunes, 1982). Among the clinical samples of men, the problematic precursors seem to be embedded in the early relationships with parents and the current relationships with the wife. A question we posed was whether some of the same dynamics would be evident in a normal sample drawn from Parkville. The initial analysis was conducted with the men, partly because the best comparative data comes from the men, and partly because men seem to have much more difficulty with gender modifications than do women. The sample included the 105 men from Parkville who completed all phases of the data collection.

The patterns in the Parkville sample were largely similar to those already observed in clinical samples. Men who showed an atypically passive and feminine profile in later years are those whose early years were characterized by powerful and still unrelinquished ties to devoted mothers. If the aging wife is willing to replicate the mother's attention and concern, then these men appear to be soothed, often immensely content, and symptom free. But if the older wife refuses to be hyper-maternal and does not match the husband's internally imprinted *magna mater,* then the dependent man either becomes depressed, or uses somatic symptoms as a cry for help. These results indicate that men who do not separate in the psychological sense from their mothers during the formative years are particularly at risk in the later years: Rendered particularly vulnerable by postparental androgyny, their own well-being is chronically hostage to their wives' shifting moods. However, men who did manage to separate from the mother survive the post-parental phase relatively unscathed by the psychic reorganizations. They are the ones who can reclaim repressed aspects of the self without feeling compromised in their basic gender integrity.

## IMPLICATIONS FOR THEORY, PRACTICE, AND FURTHER RESEARCH

### Lessons from Parkville on Gender Development

Gender remains an important dimension of self-identity and appraisals of others, even though young adults are challenging gendered expectations. Sixty percent of the young women we interviewed said they did not conform to stereotypic expectations. The young women seem to differentiate from their mothers by incorporating more assertive, purportedly masculine characteristics into themselves. However, as these young women moved into their later 20s, and/or married and became mothers, they were no longer different from their own mothers. One third of the young men describe themselves as not meeting stereotypic standards of masculinity, and some of the young men feel clearly uncomfortable seeing themselves as masculine. Overall, the young adult sons describe themselves as more masculine than do their fathers; the sons who have become fathers themselves are like their own fathers.

The ways in which midlife parents responded to potentials for modifying their gender style reflected, in part, internalized images of their own parents in gendered terms. Women and men who recollected both parents as loved and strong in different ways found it easiest to incorporate new aspects of feeling and behavior without feeling "degendered." Men who yearned to return to the role of beloved son did well in later life if their wife indulged this wish without demeaning them; if the wife resisted, such men were at risk.

The data do not offer much support for a cohort-effects model of development. Rather, young adults seem to show ways of differentiating themselves from their own same-sex parents, but this differentiation virtually disappears when the young persons marry. While there is clear variability in the ways in which the men and women in Parkville experience their own gender identity, their own children seem to follow whatever family style has been established. These patterns support the socioevolutionary model, which assumes that behaviors that are adaptive for family functioning are preserved and activated at the developmentally appropriate points in the life course. The results are also congruent with psychodynamic theories, which postulate that identification with the same-sex parent is a mark of mature, adaptive behavior. They conform, too, to cognitive social learning theories, which describe the mechanisms through which behaviors might be acquired once the emotional identification specified by dynamic theory has been accomplished.

## Gender Expansion Vs. Androgyny

Except for the minority of young adults who are having obvious difficulty in coming to terms with their basic gender, and who almost refuse to admit that being male or female has any social or psychological consequence, the men and women in Parkville are clear about the ways in which they experience themselves primarily in terms of their gender-congruent styles. Their first experience of self has to do with how they deal with their own maleness or femaleness. The persons represented here have developed varied ways of recognizing themselves as masculine or feminine, but the underlying theme is how much and how comfortably they can feel and behave in ways that they believe are congruent with their sex. The primacy of this sex-congruent gender makes good sense in terms of cognitive-schema theories, which posit that organizing perceptions by sex remains a powerful principle throughout life. The primacy of sex-congruent perceptions about the self also makes sense psychodynamically, since society needs to deal with the realities imposed by differing reproductive potentials, hormones, aggression potential, fantasies, and social-stimulus value.

Congruence to gender forms the basis for adding (or rejecting) any interests, behaviors, or other individualized traits associated with the other gender. For example, recognizing a desire or propensity to confront criticism by direct challenge is typically experienced as gender-confirming by males because it affirms a very core aspect of masculinity. Women who recognize a similar propensity in themselves generally feel ambivalent about it. They may control it in order to remain gender congruent, or act on the desire in order to demonstrate they are not limited by their gender. In either event, the choice is not neutral with regard to gender identity. Similarly, individuals are not regarded as sexless "persons" by others. The gender-associated behavior will be evaluated, and responded to, by others in terms of the sex and presumed gender of the actor. Thus, it seems unrealistic and unreasonable to think in terms of androgyny, unisex, or gender-free realities. These terms could be dropped from our conceptual vocabulary.

The degree to which behaviors and evaluations of behaviors are linked to gender certainly varies, among persons and probably by historical period and culture; in the Parkville sample, the older middle-aged men are relatively gender sensitive and the older, upper-middle-class women are relatively gender transcendent. However, the basic template for personal awareness and social interactions remains gendered.

## Clinical Implications

The ratings based on interviews about gender make it clear that adults develop varied ways of defining themselves as appropriately masculine or feminine. While acknowledging media stereotypes, they are not necessarily coerced by them. This is a positive sign, since it means that we can help persons identify the diverse ways in which they can be, and are, gender congruent. From this base of security, it seems easier to acknowledge aspects of the self that are not congruent with personal or stereotypic gender, and to take pleasure in those expansions.

Gender is more problematic for men than for women. Women, particularly midlife women, seem to be better able to incorporate what they feel are masculine characteristics without feeling compromised in their femininity. The young men who do not feel masculine are less likely to move into the adult roles of marriage and fatherhood. The consequences of psychological passivity for midlife men depends on the wife's response; if she is accepting, his passivity is not problematic, but if he feels she demeans it he is likely to feel very stressed. Clinicians and marriage counselors must remember that a husband's complaints of a domineering wife may reflect his own internalized sensitivities much more than significant change in his wife's behavior. Such sensitivities are likely to reflect his own early developmental problems in separating from his mother.

## Future Research Suggestions

We need to develop measures that are sensitive to the ways that gender-congruent, gender-compromised, and gender-expanded styles are developed, maintained, and modified. We need to reemphasize that the important distinctions between socioevolutionary patterns and cohort influences can be addressed fully only with cross-sequential, cross-cultural research. The patterns identified here should be explored in groups that differ from the Parkville sample in terms of age, marital and family history, sexual orientation, ethnicity, and other characteristics that may well influence gender development over the life course.

## ACKNOWLEDGMENTS

The intergenerational research project "Aging Parents, Young Adult Children and Mental Health" was funded by a U.S. Public Health Services grant from the Center on Aging, National Institute of Mental Health, Grant Number ROI MH36264, to the Illinois Institute of Technology from 1982–1986, M. Huyck and S. Frank, co-principal investigators. We especially appreciate the guidance of Dr. Nancy Miller and Dr. Barry Lebowitz from NIMH for their guidance in establishing the project. I would like to thank all the respondents who participated: Susan Frank for her contributions in establishing the data set; Amy Shapiro for her work as project coordinator; and the students who have helped collect the data and prepare it for analysis. Interviewers included Cathy Butler

Avery, Scott Andrews, Jeffrey Angevine, Larry Antoz, Mike Bloom-
quist, Yael Buchsbaum, Paul Carney, Lidia Cardone, Rita Decker, Jim
Duchon, Helen Dredze, Susan Frank, Gail Grossman, Dee Heinrich, Jeri
Hosick, Margaret Huyck, Mark Laman, Hunter Leggitt, Bill Pace, Kate
Philben, Timothy Pedigo, Martha Scott, and Mary Jane Thiel.

# REFERENCES

Angelaccio, C. (1990). *Gender identity of young adults.* Unpublished master's
    thesis, Illinois Institute of Technology, Chicago.
Berzins, J., Welling, M., & Wetter, R. (1978). A new measure of psychologi-
    cal androgyny based on the Personality Research Form. *Journal of
    Consulting and Clinical Psychology, 46*(1), 126–138.
Cross, S. E., & Markus, H. R. (1993). Gender in thought, belief and action: A
    cognitive approach. In A. Beall & R. J. Sternberg (Eds.), *The psychology
    of gender* (pp. 55–98). New York: Guilford.
Erikson, E. (1963). *Childhood and society.* New York: Norton.
Frank, S. F., Avery, C. B., & Laman, M. (1988). Young adults' perceptions of
    their relationships with their parents: Individual differences in connected-
    ness, competence, and emotional autonomy. *Developmental Psychology,
    24,* 729–737.
Geis, F. L. (1993). Self-fulfilling prophecies: A social-psychological view of
    gender. In A. Beall & R. J. Sternberg (Eds.), *The psychology of gender*
    (pp. 9–54). New York: Guilford.
Gutmann, D. L. (1975). Parenthood: A key to the comparative study of the life
    cycle? In N. Datan & R. Levine (Eds.), *Life-span developmental psychol-
    ogy: Normative life crises.* New York: Academic Press.
Gutmann, D. L. (1977). The cross-cultural perspective: Notes toward a com-
    parative psychology of aging. In J. E. Birren & K. W. Schaie (Eds.),
    *Handbook of the psychology of aging* (pp. 302–306). New York: Van
    Nostrand Reinhold.
Gutmann, D. L. (1987). *Reclaimed powers: Toward a new psychology of men
    and women in later life.* New York: Basic. Reissued 1994 by Northwestern
    University Press, Chicago.
Gutmann, D. L., Griffin, B., & Grunes, J. (1982). Developmental contributions
    to the late-onset affective disorders. In O. Brim, Jr., & P. Baltes (Eds.),
    *Life-span development and behavior* (Vol. 1, pp. 243–261). New York:
    Academic Press.
Gutmann, D. L., & Huyck, M. H. (1994). Development and pathology in post-

parental men: A community study. In E. Thompson, Jr. (Ed.), *Older men's lives* (pp. 65–84). Thousand Oaks, CA: Sage.

Huyck, M. H. (1989a). Midlife parental imperatives. In R. Kalish (Ed.), *Midlife loss: Coping strategies* (pp. 115–148). (Reprinted in 1991 as Parents and children: The "postparental imperatives." In B. Hess & E. Markson (Eds.), *Growing old in America* (4th ed., pp. 415–426). New Brunswick, NJ: Transaction.

Huyck, M. H. (1989b). Models of midlife. In R. Kalish (Ed.), *Midlife loss: Coping strategies* (pp. 10–34). Newbury Park, CA: Sage.

Huyck, M. H. (1990). Gender differences in aging. In J. E. Birren & K. W. Schaie (Eds.), *Handbook of the psychology of aging* (3rd ed., pp. 124–134). New York: Academic Press.

Huyck, M. H. (1991). Gender-linked self-attributions and mental health among middle-aged parents. *Journal of Aging Studies, 5*(1), 111–123.

Huyck, M. H. (1994). The relevance of psychodynamic theories for understanding gender among older women. In B. Turner & L. Troll (Eds.), *Women growing older: Theoretical directions in the psychology of aging* (pp. 202–238). Newbury Park, CA: Sage.

Huyck, M. H., & Gutmann, D. L. (1992). Thirtysomething years of marriage: Understanding husbands and wives in enduring relationships. *Family Perspective, 26*(2), 249–265.

Huyck, M. H., Zucker, P., Angelaccio, C., & deGrange, C. (1991). *Gender and the family.* Provo, UT: Brigham Young University Women's Research Center.

Pleck, J. (1975). Masculinity-femininity: Current and alternative paradigms. *Sex Roles, 1,* 161–178.

Plomin, R. (1990). *Nature and nurture: An introduction to human behavioral genetics.* Belmont, CA: Brooks/Cole.

Rebecca, M., Hefner, R., & Olesanky, B. (1976). A model of sex-role transcendence. *Journal of Social Issues, 32,* 197–206.

Schaie, K. W., Campbell, R. T., Meredith, W., & Rawlings, S. C. (Eds.). (1992). *Methodological issues in aging research.* New York: Springer Publishing Co.

Turner, B. F. (1994). Introduction. In B. F. Turner & L. Troll (Eds.), *Women growing older: Theoretical directions in the psychology of aging* (pp. 1–34). Newbury Park, CA: Sage.

Zucker, P. (1988). *A typology of gender styles applicable to the second half of life.* Unpublished doctoral dissertation, Illinois Institute of Technology, Chicago.

# Comments

## Deborah T. Gold

Margaret Hellie Huyck utilizes data from her Parkville study of adulthood to examine continuities and discontinuities in gender identity. Parkville data have been collected from two generations in families: young adults and their middle-aged or aging parents. One unique aspect of this sample is its relative demographic homogeneity, an advantage Huyck uses to its fullest. She asks questions about the effects of personality, generation, or stage of development on gender identity while ruling out potential confounders such as ethnicity, residence, and social class.

Huyck initially reminds her readers that gender is a complex and multidimensional construct relevant to individuals throughout the life span. In examining ways in which adults understand their own gender, as well as the gender of others, Huyck notes that individual characteristics can be at odds with a self-conceptualization of gender. Further, she challenges Gutmann's cross-cultural and clinical analysis of a late-life gender identity shift, with men moving from active to passive mastery while women shift from passive to active mastery. Here, Huyck suggests that we should not view such a shift as a crossover or a step toward androgyny.

One of the important and difficult questions raised in this chapter is whether there is a generation gap in gender. In looking for an answer to that question, Huyck finds that there is relative similarity between young adult women and their mothers, except when the young adult remains unmarried. The striking similarities between young married women and their mothers, Huyck posits, are affected by three processes: the daughter's maturation into the wife/mother role, the mother's own developmental changes, and reciprocal socialization by the two women as well as by broader social forces.

Comparisons between young men and their fathers, however, differ from those between mothers and daughters. In general, Huyck comments that young adult males report higher levels of masculinity than do their fathers, with the exception of sons who are fathers themselves. Huyck also explores the reluctance of some young men to take on gender-related roles such as husband and father.

Although there is some support for a gender generation gap among both men and women, Huyck cautions us not to be taken in by apparent differentiation in gender between young adults and their parents. Instead, she suggests that the gender gap disappears as the young person moves into family roles of adulthood. In her opinion, the data support a family developmental model of gender style.

Huyck argues strongly that gender is a critical aspect of self-identity, even if traditional views of gender are being contested. One of the most important of Huyck's points is that changes in gender identity throughout the life course do not appear to be an approach to androgyny. This chapter offers a major reconceptualization of gender development in middle and late life and is an important step forward in this area of investigation.

# CHAPTER 6

# A Non-Normative Old Age Contrast: Elderly Parents Caring for Offspring with Mental Retardation

## Sheldon S. Tobin

### INTRODUCTION

To make a non-normative contrast necessitates a delineation of normative old age. In normative old age, particularly in advanced old age, the adaptive life task is to preserve the self against losses of others and health, losses that can corrode the self. Stated another way, if the task of the youngest years is to preserve the self and the task of the adult years is to use the self for adaptation and to enhance gratification, the task of the oldest years is to develop the self (Lieberman & Tobin, 1983). The processes used to preserve the self at the end of the life course form the content of the normative psychology of old age.

My quest to understand these processes began in 1959 when Bernice Neugarten and Robert Havighurst asked me to assist them in composing the next interview protocol for the Kansas City Study of Adult Life. The task immersed me in reading innumerable interviews and a thick file of memos, many of which formed the basis for the 1961 book by Elaine Cumming and William E. Henry, *Growing Old: The Process of Disengagement.* Concurrently, I began being mentored at Drexel Home for the Aged by the insightful geropsychoanalyst, Jerome Grunes.

Given my simultaneous exposure to very old residents in Drexel Home and to community-dwelling Kansas City residents, some of whom were also quite old, it was natural for me to compare the two groups of persons of advanced old age. Although one group was living at home and the other in an institution, there were many similarities. One similarity was a persistence of identities, of the senses of self.

A resident in Drexel Home, when asked whether she had changed much over the years, extracted a photo from a stack in her dresser drawer, one taken when she was in her early twenties and said, "That's me but I changed a little." She had indeed changed. She was now neither curvaceous nor animated but was physically distorted from crippling arthritis and sullen from pain. To herself, however, she was still the same person she had always been. Persistence of the self was also evident for the Kansas City octogenarian who said, "Once a master brewer of the hops, always a master." Why not? At the turn of the century in Kansas City it was one of the most prestigious of professions.

What I did not understand as I began my quest was that the portrait I was drawing necessitated the completion of self-assigned life tasks; that is, that there was no unfinished business yet to be attended to. Some do have unfinished business, such as visual artists who often say when well past 80 that they are just beginning to see the essence of their vision (Tobin, 1991). Hokusai, the greatest of Japanese woodcutters, said on his deathbed at 94, "I am just beginning to learn my craft." Another group with work not yet complete are older perpetual parents, caring at home for adult daughters and sons with mental retardation. Having now studied 235 of such mothers, aged 58 to 96, it is apparent that they age quite differently from persons of normative old age. As perpetual parents, social time is different for them. They continue active child caring throughout their advanced aging without experiencing the empty nest that follows after the launching of children into adulthood. Before focusing on their non-normative aging as perpetual child caring parents, normative aging in advanced old age will be considered.

## NORMATIVE AGING

When I began my studies in the late 1950s, old age was divided between younger old age and the frail years beginning at 70. Then in the 1970s, Neugarten (1974) used existent disability data to distinguish between the young-old and old-old years, with the old-old years beginning at 75. By the mid-1980s, data led demographers to designate 85 as the beginning of the extreme aged years, the oldest-old years (Suzman & Riley, 1985). Colleen Johnson simply entitled the investigation she conducted with Barbara Barer and Lillian Troll (Johnson & Barer, 1992, 1993) the *85+ Study*. That study and the life and work of Erik Erikson have greatly informed me on advanced old age.

Erik Erikson is instructive in his own aging. In his original theorizing on the last stage of life in *Childhood and Society* (1950), Erikson postulated that integrity is achieved and despair avoided by accepting life as it has been lived and by investing in the continuity of generations. Then, in his advanced old age, Erikson reformulated the last stage of life in his book, *The Life Cycle Completed* (1982), and wrote that integrity is under "supreme risk" from terminal conditions demanding "integrality," which is a tendency to keep things together (pp. 64-65). Integrality, like the preservation of the self, suggests a new developmental task.

The motive to maintain a sense of coherence and wholeness, however, is apparently continuous after the development of the self, a motive that Lecky (1945) has referred to as *self-consistency*. Given that a lifetime has been lived and that there has been an accretion of losses, the psychological processes deployed to maintain self-consistency and integrality and to preserve the self in advanced old age may be different from those processes in younger years. Continuity, however, does not necessarily mean that changes do not occur. Continuity and discontinuity are not mutually exclusive but rather are complementary (Shanan, 1991). Change is always occurring as humans, and all living systems, adapt to environmental and developmental forces; but adaptation occurs within limits, in order to retain coherence and wholeness.

If continuity and discontinuity are inextricably interwoven throughout adult life, we must next ask: Are there some commonalities among ordinary people of advanced old age in the pattern of the weaving? In this exercise, however, a further question is: Are there some aspects of adaptation that particularly reflect discontinuity? And how so? These were not the kinds of questions I set out to answer when I wrote my 1991 book, *Personhood in Advanced Old Age: Implications for Practice*. The dimensions associated with preservation of the self discussed in that book, however, lend themselves to consideration of continuity and discontinuity, encompassing environmental mastery through active control and assertiveness (the obverse of passivity), the uses of reminiscence, religiosity, acceptance of death, and the maintenance of subjective well-being.

## Environmental Mastery

Mastery of the environment through active control and assertiveness (nonpassivity) are important to adaptation and survival itself. In a classic study, Cannon (1942) documented how healthy young people who believe in voodoo can deteriorate and die if hexed. In our longitudinal studies of relocation of the elderly (Lieberman & Tobin, 1983; Tobin & Lieberman, 1976), the inability to exert control over the situation and the giving in to passivity, although related, were independent predictors of adverse outcomes.

Control is as American as apple pie. Independence, self-determination, and autonomy are cherished throughout life. But control is different in advanced old age. Johnson and Barer (1992, 1993), in making control the centerpiece of their 85+ Study, discuss disengaging from superfluous roles, outliving conventional concerns, reframing time to focus on the here-and-now, and constricting control to day-to-day activities. Associated with these late-in-life changes is the shift in adulthood from primary control (controlling by actively changing the situation) to secondary control, achieved by reducing expectations of what can be controlled. This shift occurs when, for example, age-associated losses from deaths of family members and close friends and incapacities from physical changes necessitate modifications in what can be controlled. The wheelchair-bound formerly vigorous athlete of 85 who can control his movements only on the first floor of his ranch house, where his bed has been placed because he cannot mount the stairs to his bedroom, retains a sense of control.

A little sense of control goes a long way. Rodin and Langer (1977) found that a group of nursing home residents given as little as a plant to care for, or free to choose when and where to see visitors, survived longer than a control group. So too, we (Lieberman & Tobin, 1983; Tobin & Lieberman, 1976) found that elderly persons about to be relocated who transformed an unwelcomed, involuntary relocation into a welcomed, voluntary relocation situation were more likely to survive intact one year after relocation. Manifest feelings of control provide for latent feelings that one is in control and that the world is controllable. Among the very old whose power to control is limited, there is likely to be *magical mastery* (Gutmann, 1964, 1987). Goldfarb (1959), a psychoanalyst, assisted a person of advanced old age who was in acute crisis to move "toward inflating his belief that he can and does master current problems" (p. 386). Enhancing belief in mastery facilitates reintegration. Yet, the process by which manifest, even modest, control facilitates latent beliefs in control and controllability is continuous throughout life. A world that is unmastered is a precarious and dangerous world. It is human to overevaluate how much can be controlled. What is discontinuous, however, is the contraction of control while continuing to harbor beliefs in controllability.

A similar situation pertains to ill younger persons confronting a foreshortened life span. It is best to feel in control, to have Taylor's (1989) cognitive illusions and not to relinquish control to a lethal disease. Another parallel is that in order for manifest control to be effective for latent control, control must be exerted over something that is personally meaningful. The ill person facing a premature death must control the illness whereas the very old person must transcend illness, to control essential activities of daily living, and also control specific activities or people that provide for a persistent sense of meaningfulness.

The importance of assertiveness for the very old was also demonstrated many years ago by Brody, Kleban, and their colleagues (Brody, Kleban, Lawton, & Silverman, 1971; Kleban, Brody, & Lawton, 1971). This group found that aggressiveness was necessary to reduce excess disability among mentally impaired elderly persons institutionalized in a home for the aged, the Philadelphia Geriatric Center. Excess disabilities, which refer to levels of functional incapacity that are greater than warranted by actual impairments, were identified for 32 pairs of female residents in the experimental study. An individualized treatment plan was designed for one of each pair (the experimental group), aimed at reducing their excess disabilities. Only among those who were nonpassive and sufficiently aggressive were excessive disabilities reduced. Moreover, the factor of "aggressiveness" that was associated with therapeutic success was not simply mobilization, or nonpassivity, but rather a kind of determined nastiness that usually alienates others.

We (Turner, Tobin, & Lieberman, 1972) found that the same kind of determined nastiness facilitates adaptation to relocation, including survivorship. One aspect of facilitory aggressiveness is the functional paranoia of old age (Pearlin & Butler, 1963). The propensity to blame others, which may not have been evident in younger years, apparently becomes functional as age-associated losses occur. For some, the nastiness and distrust of others is thus newly acquired, reflecting discontinuity in adaptive coping. Or it could be argued that these behaviors are not new at all but rather are characteristic of adaptive coping under situational duress. Externalizing blame for misfortunes is always more adaptive than self blame and depression.

## Reminiscence

The personal narrative continually changes, but two attributes of reminiscence become different in advanced aging: the past become interchangeable with the present in validation of the self-picture and is dramatized to make the self vivid and vitalized.

When listening to personal narratives of very old people, themes emerge that make whole lives consistent and coherent. If, for example, an 85-year-old woman perceives herself as a take-charge person, this theme will be echoed throughout her reportage beginning with her earliest years, continuing through her adult life, and persisting until now. Because of losses of others and incapacities, the reportage of the here-and-now may contain only mild support for her life theme but invariably she will be able to interpret current interactions with others to be congruent with her self picture.

If we approach the validation of self-pictures from another perspective, a difference emerges between the validation of older and younger people. When a young woman is asked to provide an example in the present for the take-charge aspect of her self-picture, she will be readily able to do so (Lieberman & Tobin, 1983; Rosner, 1968). She may say something like, "I am organizing the bridal shower for my friend Suzie." Indeed, she will construct and also interpret current interactions to support who she believes she is. The octogenarian, however, when asked for an example in the present is just as likely to give an example in the past, such as "When my husband died, I took over the business," as to give an example in the present, such as "Everyday I make sure my neighbor Mollie is okay." In composing her personal narrative that contains a dominant theme of taking charge, past examples become as convincing and self-validating for her as current examples.

The telling of a personal narrative entails reconstructing reminiscences. What is different between middle-aged and oldest-old people is the dramatization of the past. Lopata (1979) found that widows mythicize deceased husbands. But very old people also mythicize deceased persons from their earliest life. In a comparison of reminiscences gathered by a focused life interview, we (Revere & Tobin, 1980/1981) found that very old people dramatized their past more than middle-aged people, making significant others bigger than life, often more perfect that can be believed but sometimes more cruel than even the wickedest of wicked stepmothers.

The mythicizing of parental figures is revealed by Erikson (1982) who in his latest years discussed the necessity of perceiving the true and timeless love of one's mother as a means of counteracting the narcissistic assaults on the self in aging, and a means of achieving integrality. The recognition of the importance of retaining a vividly coherent reconstruction of earlier life led Grunes (1982) to base his psychotherapy with oldest people in acute crises on recapturing memories:

> The patient, bewildered and in need of touchstones, can find, with the uncovering and the attempt to reestablish memories from his own life with a nonjudgmental person, a recathexis of his own past and a sufficient organization of the historical sense of self, perhaps less subtly organized but organized nonetheless, to function as a unified personality. . . . It is the recathectic memories reincorporated with the sense of worthwhileness that the patient receives from the therapist. (p. 547)

## Use of Religiosity

The extent of religiosity in our society is indeed impressive. For example, Gallup and Castelli (1989) reported that 93% of Americans agree that they have a personal relationship with their God, four of five believe that God still performs miracles, and three of four believe in a hereafter; the findings are independent of educational level. Given the extent of religiosity, it is apparent that people do not become more religious as they age but, rather, religious coping and religious beliefs may, in becoming more salient, appear to increase among the current cohort of oldest people (Koenig, George, & Siegler, 1988). Praying, a lifelong form of religious coping used by those who are observant in order to relieve anxieties, becomes more evident among the oldest old, not only because of anxieties but also because there is now more time for reflection in solitude and because of their wishes for three of God's blessings.

The three blessings of God that are learned early in life, which become particularly salient toward the end of the life cycle, are relief from unendurable suffering, a long life as a divine reward for prior service, and a hereafter that contains reunions with departed loved ones (see, for example, Deuteronomy 4:40, Psalm 91:16, and Proverbs 9:11). The belief that God relieves the just of unendurable suffering can cause religious persons difficulties when they are suffering and wish to be taken to their final resting place but persist in remaining alive. God's blessing of a long life for services is obviously helpful when living beyond the biblical three score and ten. To live beyond 70 is so commonplace now that the solace provided by this belief is practically ubiquitous among the oldest-old. Ubiquitous also is the looking forward to reunions. The most common picture of the afterlife cherished by the old is not sitting on a heavenly cloud strumming a harp. Rather, it is of meeting one's Maker and being surrounded by loved ones.

Possibly the clearest expressions of reunions in the hereafter are heard in African American spirituals:

I looked over Jordan and what did I see?
A band of angels comin' after me,
Comin' for to carry me home.

## Acceptance of Death

When Munnichs (1966) reported that most older people find death acceptable, I interpreted his finding as reflecting avoidance of thoughts of nonbeing and recalled Kierkegaard (1844/1957), who wrote that the price paid for being human is the dread of death. Over the years, I have become convinced that death itself (as nonbeing) becomes acceptable if life tasks have been completed and there is no unfinished business. There is a shift from the fear of nonbeing to the fear of the process of dying. This shift from the fear of nonbeing to the fear of the process of dying is clearly a discontinuity.

## Subjective Well-Being

Another kind of discontinuity is inherent in how the past is used for self-assessments of feelings of well-being. In the interiority of the middle years (Neugarten & Datan, 1973, 1974) there is introspection on what has been accomplished, and what can be accomplished in the remaining years. When, however, there are few remaining years, past accomplishments gain ascendancy as the congruence between expected and achieved life goals is contemplated. The here-and-now still matters, as discussed in the section on *environmental mastery,* but not only is the past used to validate the self-picture and mythicized to reinforce the self, but it also serves as a guidepost for the meaningfulness of one's life. Many, if not most, in the current cohort of the oldest-old feel that they have fulfilled the expectations with which they were reared. Indeed, many feel that they have exceeded expectations. Their earliest years may have been very difficult, especially if they were immigrants or the first generation born of immigrants, and then later experienced the Great Depression while raising their children. Elder (1974) provides a poignant portrait of the hardships of the Great Depression and how these bleak years during child rearing thwarted expectations. If later in advanced old age they can feel that their children have successfully traversed their own lives and if they themselves have a modicum of security, these elders are likely to evaluate their lives as meaningful. Albeit current discussions laud productive aging, ordinary oldest people do not need to feel that they are productive to know that their lives have been meaningful and successful.

## THE NON-NORMATIVE CONTRAST

Our sample of 235 mothers, 58 to 96 years of age, each caring for an adult daughter or son with mental retardation, varied not only by age but also other demographic variables (see Smith, Fullmer, & Tobin, 1994). Most (72.7%) of the mothers had minimal or no activities of daily living (ADL) incapacities and (by intention of the study) one of four had offspring who did not participate in available day care programs, but stayed at home all day, usually watching TV and assisting in household chores. Our best estimate is that one of two potential respondents who were asked to partici-

pate refused the request. The interview consisted of standardized instruments, as well as fixed and open-ended queries, in six dimensions:
demographics, care-related variables, service use, informal supports,
permanency planning for the offspring's future, and subjective well-being.

An example of how our elderly mothers who have mentally retarded
offspring at home differ from the portrait of normative aging is Mrs.
Molly Jones.

Mrs. Jones at 86 feels "old" because of her waning physical energies,
and, also, from caring for her quite ill 87-year-old husband. She is
poignantly aware of not being her former self. She says, "I'm not like I
was. I don't have the energy anymore. I just don't have the patience." She
can, however, preserve her sense of self because she continues to care at
home for her eldest son Jim who, at 59, is moderately retarded.

Her other son, 58-year-old Tom, resides less than a block away; and
Tom, his wife, and their children form a close-knit family with Mrs.
Jones. She is proud of them, particularly of their closeness and attentive-
ness to Jim. Thus like other elderly people, Mrs. Jones feels she has successfully mothered and launched the next generation. Yet with Jim at
home and necessitating daily care, a lifelong task remains. Having cared
for Jim for more than half a century, she feels that placing him in a group
home would be to abandon him. Although she would prefer that Tom
make a home for Jim, she wishes not to burden him and his wife. She
says, "It would be too much of a burden. They should live their own lives
and enjoy their children and then their grandchildren."

Noticeably absent is use of the past for preservation of the self. She
never mentions anyone from her family of orientation. She can think
about the past only as it pertains to Jim, and to the fact that caring for Jim
has been meaningful to her since his birth and that the successful rearing
of her other child is best reflected in his and his children's closeness to
Jim. Never does she describe any attributes or successes of Tom or her
grandchildren other than closeness in the family. She communicated that
Tom's wife is special too because she also is fond of Jim. (Although the
interview focused on the mother's relationship with her retarded offspring, there apparently were sufficient open-ended queries to elicit comments on children's and grandchildren's accomplishments, had Mrs.
Jones wished to make them.)

Caring for Jim, however, is not without its rewards. She says, "He is
still my baby. I don't know what I would do without him. Caring for him
. . . I just don't have the energy and my husband is so sick. . . . It is so
hard but it's what I do." Indeed, she does it well.

Mrs. Jones obtains gratification from caring for her retarded son Jim as do mothers of young children but, in common with other mothers now old, when she thinks about her other son Tom and his family she reaps the rewards of achieving lifelong goals. Yet, although she has agreed with the case manager at the day program that a group home is sensible for Jim, she knows that it can never be like the home she has made for him. She worries about the future, is unable to foster inflated beliefs in control, and, dreading the eventuality of Jim's uncertain future, she cannot face death with equanimity. She not only says that she cannot let herself think about dying but, as she ponders the subject, adds, almost inaudibly, "I can't die." Unlike other elderly mothers, she has "unfinished business" that preoccupies her thoughts.

Religion sustains Mrs. Jones in her caregiving. Jim is God's special gift to her, not as a cross to bear but as a special child to care for and to mother. Like other mothers who live to advanced old age, she has a feeling of specialness. But although she shares with others beliefs in being personally blessed by God by a long life, and in a hereafter with reunions, she cannot use these beliefs to her advantage, as mothers can who exhibit normative aging when very old. If she were certain that she would outlive Jim, she could feel blessed for her long life. Also, she cannot consider reunions with lost loved ones, particularly her parents, while immersed in caregiving. Because of her unfinished tasks, she cannot sleep peacefully and accept her approaching death.

Mrs. Jones reveals the paradoxical aging that is characteristic of the mothers in our study. Like younger mothers nurturing young children, she accrues gratification in caregiving. In turn, if the adaptive task in aging is to preserve the continuity of the self, this task is assured because of perpetual motherhood. Enhancement of the self and well-being is further bolstered by perceptions of having successfully launched other children. Yet, these foundations are undermined by awareness of unfinished business, which will remain unfinished following her death.

## Environmental Mastery

Mastery of the environment is assured through moment-to-moment caregiving. Indeed, the interpersonal world of perpetual parenthood necessitates a persistence of control in everyday life, including a mobilization of assertiveness for carrying out the essential tasks of daily living. Because thoughts of the future threaten feelings of mastery, these thoughts are actively suppressed, while feelings are sustained that one is in control and that the world is controllable. Even when there are incapacities in daily living and retarded offspring are now caring for their mothers, feelings of efficacy (using the Duncan and Liker, 1981, scale) are indeed very high. In contrast with normative aging, there is not a contracting of the world of the perpetual parent, and the mechanisms of magical coping, aggressiveness, and functional paranoia are absent.

## Reminiscence

Reminiscences focus mostly on the offspring with mental retardation, particularly the rearing experience. When asked to consider their family's child-rearing experiences, less than one of three make negative comparisons with mothers who do not have offspring with mental retardation. The usual positive comparisons are that their family is closer, more sensitive, and more caring. Moreover, when asked to compare their family to other families with offspring with mental retardation, somewhat more than one third perceive their family to be better. In turn, almost three fourths are positive about their rearing experience: one half characterize it as very positive, and more than one in five as somewhat positive.

## Religiosity

Of the 235 mothers, about one half responded to the query "Are you religious?" by choosing "very religious" and about another one half chose "somewhat religious" with only a few choosing "not religious" (Tobin, Fullmer, & Smith, 1994). It is apparent however, that the "somewhats" often reflected their nonparticipation in formal religious activities rather than their intrinsic religiosity. Because of stigma attached to the mentally retarded when these mothers had their children, many neither attended church services nor had their sons or daughters attend Sunday school. Given the level of religiosity of the sample, it would be expected that religious beliefs inculcated earlier in life that are salient to the older years would be in evidence. But salient religious beliefs were not very evident. Nor was the expected association between religiosity and these beliefs evident.

## Religiosity and Acceptance of Death

Mrs. Smith exemplifies the difficulty for these mothers, who are experiencing non-normative aging, of using their religiosity to help them accept death:

> At 87 and twice widowed, Mrs. Smith lives an isolated rural life caring for her 62-year-old retarded daughter, Janey. Her other daughter, aged 70, lives two miles away and is expected to make a home for Janey when their mother dies. Mrs. Smith said that she is very religious and the interviewer wrote, "She is very religious and feels that God gave her the responsibility of caring for her mentally retarded daughter and she will live up to that responsibility until the day she dies. I believe she will do this." She will do so because, Mrs. Smith says, "God gave me this cross and I have to carry the cross."

The four mothers over 90 years of age in our sample are similar in their resistance to death and their determination to persist despite physical deterioration. All four acknowledge that their capacity for self-care is diminishing. Aware that death will separate them from their offspring, they are not yet ready to die. Whereas they appear to believe in the hereafter, they are unable to complete a sentence completion test (SCT) stem, "Death is . . ." by introducing this belief because of how thoughts of death are intimately associated with separation from their offspring.

> Mrs. Angel at 96 says about her severely retarded daughter Amy (who is 50), "She is still a child." Although she considers herself a very religious convert to Catholicism, the SCT "Death is . . ." stem was completed with "I don't know. I never went through it or thought about it." She is also not ready to think about future plans: "I'll think about that in due time." The interviewer wrote, "She is very busy performing as much as she can until she can no longer do so." She is now having trouble doing so because she can neither bathe nor dress herself, uses a cane since suffering a broken hip two years ago, and has a pacemaker. Although she has begun to feel "old," she says that she is still in late middle age.

When is "due time" for Mrs. Angel? She certainly will not accept that it has arrived—even though she is 96 and has age-associated health problems and difficulties in activities of daily living. With a determination that the interviewer describes as "feisty," Mrs. Angel resists death, which will sever a lifetime of caring. Whereas these ninety-plus-year-old women are religious in ways similar to all but a few in our sample, they do not plead to God to outlive their dependent offspring. Rather, it appears that their continued survival is energized by an indomitable, highly personal will to survive that is uncharacteristic of the majority of elderly persons among the current cohort of the oldest-old.

Three aspects of religiosity warrant synthesizing. First, these mothers are likely to use prayer for coping; second, they are likely to introduce God when talking about birthing and rearing an offspring with mental retardation; and third, although they have religious beliefs inculcated early in life that are particularly useful in normative aging, they have difficulty using these beliefs. All three aspects reflect the intrinsic religiosity of the mothers. Prayer is used particularly to request the health and strength to continue to care at home for their offspring. As one mother said, "Everyday I ask God to stay on earth so I can help him." For most of these mothers, their offspring are "God's special gift" to them, but for some, "It is a cross I must bear." Note that "bearing a cross" is a religious referent.

The blessing most focused upon in this chapter is one's heavenly reward. Only a handful of our mothers could talk favorably of a here-after, specifically those mothers who had made future plans for their offspring with which they were comfortable. Mrs. Green, at 83, could say to her 63-year-old daughter, "I don't mind dying. You'll be in a wonderful atmosphere." She felt that adequate plans had been made for the future. Similarly, Mrs. Brown, at 89, because she had made plans for her 53-year-old daughter to live with another daughter in their trailer on the grounds of a church-related retirement community, completed the SCT "Death is" stem by saying "going to heaven." Most, however, were not comfortable with plans they had made, and many could not even allow themselves to make plans. Mrs. Kane commented, "Death is surrendering my life to God. A long rest. Going to another level of my life." But at 91 she is not yet willing to surrender her life to God "because I leave someone behind who I love and needs me."

Another blessing, a long life (three score and ten) as a divine reward for service, gives little comfort because it is not enough to live to 70. Living to 90, on the other hand, gives religious people a sense of being personally blessed by God. The wish, even at age 96, is to outlive their offspring; Mrs. Angel would welcome death if she could outlive her 50-year-old daughter, of whom she says, "She is still a child."

Of interest is that a typical third belief, that a merciful God will relieve us from unendurable suffering, is relatively absent in our data, which confirms our observations that the mothers tolerate physical suffering very well. Some do, however, endure enough physical suffering to become physically dependent on their offspring for daily care. Fear of a final separation from their offspring seems to inhibit invocation of this blessing. A mother who did say that death would be a "relief" also said, "I want to be here forever to give care."

## Subjective Well-Being

Satisfaction with caregiving is exceptionally high. Four items were created such as "I really enjoy being with (name of offspring)" and "(Name of offspring) shows real appreciation for what I do for her/him." When responses to each item were scored on 4-point scales from "not at all" to "very much" and summed, almost one third of the mothers received maximum scores of 12. More than one third had very high scores (11 and 10), and only about one of ten scored low (7 or less). Echoing their satisfaction with caring, as well as their positive evaluations of their rearing experiences, their current affect states and life satisfaction ratings were quite high, higher than in the community sample. On the Bradburn Affect Balance Scale (BABS, of Bradburn, 1969), the sample revealed high current positive affect, and only one of ten had a negative affect balance score. In turn, the mean on our life satisfaction rating scale (the LSR; Neugarten, Havighurst, & Tobin, 1961) was higher than the mean we had found in Kansas City (19.1 compared to 17.8); also, the interquartile range (17 to 22) for mothers in this sample reflects rather high feelings of well-being.

These feelings of well-being, however, occur in the context of fears of the future. These fears were assessed, for example, by an item "I cannot accept the fact that (name of offspring) could learn to live without me." Almost three of four agreed with this statement. Confronted with this future, a very religious mother, when asked how her retarded daughter affected her attitude toward death, recalled a solution offered in the Bible: "Perhaps Armageddon will come and I will not have to worry." She will not have to worry about her daughter's future as they both enter heaven together, even if the only way to do so is through the end of both of their current lives on earth.

## SYNTHESIS

Social time is radically different for these 235 mothers, 58 to 96 years of age, who continue to care at home for their adult children with mental retardation. In contrast to normally aging parents, they have not launched all their children to adulthood and then experienced an empty nest. Rather, these perpetual parents persist in child caring and never is their nest empty.

Moreover, in common with parents of young children, they must be concerned about the future of their dependent offspring. Indeed, they are threatened by unfinished business as the life cycle nears its end. When they become too incapacitated or die, others will have to assume responsibilities for care, others who they know can never provide the loving care that they have provided throughout their lives.

Their perpetual parenting permits the maintenance of a persistent sense of self when confronting age-associated losses that corrode the self, particularly losses of meaningful others and losses in functioning. People in normative aging are able to transcend these losses and preserve their sense of self, their identities, by an environmental mastery characterized by a narrowing of the focus of control: Focusing on what can be controlled supports latent beliefs that one is in control and that the world is controllable. In doing so, they mobilize sufficient assertiveness to resist lethal passivity. Perpetual parents, however, need not narrow their focus of control as they persist in child rearing and also maintain assertiveness inherent in the daily tasks of caregiving. Even when their frailty necessitates care by their dependent adult children, these elderly parents maintain mother–child caregiving and intimacy, as well as control and assertiveness. Thus, focusing on their current parenting, they are able to maintain a persistence of the self when confronting age-associated losses. The sense of control is assured without the kinds of aggressiveness, magical coping, and functional paranoia found in normative aging.

Reconstructions of the past focus largely on their offspring. The past, however, is neither used nor made vivid to validate the self, as is common in normative aging.

Some religious beliefs are unusable, particularly the belief in reunions in an afterlife, because the reunions they wish are with offspring who are expected to outlive them. Death cannot be accepted. In normative old age, when there is no unfinished business, death becomes acceptable as concern shifts to the process of dying—to not dying alone, in intractable pain, bedridden, and irreversibly confused.

Yet, because of their current gratification through caregiving, and also their appraisal of their lifetime of caregiving as very meaningful, the mothers in our sample have high levels of life satisfaction, higher than those aging normatively. Still, fears of the future must be, and usually are, valiantly suppressed. With containment of threatening fears of the future, social time is radically different than in normative aging. These elderly parents who are suspended in social time are able to persist in caring for their children, reaping gratifications from knowing that their lives are meaningful in ways that the lives of their age peers are not. Perpetual parenthood has its rewards in spite of the threat of the future.

## REFERENCES

Bradburn, N. (1969). *The structure of psychological well-being*. Chicago: Aldine.

Brody, E. M., Kleban, M. H., Lawton, M. P., & Silverman, H. A. (1971). Excess disabilities of mentally impaired aged: Impact of individualized treatment. *The Gerontologist, 11,* 124–133.

Cannon, W. B. (1942). "Voodoo" death. *American Anthropologist, 44,* 169–181.

Cumming, E. M., & Henry, W. E. (1961). *Growing old: The process of disengagement.* New York: BasicBooks.

Duncan, G. J., & Liker, J. K. (1981). *Disentangling the efficacy-earnings relationship.* Unpublished manuscript.

Elder, G., Jr. (1974). *Children of the Great Depression.* Chicago: University of Chicago Press.

Erikson, E. H. (1950). *Childhood and society.* New York: Norton.

Erikson, E. H. (1982). *The life cycle completed.* New York: Norton.

Gallup, G., Jr., & Castelli, J. (1989). *The people's religion.* New York: Macmillan.

Goldfarb, A. I. (1959). Minor maladjustment in the aged. In S. Arieti (Ed.),

*American handbook of psychiatry* (Vol. 1, pp. 378–397). New York: BasicBooks.

Grunes, J. M. (1982). Reminiscence, regression and empathy—A psychotherapeutic approach to the impaired elderly. In S. I. Greenspan & G. H. Pollock (Eds.), *The course of life* (Vol. 3, pp. 545–548). Washington, DC: National Institute of Mental Health.

Gutmann, D. (1964). An exploration of ego configurations in middle and later life. In B. L. Neugarten (Ed.), *Personality and later life* (pp. 114–148). New York: Atherton.

Gutmann, D. (1987). *Reclaimed powers: Toward a new psychology of men and women in later life.* New York: BasicBooks.

Johnson, C. L., & Barer, B. M. (1992). Patterns of engagement and disengagement among the oldest old. *Journal of Aging Studies, 6,* 351–364.

Johnson, C. L., & Barer, B. M. (1993). Coping and a sense of control among the oldest old: An exploratory analysis. *Journal of Aging Studies, 7,* 67–80.

Kierkegaard, S. (1957). *The concept of dread* (Walter Lourie, Trans.). Princeton: University Press. (Original work published 1844.)

Kleban, M. H., Brody, E. M., & Lawton, M. P. (1971). Personality traits in the mentally impaired aged and their relationship to improvements in current functioning. *The Gerontologist, 11,* 134–140.

Koenig, H. G., George, L. K., & Siegler, I. C. (1988). The use of religion and other emotion-regulating coping strategies among older adults. *The Gerontologist, 28,* 303–310.

Lecky, P. (1945). *Self consistency: A theory of personality.* New York: Island.

Lieberman, M. A., & Tobin, S. S. (1983). *The experience of old age: Stress, coping and survival.* New York: BasicBooks.

Lopata, H. A. (1979). *Women as widows: Support systems.* New York: Elsevier.

Munnichs, J. M. (1966). *Old age and finitude.* New York: Karger.

Neugarten, B. L. (1974). Age groups in American society and the risk of the young-old. In F. Eis (Ed.), *Political consequences of aging* (pp. 189–198). Philadelphia: American Academy of Political and Social Sciences.

Neugarten, B. L., & Datan, N. (1973). Sociological perspectives on the life cycle. In P. B. Baltes & K. W. Schaie (Eds.), L*ife span developmental psychology: Personality and socialization* (pp. 53–69). New York: Academic Press.

Neugarten, B. L., & Datan, N. (1974). The middle years. In S. Arieti (Ed.), *American handbook of psychiatry* (pp. 592–606). New York: BasicBooks.

Neugarten, B. L., Havighurst, R. J., & Tobin, S. S. (1961). The measurement of life satisfaction. *Journal of Gerontology, 16,* 134–143.

Pearlin, S., & Butler, R. N. (1963). Psychiatric aspects of adaptation to the aging experience. In J. E. Birren, R. N. Butler, S. W. Greenhouse, L.

Sokoloff, & M. R. Yarrow (Eds.), *Human aging: A biological and behavioral study* (pp. 143–156). Washington, DC: National Institute of Mental Health.

Revere, V., & Tobin, S. S. (1980/1981). Myth and reality: The older person's relationship to his past. *International Journal of Aging and Human Development, 12,* 15–26.

Rodin, J., & Langer, E. (1977). Long-term effects of a control-relevant intervention with the institutionalized aged. *Journal of Personality and Social Psychology, 35,* 897–902.

Rosner, A. (1968). *Stress and maintenance of self-concept in the aged.* Unpublished doctoral dissertation, University of Chicago, Illinois.

Shanan, J. (1991). Who and how: Some unanswered questions in adult development. *Journal of Gerontology: Psychological Sciences, 46,* P309–P316.

Smith, G. C., Fullmer, E. M., & Tobin, S. S. (1994). Living outside the system: An exploration of families who do not use daycare. In M. M. Seltzer, M. W. Krauss, & M. P. Janicki (Eds.), *Life course perspectives on adulthood and old age* (pp. 183–202). Washington DC: The American Association on Mental Retardation.

Suzman, R., & Riley, M. W. (1985). Introducing the "oldest old." *Milbank Memorial Fund Quarterly/Health and Society, 63,* 177–186.

Taylor, S. E. (1989). *Positive illusions: Creative self-deceptions and the healthy mind.* New York: BasicBooks.

Tobin, S. S. (1991). *Personhood in advanced old age: Implications for practice.* New York: Springer Publishing Co.

Tobin, S. S., Fullmer, E. M., & Smith, G. C. (1994). Religiosity and fears of death in non-normative aging. In E. Thomas & S. A. Eisenhandler (Eds.), *Aging and the religious dimension* (pp. 183–202). Westport, CT: Auburn House.

Tobin, S. S., & Lieberman, M. A. (1976). *Last home for the aged: Critical implications of institutionalization.* San Francisco: Jossey-Bass.

Turner, B. F., Tobin, S. S., & Lieberman, M. A. (1972). Personality traits as predictors of institutional adaptation among the aged. *Journal of Gerontology, 27,* 61–68.

# Comments

## Boaz Kahana and Eva Kahana

Continuity and discontinuity are the themes of this volume's celebratory essays for Bernice Neugarten. Sheldon Tobin's chapter not only addresses some key elements of continuity and discontinuity in personal development but also illustrates these concepts in terms of the evolution of his ideas. They are familiar themes in his essay, reminders of the pioneering research that he and Morton Lieberman conducted to understand the impact of institutional living and the development of self in late life. We first heard these ideas as new students at the University of Chicago. Yet in a field of institutional care in which there have been new and exciting research developments, these ideas are still fresh and we include the publications that set them forth in our class reading lists.

There are also broad new ideas along with reappraisals of earlier views reflected in Tobin's chapter. As we see it, the fundamental and continuing contribution of his research and thinking concerns the unique processes by which old-old individuals attempt to maintain continuity of the self. A new and very valuable aspect of this work relates to consideration of non-normative life situations such as the care needs of an adult retarded child, which can result in the ongoing and unfinished business of parenting. Here, Professor Tobin undertakes an important step toward identifying how contextual and environmental factors may alter even very fundamental processes related to the acceptance of one's impending death. Mothers of developmentally disabled adult children alter the very process of self-maintenance that prevails among older persons who live in a normative context of aging. The latter group have finished their developmental tasks of parenting and can go on to the processes of self-maintenance that occur in old age.

We would like to pick up two interesting threads that are implicit in Dr. Tobin's chapter. The first is a temporal component. He notes that processes of self-maintenance in late life include dramatization of the past, reminiscences, and vividly coherent reconstructions of earlier life. All of these methods of self-maintenance tie the normative ager to the past rather than to the present or the future. In contrast, those with unfinished parenting cannot accept their impending death. Instead, their continuing self is maintained by heroic attempts to go on living productively, and they continue to propel themselves into the future.

The second implicit thread, which is distinctly different for Dr. Tobin's normative and non-normative agers, refers to the dimension of self- versus other-directedness. This is the spatial rather than the temporal dimension of the self. Normative agers are very much focused on the self. Their goal is that of self-preservation. They appear inner-directed and succeed in maintaining their integrity in ways that range from asocial (magical coping, religiosity) to antisocial (determined nastiness and functional paranoia).

In contrast, the non-normative or unfinished business group appears other-directed. Their desire to continue to be nurturers is what gives meaning to their lives. They continue to maintain high levels of satisfaction in spite of "tenacious goal pursuit," in Brandtstadter's and Renner's (1990) term. We should also remember that this group is a highly select one. Not only did they face the adversity of having a developmentally disabled offspring but they opted to continue caring for that offspring at home throughout their adult lives. These elderly fit profiles of altruistic orientations toward aging that have been the focus of our own work.

Dr. Tobin does not place an evaluative judgment on the success of normative or non-normative aging, although the latter appears deviant. In our own work, we have referred to alternative pathways to achieving Erikson's (1950) stage of *integrity* among non-normative agers who undertook long distance moves to Florida or Israel. The first group noted, in describing their life goals, "All my life I have done for my children and for my family, now it is time to do for me!" The second group described an alternative orientation, "All of my life I have done for my family and children, now it is time that I do for others!" Both of these groups sought discontinuity. This is in contrast to Dr. Tobin's group, who seek to maintain continuity of the self using alternate pathways. Perhaps, if our examples comprise alternative pathways to integrity, Dr. Tobin's groups comprise alternative pathways to integrality.

We started our discussion in noting both continuities and discontinuities in Dr. Tobin's own formulations, starting with his early ideas and recognizing his later contributions. We will end our remarks by referring to Dr. Tobin's quote from Professor Yoel Shanan (another of Bernice Neugarten's students). Shanan (1991) pointed out that continuity and discontinuity are, in fact, complementary rather than opposite concepts. The adaptations Dr. Tobin discovered among older persons who experienced non-normative life situations complement Bernice Neugarten's early contributions regarding age norms and age constraints. There is a remarkable and surely welcome continuity between the pioneering work of the mentor and the innovations of Dr. Tobin.

## REFERENCES

Brandtstadter, J., & Renner, G. (1990). Tenacious goal pursuit and flexible goal adjustment, explication and age-related analysis of assimilative and accommodative strategies of coping. *Psychology and Aging, 5,* 58–67.

Erikson, E. (1950). *Childhood and society.* New York: Norton.

Shanan, J. (1991). Who and how: Some unanswered questions in adult development. *Journal of Gerontology: Psychological Sciences, 46,* P309–P316.

# CHAPTER 7

# Perspective on Adult Life Crises

## Morton A. Lieberman

### INTRODUCTION

How do we determine what external life events or inner manifestations are appropriately designated adult life crises? By definition, life crises are normatively delineated by each society. Crises otherwise ignored by society are relegated to, and become the province of, certain institutions that deal with the marginal, the ill, and the disabled. Thus psychiatry and its allied professions have become the repository for those individuals whose disrupted emotional lives receive no other succorance or aid. One approach, then, for defining the current arena of adult life crises is to examine the array of institutions that society has made available to ameliorate the psychological consequences of life stresses. Psychiatry has historically functioned to contain, as well as to heal, those who are the most ill; community-based psychological resources, such as self-help groups and adult education, however, have become newly available to minimize or master the consequence of psychiatric control, by supporting adults who are confronting issues beyond the individual's capacity to resolve. This definition of adult crises based on community response has changed historically and, of course, does not produce a fixed and eternal list.

The usual academic definition of adult life crises involves discrete changes in life events that are consensually recognized as entailing some degree of distress, challenge, or hazard by the individual and members of his or her social group. The common-sense meaning is contained in the list of major life events, both normative (marriage, birth of a child, retirement) and those unscheduled but all too common milestones, such as divorce and widowhood. Many investigators have shown interest in a particular event (widowhood, retirement, marriage, divorce), a class of events (losses), or the accumulation of life events (life stress). Numerous modifiers may also be invoked to explain the linkages between life crises and responses. Often the point of departure for a research study is not the event, but the modifier.

A phenomenological perspective has guided the life events research of several investigators. Although they begin with real external events that have an objective definition in time and place, their interest is in the processing of these events rather than the events themselves.

Life crisis research is also represented by a distinct developmental position. The work of Buhler (1935), Jung (1933), Erikson (1982), Levinson, Darrow, Klein, Levinson, and McKee (1978), Gutmann (1987), and Gould (1978) articulate a broad formulation of crisis as engendering major transformations. Adult life crises are seen as representing or inaugurating distinct psychological stages, which require energy and effort for salutary change. Although developmentalists link crises to external events, these events are not at the forefront of their theory.

Although there is considerable correspondence between these methods of defining crises, distinct differences do exist. For example, the stress of caring for a living parent by adult children has been newly legitimized by the community, as evidenced by the proliferation of self-help and adult education groups. Historically, caregiving was not defined as a crisis, but was part of the family life cycle, rather than an abrupt entrance into a new role. The profound changes in our social structure within the memory of most of us have propelled *parent caring* into the nomenclature of adult life crisis. Notice of the adult's predicament of simultaneously caring for children and parents (the predicament of the so-called sandwich generation) has also become a sign of wider community commitment to social and economic justice. Such societal recognition moves the problem from an individual focus to a social issue involving both the person and society's structures.

I have chosen one life crisis to illustrate the issues confronting investigators who study adult life crises from an adaptational perspective. The loss of a spouse exemplifies the conceptual and methodological promise and problems inherent in the study of adult life crises. I will use some of the findings from my studies to contrast two opposing perspectives on adult events as turning points—the *life course model* and the *illness model.*

The contemporary singular concern with widowhood as an illness reflects a tradition hundreds of years old. Robert Burton, an English clergyman of the 17th century, authored a widely read book, *The Anatomy of Melancholy* (1896), that advocated the view that grief could adversely affect a widow's health. Burton's view was widely shared by the medical profession of his day. In 1809, Benjamin Rush, a prominent American physician, went so far as to suggest that an individual could even die of grief. He based his conclusions on autopsies of widows and widowers who showed "congestion in and inflammation of the heart, with rupture of its auricles and ventricles." In the 20th century many scientists have researched possible connections between widowhood and mental illness. Their work has been largely inspired by Freud's well-known 1917 paper, "Mourning and Melancholia" (1917/1957). It was Freud who advanced the idea that many psychiatric illnesses are caused by pathological mourning. Both excessive grief and the failure to grieve define such mourning. Contemporary thinking about grief still relies on these ideas.

The tenets of the illness model may be summarized as follows:

- A widow's principal task is to appropriately grieve so that she can become "whole" again.
- Help for widows necessitates an exploration of the meaning of the loss to unlock her grief.
- Recovery occurs when the widow's life is restored to its previous status quo.
- Failure to recover is a consequence of inadequate or inappropriate grieving.
- Deficiencies in grieving often lead to physical and mental illness.
- Many widows fail to recover and require professional help.

If, on the other hand, we view widowhood as part of the life course, we can see the loss of a spouse as one of the normal, expectable stages of existence. This perspective may be summarized as follows:

- Grief is only one of many tasks and challenges facing widows.
- The absence of protracted grief is not a sign of pathology.

- Successful "resolution of grief" can follow many different pathways.
- Recovery is not the end point. Beyond it, growth and meaningful change occur for many widows.
- Most widows do not require professional help.

Beyond grieving and loss of the partner, the spousally bereaved are faced with a set of challenges and alternative paths. Widowhood disrupts plans, hopes, and dreams for the future. The loss also challenges individuals' beliefs and assumptions about their world. Social supports and social networks must be renegotiated. Furthermore, widows must reexamine their self-image, which has been embedded in a long-term relationship, and move to a self based on an "I" rather than a "we." Many of the spousally bereaved are faced with inner psychological tasks that can be described by the label "existential dilemmas": confrontations of their regrets not only in regard to the deficits of their past marital relationships but to undeveloped aspects of their own lives. Such confrontations lead some from a sense of aloneness to the "closeness" of their own death, and then to seeking new meanings in life. Such challenges can be a source of distress for many; for others, however, it can provide a sense of accomplishment.

## ILLUSTRATIONS OF THE CHALLENGES FACING WIDOWS

### Self-Revisions

Jane is a young-looking, 45-year-old widow. This soft-spoken mother of two adolescents described her new-found self:

> When I was married, I always used to defer to my husband's decisions in everything, but in the year and a half since his death I've discovered that I really enjoy being in charge. I never knew I was such an independent person. I own an apartment building and I enjoy being the boss. I rent out the units, spruce them up, and tell the manager what to do. When I was married I was always torn between wanting to be taken care of and wanting independence. In the past year, I've lived alone and found that I can

manage fine. No one is taking care of me financially and I pay my own bills. I even joined Weight Watchers and a fitness program. My self-confidence has really taken off. What a difference! I live very much in the present and no longer postpone things until the future. I'm aware that my life is my responsibility and no one else's, not only now but in the past as well. I was my own jailer. I wouldn't let myself change, but now I relish the changes I've already made and those that will come later.

## A New Identity

A widow must move from the psychological space of thinking of herself as married to thinking of herself as being single again. An important symbol of being single comes into play in the difficult decisions women face after the death of a spouse of what to do with their wedding bands. For many widows the clearest symbol of their marital status resides in their wedding ring. Some wear their bands on their left hand, others on their right.

Linda, a 37-year-old who had been widowed for two years, told me that some days she wore her ring on her left hand, and some days on her right. Although Francis had been widowed only half as long as Linda, she felt that widows should acknowledge their "I-ness": "Since we are, in reality, no longer married, it's better to move the ring to the right hand as a sign of recognition we are single again," she said.

For Muriel, a recently widowed 64-year-old, keeping her wedding band on her left hand for now was important: "I'm comforted just by looking at my wedding band. It's a reminder of the love Joe felt for me."

The length of time one has been widowed has nothing to do with the willingness to embrace "single" identity again. Each woman, in her own way, struggles with the questions of how and when she is willing to let go of the idea of being married, and each moves along the path of healing at her own unique pace. None of the choices described above is inappropriate. All the women who spoke believe that they have to move on eventually and completely accept the fact of being single. But how and when to do so is a matter of personal choice.

## Separating the "We" from the "I"

Lisa, a widow in her late 50s, told me how her husband had provided them both with the assertiveness they needed for dealing with the outside world. After his death she began to recognize parts of herself that had lain dormant for over thirty years.

> I haven't pushed and pulled at the world since my early 20s. I left that for Bob to do. Since his death six months ago, I've rediscovered that part of myself. I've found I can be tough and I'm enjoying this new feeling. I realize now that during our marriage I believed it wasn't proper for a woman to be hard, even when circumstances called for it. At the very least, I wouldn't allow myself to admit it or be obvious about it. Bob and I faced the world as a team. He provided the toughness for both of us. At first it wasn't easy for me to see myself as an aggressive person, but gradually I've come to accept and even cherish this new me.

## Existential Confrontation

> My husband was only 49 and we never had a chance to say good-bye to each other. I was hearing, "I'm going to become an old woman." All I could think of was what my husband, now caught in eternity, would think of me. He'd be handsome and passionate, a Roman whose face is classical enough to been stamped on an ancient coin. I had been singled out too. Much older widows eagerly embraced me, clairvoyance whispering into my ear. I didn't need their prognostications. I knew then instinctively. I was struck with the conviction that by dying too young, he had aged me overnight. . . . Yet I had no conjugal regrets or animosity, just incredulity; I had no flesh and blood to hate nor even secretly to desire. I didn't have that one chance in a million to work things out. I was bringing news from a different front, a more remote posting where most of my contemporaries had never been. I felt there was something shameful about my condition, inappropriate, abnormal, widowed at the wrong age. I had not only grown up, grown old, as I expected, I had died in my own way and been reborn a different human being. This new person crawled out, waited with sadness, then, weak in the knees, began walking towards the future. By now, I feel like a middle-life adolescent; confused, sometimes angry, frightened, yet amazed by my shaky independence; I had the same inchoate longings, those wild curiosities and romantic yearnings, the needs to find meaning and connection in the world. But what I know now is that even if you love them inordinately, people are not ours to possess; they are only loaned to us. In fact, we barely own ourselves, and we need to keep re-inventing our lives in order to keep moving. (Tagliasozzo, 1988, p. 12, 21)

# THE STUDIES

## Methods

My findings are based on two nonclinical samples of widows and widowers. Questionnaires, multiple intensive clinical interviews, and observations of groups were used to generate data.

### *Description of the Samples*

SAMPLE 1.   Using lists of recently bereaved individuals provided by two self-help organizations, 696 widows/widowers were recruited. Individuals were assessed at three points in time: first at baseline, the second a year later, and the last 6.5 years after the initial assessment. Of the total of 696, 597 were women; 16% were under age 40, 24% in their 40s, 40% in their 50s, and 20% were 60 or over. There were 437 who were or became members of the self-help group, 159 who did not. Regarding education, 8% had not completed high school, 53% were high school graduates, 16% had some college, 17% were college graduates, and 6% had gone beyond college to either graduate or professional schools. Ninety-three percent had children, of whom slightly more than half (54%) were still living at home. Approximately three quarters of the men and half of the women were working prior to the spouse's death. After the spouse's death, employment status increased for the women by 14%.

SAMPLE 2.   A consecutive sample (*N*=80) of all surviving spouses of individuals who died of cancer 4 to 10 months before at two local medical centers were targeted for a random clinical trial of psychotherapy. A subsample of 20 were randomly selected as controls; the remainder participated in brief group therapy.

### *Measures*

RECOVERY.   Measures of recovery are embedded in a homeostatic framework, which assumes that the person perturbed by life crises seeks to rectify disequilibrium by returning to prior levels of adaptation.

ADAPTATION.   Four conceptually relevant areas for quantifying adaptation were chosen: mental health, positive states, role functioning, and grief intensity. *Mental health* measures reflect indices typically used to assess the effects of spousal bereavement—depression, anxiety, somatic symptoms, health, and substance abuse. *Positive states* measures include self-esteem, coping mastery, positive well-being, and life satisfaction. *Role functioning* provides a behavioral assessment of adaptation. It asks how well the person is performing in the major role areas—economic and parental—and in the newly acquired "single role." Phenomenological measures for indexing levels and intensity of grieving are based upon self report on grief intensity and the frequency of intrusive thoughts about the lost spouse. At baseline, 12% reported little or no grief, 30% reported mild grief, 43% moderate grief, and 15% intense grief.

GRIEF PATTERNS.    Scores on grief intensity at baseline and one year later (Time 2) were used to develop four grief types. *Typical* or normative grief was defined as the pattern of those widows/widowers who at baseline showed high levels of grief (moderate to intense) but at Time 2 demonstrated little or very mild grief (21%). These widows and widowers showed the prototypical "healthy" pattern of grief described in the loss literature. Three atypical grief patterns were defined: (1) widows/widowers who showed little or no grief both at Time 1 and Time 2—*limited grievers* (25%); (2) *delayed grievers,* who reported little or no grief at baseline but one year later demonstrated moderate to intense grief (11%); and (3) a group of widows/widowers who showed moderate to intense grief both at Time 1 and Time 2, who were designated as *prolonged grievers* (43%).

MEASURES OF GROWTH.    Measures used to index developmental changes focused on *personal growth* and *self-concept revisions.* Based on tape-recorded interviews, individuals were rated on growth. "High growth" is characteristic of a widow who is obviously stretching (doing new things, taking educational courses, struggling to find her own identity and own roots), is more aware of being an "I" rather than a "we," has developed new interests, has visited new places, and is willing to explore new relationships. She may be more self-sufficient, taking care of her finances, car, and house. She may be engaged in a new or renewed form of creative expression like painting or writing.

MEASURES OF SELF-CHANGE.    The abrupt and unanticipated thrust into widowhood compels a self-exploration because of the numerous changes linked to the death of a spouse. Two conditions are pivotal in obliging widows to begin such an exploration: the prior existence of a couple's self image and changes in the source of reflections on the self from others. Widowhood magnifies and focuses attention on readdressing the question, "Who am I?" Spouses, throughout a marriage, provide a unique source of self-image information. Opposed to these forces demanding self-image revision is a compelling drive within all people to preserve a stable self, to see our reflections in the mirror as we have always seen them.

The *self-sort* questionnaire and interview were used to assess self-concept revisions. Respondents using 48 interpersonal statements were asked to decide which items were like themselves and which were unlike themselves. They were then asked to indicate, for those self-descriptive items currently like themselves, which of the items they selected reflected new self-images. Similarly, they were asked to look once again at items they had selected and indicate those items not currently characteristic of the self but that used to be like themselves. Finally, respondents were asked to provide examples from their current life that supported their current self-image. These open-ended responses were coded on an 11-point scale assessing the quality of support for self-image.

## Some Findings

Most widows showed recovery within one year after the loss. Figure 7.1 shows the changes in grief intensity over one year; Figure 7.2 shows changes in outcomes measures. Widows who demonstrated little or no grief (limited grief) were, over the 7 years studied, doing the best. These findings do not fit the expectations of the illness model's basic tenet, that intense grief is required for recovery. The course of bereavement for widows designated as typical grievers matches our common-sense expectations. They showed intense grieving early in widowhood with significantly decreased grief intensity within a year. Their recovery and adaptation several years after their husbands' death was complete. Prolonged grievers failed to show much recovery, even after 7 years. The last grief type, delayed grievers, closed off their feelings in the early months of bereavement. Later on they were overwhelmed with

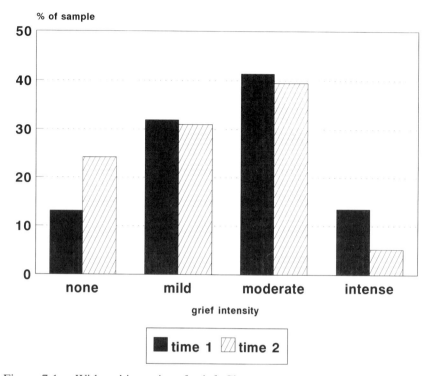

Figure 7.1. Widows' intensity of grief: Changes over one year.

grief and struggled to finally accept their loss. After a lengthy period, most delayed grievers were able to achieve a reasonable balance in their lives.

The homeostatic model has limitations. It is not sensitive to some important phenomena such as the powerful and highly individualized meaning of loss to bereaved individuals and the deep capacity within each individual for self-exploration and personal change. The bereaved person is faced with a number of significant challenges beyond the traditional confrontation with loss. To illustrate these limitations, I will turn to some findings based on the alternative perspective.

Over one third of the widows I studied showed clear-cut evidence of growth. They engaged in a search for their forgotten selves. Frequently they discovered new strengths and talents. Many of them took risks in trying new things and entering fresh relationships. Some returned to their distant pasts to resuscitate long-forgotten talents. Most made a

MEASURES

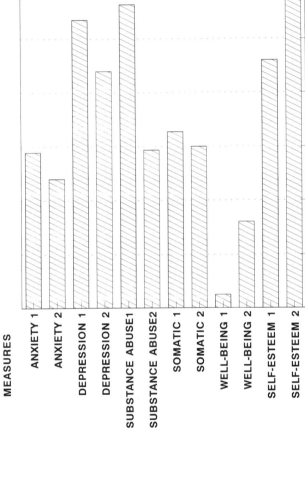

**INTENSITY**

**BASELINE AND 1 YEAR LATER**

Figure 7.2.   Changes in symptoms of grief, soon after the death compared to one year later.

decided effort to live in the present rather than postponing their lives for the vague tomorrow. The struggle to grow was not an easy one, nor did it occur instantaneously. More often than not, growth was achieved slowly, arduously, over long periods of time.

### High Personal Growth

Mrs. Dohl, a 62-year-old widow, underwent a number of changes after the death of her husband. She felt she first needed to rediscover her own identity—she had been a "we" and had long lost touch with her "I." Hence, she made a pilgrimage back to the country of her birth, searched for the house in which she had been born, and spoke to old townspeople and relatives in order to reconstruct her family and her early life. She began a number of new activities—some had been interrupted during her earlier life, some she had long yearned to do: she had braces put on her crooked teeth, took swimming and piano lessons, attended poetry-writing workshops, sold a house she had never liked and designed a new one, and enrolled in the freshman class of a nearby university's intergenerational program.

### Growth and Existential Awareness

What facilitates growth? Why are some widows able to render from the pain of loss and the anxiety of an unknown future a new beginning while others struggle but remain in place? What are the psychological processes that promote growth? An answer to these questions can be found in the ways widows involved themselves in inner explorations. Did they, spurred by their husband's death, explore existential life issues? Did they look inward and ask themselves, "What is the meaning and measure of my being?" Were they dealing with such issues as finitude, the inevitability of death, life's brevity, and, hence, its preciousness? Did they attend to the fragility, capriciousness, and contingency of being? Were they exploring personal responsibility for their life and their choices? Did they attend to feelings of isolation (not social isolation or loneliness but the unbridgeable isolation inherent in existence)? What kind of struggle were they engaged in to locate meaning in life?

A CASE OF EXISTENTIAL AWARENESS.    Mrs C. is a 55-year-old woman who, since the death of her husband, reports that she thinks differently about her life. She is full of regrets about the way she has lived her life: She believes she married the wrong man and is striving now to make choices more consonant with her real wishes. She is more aware of her fear of being free and the extent to which her fear of change rules her life. She is very much aware of the brevity and preciousness of life. She doesn't buy long-term subscriptions to magazines. She no longer buys five-gallon plants but instead buys faster growing, smaller plants. "There's no guarantee I'll be here in five years." She has stopped postponing things—she knows that her life must be lived now if it is to be lived at all. She knows now that it wasn't her husband who restricted her life but that she was her own jailer. She is aware of the artificial structure she had given to her life, the stifling routine of carefully prepared dinners and her many social obligations. She is frightened by the lack of structure in her life but also exhilarated by her freedom ("I can have popcorn for dinner"). She knows that death, her death, is real and inevitable. She has begun to take care of her own body: She has stopped smoking and has begun to exercise and lose weight. She has, for the first time, made a will and made her own funeral arrangements. She decries her former materialistic way of life in which she spent much time in decorating herself and her home and in lunches and bridge. That way of life feels very empty to her now; she is searching for some way of giving meaning to her life, some way to make a difference in the world, some way to leave her mark. She realizes that previously her sense of purpose in life derived from her role as a wife. Today she believes that, even if that role were still available, she would nevertheless demand more from life.

The existential journey significantly alters the course of bereavement. It leads to a rediscovery of "who I am" and "what I want out of my life"; in short it leads to growth. Did such explorations facilitate resolution of grief and enhance adjustment? In order to determine the impact of existential awareness on recovery I compared widows high on the scale of existential search to those low on the same measures and found a relationship between existential awareness and growth (Figure 7.3). No evidence was found, however, that embarking on the existential journey aids recovery. Good adjustment and growth seem to be separate and independent routes.

Who were the widows who were involved in exploring the meaning of their lives, who confronted their regrets, and who grappled with the tenuous nature of life? I compared characteristics of widows who

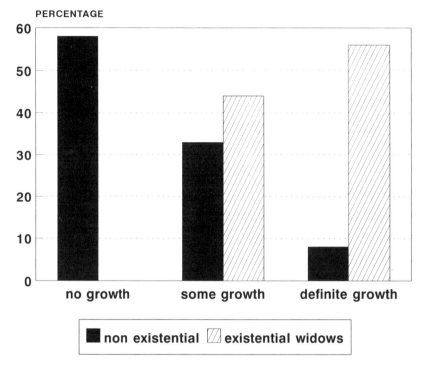

PERCENTAGE

Figure 7.3.   Existential exploration and growth. Time 1=soon after the loss, Time 2=one year later.

embarked on an existential search with those who chose not to explore their past, who did not search for new meanings in life, and who turned away from facing the inevitability of personal death.

Soon after their husband's death, searchers experienced more turmoil than did the nonexistential widows. They were more depressed and anxious and reported more loneliness. Their sense of loneliness was not based on the absence of people or activities. When I compared the level of social activity and amount of family contact of the searcher to that of the nonsearcher, I found that they were similar. They were also alike in their current relationships to men. One interesting difference is in how each of the two groups viewed these relationships. Although about the same number of the existentially and nonexistentially aware developed such relationships, widows who embarked on an existential journey were less likely to use these friendships with men to evade or diminish their grief. The sharpest differences between the searchers and nonsearchers were found in how they viewed their marriages. The existential widows evaluated their relationship as being overall a good and generally satisfying one but also a marriage that did stunt them. They felt that important aspects of their desires to fully express themselves and their interests were not permitted to flourish. In contrast the nonexistential widows were more likely to idealize their spouses, often describing their husbands and their relationship in superlatives. Despite this perception, they also suffered considerable guilt and anger towards their husbands.

One of the most challenging tasks facing widows beyond the early flood of grief is the struggle with personal identity. Everyday life, with its onrush of events, its engagement in career, children, and social relationships, rarely permits or requires a self-examination. Self-scrutiny is, however, commonly stimulated by major life crises. Among the sample widows, we saw a variety of responses in terms of self-image:

- Widows who revise their self-image by grafting on new qualities of self recover faster and better. Their grief is much lower.
- Widows who altered their self-images by letting go of important aspects of their previous selves in response to their husband's death did more poorly.
- Some widows who did not change their self-view, who maintained that they were the same person after their husband's death as they were before, did poorly, and some did well. I found that the difference between those who recovered well and quickly, compared to those whose recovery was much stormier, rested on the psychological processes each used to maintain her self. Widows who based their self-views on current reflections from others to support an unchanged image recovered rapidly and well. Widows who maintained an unchanged self-image by basing their self-view on the past, however, on a conviction that "I've always been like that," jeopardized their recovery.

One common path to growth is illustrated by the following case. Confronting past regrets and disappointments in the marriage frequently led to profound change.

A CASE OF GROWTH THROUGH LIBERATION.    Clara is a 76-year-old widow whose husband died ten months ago. She is short and very nearsighted. A sweater and skirt without adornments gave her the appearance of a simple, somewhat plain woman. Most of her life, until retirement at 65, she worked as a high-school teacher. Clara, who lives in a small town close to Boston, has been in the same house for over 50 years. One son lives in the city, but offers little solace or help. He told her that he would much rather she spend money on hired help (e.g., a gardener) and decrease his legacy than call upon him for help. She said, "I had an argument with him about this last week and felt, after the argument, that there were no helpful vibes coming from him at all."

Her style of interaction was direct, blunt, and very open. Her directness belied the intense depression she was experiencing. Although she attempts to push away her depression by being as busy as possible, she said:

> It doesn't work. I'm grieving because of Bob's death, but what I'm really angry about is the loneliness of widowhood and the fact that I see no light whatsoever at the end of the road. After he died, I was really in the state of shock for a couple of months. I was numb. It's almost like my brain was dead, and I just stopped thinking. I would unaccountably burst forth in tears, and yet, somehow I knew that wasn't enough. After Bob died and I buried him, I haven't been able, for almost a year, to visit the cemetery. Are you shocked? Do you think I did something bad? It's just that I'm not ready to do it. Visiting the cemetery would tear me apart right now, and I've really got to take care of myself. I got rid of his clothes as fast as possible. Two days after he died, I got rid of everything. The only thing I kept were some pictures of him to remind me of our travels together.

Clara was the prime caretaker of her husband. She nursed him throughout his illness until he became too ill to care for at home. He spent the last month of his life in a hospice.

> Bob was a noncommunicator; I tried many times to talk to him about his illness and what was happening to him, but he didn't seem to want to. Towards the end, I remember grabbing him and pleading with him not to leave me. He responded by buying me a present, a new luxury car. I was touched by this and his looking out for me. He knew I'd be too cheap to buy a new car for myself. At the same time, I regret that I didn't participate in the decision of which car to buy. During the last week of his life, he did reach out to tell me he loved me, and that I'd been a good wife and good nurse. That made me feel good. It's a pleasant memory. He never was before able to tell me explicitly that he loved me. I treasure that comment.

Speaking on what her marriage was like:

> The early years were pretty good. But about twenty years ago, when Bob was 58, he decided to retire, and we managed to do a lot of traveling. But throughout most of the last twenty years, it was as if I were a part-time widow. He'd go to sleep at 8:00 every night, and I'd be left alone. My husband was a great giver-upper. Why, he even gave up sex when he was at the tender age of 42. But really, our sexual life was never good before that . . .
>
> I think I wasted my life. We had no social life, we never entertained, we had no sex, and I had no real companionship from Bob. He was good to me, he was oh so boring, and I'm too bright and an energetic woman to have given up on life. Bob neglected me emotionally. He starved me emotionally. I was, and still am, a sexy woman even though I'm 76, and he never saw that. I know I could have married a lot of different men, but somehow, I think, I didn't make myself available. I could have had a much more challenging career, could have been a successful business-woman, but I somehow kept myself in an unsatisfying marriage. I never thought about me, I just marched along in life. At one point, my doctor suggested I ought to think about leaving Bob. I simply couldn't entertain that. I don't know why, I just couldn't think about ending our marriage, never.

One year later, Clara bounced into my office stating that her grief was over. She was animated and lively, and told me that the despair she felt a year ago had now disappeared.

> I don't grieve for Bob any longer. I visited the cemetery once since I last saw you. I just don't think very much about my past life, except that every so often, I feel how much of it I had wasted. I guess the best thing that has happened to me since I talked to you last, is I now have a boyfriend. I see him about twice a week, we have dinner together. He is so different than Bob, he's extremely affectionate, I enjoy being with him. He sees me as a sexy lady, and we enjoy having a relationship together. Oh no, I'm not interested at all in marrying him; it's a very nice relation-ship that makes me feel good, I just realized how much I missed. . . .
>
> I think I changed in a lot of ways. I've become much more autonomous. I had a fight with the city government over a house that I own. When Bob was alive, he tried to win with the city, but he never could. After he died, I took over this problem, and really was able to assert myself, find out what to do, and did it, and finally won the battle. I couldn't ever have done these things before. I feel I've grown and have become a changed

person. I accept things much better now, I've taken on battles and won them, never in my wildest dreams could I have done this before. I see myself as a much more effective person, I'm more serene, I'm more generous, and I'm calmer.

Clara has been able to confront the deep, unyielding depression and overwhelming regrets that she experienced, and at the age of 76 has been able to overcome them and develop into a much more comfortable, lively, commanding person, whose notions of pleasure in life have certainly increased. The death of her husband served to stimulate her feelings of profound regret and loss and at the same time freed her, liberated her, to pursue aspects of herself that had been for so long restricted by a less than adequate marriage.

A CASE WITH NO PAIN, NO GROWTH. Donna, a young-looking 62-year-old, marched into my office four months after her husband's death. She was stylishly dressed in a powder blue crepe adorned by a multi-strand set of pearls around her neck. Sitting down promptly, she appeared ready to talk about herself with no need of my prompting.

> My husband, Jonathan, owned a small manufacturing company which was good to us. I have always been active in the business. Jonathan hated paperwork and I took care of that part of the business as well as doing much of the bookkeeping. When he got sick, about two years ago, we decided to sell the business. That was done but I still spend a good deal of time in the large mass of paperwork that needs attention, both in finalizing my interest in the business as well as the estate.
>
> We have two sons, Larry and Robert. Larry lives with me, he was living at home before my husband died. We have dinner every night together. I rarely go out after dinner. It's easier to get together with my friends on the phone.
>
> The last couple of months of Jonathan's death were very, very hard. I did most of the nursing until the last few weeks. Those last few weeks were hell. Jonathan deteriorated mentally, he hallucinated and was filled with delusions. I was up almost every five minutes of the night with him. It really wore me out. I just was exhausted. The last week of his life I did hire a nurse to be with him at night.
>
> We didn't talk about Jonathan's death together. He was very brave and never mentioned these things. For the last few months before he died, we talked about the past and the good trips we used to have together and all the things we liked doing together. His last words to me were that he

loved me. He was a very thoughtful and affectionate man, and I miss him very much. I think I did most of my grieving two months before he died. I haven't felt a lot of grief since his death. I've visited the cemetery only twice, but I have a real sense that Jonathan is looking down on me, and as I work on the paper, I feel he's saying to me I'm doing the right thing.

We had a good and happy marriage. Jonathan and I spent much of our time both working and at home together. We were never separated. We weren't the kind of people who went gadding about very much. We had a marvelous marriage and I enjoyed every moment of it. There's nothing I would have done differently. Looking back, I never doubted my choice of a husband even once. They were all good years, perhaps I would say the last 15 were the best. There were no real disagreements. In fact the only one I can remember is when the children were younger we did disagree about discipline. I was the stricter one. I can't think of anything I would have changed about Jonathan and our marriage, but perhaps would have liked a little more social life and going out than he did. He liked people one-to-one, or in a very small group, but he never in his life liked large groups of people. I have no regrets about any single thing that I've done in life or regrets about things that I haven't done. It was a happy life, a happy marriage, and I feel I've really lived my life.

My life was that we did everything together. I miss him but I really don't feel lonely. I don't have a great deal of interest in meeting new people, engaging in new activities or joining clubs or those kinds of things. I never really did. I have a few good friends. They call me or I call them, and I don't seem to have any need to enlarge that group. Yes, I like the company of men very much, but I haven't decided, I think it's too early, what I'm going to do about that.

My beliefs are very important to me. I've never been a regular churchgoer, I believe in God and in the afterlife. I do feel I will see Jonathan again and be united with him. God has a plan for each of us. God's plan for me now is to test me and see if I can cope with the loss that I have to face. I think God's plan for Jonathan was to take him in order to ease his pain.

When I asked whether her husband's death stimulated Donna to think about her own life and the closeness of death, she replied

I had a dream about my death—I was in an airplane and the plane I was in hit nose to nose with another United Airlines plane. I woke up just before the real collision. I notice that I'm becoming more concerned about my health. I've decided that I really should stop smoking and take better care of myself. Jonathan's death made me think about my own limitations. I know I'm not invincible any more. I've been thinking about my own death and I've been preparing lists of instructions for the children about burial, about distribution of goods, about where the money is invested, and things like that. I never thought like that before Jonathan died.

I've been thinking about the fact that I'm a single woman, even though I think about myself as still married. No one else seems to think that of me. I haven't been thinking about remarriage although sometimes I worry that suppose I were to get ill, I'd like someone to take care of me.

Donna is a bright, articulate woman who was extremely forthright in the interview. Her grief was limited to the month or two before Jonathan's death. Although she misses him very much, she has managed to find a solid equilibrium. This is a woman who feels satisfied with her life and is particularly comfortable with the nearly 38 years of marriage they spent together. It was a good solid marriage and the memories of it are sustaining on a daily basis for her current life. She is highly self-contained and able to work effectively and plan for the future. Economically comfortable, she has been considering, once the deluge of paperwork is gone, engaging herself in volunteer work for good causes. Unlike Clara, the stimulus for looking inward and changing are not apparent for Donna. She has no regrets, she liked the life she lived, and feels comfortable with her current circumstances. Yes, loneliness is sometimes a problem for her, and she is engaged in exploring what it means for her now to recognize that life is limited and she herself is closer to death. She readily engages in these explorations but is not driven to use them for inner or outer changes.

The existentially aware are those who looked into, rather than away from, death. They were able or willing to bear and experience their aloneness. They were more willing to examine the limitations of their marriage and to view their spouse in more realistic, nonidealized terms. They grasped the idea that their loss offered an opportunity for psychological freedom and recognized and acknowledged the fact that they had been stunted by their marital relationship. This recognition does not necessarily imply that the overall quality of such marriages was poor; in fact, they were judged higher overall in marital quality.

These widows were upset about the right thing, about the real situation they faced in life. Often, individuals mired in chronic grief tend to be fixated on their loss, fixated in anger, fixated on their spouse. Not so the existentially aware: they showed less grief, and less guilt and anger toward their spouse. They did have more anxiety and depression but their dysphoria may be linked not to grief, but to death, their own death, to questions about life's meaning, and to the opportunity and challenge of freedom.

The existentially aware also have higher self-esteem and are more prone to change their self-image by taking new elements into the self. They possess a certain type of internal strength—a sureness about oneself, a relative freedom from neurotic or distorting defenses that enables them to fix their gaze on their existential situation. They are engaged in a psychosocial moratorium. They experience more loneliness and are less prone to use developing relationships with men to avoid it.

# CONCLUSION

These findings raise some important questions about the medicalization of widowhood. The traditional measures that have always been studied in bereavement research (symptoms, vicissitudes of grief, and social adjustment) represent the status quo, assuming that spousal bereavement is a stressor that upsets the equilibrium of the person. This perspective presumes that the most appropriate way to assess the consequences of the death of a husband is to examine whether or not the widow returns to equilibrium. It further presumes that, after an appropriate passage of time following spousal loss, the optimal and only meaningful outcome should consist of the resolution of depression and grief and a return to the previous level of social adjustment.

But the illness framework with its emphasis on restoration of homeostasis may overlook valid, individual responses to loss and neglects the human capacity for self-exploration and personal change. I have chosen to use a language of challenge and to posit that a widow is faced with a number of significant challenges beyond the traditional confrontation with loss. Widows are challenged in many areas but, most importantly, they are confronted with major and mortal questions about existence—about finitude, freedom and responsibility, isolation, and meaning in life.

These existential challenges always confront widows, but not all choose to attend or to respond to the challenge. My studies suggest that those who do respond ultimately have a meaningful payoff—they are very likely to undergo personal growth. Obviously not all experience the same degree of growth but the findings do indicate that all of the widows who engaged in the existential task underwent some growth.

One clear implication of these findings is that the study of spousal bereavement must be broadened and individualized; it must go beyond loss and recovery. It must be sensitive to the fact that spousal loss in mid- and late life is highly complex; it impinges both on the inner life of the spousally bereaved as well as on external tasks and adjustments. Studies of bereavement have traditionally assessed outcome by the presence or absence of such variables as physical and psychological symptoms, use of medication and drugs, crying, pining, insomnia, and intrusiveness of thoughts of the lost person. Yet our data suggest the presence of personal growth—a positive outcome of bereavement—which is empirically orthogonal to the more traditional measures of distress.

Postulating adult life crises as transformative offers a rich conceptual step in the eventual systematization of adult development. However, a number of conceptual and methodological concerns demand attention. Although transformative concepts are evocative and challenging, they are often underspecified, limiting the ability of other investigators to replicate.

The common assumption of universality is disturbing. Since the adult life crises are products of a particular social context, the attribution of universality may hinder more than help scholarship. Similarly, are we helped by the assumption that an individual's failure to address a particular crisis, defined from the point of view of the investigator, leads to untoward psychological outcomes? Too often in these theories, change is equated with the good, the true, and the beautiful; stability of psychological processes with the bad, the imperfect, or the pathological.

# REFERENCES

Buhler, C. M. (1935). *From birth to maturity.* London: Klegan Paul.

Burton, R. (1896). *The anatomy of melancholy.* London: Bell.

Erikson, E. H. (1982). *The life cycle completed.* New York: Norton.

Freud, S. (1957). Mourning and melancholia. In J. Strachey (Ed. and Trans.), *The standard edition of the complete original works of Sigmund Freud* (Vol 14, pp. 152–170). London: Hogarth Press. (Original work published 1917)

Gould, R. (1978). *Transformations: Growth and change in adult life.* New York: Simon and Schuster.

Gutmann, D. (1987). *Reclaimed powers: Towards a psychology of men and women in later life.* New York: BasicBooks.

Jung, C. (1933). *Modern man in search of a soul.* New York: Harcourt, Brace, & World.

Levinson, D., Darrow, G., Klein, E., Levinson, M., & McKee, B. (1978). *The seasons of a man's life.* New York: Knopf.

Rush, B. (1809). *Medical inquiries and observations* (3rd ed.). Philadelphia: Hopkins & Earl.

Tagliasozzo, R. (1988, July 31). The legacy of widowhood. *New York Times,* pp. 12, 21.

# Comments

## David Gutmann

R eading this important chapter, I recall seminars at Stanford with Irv Yalom and Mort Lieberman. After glumly reviewing with them many case protocols of feisty, empowered California widows, I warned Mort against revealing these unsettling findings to the world. I feared that liberated women would insist on new prenuptial contracts, garnished with clauses guaranteeing ten years of trouble-free widowhood—the minimum time in which to realize the potentials of this developmental stage.

But now that the cat is out of the bag, I must grant that the benefits of Mort's findings for widows probably outweigh any damage to still-living husbands. As in the best of developmental gerontology, he has demonstrated the potentials, rather than the usually documented losses, inherent in a normal phase of female aging.

But the prospect that Mort Lieberman depicts, of an expanded, grief- and remorse-free widowhood, may be in part an artifact of his time sampling, the restriction of his focus to the postmarital period, rather than to the marriage as a whole. When we consider the natural history of the typical marriage, we find that there are, for some women, periods of "virtual widowhood" that can precede the husband's actual demise by several years. Thus, reviewing the protocols of married women from the Parkville study (see Huyck, 1992), we identified a subsample—the "widows in waiting"—whose husbands were, in the psychological sense, already dead to them. They had long ago grieved for the disappointing husband, for the unhappy marriage, and for themselves in the marriage. Most of these precocious widows were waiting, with barely concealed impatience, for the S.O.B. to finally die and grant their freedom. Some less patient wives from the same sample had already liberated themselves into the premorbid stage we called "separate peace." They roomed with their husbands, but did not in most respects share their lives. Although still married, they are very reminiscent of Mort's sun-tanned California widows who, after minimal grieving, had moved into expansive, husband-free life ways.

My hunch is that Lieberman's widows, like our "widows-in-waiting" and separate-peace-niks, had not—as Lieberman suggests—escaped a significant bout of grief, but had done their mourning premorbidly, while the marriage was still formally in place. Thus, the Freudian paradigm of necessary grief, of mourning preceding liberation, may still apply. Widowhood is not a disease, but by the same token, it is probably not a free ride; at some point, either before or after his death, the lost husband receives his due of wifely grief.

The preemptive mourning that we found in the Parkville sample sometimes triggers mood disorders in still married women resembling those seen in Lieberman's "protracted grief" subgroup of depressed widows. Thus, among our late onset psychiatric patients, we find women whose severe depressions are reactive to their covert death wishes toward the still living husband. These are the ambivalent older wives, would-be "widows-in-waiting," so guilty about their hostile wishes that they take on themselves the depression that they think would afflict the husband if the wife's fantasies were revealed. These women are too conflicted to accept the liberation that the separate-peace-niks are able, after some difficulty, to claim for themselves. In short, older women's hidden resentments toward their husbands can have the same pathogenic consequences before widowhood as after it. Whether the outcome be liberation or pathology, the themes of the marriage as well as the wife's premorbid personality seem to determine her experience of widowhood.

I also wonder about possible life stage influences on the experience and manifestations of widowhood. There may even be a paradox here: The briefer the marriage, the greater the widow's grief. It does, after all, make intuitive sense that a bereaved young wife, left without a husband at the height of the parental emergency, will suffer harsher grief than an older, postparental wife. Their older sisters, after all, experience widowhood "on time," and they may be quite prepared to declare and enjoy a separate peace.

We cannot easily test this proposition regarding the age grading of the widow's grief with Lieberman's sample, as 60% of his subjects are over age 50, and 80% are over age 40. We do not know if the younger widow's experience is predictable from a life span developmental model; but the older widow's certainly is: The latter group seems to condense into a rather brief postbereavement period the changes toward greater female independence and assertion that normally go forward, although over a period of years, within the intact postparental marriage. Thus, we find older widows reporting that, since the husband's demise, they have come out of the marital closet in a much more assertive, managerial stance. They also claim that the radical change in their nature was imposed from without, rather than developmentally, from within. In their eyes, they are not responsible for this acquisition: the husband's death left them with no recourse but to inherit the special competencies and aggressive traits that he, in dying, had abandoned. With him gone, if she didn't do it, then it wasn't going to get done.

But I am struck by the possibility that some older widows may actually be plea bargaining, citing the husband's death to rationalize the acquisition of powers that they were in any event preparing to co-opt from a living spouse. They seem to excuse themselves, arguing that their self-expansion did not represent a hostile takeover. They had to become phallic, they claim, not because they wished to be, but because the husband no longer was. "You're not using it any more, so give it to me!"

In short, the expansion of the older widow that Mort Lieberman found may not be a side effect of widowhood per se, but may pertain to a larger context: the postparental rather than the postmarital emergence of the older woman—a normal developmental process which uses the "accident" of widowhood to speed its advance. Despite their bereavement, older widows may be showing not an absence of grief so much as the heightened morale that is part of female development in the postparental years. Lacking the phase-specific, developmental buffering that protects their older sisters, younger widows may understandably prove to be more grief-stricken, less masterful, more in conformity with the "illness" model of widowhood.

Accordingly, I recommend that Lieberman study the possibility of an age/life span effect by comparing, in terms of the grief and mastery dimensions, the youngest to the oldest widows in his sample. Because of health and financial difficulties, older widows are particularly burdened; they would be cheered to know that their cohort is at least exempted from the emotional wounds of the younger widow.

# REFERENCE

Huyck, M. H. (1992). Thirty-something years of marriage: Understanding experiences of women and men in enduring family relationships. *Family Perspective, 26,* 249–265.

# CHAPTER 8

# In Search of Continuities and Discontinuities Across Time and Culture

**David A. Chiriboga**

*Never kick a dead donkey from its*
*rear end . . .*
—ancient Ecuadorian proverb

## INTRODUCTION

The focus of this chapter is on new answers to the old question of whether or not there is continuity in personality across the adult years. In the 1960s and 1970s research furnished a fairly convincing argument in favor of discontinuity. Summing up the existing evidence, Walter Mischel (1968, p. 146) felt justified in his categorical statement that "with the possible exception of intelligence, highly generalized behavior consistencies have not been demonstrated, and the concept of personality traits as broad dispositions is thus untenable."

More recently there has been a resurgence of trait research, and in the mid-1990s a new and completely different answer has emerged. As expressed by Robert McCrae (1993, p. 577), the answer is that discontinuity has become a dead issue: "In adults, changes in personality scores across occasions are apparently due chiefly to error of measurement."

## A Need for Theoretical Guidelines

Part of the discrepancy between older and newer conclusions with regard to change may derive from the highly empirical nature of much personality research. As an example, while the personality literature is full of discussion and debate concerning whether there are 3, 4, 5, or more personality traits, there are few if any papers that even attempt a conceptual rationale for the number or content of traits. Students of adult development and aging, indeed, have long decried the lack of theoretical guidelines for investigating continuity and change over time (e.g., George, 1995; Neugarten, 1977).

The discrepancy may also reflect the fact that research on psychological traits was out of favor during the historical period when the field of life span development was showing its initial growth spurt. For whatever reason, instead of looking at continuity, considerable attention was paid to other factors that might shed light on personal development. Summarizing results obtained from the venerable Kansas City Study, and reflecting the potential breadth of inquiry into personality that characterized research at the time, Neugarten (1964, p. 200) concluded that "age-related phenomena will be better understood only as investigators isolate variables that they have reason to believe have particular relevance for a developmental psychology of adulthood."

Some ten years later, research had progressed to the point where Neugarten (1977) could remark with apparent pleasure on the wealth of contemporary scholars who were vigorously questioning accepted perspectives on personality development. However, since that time, studies of adult personality development have focused more and more narrowly on the issue of whether personality demonstrates significant continuity during middle adulthood and aging. Study after study has challenged or supported the presence of continuity, with most studies corroborating the early findings of Kelly (1955) that significant levels of continuity exist over periods of up to thirty or more years.

At present, and as evidenced by the earlier quote from McCrae, the impressive accumulation of evidence to support continuity would seem to suggest that any further research is unnecessary. According to what might be called the "neo-trait" perspective of McCrae (see also Costa & McCrae, 1994), one could conclude that personality reflects "basic tendencies" of the individual, their expression unaltered save under extreme conditions such as represented by dementia or psychosis. The existence of such basic tendencies, it has been further suggested, may derive from the primary emotions (e.g., Lewis, 1995) and therefore may have biological underpinnings.

Although the work of McCrae and Costa might appear to sound the death knell of research on change, reports of the demise of such research are premature. Indeed, what we are witnessing may be the beginning of a paradigm shift, as theory and research proceed from what in fact may be a rather trivial question (i.e., how much continuity is there?) to a more compelling concern with discovering why continuities and discontinuities can be found.

The remainder of this section reviews some models that underlie current perspectives on adult personality development. In the following sections findings are presented from four studies that each addressed issues of continuity. Several different analytic strategies are employed, each providing a slightly different perspective on continuity versus discontinuity. The intent is to demonstrate that significant levels of change may coincide with significant consistency over time, that consistency and change may or may not be predictable, and that exciting new approaches to the study of development are emerging in the literature.

## Three Competing Models of Adult Development

Three underlying models have been described as underlying existing theories of personality development. As described by Gergen (1977), these models depict development as involving, respectively, stability, ordered change, and random change.

### *The Developmental Stability Model*

In discussing findings from the Berkeley Growth Study of development some years ago, Livson and Peskin (1980) noted that while some attributes of individuals are predictable from childhood through middle age, other attributes are transformed in systematic ways. This idea was subsequently elaborated upon by Gergen (1977) and others. According to Gergen, underlying much of past and present thinking has been a *stability template*. This template reflects a commitment to the principle of stability in adult life; change is thought to exist only as a reflection of the continued development of some previously existing characteristic. The work of Freud and other representatives of the classic psychoanalytic perspective serves as a good illustration of this model since these theorists believed that the trajectory of personal development was relatively fixed by the age of five or six. Modern perspectives on personality traits also find a home in this model.

In studies of adults, stability is usually inferred either from item or scale correlations over time. However, from a statistical perspective there is perhaps a deeper level in which one can question whether the factorial structure—the pattern of correlations—of personality scales remains constant over time (Nesselroade & Boker, 1994). While the question of structural stability is intriguing, little if any attention has been paid to the question of structural stability from a developmental perspective.

### The Orderly Change Model

While the stability model would seem almost antagonistic to the idea of any real development during adulthood, a somewhat different orientation can be found in Gergen's (1977) second model, that of orderly change. Theories following this model view development at any age as a progression of orderly and perhaps invariant changes over time. This is another way of saying they usually are stage theories, one of the most popular ways of conceptualizing personality development. The reader may be familiar with the works of Piaget (e.g., 1972), Loevinger (e.g., 1976), and Kohlberg (e.g., 1986), whose stages of childhood and adolescence have been well accepted among developmental psychologists. Most such theories are heuristic but not necessarily authenticated; often they represent a blending of both orderly change and stability template models, with the individual viewed as grounded in the past but interacting with the present and with possible futures.

### The Random Change Model

There is, finally, a more recently developed model that emphasizes the role of chance in our lives. Labeled by Gergen (1977) the *random change* model, its central thesis is that human beings run out of genetic programming by late adolescence. Thereafter, the role of chance factors, such as exposure to major stress conditions or transitions, becomes more important as a shaper of personality. Support for this model can be found in the research of developmental scientists such as Klaus

Riegel (1977), Paul Baltes (1987), and Bernice Neugarten (1977), as well as in my own work (Chiriboga, Catron, et al., 1991; Fiske & Chiriboga, 1990). From the mainstream of psychological research, the sustained research of Mischel (1979, 1990) emphasizes the importance of the situational context in determining levels of stability in personality, and the very strong influence of social stress upon psychological functioning is also well-documented (e.g., Chiriboga, 1984; Fiske & Chiriboga, 1990; Turner, Wheaton, & Lloyd, 1995). However, within the field of adult development and aging no well-formulated theories of personality have yet evolved that follow this model.

### *A Comment on the Models*

Although the three underlying models of change do not really contradict each other, they are often treated as if they do by their proponents. As Nesselroade and Boker (1994, p. 125) note: "Personality researchers sometimes oversimplify matters of constancy and change." Perhaps the most reasonable approach, and the one followed in this chapter, is to assume that all three models may be operative.

## A TRADITIONAL CONSIDERATION OF CONTINUITY ACROSS TIME

While presenting further empirical evidence concerning continuity may seem about as productive as beating a dead donkey, discontinuity, in fact, may not be a dead issue. Data from four studies are presented below. The first was a 12-year, 5-contact study of 216 community-living men and women, mostly "white" American and mostly working-class to lower middle-class; all lived in San Francisco, California, and were interviewed before and after one of four major normative transitions (Fiske & Chiriboga, 1990).

The second study was a follow-up study of 333 men and women, living in the San Francisco Bay area, approximately 25% of whom belonged to racial minorities. They were studied within 8 months of marital separation and then approximately 3.5 years later; all were therefore involved in what has been called non-normative transitions (Chiriboga, Catron, et al., 1991).

The third is a three-generations study of Mexican American families; originally contacted in the early 1980s, they were recontacted approximately 11 years later, in 1993 (Chiriboga & Markides, 1994).

The fourth and final study was, like the one on divorce, focused on stress conditions. However, unlike the divorce study, it examined people experiencing conditions of chronic stress (Chiriboga, Yee, & Weiler, 1992). The sample consisted of middle-aged men and women who were primary or secondary caregivers to a parent with Alzheimer's disease.

All in all, then, the data are drawn from two longitudinal studies that each covered over a decade of life, one panel study that focused on individuals struggling with marital separation and divorce, and another panel study whose focus was on chronic distress. The question to be addressed is whether there is evidence for stability of personal functioning over different time spans, in differing stress contexts, or according to ethnicity.

## Normative Study of Transitions

The Transitions Study included four groups of men and women. At first interview, the two younger groups were facing transitions characteristics of younger adults: departure from the parental home and parenthood. Two of the groups were middle aged, and faced, respectively, departure of the youngest child from the family home (often called the "empty nest" stage), and retirement.

Like the Divorce Study to be considered later, the Transitions Study included a 70-item adjective rating list (ARL). The ARL represents a shortened (Block, 1961) version of the Gough Adjective Checklist that substitutes a range of response ("unlike me," "in-between," "like me") for the standard "yes/no" format.

In order to reduce the number of measures, the 70 ARL items from initial interviews with both Divorce and Transitions subjects were combined into a single data set. A principal components extraction with varimax rotation was used as the basis for generating unit-based scales for both studies. Although 22 factors were possible, a scree test for eigenvalues suggested a cutoff of 2.0; the result was a 7-scale solution.

The scales resemble facets from four of the five higher-order components of personality that have been identified with some regularity (e.g., Goldberg, 1993; Costa & McCrae, 1994): (1) agreeableness (rep-

resented here by the Warmth scale), (2) surgency or extroversion (represented here by Sociability and Assertiveness), (3) emotional stability or
neuroticism (represented here by Hostility, Unhappiness, and Impulsive-
ness), and (4) conscientiousness (here called Reasonableness). The one
missing component of what is called the "big five" is "intellectance" or
openness to experience.

## *Measures*

One way of examining the stability of the seven scales over the 12-year
period is by means of standard repeated measures. Using a MANOVA
approach, significant changes over time were found for six of the seven
scales, with gender and life stage differences sometimes being maintained and sometimes exhibiting variations suggestive of developmental progression, as follows:

WARMTH.   Women perceived themselves to have greater interpersonal
warmth than did men. Over time the entire sample increased significantly in self-ascribed warmth.

SOCIABILITY.   Sociability was defined in terms of whether people felt
themselves to be easily hurt or offended. Men felt themselves to be less
socially vulnerable than women, but both sexes had become less vulnerable some 12 years later.

ASSERTIVENESS.   Men viewed themselves as more assertive than women,
with the former empty-nest men scoring as the most assertive of all.
Assertiveness increased significantly over time for the entire sample,
but the two younger stages increased the most.

HOSTILITY.   The youngest group of men and women were significantly
higher than other groups on perceived hostility. All groups declined on
this attribute over the 12 years of study.

UNHAPPINESS.   Individuals in the two younger stages saw themselves
as more unhappy, but men and women of all stages showed decline
over time.

IMPULSIVITY.   Individuals in the two youngest stages endorsed impulsive attributes more often than those in the older stages. This was the only attribute of the seven in which no changes over time were found.

REASONABLENESS.    Men rated themselves higher than women on reasonableness at both contacts. The entire sample showed a significant increase, but the youngest group of men and women ended up, respectively, highest and lowest in perceived reasonableness.

While the repeated-measures analyses provided evidence for significant change on all self-concept scales but Impulsivity, correlations between Time 1 and Time 5 measures suggest a very different scenario. As shown in Table 8.1, Warmth was the only scale for which the correlation over time was not significant, and this lack of significance was found only for younger men. Demonstrating how analytic strategies can provide seemingly divergent results, for the entire sample Assertiveness was ranked highest in magnitude of correlation but demonstrated significant differences over time when subjected to the repeated-measures ANOVA. Impulsivity, the only scale found not to demonstrate change in the repeated-measures approach, was ranked second in size of correlations.

Another way of evaluating the correlations of the scales was to compute gender and stage differences in the size of the correlations found in Table 8.1. Results bear out what can be determined by simply looking at the correlations: the self-concept of the two older groups demonstrated greater stability over time ($F=15.69$, df=1/27, $p=.001$) than that of the two younger groups. From a developmental perspective, this should come as no surprise. One would assume that among the two younger groups, including people who have substantially less familiarity with their adult self, there would be greater variability. In contrast, and as Neugarten (1968) has suggested, there may be an enhanced self-awareness in the later years that results from having been an adult for decades.

To provide a context against which to contrast continuities in self-concept scales, Table 8.2 shows the 12-year stability of Bradburn (1969) positive and negative affect scales, and positive and negative life events scales. The magnitude of these correlations is generally lower than found for the self-concept scales, and fall primarily into the low-moderate range. As was the case for self-concept, the older groups exhibited a greater magnitude of correlation for the two morale scales. Given the length of time covered, it would be surprising if the correlations were

**TABLE 8.1  Correlations Over a 12-Year Period on Eight Subscales from the Adjective Rating List (Transitions Study Data)**

| | Younger | | Older | | | |
| | Men (*n*=35) | Women (*n*=43) | Men (*n*=35) | Women (*n*=38) | All *R*s (*n*=151) | Rank |
|---|---|---|---|---|---|---|
| Warmth | .00 | .39[b] | .50[c] | .70[d] | .45[c] | 5 |
| (Un)Sociable | .36[b] | .30[a] | .79[d] | .69[d] | .56[c] | 3 |
| Assertive | .24 | .71[d] | .78[d] | .72[d] | .66[d] | 1 |
| Hostility | .33[b] | .29[a] | .53[c] | .47[c] | .41[c] | 7 |
| Unhappy | .53[d] | .27[a] | .48[b] | .41[b] | .43[c] | 6 |
| Impulsive | .43[b] | .68[d] | .74[d] | .63[d] | .64[d] | 2 |
| Reasonable | .47[b] | .47[c] | .70[d] | .62[d] | .55[c] | 4 |
| Average *r* | .34 | .44 | .65 | .61 | .51 | |

[a] *p* = .05.
[b] *p* = .01.
[c] *p* = .001.
[d] *p* = .000.

**TABLE 8.2  Correlations Over a 12-Year Period on Moral and Life Event Scales (Transitions Study Data)**

| | Younger | | Older | | |
| | Men (*n*=35) | Women (*n*=43) | Men (*n*=35) | Women (*n*=38) | All *R*s (*n*=151) |
|---|---|---|---|---|---|
| Positive affect | .19 | .20 | .25 | .39[b] | .31[d] |
| Negative affect | .11 | .04 | .27[a] | .25[a] | .26[c] |
| Positive stress | .27[a] | .16 | −.16 | −.02 | .25[c] |
| Negative stress | .24 | .09 | .07 | .32 | .25[c] |

[a] *p* = .05.
[b] *p* = .01.
[c] *p* = .001.
[d] *p* = .000.

higher: Emotional and stress experiences would seem by their very nature to be more context-driven. On the other hand, older and younger subjects were roughly equal in the extent to which life events, both positive and negative, were correlated over time.

### Predicting Change over Twelve Years

Table 8.3 shows the results when self-concept scores at the 12-year follow-up were included as dependent variables in hierarchical regression analysis. The first set for this and all following regressions included initial status on the dependent variable being considered. The remaining sets each included one or two measures reflecting variables that have been suggested in the literature as possible influences on development. It should be noted that the analytic model did not take advantage of the rich amount of data actually available in each of the four studies. Instead, the measures are those for which data were generally available across the four studies.

Given the magnitude of correlations shown in Table 8.1, it will come as no surprise that the initial levels on self-concept scales were all highly predictive of where people ended up. On the other hand, the amount of explained variance varied widely: from below 20% (Warmth, Hostility, and Unhappiness) to percentages in the mid-60s on the two most stable scales (Impulsivity and Assertiveness).

What was surprising is that the social demographic measures contributed significantly to variability in self-concept only for Impulsivity and Assertiveness (which, again, were the two most stable scales). Generally unrelated to self-concept changes were the self-reports of health status and measures of how involved people were in social interactions. Negative life events, on the other hand, did play a significant role in predicting scales for traits representing neuroticism: Impulsivity, Unhappiness, and Hostility. Specifically, it was found that persons who reported more negative life events during the year prior to the final interviews were more likely to have increased in Impulsivity, Unhappiness, and Hostility.

## The Non-Normative Study of Divorce

Our Divorce Study collected data within 8 months of marital separation, and then again approximately 3.5 years later. The basic rationale for this life span study, which included subjects aged 20 to 70, was my growing recognition that the normative transitions included in the Transitions Study have relatively low impact on the majority of people, due in part to their very slowly evolving and highly expectable nature. On the other hand, unexpected transitions, and stressors, may exert great impact (Chiriboga et al., 1991; Fiske & Chiriboga, 1990).

**TABLE 8.3  Results of Hierarchical Set Regression Analyses Predicting 12-Year Follow-up Self-Concept on the Basis of Both Initial Status and Other Factors**

|  | Warmth | | Sociability | | Assertive | | Hostile | | Unhappy | | Impulsive | | Reasonable | |
|---|---|---|---|---|---|---|---|---|---|---|---|---|---|---|
|  | MR | $(r^2)$ | MR | $(r^2)$ | MR | $(r^2)$ | MR | $(r^2)$ | MR | $(r^2)$ | MR | $(r^2)$ | MR | $(r^2)$ |
| **Sets** | | | | | | | | | | | | | | |
| *1. Initial* | .41[e] | (.17)[e] | .56[e] | (.32)[e] | .65[e] | (.42)[e] | .41[e] | (.17)[e] | .43[e] | (.18)[e] | .64[e] | (.41)[e] | .54[e] | (.30)[e] |
| Base | .41[e] | | .56[e] | | .65[e] | | .41[e] | | .43[e] | | .64[e] | | .54 | |
| *2. Demographic* | .45[e] | (.04)[a] | .59[e] | (.03)[a] | .69[e] | (.06)[e] | .41[e] | (.00) | .46[e] | (.02) | .67[e] | (.03)[c] | .56[e] | (.02) |
| Gender | .03 | | .07 | | -.18[c] | | .02 | | .08 | | .06 | | -.04 | |
| Age | -.17[b] | | -.05 | | -.13[b] | | -.05 | | -.11 | | -.17[b] | | -.03 | |
| Education | -.16[b] | | -.17[b] | | .07 | | -.05 | | -.11 | | -.00 | | .13[a] | |
| *3. Health* | .46[e] | (.00) | .59[e] | (.00) | .70[e] | (.01) | .41[e] | (.00) | .46[e] | (.00) | .67[e] | (.00) | .57[e] | (.00) |
| Self-report | -.06 | | -.04 | | .08 | | .00 | | -.06 | | -.02 | | -.01 | |
| *4. Social* | .46[e] | (.00) | .61[e] | (.02)[a] | .70[e] | (.00) | .41[e] | (.00) | .46[e] | (.00) | .67[e] | (.00) | .57[e] | (.00) |
| Social | -.04 | | .17[b] | | -.06 | | -.01 | | .06 | | .03 | | .02 | |
| Activity | .03 | | -.05 | | .02 | | .00 | | -.06 | | -.05 | | -.06 | |
| *5. Stress* | .46[e] | (.00) | .62[e] | (.01)[a] | .70[e] | (.01) | .54[e] | (.13)[e] | .54[e] | (.08)[e] | .69[e] | (.03)[c] | .57[e] | (.00) |
| Events | .05 | | .13[a] | | .01 | | .39[e] | | .32[e] | | .19[c] | | .02 | |

[a] $p = .10$.
[b] $p = .05$.
[c] $p = .01$.
[d] $p = .001$.
[e] $p = .000$.

The Divorce Study was designed to capitalize on the possibility of change: Participants were first interviewed shortly after marital separation, a time during which most experienced multiple disruptions, and subsequently reinterviewed after sufficient time had elapsed to permit adaptation to have at least begun (Chiriboga et al., 1991). Given that their situation presented a strong challenge to self and personal beliefs (e.g., Ickes, 1984), it was hypothesized that the self-concept of Divorce subjects would demonstrate lower levels of stability than that of Transitions subjects. It was also expected that the most and least stable characteristics would differ between samples.

Comparisons between the Transitions and Divorce studies were made possible by the fact that subjects in both studies were drawn from the same geographic area, and that no differences between the groups were found in age, education, or occupation (Chiriboga et al., 1991).

Using the same seven scales reported for analyses with the Transitions Study, a repeated-measures MANOVA revealed striking differences from the latter study: Significant change over time was evident in only two scales, Assertiveness and Hostility.

## Analyses of Measures

WARMTH.     Like counterparts in the Transitions Study, women were more likely to acknowledge adjectives reflecting interpersonal warmth.

SOCIABILITY.     No differences were found.

ASSERTIVENESS.     Like counterparts in the Transitions Study, men viewed themselves as more assertive than women; however, middle-aged men were no different than younger men. By the second contact all subjects had increased significantly in assertiveness.

HOSTILITY.     No differences.

UNHAPPINESS.     Men and women of all ages declined in unhappiness between the two contacts.

IMPULSIVITY.     As in results from the Transitions Study, Rs in their 20s were highest in impulsivity, while those aged 40 and over were lowest. And, as in the other study, there were no changes over time.

REASONABLENESS.    No differences.

Supporting results obtained from repeated-measures analyses, the correlations over time for the seven attributes also reflected stability (Table 8.4). One curious finding was that when all subjects were considered together, the correlation ranked as greatest in magnitude was for Assertiveness—one of the two scales manifesting significant levels of change. Comparing the two studies, we find that in both samples Assertiveness was most stable (or consistent), and Hostility was least. The correlation for the Warmth domain is also very similar, and equally low, in both studies.

Contrary to expectations, there was no evidence of gender or age differences in the magnitude of the correlations. The average correlation for the Divorce Study was moderate ($r=.50$), and almost exactly the same as that found for the Transitions Study. Thus, although the Divorce Study subjects were studied during a time when they were significantly higher in nearly all indices of stress exposure (Chiriboga et al., 1991), the size of correlations was similar in the two studies.

**TABLE 8.4**   **Stability of Self-Concept Subscales Over a 3.5-Year Period: Divorce Study**

| | Younger | | Older | | | |
|---|---|---|---|---|---|---|
| | Men ($n=76$) | Women ($n=132$) | Men ($n=33$) | Women ($n=33$) | All $R$s ($n=272$) | Rank |
| Warmth | .37[c] | .53[d] | .37[a] | .30[a] | .44[d] | 6 |
| (Un)Sociable | .47[d] | .52[d] | .35[a] | .31[a] | .47[d] | 5 |
| Assertive | .63[d] | .70[d] | .68[d] | .49[c] | .66[d] | 1 |
| Hostility | .04 | .30[d] | .55[c] | .45[c] | .24[d] | 7 |
| Unhappy | .46[d] | .52[d] | .57[d] | .58[d] | .52[d] | 4 |
| Impulsive | .50[d] | .48[d] | .74[d] | .72[d] | .56[d] | 3 |
| Reasonable | .43[d] | .62[d] | .60[d] | .70[d] | .59[d] | 2 |
| Average $r$ | .41 | .52 | .55 | .51 | .50 | |

[a] $p = .05$.
[b] $p = .01$.
[c] $p = .001$.
[d] $p = .000$.

Moderating the import of this similarity are sizable differences in follow-up: 3.5 years in the case of the Divorce Study and 12 years for the normative Transitions Study. One way of interpreting the results, therefore, is that 12 years of change were collapsed into less than 4 years.

Continuity correlations for the Bradburn (1969) morale scales, and positive and negative events were also computed. All correlations fell rather consistently into the moderate range, and thus were slightly higher than the 12-year correlations reported for the Transitions Study. In this shorter time between contacts, in fact, the size of the correlations approximated those for self-concept scales.

COMPARING MINORITY VERSUS MAJORITY GROUPS.    Given the scarcity of research on continuities of personal characteristics evident among members of minority groups, I decided to examine correlations for minority subjects. Because so few were included (25 African Americans, 11 Hispanic Americans, and 12 Asian Americans), members of all three groups were combined into a single category. Clearly members of these minority groups are distinct in many ways, and therefore findings must be viewed as quite provisional.

The combined group of minority individuals demonstrated consistency correlations at magnitudes no different from persons defined (by exclusion) as members of the majority culture ($t$-test [equal variance]=.02, df=12, $ns$). Again, it should be emphasized that for expediency quite diverse groups of minority individuals were combined.

PREDICTING CHANGE OVER TIME.    Next we will consider a series of hierarchical regression analyses that included the same variables, in the same order, as those computed for the Transitions Study. Initial standing on self-concept measures again was the single best predictor of where subjects stood some 3.5 years later (Table 8.5), and again there was substantial variability in how well initial status fared as a predictor. Assertiveness was the most stable attribute, followed by Reasonableness and Impulsivity. Low stability was again found for Hostility, an attribute whose status at Time 2 was very poorly predicted: Only about 5% of its variance was explained by initial levels. And again, Warmth was not well predicted.

Compared with Transitions Study findings, the remaining predictive sets generally were not as strongly associated with long-term self-concept. Demographic measures (age, gender, education) did not play a role,

**TABLE 8.5** Results of Hierarchical Set Regression Analyses Predicting 3.5-Year Follow-up Self-Concept on the Basis of Both Initial Status and Other Factors: Non-Normative Study of Divorce

|  | Dependent Measures | | | | | | |
|---|---|---|---|---|---|---|---|
|  | Warmth MR ($r^2$) | Sociability MR ($r^2$) | Assertive MR ($r^2$) | Hostile MR ($r^2$) | Unhappy MR ($r^2$) | Impulsive MR ($r^2$) | Reasonable MR ($r^2$) |
| **Sets** | | | | | | | |
| 1. *Initial* | .46[e] | .46[e] | .66[e] | .22[d] | .53[e] | .56[e] | .58[e] |
|  | (.21)[e] | (.21)[e] | (.43)[e] | (.05)[d] | (.28)[e] | (.32)[e] | (.34)[e] |
| Base | .46[e] | .46[e] | .66[e] | .22[d] | .53[e] | .56[e] | .58[e] |
| 2. *Demographic* | .47[e] | .46[e] | .66[e] | .23[b] | .53[e] | .57[e] | .59[e] |
|  | (.01) | (.00) | (.01) | (.01) | (.00) | (.00) | (.01) |
| Gender | .09 | .04 | −.04 | −.04 | .03 | .04 | −.05 |
| Age | .07 | −.04 | .08 | .04 | .00 | .05 | .04 |
| Education | .01 | .01 | .01 | .04 | .02 | .03 | .02 |
| 3. *Health* | .47[e] | .57[e] | .47[e] | .28[c] | .53[e] | .57[e] | .59[e] |
|  | (.00) | (.01) | (.00) | (.02)[a] | (.00) | (.00) | (.00) |
| Self-report | −.04 | −.10 | −.05 | −.16[a] | −.04 | .00 | .00 |
| 4. *Social* | .48[e] | .47[e] | .67[e] | .29[c] | .54[e] | .57[e] | .60[e] |
|  | (.01) | (.00) | (.01) | (.01) | (.01) | (.01) | (.02)[a] |
| Social | −.10 | −.07 | .02 | .06 | −.03 | .03 | −.05 |
| Activity | .01 | .00 | −.08 | .05 | .08 | .08 | −.12[b] |
| 5. *Stress* | .48[e] | .49[e] | .68[e] | .31[c] | .59[e] | .57[e] | .61[e] |
|  | (.00) | (.02)[b] | (.01)[b] | (.01) | (.05)[e] | (.00) | (.00) |
| Events | −.02 | .14[b] | −.12[b] | .10 | .26[e] | −.01 | −.06 |

[a] p = .10.
[b] p = .05.
[c] p = .01.
[d] p = .001.
[e] p = .000.

187

and health was important only once: Those who earlier had reported themselves to be in better health were likely to decline in Hostility. The only other set to contribute significantly included the summary measure of negative life events for the prior year. Those who reported higher levels of negative events were more likely to have increased in unhappiness and had become less assertive and less gregarious or sociable.

PREDICTION FOR THE MINORITY SUBJECTS.   Another analysis was run just for the minority subjects. While results were generally very similar to those found for the entire sample, some differences were also found. For example, the Hostility domain of self-concept demonstrates substantially greater consistency for the minority subjects, and change in hostility was predicted not only by health status but by age as well: Older minorities were more likely to increase in their view of themselves as hostile people.

Overall, the results obtained from the first two studies, both of which included people immersed in some kind of transition, suggest that significant change can be found over time in self-concept. As evidenced by findings from the regression analyses, the change is at least in part predictable. Moreover, despite the presence of change, self-concept scales also demonstrated significant levels of stability. Finally, results from the Divorce Study provide some evidence that minority groups may exhibit levels of continuity similar to those of "mainstream" Americans.

## Mexican American Study

In 1981 and 1982 my colleague Kyriakos Markides launched an investigation of Mexican Americans living within a 50-mile radius of San Antonio, Texas. Designed as a three-generation study of families and family relationships, the study focused on cross-generational linkages but also addressed the mental and physical well-being of subjects and examined risk behaviors such as use of alcoholic beverages and tobacco products.

A total of 375 three-generation family units ($n$=1,125) were included in the baseline study. Average ages per generation were 26 for the youngest group, 54 for the middle group, and 74 for the oldest group. Overall refusal rate was approximately 15%.

During the last half of 1993, follow-up interviews were conducted (funded by the National Institute on Aging; K. Markides, Principal

Investigator). At least some information was obtained on over 80% of the original sample. More specifically, over 55% were reinterviewed ($n$=624), while proxy interviews (with spouses, children, other family members, or friends) and/or material from death certificates provided data on the remainder.

## Analyses of Measures

While no self-concept or personality measures were included in this investigation, the Center for Epidemiological Studies Depression Scale (CES-D; Radloff, 1977) was included. Often used as a screening tool for evidence of possibly clinical levels of depression, the scope of the items overlap with the depression facet of neuroticism. Over the 11-year interval, the correlation was relatively low for a measure assessing personal functioning ($r$=.28, $p$=.001), although still attaining quite significant probability levels.

PREDICTING CHANGE OVER TIME IN DEPRESSION.    While the correlation over time for the total CES-D was low, an attempt was made to determine how predictable the follow-up score might be. Once again the question at hand was how predictable might be the variance in follow-up status left unexplained by baseline status. As shown in Table 8.6, the predictive equation worked reasonably well at predicting variance beyond that explained by initial status, 11 years earlier. Older people, men, and the better educated were, at the time of the first interviews, significantly less at risk for subsequent depressive symptomatology. And, while small amounts of additional information were obtained from knowing that individuals saw themselves as being in poorer health, or were unmarried (including divorce, long-term singlehood, and widowed), an amount of variance equal to initial status on depression was contributed by the experiencing of life events, especially those clearly negative in nature.

Findings from the Mexican American Study generally correspond with what we have already seen in data from the Normative and Divorce studies: While baseline status on qualities of personal function certainly provide a wealth of information about what (on average) people will be like at some future date, other data also provide useful information with some consistency. In effect, the correlations provide evidence for consistency of function, the repeated-measures MANOVA strategies pro-

**TABLE 8.6  Prediction of CED-D Total Depression Evident at the 11-Year Follow-up, Using Hierarchical Set Regression: Three Generations Mexican American Study (N=625)**

|  | Beta | Multiple $R$ (change in $R^2$) |
|---|---|---|
| Set 1: *Baseline status* |  | .27[d] (.07)[d] |
| CES-D depression | .27[d] |  |
| Set 2: *Demographics* |  | .32[d] (.03)[c] |
| Age | −.14[b] |  |
| Gender | .08[a] |  |
| Education | −.20[c] |  |
| Set 3: *Health* |  | .33[d] (.01)[b] |
| Self-reported health | .11[a] |  |
| Set 4: *Social* |  | .34[c] (.01)[a] |
| Married (vs. not) | .09[a] |  |
| Set 5: *Stressors* |  | .43[d] (.07)[d] |
| Positive events | −.01 |  |
| Negative events | .26[d] |  |

[a] $p = .05$.
[b] $p = .01$.
[c] $p = .001$.
[d] $p = .000$.

vide clues as to the degree of change, and the regression analyses have demonstrated that other qualities of the person and their social context also play a role in shaping the future of things present.

## Caregiver Study

A group of 395 adult children were studied, all of whom were caregivers to parents suffering from Alzheimer's disease (Chiriboga et al.,

1992). The caregiving role was not a new one to most: on the average, the dementing parents had demonstrated noticeable decline for over four years, at the point when they were first interviewed. The interviews included a semantic differential type of instrument on which the adult children rated themselves on 12 items (good/bad, fair/unfair, etc.). Factor analysis generated a three-factor solution that captured components of the five personality component theory: self as nice, self as independent, self as happy. Caregivers also responded to the depression subscale of the Hopkins Symptoms Checklist, and to a modified Ways of Coping Inventory. The coping inventory factored into seven scales.

## Analyses of Measures

Between 11 and 12 months later, a subsample ($n$=200) were reinterviewed. Repeated-measures tests indicated that the subjects were stable over time in the self-concept and mental health domains, but exhibited substantial change over time in the use of coping strategies, in hassles, and in burden. There also was a general improvement in self-reported health of all subjects.

Correlating the measures over time provided another perspective. As shown in Table 8.7, quite varying degrees of consistency were evident. The scales reflecting self concept demonstrated (as might be expected) the highest levels of consistency, but morale items also were relatively stable over the admittedly brief period of time covered.

Of greater interest are the stabilities found for indices of coping, health, and stress. The health indicators demonstrated essentially no continuity over the one-year period: people healthier at the first contact were apparently just as likely to report health problems at follow-up, either mental or physical, as they were to report continued good health. Coping demonstrated low/moderate stability, an interesting finding given that much of the coping literature has emphasized the situation specificity of this construct. Perhaps most relevant, scores on hassles and caregiver burden not only reflect significant continuity, but burden was more highly correlated over time than were the personality measures. Indeed, over 60% of the variance at follow-up could be explained by initial status. One obvious possibility: As is indeed implied by their category, conditions of chronic stress, such as those found in caring for demented patients, may be relatively consistent for sustained periods of time.

**TABLE 8.7   Correlations Over a One-Year Period Among Adult Child Caregivers (*N*=170, Minimum) to a Dependent Parent with Alzheimer's Disease**

| | Under Age 50 | | 50 and Over | | All |
|---|---|---|---|---|---|
| | Men | Women | Men | Women | Subjects |
| **Semantic Differential** | | | | | |
| Self as nice person | .74[c] | .47[d] | .31 | .74[d] | .61[d] |
| Self as independent | .37[a] | .63[d] | .75[d] | .65[d] | .61[d] |
| Self as happy | .62[d] | .66[d] | .32 | .61[d] | .61[d] |
| **Bradburn Morale** | | | | | |
| Positive Scale | .23 | .47[d] | .75[c] | .68[d] | .56[b] |
| Negative Scale | .90[d] | .65[d] | .74[c] | .46[c] | .60[b] |
| **Hopkins Checklist** | | | | | |
| Depression | .78[c] | .72[d] | .78[d] | .81[d] | .77[d] |
| Anxiety | .78[c] | .46[d] | .69[b] | .73[d] | .63[d] |
| **Ways of coping** | | | | | |
| Palliative behavior | .84[d] | .37[b] | .87[d] | .46[c] | .49[d] |
| Active mastery | .72[b] | .40[b] | .33 | .40[b] | .25[c] |
| Growth/contemplation | .57[a] | .48[d] | .60[b] | .54[d] | .29[c] |
| Support seeking | .68[b] | .52[d] | .50[a] | .25 | .27[b] |
| Denial | .76[c] | .48[d] | .76[d] | .45[c] | .34[d] |
| Redirection | .76[c] | .41[b] | .62[b] | .41[b] | .35[d] |
| Passive mastery | .52[a] | .29[a] | .50[a] | .32[a] | .29[c] |
| **Health status** | | | | | |
| Health problems | .87[d] | .25[a] | .40 | .31[a] | .36[d] |
| **Stressors** | | | | | |
| Hassles | .23 | .32[b] | .14 | .71[d] | .44[d] |
| Burden | .64[d] | .81[d] | .76[d] | .83[d] | .78[d] |

[a] $p = .05$.
[b] $p = .01$.
[c] $p = .001$.
[d] $p = .000$.

PREDICTING CHANGE OVER TIME.    The prediction model for the Caregiver Study differs slightly from the previous models in that the measure of stress was not drawn from an events inventory but instead consisted of the Zarit (1994) Burden Scale, an index of chronic stress. The reason for this difference was that the caregiver study was conceptually oriented to the more chronic conditions.

Keeping in mind the use of a chronic as opposed to acute stress indicator, results are still quite similar to those found for the three other studies: Follow-up status on the three indices of self-concept was best predicted by initial status (Table 8.8). The levels of variance accounted for were higher than evident in the other studies, a finding that may be

**TABLE 8.8   Results of Hierarchical Set Regression Analyses Predicting One-Year Follow-up Self-Concept on the Basis of Both Initial Status and Other Factors: Caregiver Study**

|  | Dependent measures | | |
|---|---|---|---|
|  | Happy Self $MR$ $(r^2)$ | Independent Self $MR$ $(r^2)$ | Nice Self $MR$ $(r^2)$ |
| Sets |  |  |  |
| 1. *Initial* | .63[e] | .65[e] | .59[e] |
|  | (.49)[e] | (.42)[e] | (.35)[e] |
| Base | .63[e] | .65[e] | .59[c] |
| 2. *Demographics* | .66[e] | .66[e] | .62[e] |
|  | (.03)[a] | (.02) | (.03) |
| Gender | .06 | .08 | −.11 |
| Age | −.17[b] | −.05 | −.07 |
| Education | .00 | −.11 | −.15[a] |
| 3. *Health* | .66[e] | .68[e] | .64[e] |
|  | (.00) | (.02)[a] | (.02)[a] |
| Self-report | .05 | .14[a] | .15[a] |
| 4. *Social* | .66[e] | .70[e] | .64[d] |
|  | (.00) | (.04)[b] | (.00) |
| Close kin | −.06 | −.20[c] | −.04 |
| Friends | −.03 | .06 | .01 |
| 5. *Stress* | .69[e] | .71[e] | .64[e] |
|  | (.04)[c] | (.01) | (.00) |
| Burden | .21[c] | .09 | −.04 |

[a] $p = .10$.
[b] $p = .05$.
[c] $p = .01$.
[d] $p = .001$.
[e] $p = .000$.

a function of the relatively brief interval (slightly less than one year) between contacts. Also similar was the fact that the subsequent predictive sets often—but not always—made a contribution, with the stress indicator providing the greatest additional contribution for one of the three dependent variables.

## NEWER APPROACHES TO ASSESSING PERSONALITY DEVELOPMENT

The analyses presented in the preceding section provide an overview of some of the issues related to studying continuities and consistencies in the self-concepts of people over a period of 12 years. While the findings provide insights into forces affecting trajectories of the self-concept, they were based on more or less traditional ways of assessing personality development.

More recently developed perspectives assume that personality is a relatively fluid characteristic and that its actual attributes may depend both on context and the individual's need for meaning. For those who use this perspective, which draws heavily on the prior work of pioneers like Murray (1938), a focus on continuity is overly restrictive in that it ignores the adaptive and changing aspects of personality (McAdams, 1992).

In this last section, one alternative perspective on personal development will be presented. The perspective is based on the idea that the stability or "traitedness" of personality attributes may be very much an individual matter, with variations in stability being dependent on the salience or meaning of the attribute to the individual (e.g., Baumeister & Tice, 1988; Britt, 1993). Baumeister and Tice (1988) operationalize what they call *metatraits* by computing inter-item variability over time for specific items, for specific individuals. If an individual demonstrates little variability in the items that traditionally make up a trait such as introversion, then that individual would be seen as "traited" for introversion. Conversely, someone untraited in introversion would demonstrate substantial variability in introversion-related items over time.

The approach that will be presented here represents a variant of the inter-item variability method. Using Transitions Study data, an overall Time 1 versus Time 5 variability or discrepancy score was computed, for each individual, on the basis of how correlated their scores were on the 70-item Adjective Rating List. For each subject, in other words, data were treated as if we broke the person into 70 different pieces and tried to see if all these parts were more or less in the same place at two different times. In comparison with the method used by Baumeister and Tice (1988), this approach could be said to ask whether some people are generally traited (i.e., are consistent in how they respond to every item) or untraited (i.e., tend to be highly variable in all times). My hypothesis—based on Neugarten's (1964) conclusion that people become more like themselves with age—was simply that in comparison with the two younger groups, older individuals in the Transitions sample would give evidence of being more traited.

Overall, the average traitedness correlation for the entire sample was .65, and there were neither gender differences nor interactions by gender and stage. There was, however, a rather clear-cut stage difference. The former high school subjects (average correlation $r=.50$) were significantly lower than all other stages, while the former newlyweds (average $r=.58$) were significantly lower than the empty nest ($r=.67$) and retirement transition stages ($r=.68$).

The findings reported earlier are corroborated by these results, suggesting that the older groups generally give evidence of greater stability in self concept. To demonstrate the potential significance of traitedness as an overall characteristic of individuals, a final set of analyses considered whether traitedness was associated with psychological symptoms reported at the twelfth-year contact. It was predicted that traitedness would be an important and expected developmental characteristic of older persons, but would, from a developmental perspective, be of little consequence for younger subjects.

The results were as anticipated. For the former high school seniors and the newlyweds, the correlations were insignificant. For the former empty nest subjects, on the other hand, the correlation was $-.37$ ($p=.01$) and for the retired subjects it was slightly higher ($r=-.44$, $p=.00$). Thus, the adaptive quality of traitedness differed systematically by stage of life.

## DISCUSSION

Some years back, in a retrospective on disengagement theory presented at the Gerontology Society, Bernice Neugarten asked whether in addressing disengagement we might in fact be kicking a dead donkey. Does change fit the same metaphor? There are some who strongly suggest that it does. As represented by McCrae (1993), for example, there is now definitive evidence that personality is a continuous aspect of the individual, barring such things as the onset of a dementing illness or clinical depression, and we should now be moving on to consider such issues as role and relationship continuities.

The findings reported here, however, suggest that, rather than having reached the point where the evidence is conclusive and we can lay the issue to rest, exciting new avenues of exploration are opening up. What we may have reached, indeed, is the beginning of a paradigm shift. Indeed, as someone who only recently returned to research on personality development, I have been struck by the remarkable vigor and diversity of current research on personality.

In the preceding pages I have attempted to capture some of the nuances of personal continuities and discontinuities as evidenced by individuals facing often quite different social conditions. Is the glass half full, or half empty? Naturally, both are true. Which is the more important question? Probably neither. While the more popular conceptualizations of personality, especially those representing the semimythical "Big Five" traits, would seem to assume that personality is a predisposing factor with inherent stability, there is a growing documentation of the notion that personality attributes have characteristics of both state and trait (e.g., Headey & Wearing, 1991). In one comparison of structural equation models based on "top down" (i.e., trait) versus "bottom-up" (i.e., state) approaches, Feist, Jacobs, Miles, and Tan (1995) argue that both types of model fit longitudinal data of psychological well-being equally well. The long-sustained research efforts of Mischel (1990) now suggest compellingly that personality attributes can exhibit continuity over time as well as discontinuities across situations. What his research, and that of many others, implies is not that continuity is the rule, and not that discontinuity is the rule, but rather that there would seem to be some rules, or, as McClelland (1992) suggests, lawfulness in how things turn out.

Thus, by discounting evidence for change in quest of stability, we may, in effect, be trying to kick an apparently dead donkey from its rear end. As an old Ecuadorian proverb notes, that's not necessarily a good idea. The idea of change remains alive and well in personality research—as indeed does the idea of continuity.

# ACKNOWLEDGMENT

Preparation of this chapter was supported in part by funding from the Henry A. Murray Center and in part by the National Institute of Aging grants AG00002, AG08633, and MH33713.

# REFERENCES

Baltes, P. B. (1987). Theoretical propositions of life-span developmental psychology: On the dynamics between growth and decline. *Developmental Psychology, 23,* 611–626.

Baumeister, R. F., & Tice, D. M. (1988). Metatraits. *Journal of Personality, 56,* 571–598.

Block, J. (1961). *The Q-sort method in personality assessment and psychiatric research.* Springfield, IL: Thomas.

Bradburn, N. (1968). *The structure of psychological well-being.* Chicago: Aldine.

Britt, T. W. (1993). Metatraits: Evidence relevant to the validity of the construct and its implications. *Journal of Personality and Social Psychology, 65,* 554–562.

Chiriboga, D. A. (1984). Social stressors as antecedents of change. *Journal of Gerontology, 39,* 468–477.

Chiriboga, D. A., Catron, L. S., & Associates. (1991). *Divorce: Crisis, challenge or relief?* New York: New York University Press.

Chiriboga, D. A., & Markides, K. (1994, November). *The stressors of older Mexican Americans.* Paper presented at the annual meeting of the Gerontological Society of America, Atlanta.

Chiriboga, D. A., Yee, B. W. K., & Weiler, P. G. (1992). Stress and coping in the context of caring. In L. Montada, S.-H. Filipp, & M. J. Lerner (Eds.), *Life crises and experiences of loss in adulthood* (pp. 95–118). Hillsdale, NJ: Erlbaum.

Costa, P. T., Jr., & McCrae, R. R. (1994). Set like plaster? Evidence for the stability of adult personality. In T. F. Heatherton & J. L. Weinberger (Eds.), *Can personality change?* (pp. 21–40). Washington, DC: American Psychological Association.

Feist, G. J., Jacobs, J. F., Miles, M., & Tan, V. (1995). Insulating top-down and bottom-up structural models of subjective well-being: A longitudinal investigation. *Journal of Personality and Social Psychology, 68,* 138–150.

Fiske, M., & Chiriboga, D. A. (1990). *Change and continuity in adult life.* San Francisco: Jossey-Bass.

Freud, S. (1933). *New introductory lectures on psychoanalysis.* New York: Norton.

George, L. (1995). The last half-century of aging research—and thoughts for the future. *Journal of Gerontology: Social Sciences, 50B,* S24–S34.

Gergen, K. J. (1977). Stability, change, and change in human development. In N. Datan & H. W. Reese (Eds.), *Life span developmental psychology: Dialectical perspectives on experimental research* (pp. 136–158). New York: Academic Press.

Goldberg, L. R. (1993). The structure of phenotypic personality. *American Psychologist, 48,* 26–34.

Headey, B., & Wearing, A. (1991). Subjective well-being: A stocks and flows framework. In F. Strack, M. Argyle, & N. Schwarz (Eds.), *Subjective well-being: An interdisciplinary perspective* (pp. 40–71). Oxford, England: Pergamon.

Ickes, W. (1984). Personality. In A. S. Bellack & M. Hersen (Eds.), *Research methods in clinical psychology* (pp. 157–178). New York: Pergamon.

Kelly, E. L. (1955). Consistency of the adult personality. *American Psychologist, 10,* 659–681.

Kohlberg, L. (1986). *The psychology of moral development.* New York: Harper & Row.

Lewis, M. (1995). Self-conscious emotions. *American Scientist, 83*(1), 68–78.

Livson, N., & Peskin, H. (1980). Perspectives on adolescence from longitudinal research. In J. Adelson (Ed.), *Handbook of adolescent psychology* (pp. 47–98). New York: Wiley.

Loevinger, J. (1976). *Ego development: Conceptions and theories.* San Francisco: Jossey Bass.

McAdams, D. P. (1992). Unity and purpose in human lives: The emergence of identity as a life story. In R. A. Zucker, A. I. Rabin, J. Aronoff, & S. J. Frank (Eds.), *Personality structure in the life course: Essays on personality in the Murray tradition* (pp. 323–375). New York: Springer Publishing Co.

McClelland, D. C. (1992). Is personality consistent? In R. A. Zucker, A. I. Rabin, J. Aronoff, & S. J. Frank (Eds.), *Personality structure in the life course: Essays on personality in the Murray tradition* (pp. 22–53). New York: Springer Publishing Co.

McCrae, R. R. (1993). Moderated analyses of longitudinal personality stability. *Journal of Personality and Social Psychology, 65,* 577–585.

McCrae, R. R., & Costa, P. T. (1990). *Personality in adulthood.* New York: Guilford.

Mischel, W. (1968). *Personality and assessment.* New York: Wiley.

Mischel, W. (1979). On the interface of cognition and personality: Beyond the person-situation debate. *American Psychologist, 34,* 740–754.

Mischel, W. (1990). Personality dispositions revisited and revised: A view after three decades. In L. A. Pervin (Ed.), *Handbook of personality: Theory and research* (pp. 111–134). New York: Guilford.

Murray, H. A. (1938). *Explorations in personality.* New York: Oxford University Press.

Nesselroade, J. R., & Boker, S. M. (1994). Assessing constancy and change. In T. F. Heatherton & J. L. Weinberger (Eds.), *Can personality change?* (pp. 121–147). Washington, DC: American Psychological Association.

Neugarten, B. L. (1964). Summary and implications. In B. L. Neugarten & Associates (Eds.), *Personality in middle and late life: Empirical studies* (pp. 188–200). New York: Atherton.

Neugarten, B. L. (1968). Awareness of middle age. In B. L. Neugarten (Ed.), *Middle age and aging: A reader in social psychology* (pp. 93–98). Chicago: University of Chicago Press.

Neugarten, B. L. (1977). Personality and aging. In J. E. Birren & K. Warner Schaie (Eds.), *Handbook of the psychology of aging* (pp. 626–649). New York: Van Nostrand Reinhold.

Piaget, J. (1972). Intellectual evolution from adolescence to adulthood. *Human Development, 15,* 1–12.

Radloff, L. S. (1977). The CES-D Scale: A self-report depression scale for research in the general population. *Journal of Applied Psychological Measurement, 1,* 385–401.

Riegel, K. F. (1977). The dialectics of time. In N. Datan & H. W. Reese (Eds.), *Life span developmental psychology: Dialectical perspectives on experimental research* (pp. 3–45). New York: Academic Press.

Turner, R. J., Wheaton, B., & Lloyd, D. A. (1995). The epidemiology of social stress. *American Sociological Review, 60,* 104–125.

Zarit, S. H. (1994). Methodological considerations in caregiver intervention and outcome research. In E. Light, G. Niederehe, & B. D. Lebowitz (Eds.), *Stress effects on family caregivers of Alzheimer's patients: Research and interventions* (pp. 351–369). New York: Springer Publishing Co.

# Comments

## Steven H. Zarit

To continue with the Ecuadorian proverb that David Chiriboga introduced, let's give the donkey one more kick. The main thrust of Chiriboga's chapter is that it is time to question the orthodoxy that has grown up around the issue of stability of personality in the adult years. According to that orthodoxy, all we need to know is that personality is comprised of five factors, which are stable over time (neuroticism, extroversion, openness to experience, agreeableness, and conscientiousness). McCrae and Costa (1984; McCrae, 1993) have made notable contributions to our understanding of personality across the adult years, including providing impressive evidence regarding stability of personality, but as Chiriboga has pointed out, the issue may not be as settled as many in the field have argued. Instead, he argues that the answer to the question about whether personality is stable or changes depends on at least three factors: (1) the type of measures used, (2) the timing of assessments, and (3) how much of a difference represents meaningful change. These points are worth examining in more detail.

Although it is not a main point in his chapter, Chiriboga shows that estimates of stability of personality vary, depending on the measurement approach used. This issue has previously been stressed by Whitbourne (1986; Whitbourne & Angiullo, in press), among others. Most of the evidence for stability in personality rests on findings from the use of self-report inventories. An older tradition, typified by research by Bernice Neugarten and other Chicago investigators (e.g., Neugarten, 1964; Neugarten, Havighurst, & Tobin, 1968), used a multimethod approach to personality, which included self reports, ratings of interviews, and, on occasions, results of projective tests. Chiriboga's work draws from that tradition by providing a multifaceted perspective on personality.

Beyond the specifics of measurement, however, the heart of the matter is what we mean by *personality*. We may believe that self-reports of traits are sufficient to characterize this construct. Multitrait personality inventories are easy to administer and have appropriate psychometric properties, that is, they are reliable and form interpretable factors that can be replicated across samples and over time. Nonetheless, there may be more to personality than people are willing or able to tell researchers in their responses to a questionnaire. In particular, an interviewer who first establishes rapport and then guides and probes respondents about critical themes may obtain a very different perspective about someone than he would from quick responses to a personality inventory. Structured observations and reports by the respondent's family and friends can add still other dimensions. It may be useful to think about responses to self-report inventories as how we wish to be perceived by other people, and, to an extent, by ourselves. That those reports show a high degree of consistency over time is an important and interesting observation. But self-reports represent only one level of personality. There are other dimensions that we do not typically reveal to a casual inquiry, but which may be disclosed in situations that involve a more intimate encounter. There may also be dimensions of which we are not fully aware or which we cannot articulate, but which may be accessible through ratings of interview material.

The gerontological field as a whole has been pulled increasingly toward use of large samples and simple measures in its research. Although meeting minimum criteria for reliability and validity, these measures may not be sufficient for encompassing the most essential or pertinent meaning of a given construct, especially for complex constructs such as personality. We may be spending too much time asking closed questions, and not enough time discussing with people how they live or what they do, think, and feel. There needs to be more room for multimethod approaches, such as Chiriboga uses, especially on a topic like personality. These other measures can inform and challenge the findings from questionnaire studies, and can ultimately broaden our understanding of personality processes over adulthood.

The second issue, which is addressed more directly in Chiriboga's chapter, has to do with the timing of assessments of personality. In a larger sense, this issue gets at the heart of concepts and models of development in the adult years. Do we believe that development in adulthood is tied to chronological age, or that change is likely to occur around critical events or transitions? Certainly a consistent theme in Bernice Neugarten's work is that chronological age is not an important explanatory variable, except as it is linked to specific social norms or events. Chiriboga's chapter represents a very creative exploration of this issue. Rather than assuming that change occurs in regular increments over time, he has examined a series of key transitions. In doing so, he has found that the extent of change varies, depending on the transition. Furthermore, there are different patterns of change for men and women, for younger and older respondents, and across measures.

This type of work underscores the need for conceptual models of personality and aging that go beyond simple questions of stability versus change. We should follow Chiriboga's example by asking under what conditions we would expect any particular dimension of personality to be stable or to change and what might account for stability or change. People may have little reason to change in a stable social situation in which they function reasonably well. Similarly, there may be different patterns of response to undesirable or uncontrollable changes (e.g., becoming a caregiver) than for a desirable transition.

Finally, a basic issue that has been given surprisingly little attention is how much change is meaningful change. In other words, What constitutes stability and what is change? The dependence of research on tests of statistical significance has sometimes deadened thought about the meaning of any particular result. Because significance tests are so heavily dependent on sample size, it is important to extend our analyses to include consideration of effect size. But that still does not address how much change is a meaningful amount. Studies of developmental processes need to posit how much change is expected or would represent a meaningful difference from baseline scores. In other words, what amount of change constitutes a significant shift or alteration in personality. Unfortunately, standardized personality measures offer few clues about how much change might be associated with a meaningful alteration in how one behaves, or thinks about oneself or the world. Scores between one time of measurement and another could correlate highly (e.g., .60 to .80), yet this small amount of change might be meaningful. Conversely, a lower degree of stability on a measure might not indicate a particularly meaningful or interesting degree of change.

The issue of how much change is meaningful brings us back to the earlier point about the need for multimethod approaches to the study of personality. By having in-depth conversations with people and making multiple levels of observation, it is possible to define stability and change more precisely and in terms of meaningful qualitative shifts.

Chiriboga, then, has presented a challenging and important chapter that continues the traditions developed by Bernice Neugarten and the other Chicago investigators. His chapter demonstrates the value of multimethod approaches to personality, questions the wisdom of equating development and chronological age, and, above all else, expresses the willingness to go beyond the orthodoxy of current thinking. In the end, that is the most important lesson we learned from Bernice Neugarten.

## REFERENCES

McCrae, R. R. (1993). Moderated analyses of longitudinal personality stability. *Journal of Personality and Social Psychology, 65,* 577–585.

McCrae, R. R., & Costa, P. T., Jr. (1984). *Emerging lives, enduring dispositions: Personality in adulthood.* Boston: Little Brown.

Neugarten, B. L. (1964). Summary and implications. In B. L. Neugarten & Associates (Eds.), *Personality in middle and late life: Empirical studies* (pp. 188–200). New York: Atherton.

Neugarten, B. L., Havighurst, R. J., & Tobin, S. S. (1968). Personality and patterns of aging. In B. L. Neugarten (Ed)., *Middle age and aging: A reader in social psychology* (pp. 173–177). Chicago: University of Chicago Press.

Whitbourne, S. K. (1986). *The me I know: A study of adult identity.* New York: Springer-Verlag.

Whitbourne, S. K., & Angiullo, L. M. (in press). The developing self in midlife. In S. L. Willis & J. D. Reid (Eds.), *Life in the middle.* New York: Academic Press.

# CHAPTER 9

# On-time, Off-time, Out of Time? Reflections on Continuity and Discontinuity from an Illness Process

## Gunhild O. Hagestad

*When I had journeyed half of life's way, I found myself*
*within a shadowed forest, for I had lost the path*
*that does not stray.*
—Dante, *The Divine Comedy, Inferno,* canto 1

### THE SOCIAL STRUCTURING OF TIME

What follows are reflections from an illness journey that started with a cancer diagnosis in 1993 and continued with complex infections until the spring of 1994. My purpose is not primarily to discuss the experience of life-threatening illness, but to illustrate how it sheds light on the sociocultural construction of time and lays bare some core assumptions that we live by in our society. Like my social science colleague and fellow cancer patient Arthur W. Frank (1991), I see illness as "a dangerous opportunity" (p. 1), an opportunity for reflection and insights.

Ever since I read Durkheim's *Elementary Forms of Religious Life* (1912/1915) as a young graduate student, I have been intrigued by his description of time as "an endless chart before our minds," a chart which takes on structure and meaning through the schedules and calendars that both *reflect* and *maintain* the rhythms of social life. The theme of social calendars was further developed by Sorokin and Merton (1937) in the 1930s. Whereas these sociological men were mostly concerned with the integration and continuity of society, Bernice Neugarten applied ideas of social clocks and calendars to the integration and continuity of persons and their lives. In pioneering work, which started with the Kansas City Study of Adult Life (Neugarten & Peterson, 1957) and culminated with several projects in the 1960s (Neugarten, Moore, & Lowe, 1965), she argued that the schedules provided by our social world give us scripts not only for the normal day, but also for the *normal, expectable life* (Neugarten, 1969). Our personal sense of time and timing is inextricably linked to the pulse of the human groups in which our lives are embedded. In the same decade, Julius Roth (1963) wrote the sociological classic on social timetables in a formal organization, the hospital.

Discussions of schedules in everyday life and the life course build on two key assumptions: That we human beings have a fundamental need for predictability and continuity, and that this need to an important extent is met through social time rhythms and schedules. As Zerubavel (1981) points out, the temporal regularity of our social world provides us with a reliable repertoire of what is expected, what is likely or unlikely to take place, and "adds a strong touch of predictability to the world around us, thus enhancing our cognitive well-being" (p. 12). In everyday life as well as the course of life, temporal ordering means that we have some sense of where we have been and what lies ahead (Strauss, 1959). Socially constructed timetables become internalized and used as benchmarks for our own life journey.

In some of my own work, I have explored contrasts between off-time and on-time life changes (Hagestad & Burton, 1986; Hagestad, Smyer, & Stierman, 1984). I have also discussed how it is necessary to see families as bundles of interwoven lives and interconnected timetables (Hagestad, 1986). The last year and a half of my own life has taught me that being *out of time* also needs to be considered. Critical illness not only presents you with the issue of finitude, but more importantly, it threatens the very foundations of time structuring by removing you from life's comforting rhythms. It becomes a struggle not to *fall out of time.* What follows is a personal ethnography from an illness journey, which took me to places where I gained new understanding of the importance of schedules. I also had flashes of insight into what it means to no longer be in time, but to live out of time. Starting with four snapshots from the illness process, I attempt to discuss being off-time and out of time and how these experiences are connected to social time systems.

# FOUR GLIMPSES

1. *Facing a year of uncertainty.*  It is New Year's Eve, the end of a year that has brought a cancer diagnosis and a lengthy treatment protocol. I am with my two daughters, both in their twenties, at our house in a snowy Norwegian countryside. Even though it is a festive occasion, we all know that I have been ill for three weeks—too long and too severely to make flu a reasonable explanation. Instead of flying to the United States as had been the plan for January, I will go into the hospital again. After good food and champagne, my daughters want to know my New Year's resolutions. I burst into tears, saying that resolutions make no sense without assuming predictability. To my daughters, it seems that I have given up, but what I am experiencing is the unsettling loss of an illusion that serves as an unspoken premise of everyday plans, ambitions, and evaluations in our society. I am entering a year when I lose, as did Frank (1991), "an innocence about the normal expectations of life" (p. 39).

2. *The importance of schedules.*  For several weeks, I am critically ill with no clear diagnosis. After about a month in the hospital, I move to a rehabilitation center in Spain. The people around me have functional capacities similar to mine. Their average age is 85. In this sunny place of relaxation, I find that I make a rigid, almost military schedule for my day. Times for meals, simple exercise, rest, and reading are defined with no margins. The strict schedule seems right and necessary.

3. *Interconnected timetables.*  After Spain, I again have a long hospital stay, with new threatening, unexplained symptoms. Since the nature of my problems is not understood, I cannot count on improvement. It is clear that some members of the medical staff think that the cancer has spread. My oldest daughter writes in a letter, "Mom, this would have been so much easier if I were older." My immediate response is, "Me too!" In communications with both my daughters, I sense an underlying frustration, sometimes anger—a reaction of "this isn't fair!"

4. *The importance of completing projects.*    After a four-month-long siege, a diagnosis makes treatment possible and I am finally on an upward spiral. Weeks of care from family and friends make it possible for me to do a little academic work, including supervision of students. The student I have been advising the longest finishes the PhD, with one of my colleagues substituting as committee chair. Nobody informs me of the changes or the final defense, "because they do not want to bother me." When I find out, I feel totally crushed.

## LIVING WITH UNCERTAINTY

In our society, we emphasize metered time, expressed as a diachronic axis—a line (Albert & Cattell, 1994; Elias, 1987). Often, time seems objectified and becomes a "place." After all, fairy tales start with "once UPON a time"! The close connection between our everyday concepts of time and space is captured in a book title by Lynch (1972): *What Time Is This Place?* The present is a place "under" us. It is in part defined by a known past, which we think of as being behind us—and an unknown future, which, we say, lies ahead (Mead, 1932). In our bureaucratized, so-called rational society, for most of our lives the future is more important in defining the present than is the past. Indeed, some authors have suggested that a preoccupation with the past may be a sign that life is coming to an end (Butler, 1968). It is more common to ask people about their plans than about their past, unless they are in advanced old age. The frequency with which we ask about plans becomes painfully clear to you when you cannot make any. There is also a realization that you become troublesome to some of the people in your social world, because without assumptions of predictability, they do not know how to take you into account. Frank (1991) writes of avoiding commitments he was not sure he could meet, commenting that this created distance from some friends: "My body was taking me out of their natural flow of plans and expectations. Others took planning for granted; my future was pervaded by uncertainty. I lost my sense of belonging" (p. 36). In our line of work, such distancing often means not being invited to future meetings or asked to contribute to upcoming publications.

In the middle-class world, individuals who act as if they hold a deed to the future are admired as "goal-directed" and "up n'coming"; people who do not have plans are seen as lacking direction and are defined as social problems. With the loss of an assumed, predictable future, maintaining a hold on the present becomes a struggle, and it is easy to end with a sense of having lost your footing on the time line. In my case, this situation represents a discontinuity with the other fifty years or so of my life, but the experience reminds me that in many societies that we call advanced, such as the United States, whole segments of the population grow up with so much chaos and so little order that *planning* is a foreign word.

It was not long ago that people in this society were much more hesitant to act as if they owned the future. Demographic change has rapidly made us assume a good deal of certainty about life and death. As Blythe (1979) states it, "We place dying in what we take to be its logical position, which is at the close of a long life, whereas our ancestors accepted the futility of placing it in any position at all" (p. 4). The 80-year life has not only become statistical reality, but also a part of our map for the normal, expectable life journey. Parents and children anticipate 40 to 60 years of shared lives. Young adults expect to have grandparents at their wedding.

The illness, in some ways, throws me back to life in the fishing village where my mother grew up, a place where old people still do not make plans without adding, "if we live." In the Islamic world, one often adds "God willing." I have been told that in Madagascar people think of the past as being in front of us, since *it* is known. The unknown future is seen as being behind us, something we cannot see. I feel a new kinship to the inhabitants of the African island, as well as to Portuguese speakers. In the language of *Fado* songs, the English expressions "to wait for," "to hope for," and "to expect" are all translated as *esperar* (Levine & Wolff, 1985). After 6 months in the fogs of uncertainty, I no longer use the word *plans*. As my strength slowly returns, I gingerly speak of *hopes*.

## THE LOSS OF SCHEDULES

My experiences in the rehabilitation center illustrate different ways in which socially created schedules bring solace. Time structuring has four key dimensions: *timing, sequencing, duration,* and *prevalence,* or rate of occurrence (Elder, 1985; Hagestad, 1992; Zerubavel, 1981). We find these dimensions on three levels of social time under consideration here: the round of daily activities, the yearly cycle of seasons and holidays, and the seasons of life.

If we see social time as a series of activities or states, timing describes *when* there is a transition from one state to another. In our culture, we mark such temporal location in metered time with the help of clocks and calendars. Sequencing is a question of the relative order of states; duration defines how long a given state lasts. Finally, prevalence has two aspects: the frequency with which a state occurs to members of a social group (how likely it is that they experience it sooner or later), and the likelihood that it will recur. Some transitions and states are experienced by all, and their occurrence has a clear pattern of timing, sequencing, and duration.

Many of the schedules of everyday life have nearly universal prevalence, regular timing, marked sequencing, and fixed durations. We wake up, eat, work, relax, and sleep within a predictable structure. Even though we sometimes refer to these rhythms as "the rut," we also recognize somewhat apologetically, after holidays or travels, that it feels good to be back in the daily routine. Children are quite young when they begin to grasp and enjoy time rhythms. As soon as the words are there, the wish for "one more time!" is expressed often. Enjoyable durations are used as yardsticks: a visit to the dentist is shorter than Sesame Street. Sequences are built around important events: first comes my birthday, then Christmas, then Valentine's Day.

In a given cultural group, the year has a predictable rhythm of timing, sequencing, and durations. Calendar time has punctuations made of seasonal changes and holidays, which we experience collectively. From our culture and social structure, we also develop a sense of life's seasons (Neugarten, 1969). We have what Plath (1982) calls an "ethnotheory of the life cycle" and can name life stages, such as childhood, youth, and middle age. Furthermore, our culture has shared expectations regarding the timing and sequencing of key life changes, what Neugarten (1969) and Roth (1963) call *timetables.* "The life course has become a principal cultural connection between individual lives and the larger society through an image not only of the good life, but of the timetable according to which it should be achieved," conclude a group of anthropologists who have examined the social meanings of age in societies on four continents (Keith et al., 1994, p. 196). There is a good time to marry, and partnerhood precedes parenthood. Such cultural scripts also include normal durations. We anticipate that parent–child bonds will last many decades, but do not expect children's financial dependency to span more than two decades.

A socially structured life course creates a sense of peership, because many life changes are experienced by most members of a birth cohort within a limited span of years. In our society, peership is to a great extent linked to chronological age, since so many of our prescriptions, proscriptions, and permissions for social participation are age based, starting with rigidly age-graded school systems.

Dimensions of social time structuring, especially timetables, serve four key functions for the individual:

- *Reducing uncertainty,* because "they help us plot where we are in the confused currents of time, so that we can project where we yet may go" (Plath, 1982, p. 9). Such a sense of direction can be found in everyday life, the yearly cycle, and the life course.
- *Enabling us to prepare for what lies ahead,* because daily life is inconceivable without predictable pulses of timing, sequencing, and durations, from bus schedules to mealtimes. In the sociology and social psychology of work, a literature on shiftwork, especially irregular shifts, documents the stresses of not having predictable schedules.

In discussions of the life course, Neugarten took issue with some of her psychologist colleagues who spoke of life events as "crises." She argued that changes that occur "on schedule" do not deserve the label *crisis,* because individuals are to some extent prepared for them. An example she used was "rehearsal for widowhood" among women. Off-time or unscheduled transitions, on the other hand, often take us by surprise and catch us unprepared. Such changes also leave us with limited social support.

- *Providing social support,* from peers who are "in the same boat at the same time" (Seltzer, 1976). Untimely life changes make individuals out of step with their peer group and make it difficult to find others who know what they are going through.
- *Marking and evaluating progress* in the life course, because we have some sense of how our movement compares to timetables, whether we are "on time," "early," or "late" (Neugarten et al., 1965; Sofer, 1970). In cases of illness, a sense of improvement can be based on "being back

on track" and having regained peership: being able to return to the rhythm of activities that is typical of your age group. In everyday life, altered durations may mark progress. More time for family meals can reflect desired reorganization of priorities. For me, shortened durations marked small victories. Walking my daily round in two minutes less than the day before brought encouragement. A friend who has experienced debilitating illness recently exclaimed as she was dashing off to an appointment, "Isn't it wonderful to be able to hurry!"

When you are seriously ill with an uncertain diagnosis, to some extent you "fall off the timetrack," to use Lyman and Scott's (1970) terminology. You become "untimely" on all three levels of social time, and the deviations may involve timing, sequencing, duration, and prevalence. Illness makes you disoriented in the currents of biographical time, because you have lost the illusion of a predictable future and you are "out of" an expected developmental sequence. As a result, you lose aspects of peership. You are unable to participate in roles that define your social age and you feel older than your years because of physical limitations. Middle-age struggles to maintain the body's continuity with its younger self multiply, especially when treatment such as surgery and chemotherapy leave physical reminders that you will never be the same (Frank, 1991).

Disability shows how closely our culture links expectations about the timing of frailty and debilitating illness to chronological age. With my fellow clients at the rehabilitation center, I had constant reminders that I was "out of age." It was enough to look around me, but I also had innumerable reactions of "What are you doing here? You're so young!" It was no easier to talk to my fellow residents about my fear and pain than it was to find empathy from my age peers. After my stay among octogenarians, I had new sympathy for young accident victims in our society who not only have experienced a loss of anticipated future, but whose only residential option is a nursing home.

The social microcosms of the nursing home and the hospital are both what Goffman (1961) called *total institutions.* Residents spend all 24 hours in them and the institution regulates all facets of daily life. However, they differ on some of the dimensions of time structuring. The nursing home is often seen as a terminal location, representing a state with clear, expected temporal placement in the life course. It is, as Tobin and Lieberman (1976) described it, *a last home for the aged.* Hospitalization can happen at any age, and in the life course of women there are normal, expectable stays during the childbearing years. However, all stays are in principle temporary. For many types of physical problems, there are clear, shared expectations for the course of treatment and the length of stay. Under systems of "managed care" in the United States, such expectations are rigidly formalized in so-called *diagnosis-related groups* (DRGs). When you are seriously ill without a clear diagnosis, you become unmanageable and disorderly.

After twice having entered the hospital with an expectation of staying a few days and ending up spending a month, I was struck by how it is assumed that hospital stays have predictable durations. Over and over again, I would face the question of how long I was going to stay. When I shrugged my shoulders and said I had no idea, people looked puzzled, even irritated. In cases of ambiguous illness and uncertain prognoses, you do not know how long your stay will be and there are no benchmarks for marking progress. Roth (1963) cites a fellow patient, "The jailbirds got it better than we do. They at least know when they are getting out" (p. xvi).

Ambiguous and life-threatening illness not only leaves you with no sense of expected duration, but the timing, sequencing, and durations of your everyday life also disintegrate. You lose "the wholeness that is the natural cycle of life among others" (Frank, 1991, p. 31). Tests interfere with breakfast; exhaustion makes you sleep through lunch; pain makes night like day. Reflecting on how his pain created a sense of incoherence, Frank (1991) says, "I was neither daily nor nocturnal, but suspended outside the limits of either existence. I was neither functionally present nor accountably absent. I lived my life out of place" (p. 32). I understand his use of a spatial reference, his sense of having fallen out of place.

The pain of life without schedules and timetables is the key concern of Roth's (1963) book. As a fresh PhD, he was diagnosed with tuberculosis and placed in a sanitarium. The hospital stay showed him that Durkheim's *endless chart* is uncomfortable and unsettling. "People will not accept uncertainty," he proclaims (p. 93); and he discusses how patients go to great lengths to make existence more structured, with at least a minimum of predictability. In such efforts, they will search for benchmarks to make the journey seem less endless and aimless.

From cancer patients, it is common to hear that treatment protocols create comfort, even though they can be very uncomfortable. You know exactly what lies ahead, and you prepare for chemotherapy, surgery, and radiation as hurdles to be jumped. Crossing treatments off a list gives a sense of accomplishment and progress. Along the track, you are supported by a professional staff, and by fellow patients who have also run the course. After finishing the protocol, people often experience intense anxiety and depression, as they are left with the fundamental question of "now what?" The illness is still potentially there, and ahead lies Durkheim's endless, open chart. As are the long-term unemployed or pupils placed in the ungraded group, you are on what Roth describes as a permanent, poorly marked chronic sidetrack, or off the track completely. Not having any sense of forward movement creates anxiety, even a sense of failure.

It seems reasonable to assume that with a loss of life course predictability and order, the rhythms of everyday life take on new magnitude and significance, as they did for me in the rehabilitation center. Daily routines took on a ritual quality. To my knowledge, little or no work exists on the connection between what we might call "micro schedules" and "macro schedules." Do people who have disorderly careers also lead disorderly daily lives? Research on unemployed men seems to suggest that with the loss of predictable careers and work spells, disorganization often permeates other realms of life, such as family careers and the rhythms of domestic life. Straw and Elliot (1986) discuss the high salience of time in the everyday life of British working class women: "Much of the orderliness, the routinisation of working class life can be seen as an attempt to hold chaos at bay, to provide a measure of security in a very uncertain world and create opportunities for sociability and enjoyment. Women are the principal architects of this protective temporal structure" (p. 44).

I am reminded of Hetherington's (1989) impressive research on children of divorce. The research team timed drop-off and pick-up of children in schools and used unreliable schedules as an indicator of family disorganization. For some children, arrival and departure were quite unpredictable. In a presentation of her findings, she commented that the last thing such children need is an unstructured school! *Can* one level of time structuring indeed compensate for disorder on another level, as I clearly seemed to think it could when I created my rigid daily schedule? If so, there are some clear implications for professional practice, intervention, and social policy.

## FAMILY RIPPLE EFFECTS: INTERCONNECTED TIMING, SEQUENCES, AND DURATIONS

We do not move through time alone. Norbert Elias (1987) points out that long chains of interdependencies, requiring attention to synchronization, are typical of modern societies. Within a culture, we build expectations not only about our own life paths, but also about the life paths of those around us. Alfred Schutz (1971) called such fellow life travelers *consociates*. Especially in the family realm, we find this intertwining. Each family creates its own web of durable ties in a complexly textured weave of needs and resources. In a fabric of interwoven lives, pulling one thread snags others and may even create holes. We experience *countertransitions:* life changes brought on by other members' transitions. Marriage creates in-laws; parenthood brings grandparenthood; divorce produces "exes." We hold expectations regarding family stages, sequences of generational turnover, and the durations of bonds.

Families are arenas in which autobiographies get shaped. In temporal constructions and reconstructions, family members play key parts: "It was the year Mary graduated, so it must have been . . ." Stories we have heard many times become like our own memories. In some instances, older family consociates know parts of our own past better than we do. The reason they do is that *we* constitute integral facets of *their* life stories. It is possible that a new awareness comes with middle age of how significant family consociates are in the construction of a life story, when most of us face the loss of "key informants."

Anthropology and history provide vivid illustrations of how societal norms make life careers of family members contingent on one another. Among the Kikuyu of Kenya, the highest status for men, that of ritual elder, could not be reached until their youngest sons were circumcised and their wives had gone through menopause (Prins, 1953; Whiting, 1981). In Europe, systems of primogeniture made it impossible for first-born sons to marry and start families until their fathers died or relinquished the farm.

Our modern society has few formal norms stating such career contingencies. Nevertheless, we recognize that our own life course progress hinges on the progress of others. Children count on strength and potential support from parents until they themselves are well established in adult roles. Facing the death of parents becomes a key marker of middle age, bringing a new sense of finitude, often a sense of vulnerability. A colleague who is represented in this volume lost both parents before he turned 40. After the second death, he walked into the office exclaiming "I'm an orphan!" When someone remarked that he was too old to be an orphan, the response came quickly: "That may be, but I'm too young to be next in line." For many, it is difficult enough when the transition comes on time. From another colleague came a recent e-mail sigh: "My father is failing and it's still hard to abandon the old expectations for what parents can and can't do at 75." His message assumed a sense of peership, a feeling of "you know what I mean." Somewhere in the forties, social conversations begin to include the question "Are your parents still living?" We do not ask it of people in their twenties. For the first two decades of adulthood, we count on some undisturbed durations and a normal rhythm of generational turnover. This is a time to add a generation, not to lose one. In aging societies, many women now expect that they will have grandchildren before they lose their mothers.

There are some indications that generational turnover can also be too late; durations too long. When parents' longevity goes far beyond expectations and families have two generations of pensioners, conflict may arise over who has the right to be needy and whose duty it is to make sure needs are met. Such situations were observed in Ursula Lehr's study of German five-generation families (Lehr & Schneider, 1983). We have also observed it in a longitudinal study of the oldest old and their caregivers in a Norwegian community (Romøren & Hagestad, 1988). Among careproviders who experienced burnout or overload, it was common to face care needs from three generations: parent, spouse, and grandchildren. A poet from Japan, a country with strong traditional expectations about filial responsibilities, wrote "I have concealed for one more year today / from aging parents that my hair is gray."

Parents anticipate a new freedom after the children are launched, on time and in the right sequence: finishing school, starting work, marrying, and becoming parents. Recent research on "the empty nest" is a far cry from earlier descriptions of depressed, abandoned mothers. It is when the children *do not* leave that Mom becomes depressed!

In the later part of his ouvre, Erik Erikson (1982) focused on family webs of interacting developmental tasks, in which one member's resolution affects other members' handling of *their* tasks. He also argued that by watching lives around us, we preview tasks that are still ahead and review those that we have already been through. The concept of generativity, central in his discussion of middle age, is linked to the younger generation's successful mastery of the tasks of young adulthood. Children who are "off course" leave parents with a sense of not having mastered their own life tasks. In this volume, Tobin gives moving descriptions of parents whose developmentally disabled offspring keep them from tending to issues related to their own aging.

Thirty years ago, Blenkner (1965) used the term *filial maturity* to describe middle-aged individuals' readiness to accept new dependence from aging parents. Since her discussion, we have come to realize that such maturity rests not only on a gradual transformation of the relationship between the old and their offspring, but also on changes in this Janus generation's ties to their children (Hagestad, 1984). Smith (1983) found that middle-aged women who experienced stress and overload in caring for parents tended to have children whose adult lives were "off track." Some of them were unemployed, others had marriages breaking up.

My illness catapulted me into developmental issues that are "normally" faced decades later. I felt unprepared to work on the task of ego integrity, the last developmental hurdle named by Erikson (1963): an acceptance of my life as inevitable, appropriate, and meaningful. I think how my father and grandfather, both of whom died in their eighties, spent their last year or so putting together their life stories. Both concluded that life had been good, and long enough. Younger generations were left with the comforting feeling that, over time, things work themselves out. Erikson (1963) captures the interdependence of trust: "children will not fear life if their elders have integrity enough not to fear death." I do not feel ready to be an elder yet. After intense years of work and parenting, I had, it seemed, just started on issues of generativity: an expansion of ego interests, a sense of contribution to the future, including new ways of needing to be needed. My off-time critical illness cut short expected durations, threatened hoped-for sequences, and disrupted peership. The worst part was not facing death, but losing a future with others (Frank, 1991). A recurring thought was that I might not see my daughters as mothers, not share retrospections of adult experiences with them, not ever hold a grandchild. Most importantly, it left me with a sense that I might be "tripping up" my children in their adult progress.

My daughters are still working on the tasks and issues of young adulthood: shaping a sense of uniqueness, building intimacy, finding meaningful work. For most of their peers, this process takes place within a family context with healthy parents. Demographer Winsborough (1980) estimates that by the time my youngest daughter turns 40, 90% of her peers will have their mothers living. One important aspect of generativity is what Gutmann (1987) calls being an *emeritus parent:* to serve as a back-up, a source of potential help should it be needed. In a culture marked by strong individualism and an emphasis on autonomy, proclamations of independence can be made with the unspoken, implicit understanding that we have a "fall-back" in the parental generation. Recent work on "the refilling of the nest," as well as court decisions stating parental responsibility for needy adult children, illustrate that parents indeed provide a safety net. Part of a middle-age experience is giving up the fantasy that if all else fails, we can always go home, and instead being ready to offer such potential refuge.

As both my children and I face an off-time emergency, I hear in some of their responses echoes of reactions from a study of young adults whose parents had just divorced (Cooney, Smyer, Hagestad, & Kock, 1986). One young man said, "This just isn't fair—instead of me leaving home, home left me!" Another student complained that his mother wanted to talk of her dating problems: "It is her job to listen to my problems, and not vice versa. She is my mother. I am not her father." One way to describe these reactions is that they reflect the problems of facing off-time filial maturity demands. Such a situation, in which needs or expectations are not met on either side of the parent-child dyad, can easily create feelings of inadequacy and guilt. Good parents and children should be there for one another.

Plath (1980) and Roth (1983), both of whom have reflected on life careers in modern Japanese society, urge us to study interacting timetables, what Pruchno, Blow, and Smyer (1984) call the "bumping and grinding of lives in interaction." My daughters and I have found such interaction during the illness process to be very grinding.

## INTERRUPTED PROJECTS

Although we academics may be extreme in this regard, most people make lists of "things to do." Some of our lists contain tasks which must be completed, others are activities we would like to be part of in the future. Being able to cross things off lists brings a sense of satisfaction and mastery. Many PhD students choose to take a master's degree along the way, not because it is required, but because it gives a sense of progress and achievement in a process which at times seems rather endless.

When the illusion of owning the future is lost, the present looks to the past for meaning, continuity, and a sense of minimal forward movement. Finishing projects from the past becomes highly significant when many of life's lists have gone by the wayside and the best-laid plans from the past never come to fruition. In the hospital, I saw women who were intent on completing embroidery which had been "in progress" for years. Others supervised, with the help of samples, letters, and telephone calls, redecorating of the living room or the summer cabin. I had no difficulty understanding their anger when well-meaning friends told them not to trouble themselves with such "unnecessary" tasks. Sometimes, close consociates can unwittingly, with the best of intentions, take away patients' precarious sense of control and continuity in their life and in the process "push them out of time." Some striking examples emerged in the dissertation research of Rubin-Terrado (1994), who studied life satisfaction and adjustment to living in a nursing home, comparing mothers and childless women. The most vulnerable, individuals who lost nearly all sense of control over their own lives, were mothers whose children made all critical decisions for them. One woman in her 80s described how the children, without consulting with her, sold her home and belongings and later told her that this was done "so that she wouldn't have to worry about it"!

Critical illness presents a threat to continuity of the self on many fronts. An altered and weakened body makes it hard to maintain "a sense of sameness," the key ingredient in Erikson's concept of identity. The loss of predictability undermines the life plan, what Berger, Berger, and Kellner (1973) call "the organizing principle par excellence of the biography." Weakened everyday rhythms make it hard to maintain a minimal sense of control over your life. Under such circumstances, it is far from helpful when others make decisions for you and rob you even of the control involved in delegating. For consociates and professionals, positive support could come from searching for ways to maintain some continuity, to see projects come to fruition. A list of examples of such help could include making it possible to see a child or grandchild (biological or academic!) graduate, completing domestic projects, putting together photo albums, and editing an old manuscript for publication.

## AN ATTEMPT AT SUMMING UP

I started this essay with a brief mention of classical contributions to the sociology of time. The authors saw social time schedules as indispensable to the maintenance of societal integration and continuity. Since then, a sociology of the life course has emerged, attempting to link society's need for a division of labor with individuals' need for predictability and continuity. The latter was the focus of Bernice Neugarten's social psychology of the life span. There is little doubt that she struck a responsive chord. In our life journey and everyday activities, the need for predictable rhythms is compelling. How integral that predictability is for our sense of personal control and continuity of self becomes painfully clear when the socially created time structure of your own life begins to fall apart.

There are also strong potential gains from the dangerous opportunity of falling out of time, but that is another story—another paper.

## REFERENCES

Albert, S. M., & Cattell, M. G. (1994). *Old age in global perspective.* New York: G. K. Hall & Co.

Berger, P., Berger, B., & Kellner, H. (1973). *The homeless mind: Modernization and consciousness.* New York: Random House.

Blenkner, M. (1965). Social work and family relationships in later life, with some thoughts on filial maturity. In G. F. Streib (Ed.), *Social structure and the family* (pp. 46–59). Englewood Cliffs, NJ: Prentice-Hall.

Blythe, R. (1979). *The view in winter.* New York: Harcourt, Brace, Jovanovich.

Butler, R. (1968). The life review: An interpretation of reminiscence in the aged. In B. L. Neugarten (Ed.), *Middle age and aging* (pp. 486–493). Chicago: University of Chicago Press.

Cooney, T., Smyer, M. A., Hagestad, G. O., & Kock, R. (1986). Parental divorce in adulthood: some preliminary findings. *Journal of Orthopsychiatry, 58,* 470–477.

Durkheim, E. (1912). *Les formes élémentaire de la vie religieuse* [Elementary forms of religious life]. Paris: Alcan.

Elder, G. H., Jr. (1985). Perspectives on the life course. In G. H. Elder (Ed.), *Life course dynamics, trajectories, and transitions: 1960–1980* (pp. 23–49). Ithaca, NY: Cornell University Press.

Elias, N. (1987). *Über die Zeit* [Time: An essay]. Oxford: Blackwell.

Erikson, E. H. (1963). *Childhood and society* (2nd ed.). New York: Norton.

Erikson, E. H. (1982). *The life cycle completed.* New York: Norton.

Frank, A. W. (1991). *At the will of the body.* Boston: Houghton Mifflin.

Goffman, E. (1961). *Asylums.* Garden City, NJ: Doubleday.

Gutmann, D. (1987). *Reclaimed powers: Towards a new psychology of men and women in later life.* New York: BasicBooks.

Hagestad, G. O. (1984). The continuous bond: A dynamic, multigenerational perspective on parent-child relations between adults. In M. Perlmutter (Ed.), *The Minnesota symposium on child psychology: Vol. 17. Parent-child interaction and parent-child relations in child development.* (pp. 129–158). Hillsdale, NJ: Lawrence Erlbaum.

Hagestad, G. O. (1986). Dimensions of time and the family. *American Behavioral Scientist, 29,* 679–694.

Hagestad, G. O. (1992). Assigning rights and duties: Age, duration, and gender in social institutions. In R. Heinz (Ed.), *Theoretical advances in life course research: Vol. III. Status passages, institutions, and gatekeeping* (pp. 261–279). Weinheim: Deutscher Studien Verlag.

Hagestad, G. O., & Burton, L. (1986). Grandparenthood, life context, and family development. *American Behavioral Scientist, 29,* 471–484.

Hagestad, G. O., Smyer, M. A., & Stierman, K. (1984). Parent-child relations in adulthood: The impact of divorcing in middle age. In R. Cohen, S. Weissman, & B. Cohler (Eds.), *Parenthood: Psychodynamic perspectives* (pp. 246–262). New York: Guilford Press.

Hetherington, E. M. (1989). Coping with family transitions: Winners, losers, and survivors. *Child Development, 60,* 1–14.

Keith, J., Fry, C. L., Glascock, A. P., Ikels, C., Dickerson-Putman, J., Harpending, H. C., & Draper, P. (1994). *The aging experience.* Thousand Oaks, CA: Sage.

Lehr, U., & Schneider, W. (1983). Fünf-Generationen-Familien: Einige Data Über Ururgrosseltern in der Bundesrepublik Deutschland. *Zeitschrift fur Gerontologie, 5,* 200–204.

Levine, R., & Wolff, E. (1985, March). Social time: The heartbeat of culture. *Psychology Today,* 29–35.

Lyman, S. M., & Scott, M. B. (1970). *A sociology of the absurd.* New York: Appleton-Century-Crofts.

Lynch, K. (1972). *What time is this place?* Cambridge, MA: The Massachusetts Institute of Technology.

Mead, G. H. (1932). The philosophy of the present. La Salle, IL: Open Court.

Neugarten, B. L. (1969). Continuities and discontinuities of psychological issues into adult life. *Human Development, 12,* 121–130.

Neugarten, B. L., Moore, J. W., & Lowe, J. C. (1965). Age norms, age constraints, and adult socialization. *American Journal of Sociology, 70,* 710–717.

Neugarten, B. L., & Peterson, W. A. (1957). *A study of the American age grading system.* Proceedings of the Fourth Congress of the International Association of Gerontology, vol. 3, 1–6.

Plath, D. W. (1980). Contours of association: Lessons from a Japanese narrative. In P. B. Baltes & O. G. Brim, Jr. (Eds.), *Life-span development and behavior* (Vol. 3., pp. 287–305). New York: Academic Press.

Plath, D. W. (1982). *Arcs, circles and spheres: Scheduling selfhood.* Paper presented at the Midwest Regional Seminar on Japan, Richmond, Indiana.

Prins, A. H. J. (1953). *East African age-class systems.* Groningen, Netherlands: J. B. Walters.

Pruchno, R. A., Blow, F. C., & Smyer, M. A. (1984). Life events and interdependent lives. *Human Development, 27,* 31–41.

Romøren, T. I., & Hagestad, G. O. (1988, November). *Careers of care: A study of Norwegian oldest-old.* Paper presented at the annual meeting of the Gerontological Society of America, San Francisco.

Roth, J. A. (1963). *Timetables.* Indianapolis: Bobbs-Merrill.

Roth, J. A. (1983). Timetables and the life course in postindustrial society. In D. W. Plath (Ed.), *Work and the life course in Japan* (pp. 248–260). Albany: State University of New York Press.

Rubin-Terrado, M. (1994). *Social support and life satisfaction of older mothers and childless women living in nursing homes.* Unpublished doctoral dissertation, Northwestern University, Evanston.

Schutz, A. (1971). *Collected papers.* The Hague: Nijhoff.

Seltzer, M. M. (1976). Suggestions for the examination of time disordered relationships. In J. F. Gubrium (Ed.), *Time, role, and self in old age* (pp. 278–304). New York: Human Sciences Press.

Smith, L. (1983). *The kin-keeping roles of middle generation women in middle and later adulthood.* Unpublished master's thesis, Pennsylvania State University, State College.

Sofer, C. (1970). *Men in mid-career.* New York: Cambridge University Press.

Sorokin, P., & Merton, R. K. (1937). Social time: A methodological and functional analysis. *American Journal of Sociology, 42,* 615–629.

Strauss, A. L. (1959). *Mirrors and masks.* New York: Free Press of Glencoe.

Straw, P., & Elliot, B. (1986). Hidden rhythms: Hidden powers? Women and time in working class culture. *Life stories/Recits de vie, 2,* 34–46.

Tobin, S., & Lieberman, M. (1976). *Last home for the aged.* San Francisco: Jossey-Bass.

Whiting, J. W. M. (1981). Aging and becoming an elder: A cross-cultural comparison. In R. W. Fogel, E. Hatfield, S. B. Kiesler, & E. Shanas (Eds.), *Aging: Stability and change in the family* (pp. 83–90). New York: Academic Press.

Winsborough, H. H. (1980). A demographic approach to the life cycle. In K. W. Back (Ed.), *Life course: Integrative theories and exemplary populations* (pp. 65–76). Boulder, CO: Westview Press.

Zerubavel, E. (1981). *Hidden rhythms.* Chicago: The University of Chicago Press.

# Comments

## Vern L. Bengtson

unhild Hagestad's chapter is a brilliant example of what C.
Wright Mills (1959) has called the *sociological imagination:*
looking at individual behavior and life events in the context of
the social forces and institutional arrangements that shape them. She
presents a personal ethnography from what she describes as "an illness
journey," which took her as an accidental traveler (and sociological par-
ticipant-observer) to psychosocial places and social settings. There she
gained a new and highly personal understanding of what she had written
about early in her career as a scholar: the importance of social schedules
during the life course.

Hagestad's account is also a case study of how some of the most basic
conceptual tools of social psychological analysis—social norms, social
roles, reference groups, and social stratification—can be used to understand the social construction of the life course. These concepts are especially useful in assessing the negotiations of meanings that are required
when an individual must cope with life crisis events.

## SOCIAL NORMS

Hagestad begins by pointing out two underlying issues concerning the
social structuring of time: first, that humans have a fundamental need
for predictability and continuity; second, that this need is met through
socially constructed time rhythms and schedules of which we are often
unaware. During the course of our life these informal expectations can
become normative timetables, establishing when we are on-time and
off-time in life's journey.

Such temporal ordering is an example of social norms—the common expectations about what should or should not happen in the course of life. Sociologists point out that we can live without much awareness of the norms that govern our day-to-day interactions until they are questioned or violated: Then we become aware of, and are often perplexed by, departures from what we had considered normal in the life flow of events and interactions. This is what happened to Hagestad when she was confronted with a life-threatening illness at a relatively young age. Hers is a compelling illustration of the existence of age-related social norms continuing into middle and later life, of which we become aware only when they are confronted by off-time events.

## SOCIAL ROLES

Hagestad's chapter directs our attention to a second crucial sociological construct, social roles, and to their creation and maintenance within the context of temporal expectations. Roles can be defined as positions in a social structure with which normative expectations are associated. But as Goffman (1959) has suggested, roles—whether in real life or on the stage—involve a complex negotiation of socially constructed meanings. They constitute performances, including not only the prepared script (the part assigned), but also the individual role player (the actor's interpretation of the script) and those witnessing the performance (an audience, which changes over time).

Hagestad's account suggests how quickly an individual's ongoing performance of social roles—whether as university professor or friend or mother—can be suddenly threatened as a consequence of a critical and unscheduled life event, such as severe illness. The event disrupts the informal and taken-for-granted calculus of obligations, rights, and reciprocities associated with the previous pattern of role behaviors; it upsets expectations about the normal course of role performances and careers. Hagestad found herself suddenly thrust into an "illness role," with the script unwritten, the audience continually changing, and the actors uncertain.

Moreover, Hagestad's examples indicate how difficult the negotiation process can be in the restructuring of previous roles following recovery from the illness role designation. Her long-term student finishes the PhD with a colleague substituting as committee chair, with no one informing Hagestad of the change "because they did not want to bother her" in her illness. This again suggests a Goffmanesque carica-ture: The script, actors, and audience suddenly find themselves in dis-array, embarrassed by an unscheduled life event that has intruded into a common, previously rehearsed performance within university life.

## REFERENCE GROUPS

Merton (1968) coined the term *reference group* in the 1940s to indicate that we take on the standards of groups that are especially important to us in making evaluations concerning our own behaviors. Reference groups can be assigned (by birth) or achieved (through choices). They may be "significant others" (Merton, 1968), to whom we are intimate-ly bonded by ties of love or kinship; or they may be generalized social peers to whom we are more loosely connected by similar social status, age, gender, or interests (such as bird-watching, target-shooting, or pre-senting papers at the Gerontological Society's annual meetings).

Hagestad's account indicates how important reference groups are in our sense of an appropriate and desired life course, as well as how prob-lematic reference groups may be in the context of an unscheduled life event. On the one hand she recounts the examples of her father and grandfather, both living until their eighties, who spent their last years of life putting together their life stories, and who concluded that "life had been good enough, and long enough." She notes that the worst part of her off-time critical illness was not facing death, but the thought that she might not live to see her daughters as mothers; not share retrospec-tion of adult experiences with them; and might in fact be "tripping up" her children in their adult progress by her untimely death. These are powerful examples of the importance of the positive reference groups comprised of our significant others to the assessments we make of our life course progression, and how the challenge to our self-assessments when a life event such as a critical illness causes us suddenly to be off-time.

On the other hand, Hagestad's illness placed her temporally in another setting that involved a problematic reference group. She found herself in a convalescent hospital populated mostly by octogenarians, resulting in constant reminders that she was temporally misaligned. This made it difficult to talk to fellow residents about common experiences of fear and pain, and to deal with her own uncertain diagnosis; was she indeed dying, or just in transition during remission? She notes the "lack of a future" as a shared characteristic of elderly residents of nursing homes. She also notes that younger persons who are hospitalized as seriously ill without a clear diagnosis become labeled as "unmanageable and disorderly" if they overstay their time and question their treatment.

## SOCIAL STRATIFICATION

Karl Marx (1867/1967) created the first modern theory of how social categories (reflecting control over the means of economic production) influence individuals' behavior. Max Weber, several decades later, further operationalized social categories as the unequal distribution of power (position, privilege, and prestige) that determines social action, and developed analyses of authority and bureaucracy as case examples (Weber, 1904/1930). Hagestad's account reminds us of how pervasive social inequalities are, especially in terms of those at risk of off-time behavior. The medical staff are in positions of formal authority during her illness; yet they are powerless to confirm either a diagnosis or a course of treatment. Members of a powerful bureaucracy, they are just as helpless as she is to cope with the loss of an assumed, predictable future.

Her puzzling illness confronted Hagestad not only with a profound discontinuity with her previous life, but also as an example of how whole segments of the population grow up with so much chaos and so little order that "'planning' is a foreign word." In living with uncertainty, authorities become crucial. But often the authorities have little power; they too become impotent. This sets the whole order of social stratification on its head.

## CONCLUSION

Hagestad's account of her illness journey is an instructive case study in the social construction of time. Moreover, it illustrates how social norms, roles, reference groups, and stratification—key concepts in sociological analysis—both shape and are affected by the social construction of the life course. The continuities and discontinuities of development are reflections of these social forces, and we use them to negotiate the triumphs and tragedies of adult life.

# REFERENCES

Goffman, E. (1959). *The presentation of self in everyday life.* New York: Doubleday.

Marx, K. (1967). *Capital: A critique of political economy.* New York: International Publishers. (Original work published 1867)

Merton, R. K. (1957). The role set: Problems in sociological theory. *British Journal of Sociology, 8,* 106–120.

Merton, R. K. (1968). *Social theory and social structure* (Enlarged ed.). New York: Free Press.

Mills, C. W. (1959). *The sociological imagination.* London: Oxford University Press.

Weber, M. (1930). *The Protestant ethic and the spirit of capitalism.* New York: Scribner's. (Original work published 1904)

# CHAPTER 10

# Continuities and Discontinuities in Sibling Relationships Across the Life Span

## Deborah T. Gold

Family relationships are extremely important to the elderly. Unfortunately, studies of aging and family relations have typically paid little attention to the nature of sibling relations in old age. However, the small but growing literature focusing on the late-life sibling bond reveals that brothers and sisters occupy an important position in the lives of many older adults (e.g., Bedford, 1989; Gold, 1987, 1989b).

Recent research on the siblings of the elderly has characterized the nature of the bond between them and the significance of that bond. These studies have defined sibling relations in terms of *closeness.* Closeness has been found to be greater in dyads that include women, with pairs of sisters consistently reporting the greatest closeness (Cicirelli, 1988; Gold, 1989b). Unmarried siblings (i.e., never married, widowed, divorced) also report closer relations with siblings than do those currently married (Gold, 1989b). Further, sibling dyads defined as "closest" typically report more frequent exchanges of instrumental and emotional support (Cicirelli, 1980; Connidis, 1989; Gold, 1989).

Until now, studies of elderly siblings have relied on cross-sectional data. That snapshot of sibling interactions cannot address questions about the changing nature of sibling relations across the life span. In this study, retrospective data from a sample of elderly siblings are analyzed to examine potential changes in sibling closeness in adulthood. We would expect that feelings about and interactions with siblings would differ as an individual meets the challenges of adulthood. Adults face different psychological issues at different life stages (Neugarten, 1969), and these issues might have a strong impact on interactions with sisters and brothers. For example, in young adulthood, issues of intimacy and family formation are salient, and the development of the family of procreation takes precedence over the family of orientation. Middle age brings new issues relating to the creation of a legacy and to the development of relations with the young. Again, these issues keep individuals focused on the future rather than on the past. However, in late life, there seems to be some evidence suggesting that brothers and sisters return to a level of closeness not seen since childhood or early adolescence (Gold, 1989a, 1989b).

Adults also face a series of life events that are important in shaping the nature of sibling interactions. Some of these life events, such as marriage, parenthood, and employment, typically occur during young adulthood; others, such as the empty nest and parental death, usually occur in middle age. Finally, old age begins with retirement, and widowhood often follows; this is also the life stage in which death of siblings may occur.

It is not yet clear whether psychological issues or life events really have any impact on sibling closeness. Furthermore, we do not understand the ramifications of sibling closeness or lack thereof. The purpose of this study is to examine patterns of closeness between siblings in adulthood. Because psychological issues are difficult to define and operationalize, we focus on the association of age, demographic factors, and life events with sibling closeness. Four research questions are addressed. First, does sibling closeness change across the adult life course? Second, if change occurs, is it related to chronological age or demographic factors? Third, are there identifiable patterns of change in sibling closeness? And fourth, are specific life events associated with changes in sibling closeness in adulthood? A systematic evaluation of patterns of change in adult sibling closeness should establish a frame of reference in which sibling support in late life can be better understood.

# SAMPLE

We conducted lengthy individual interviews with 30 men and 30 women age 65 and over about their sibling relations across the life course. Most participants were identified through senior centers and health maintenance organizations in Chicago and its surrounding suburbs. Although the sample is not random, it does represent different ethnic, religious, and social backgrounds. All respondents were white, healthy, well-functioning individuals living independently. Most were middle-class as well. Potential respondents were excluded if they had never married, had no living siblings, were childless, or were twins. This precaution minimized the inclusion of older adults whose sibling relations had been enhanced by structural factors.

## METHODS

### Interviews

Each interview included both structured and open-ended questions designed to elicit perceptions about sibling interactions throughout life. Within the interview, each respondent discussed all of his or her sibling relationships. Thus, although there were 60 members of the sample (30 men and 30 women), the data reported here include 89 sibling relationships.

The interviews included multiple aspects of the sibling relations and were transcribed verbatim. Respondents began by briefly describing a current sibling relationship, then tracing each relationship from childhood through old age. At the end of the retrospective report on life course relationships, respondents reviewed the current nature of the relationship in detail. There are, of course, concerns about accuracy of retrospective data. In order to minimize the effects of selective memory, the data reported here are limited to the three adult life stages: young adulthood, middle age, and old age.

### Variables

Two independent raters read all interview transcripts and coded closeness on a 4-point scale for each of three adult stages. A score of 4 indicated unusual closeness between siblings. A score of 1 indicated no closeness in the relationship. Raters achieved 96% agreement on closeness ratings for the three adult life stages.

Other variables of interest include sex of respondent and sibling, age of respondent and sibling, education of respondent and sibling, marital status of respondent and sibling, number of siblings ever in the family, number of siblings alive at the time of the interview, and dyadic gender composition which indicated whether the dyad included sisters, brothers, or a cross-sex pair.

# FINDINGS

## Sample Demographics

Demographic characteristics of the sample members and their siblings are presented in Table 10.1. Mean age of both sample members and siblings was 73 years. Of the 89 sibling dyads, 51% had a female respondent, and 54% of the siblings were female. Both respondents and siblings were highly educated, with 77% of respondents and 53% of siblings having some college experience. Although no unmarried older adults were included as sample members, 5% of the siblings were never married, with 2% divorced and 30% widowed. Mean ratings of closeness for the sample as a whole increased during adulthood from 2.07 (SD=0.84) in young adulthood to 2.16 (SD=0.83) in middle age and 2.65 (SD=1.02) in late life. (The differences between the mean rating of the oldest group and those of the young adult and middle-aged groups are statistically significant at the $p<.05$ level.)

## Closeness

Changes in closeness were determined by comparing closeness ratings throughout adulthood. The many unique configurations of closeness reported by these respondents reflect the naturally occurring heterogeneity in the older population. In all, 68 dyads reported some change in sibling closeness during adulthood.

Respondents explicitly verbalized their pleasure at increased closeness. One man said of his relationship with his brother: "I feel closer now than maybe at any time in my life because he needs to be close; so do I." Several of the women commented that increasing sibling closeness as people aged was an expected change. One woman said of her interactions with her sister:

**TABLE 10.1  Demographic Characteristics of the Sample**

| Variable | % (n) | Mean (SD) |
|---|---|---|
| Age of respondent | | 73.35 (4.67) |
| Sex of respondent | | |
| Male | 49.4 (44) | |
| Female | 50.6 (45) | |
| Education of respondent | | |
| Less than high school | 6.7 ( 6) | |
| High school | 15.7 (14) | |
| Some college | 18.0 (16) | |
| BA–BS degree | 44.9 (40) | |
| Graduate degree | 14.6 (13) | |
| Marital status of respondent | | |
| Married | 64.0 (57) | |
| Widowed | 32.6 (29) | |
| Divorced | 3.4 ( 3) | |
| Number of siblings ever | | |
| 1 | 13.5 (12) | |
| 2–5 | 66.3 (59) | |
| 6–11 | 20.2 (18) | |
| Number of living siblings | | |
| 1 | 37.1 (33) | |
| 2–4 | 50.6 (45) | |
| 5–7 | 12.3 (22) | |
| Age of sibling | | 72.73 (7.18) |
| Sex of sibling | | |
| Male | 46.1 (41) | |
| Female | 53.9 (48) | |
| Education of sibling | | |
| Less than high school | 5.6 ( 5) | |
| High school | 41.6 (37) | |
| Some college | 10.1 ( 9) | |
| BA–BS degree | 30.3 (27) | |
| Graduate degree | 12.4 (11) | |
| Marital status of sibling | | |
| Married | 62.9 (56) | |
| Widowed | 30.3 (27) | |
| Divorced | 2.2 ( 2) | |
| Never married | 4.5 ( 4) | |
| Closeness | | |
| Young adulthood | | 2.07 (0.84) |
| Middle age | | 2.16 (0.83) |
| Old age | | 2.65 (1.02) |

I can remember the years when we were chasing our kids, keeping our houses clean, and playing bridge together one afternoon a week. I thought then how nice it would be not to have all those responsibilities—to be able to spend more time together.

Although the majority of respondents reported that change in sibling closeness was positive, 8% indicated that sibling closeness had decreased over time. One woman indicated that relations with her sister had been, in her words,

A disaster. We were close enough right after we married and were both having kids; I guess there was something to share. But it seemed that each year brought new things to argue about, new disagreements, and we just got further and further apart.

A retired architect commented about his brother, "When we were younger, we did things together—played golf or tennis . . . go fishing . . . Now we're strangers who don't give a damn about each other."

## Chronological Age and Demographic Factors

In this sample, there was no statistically significant relationship between chronological age and change in closeness. The correlation between these variables was 0.09 ($p$=.37) for respondents' age and 0.06 ($p$=.59) for siblings' age. As shown in Table 10.2, no statistically significant associations were found between change and the demographic factors of marital status, education, and gender.

**TABLE 10.2   Comparison of Change/No Change in Closeness Status by Demographic Variables**

| Variable | Chi square | df | $p$ |
|---|---|---|---|
| Gender of respondent | 3.41 | 1 | 0.07 |
| Gender of sibling | 2.09 | 1 | 0.15 |
| Marital status of respondent | 0.05 | 1 | 0.82 |
| Marital status of sibling | 0.27 | 1 | 0.60 |
| Respondent education | 0.01 | 1 | 0.92 |
| Sibling education | 0.01 | 1 | 0.96 |

## Patterns of Change

Although no two sibling relationships were identical in their patterns of change in closeness, three subgroup patterns could be identified. Respondents whose closeness was consistent throughout adulthood were categorized as the "no change" group (NoC; $n=32$). Second, respondents whose closeness increased in late life were classified as a "positive change" group (PosC; $n=41$), while those whose closeness decreased in late life were assigned to a "negative change" group (NegC; $n=16$).

Descriptive statistics for the three subgroups defined above are presented in Table 10.3. In both the NoC and NegC groups, respondents were predominantly male (63% and 56%, respectively). NegC siblings were more likely to be female (63%). In the PosC group, two thirds of the respondents were women as were 59% of the siblings. All groups included dyads with all three gender compositions (i.e., sisters, brothers, and cross-sex). In terms of marital status, the NoC and NegC groups included primarily married respondents and siblings. The PosC group also included divorced and widowed respondents. The subgroups did not differ in terms of respondents' ages, siblings' ages, or number of siblings alive. Mean ratings of closeness for the three subgroups (NoC, PosC, NegC) during young adulthood, middle age, and old age are also presented in Table 10.3.

The 32 respondents reporting constant closeness over time could be divided into two subgroups: stable close siblings and stable distant siblings. One stable close sister said:

> Our closeness has been the most important part of both our lives since I can remember. We have always had a special feeling for each other. I know that I miss her terribly on days when we don't talk. . . . even though those are few and far between.

Nearly half (44%) of the stable dyads are cross-sex dyads, and this gender mix may contribute to stability over time. Although cross-sex sibling dyads appear to have relationships more like those of sisters than brothers (Gold, 1989b), gender differences may set up artificial boundaries and predetermined limits on closeness. In other words, same-sex siblings may naturally be able to feel closer because of the homogeneity of their life experiences.

**TABLE 10.3 Demographic Characteristics of the No Change, Positive Change, and Negative Change Groups**

| Variable | NoC group (*n*=32) | PosC group (*n*=41) | NegC group (*n*=16) |
|---|---|---|---|
| | % (*n*) | | |
| Age of respondent | 74.0 (3.7) | 72.8 (4.9) | 73.5 (5.8) |
| Sex of respondent | | | |
| Male | 62.5 (20) | 36.6 (15) | 56.3 (9) |
| Female | 37.5 (12) | 63.4 (26) | 43.8 (7) |
| Marital status of respondent | | | |
| Married | 65.6 (21) | 61.0 (25) | 68.8 (11) |
| Widowed | 34.4 (11) | 31.7 (13) | 31.3 (5) |
| Divorced | | 7.3 (3) | |
| | Mean (SD) | | |
| Number of living siblings | 2.4 (1.6) | 2.5 (1.9) | 2.0 (1.4) |
| Age of sibling | 73.3 (7.3) | 72.0 (7.5) | 73.6 (6.4) |
| | % (*n*) | | |
| Sex of sibling | | | |
| Male | 56.3 (18) | 41.5 (17) | 37.5 (6) |
| Female | 43.8 (14) | 58.5 (24) | 62.5 (10) |
| Marital status of sibling | | | |
| Married | 59.4 (19) | 58.5 (24) | 81.3 (13) |
| Widowed | 31.3 (10) | 36.6 (15) | 12.5 (2) |
| Divorced | 3.1 (1) | 2.4 (1) | |
| Never married | 6.3 (2) | 2.4 (1) | 6.3 (1) |
| Gender composition of dyad | | | |
| Brothers | 37.5 (12) | 9.8 (4) | 18.8 (3) |
| Sisters | 18.8 (6) | 31.7 (13) | 25.0 (4) |
| Cross-sex | 43.8 (14) | 58.5 (24) | 56.3 (9) |
| Closeness | | | |
| Young adulthood | 2.03 (1.0) | 2.00 (0.7) | 2.19 (0.8) |
| Middle age | 2.03 (1.0) | 2.30 (0.7) | 1.94 (1.0) |
| Old age | 2.03 (1.0) | 3.17 (0.6) | 1.50 (0.6) |

## Life Events

Throughout the interviews, respondents experiencing significant changes in sibling closeness over time reported that those changes often occurred concurrently with major life events. Table 10.4 lists the major life

**TABLE 10.4   Life Events Associated With Changes in Closeness of Sibling Relations (*n*=57)**

| Life event | Percentage reporting change at that event (*n*) | Number positive change/Number negative change |
|---|---|---|
| First employment | 16 (9) | 7/2 |
| Marriage | 63 (36) | 9/27 |
| Birth of children | 37 (21) | 4/17 |
| Empty nest | 56 (32) | 27/5 |
| Marriage of children | 18 (10) | 6/4 |
| Birth of grandchildren | 21 (12) | 6/6 |
| Death of first parent | 42 (24) | 21/3 |
| Death of second parent | 95 (54) | 49/5 |
| Retirement | 51 (29) | 26/3 |
| Serious illness of sibling | 49 (28) | 24/4 |
| Death of a sibling | 54 (31) | 29/2 |
| Serious illness of spouse | 61 (35) | 31/4 |
| Widowhood | 81 (46) | 41/5 |

events that sample members associated with changes in sibling closeness. Young adulthood included three primary life events associated with changed closeness: the first job, marriage, and birth of children. In middle age, life events associated with changes in sibling closeness included the empty nest and marriage of children, parental death, and birth of grandchildren. Without question, the life event having the greatest impact on sibling closeness in midlife was parental death, with 95% of the sample reporting changes in sibling relationships when the second parent died.

Old age includes multiple life events, many of which are losses. Those events associated with changes in sibling closeness at this life stage include retirement, serious illness and death of a sibling, serious illness of a spouse, and widowhood. Retirement was a precursor to changes in sibling closeness for 51% of respondents reporting such changes. Serious illness and death of a sibling also affected sibling closeness, with over half of the respondents (54%) indicating that the death of one sibling affected closeness to others. Spousal illness and widowhood also were strongly associated with changes in sibling closeness, with 81% of respondents reporting changes in closeness at widowhood.

The nature of the changes in closeness also appears linked to the life event. Employment, marriage, and birth of children appear to lead to diminishing closeness, a change logical in light of the independence and intimacy goals of young adulthood. In this sample, marriage was associated with decreased closeness in 63% of relationships. One man told of his separation from his brother in young adulthood by saying,

> We had been close during our teen years, but the challenges of growing up—of becoming adults—interrupted our closeness. Instead of worrying just about ourselves and each other, we each had a job, a wife, and a family to worry about. We weren't as close any more, that's true, but we didn't hate each other either—we were running as fast as we could to keep up with things.

However, some sample members, primarily pairs of sisters, noted that the events of young adulthood led to greater closeness. A woman whose relationship with her sister had been moderately close during adolescence said:

> When each of us had our first child, it was as if we shared a remarkable experience that husbands and brothers couldn't understand. We were both adults, both doing the same things and having the same goals.

Because many of the female respondents in this study did not work outside the home, they may have had time for siblings in young adulthood that brothers or cross-sex dyads did not.

Middle age is not as clear-cut as young adulthood or old age in terms of major life events. The empty nest and marriage of children might lead sisters and brothers to think more about each other. As one man remarked about his sister,

> It helped our relationship when her children were out of the house and married. I don't think she didn't care about me during the earlier part of our adult lives—I think she just didn't have time!

On the other hand, birth of grandchildren might enhance vertical relationships in the family and emphasize intergenerational relationships again. A woman commented about her brother's interest in his grandchildren:

He pays much more attention to the grandkids than he ever did to his own kids. He carts them around, showing them off. I see him more than before, but I almost never see him alone. We can't talk when the kids are there; he just stands and beams at them. I'm sure when they grow up, we'll be close again.

As noted above, the impact of parental death on sibling closeness is profound, regardless of when that death occurs. The loss of the first parent often rallies siblings, particularly if the remaining parent is a dependent older adult. Although conflicts can arise over parental care, there still seems to be a sense of unity that grows when one parent dies. An oldest son with three younger sisters said:

We all worried about our mother, about how we could help her cope with being alone when Dad died. We worried about each other too. I never realized how powerful Dad was in our family. When he was gone, I stepped forward and told them that we needed to remember how important being brother and sisters was.

The loss of the first parent may serve as a warning to adult siblings of the temporal proximity of becoming the omega generation.

Although the death of the first parent has a powerful effect on sibling closeness, the death of the last parent is even more potent. This death finalizes the entry into the omega generation that was started by the first parental death, and individuals become more aware of their own mortality. Because a sibling is an age peer as well as a family member and is someone who experiences the transition into the omega generation at the same time, it seems intuitive to expect that sibling closeness would be enhanced at this time. The oldest of three sisters said:

When Mom finally died after a long and difficult illness, I thought it was up to me to try to stay close to my sisters. I was surprised—and pleased—when I realized that we all naturally looked to each other.

In addition, the youngest brother in a family of six said:

When our mother died, a big shift happened in our family. Instead of counting on Mom to arrange family gatherings or parties, we all realized we would have to do that ourselves. It's true that Emily [the oldest] has become a "surrogate Mom" and takes responsibility for remembering all the birthdays and arranging who would bring what for Thanksgiving dinner. But all of us feel closer.

But when a parent is the glue holding a family together, adult siblings can also drift apart when that parent dies. One man said of his siblings

When Mom died, it was as if our family just fell apart. I mean, the closeness I thought we shared seemed to evaporate. I would call my sister and brothers and ask if we could get together, but they weren't interested any more. Once Mom was gone, they couldn't see any reason for staying close.

Another man said:

We didn't deliberately try not to be close once our parents died. But no one organized holidays and family celebrations for the group, and each of us began to be with our own families and friends. I'm not sure anything can be done about it. You can't make people close again.

Like parental death in middle age, the life events of old age affect sibling closeness differently. The events mentioned by these respondents fall into three categories: job loss (i.e., retirement), sibling loss (illness or death), and spousal loss (illness or widowhood). Retirement was seen as an event typically associated with increased closeness in sibling relationships. A man who retired after working for 51 years at the same company said:

I was really worried as retirement came closer. What was I going to do all day? Who was I going to talk to? I also worried about losing my income because Social Security isn't a lot. But my brother had retired three years before me, and he's been terrific. We meet for breakfast every morning, and he's introduced me to a lot of people he knows who are also retired. We joined the seniors group together and go to some of those things pretty frequently. I wish he could help with the income end too, but he says he hasn't figured that out yet!

A woman says of her sister,

I never had a job, but Elizabeth always did. Before she retired, we had a hard time doing things together because her work was always in the way. But since she retired, we've been able to try new things. Time really helped make us closer.

Few respondents saw retirement as having negative consequences for their sibling relations. One man, however, said:

> My brother and I had been pretty close all along. I really thought that when we both retired, we could do some of the things we'd been talking about—like buying a boat together. I didn't realize that he and my sister-in-law would go gallivanting around and leave me sitting at home alone.

This man also said that his wife's death had limited his postretirement interactions with his brother. "We could have all four gone on trips. But I don't want to be a third wheel," he explained. Retirement may be a more potent factor in sibling closeness for older adult brothers and sisters who are not currently married.

Events that relate specifically to siblings also have an impact on sibling closeness in late life. Both the serious illness and the death of a sibling reportedly influence changes in closeness. A woman said:

> When Arthur had his heart attack, I was so scared. We hadn't been close earlier in our lives but had been getting closer since our children grew up. But I was so afraid that he would die before we had a chance to be as close as we could. I spent hours at the hospital. When he was able to leave, I convinced him to come to my house so that I could take care of him. I was really proud that he said yes.

The sense of potentially unfinished relationship business encouraged many of these older brothers and sisters to be closer.

When a sibling died, the impact was obviously on relationships with remaining siblings. A woman spoke of her sister's death and said:

> We were in shock—all five of us. She had been the youngest, the most outgoing, and to have her die just wasn't fair. But it did make us realize how valuable we were to each other. I'm certain every one of my brothers and sisters would say that we've become lots closer since Dorothy's death.

Issues of survivorship became critical as well. When parents and some siblings had died, the remaining sisters and brothers saw themselves as the perpetuators of the family name. One man whose two brothers had died but whose two sisters were still alive remarked:

I used to be flippant about my brothers and sisters, taking advantage of them always being there. But when Jack and Willard died, I realized that we weren't going to live forever.

A woman, one of two remaining siblings in a family of ten, commented:

We call every other day . . . sometimes every day. There's no one else left. We are the family survivors, and that's made us much closer.

Finally, spousal illness and widowhood served as a springboard for increased sibling closeness. Eighty percent of respondents reporting change said that widowhood was a precipitating event. Illness seemed to accelerate the reconfiguration of sibling relations. For example, one woman said:

When my husband became very ill, I just couldn't do everything for him . . . My sisters came over to stay with him when I needed to get out, to help me bathe him and change his sheets. Without them, he would have had to go to a nursing home.

Here, sibling closeness helped one wife avoid institutionalizing her husband.

Some of those respondents indicated that a sibling "took over" some spousal duties or provided emotional support that had previously come from a husband or wife. One woman indicated:

When my husband died, I had much more free time. I also had many more responsibilities, some of which I had never done before. My brother jumped right in and helped with taxes, checkbooks, lawn mowing . . . all the male things. His willingness to help made us closer, and I was glad.

One of the men remarked:

I thought that my life would end when my wife died. She had been my best friend and the person I always talked to. But Nancy was so sympathetic and understanding that pretty soon I started talking to her about my wife and my feelings. She's been a real blessing in my life, and I like to think that my caring about her has been good for her too.

The few respondents who felt that spousal illness or widowhood had resulted in decreasing closeness with siblings reported that their brothers or sisters had let them down during times of need. One woman said:

> When my husband died, I guess I expected my brother and sister to help, to be available, to give me some sympathy. In my opinion, they didn't. If I couldn't count on them in a crisis like that, I can't count on them for anything. We're finished.

Another woman felt that her sisters were self-centered when her husband died.

> All they could think of was them, what would happen when their husbands died. They didn't seem to have time to talk to me or help me. I thought I could depend on them, but I sure learned a hard lesson.

Although these few people felt that their siblings had betrayed them or let them down, distancing of siblings at spousal illness or death was a rare occurrence in this sample.

## IMPLICATIONS

Each sibling relationship described by respondents in this study has its own distinct configuration of closeness, affected by unique life experiences and individual personalities. Yet within this overall heterogeneity, changes in adult sibling closeness occurred in the majority of sibling relationships. Only 35% of the sample indicated no change. This NoC group was slightly younger than the two change groups and may not yet have experienced life events or intrapsychic changes that would lead to increased or decreased closeness.

Sixty-five percent of the sample did undergo change in closeness at some time during the adult phase of their sibling relationships. Chronological age and demographic factors appear to have little influence on changes in closeness. For some siblings, the changes occurred early in middle age as careers spiraled and family of procreation responsibilities soared. Others experienced changes in late life.

Does this examination of patterns of change in closeness of adult sibling relations permit us to extrapolate findings to issues of support exchange between siblings across the adult life course? Further, can we conclude that the impact of discontinuities in the form of life events clarify whether siblings can be counted on as sources of support in late life? This is a particularly salient issue for baby boomers who, as Seltzer (1989) said, have more sibs than kids as potential support providers. Presumably if siblings in late life are to be mobilized as part of a support network, their relations with sisters and brothers must, at minimum, not be negative.

We still have much research to complete before we understand the dynamics of late-life sibling relations. However, if discontinuities do trigger changes in sibling closeness, we need to examine the timing of those events in the lives of older adult siblings. Finally, we must determine why a particular life event influences one sibling dyad to grow more distant while influencing another sibling dyad to become emotionally closer.

## REFERENCES

Bedford, V. H. (1989). A comparison of thematic apperceptions of sibling affiliation, conflict, and separation at two periods of adulthood. *International Journal of Aging and Human Development, 28,* 53–66.

Cicirelli, V. (1988). Interpersonal relationships among elderly siblings. In M. D. Kahn & K. G. Lewis (Eds.), *Siblings in therapy: Life-span and clinical issues* (pp. 435–456). New York: Norton.

Connidis, I. A. (1989). Siblings as friends in later life. *American Behavioral Scientist, 33,* 81–93.

Gold, D. T. (1987). Siblings in old age: Something special. *Canadian Journal on Aging, 6,* 199–215.

Gold, D. T. (1989a). Generational solidarity: Conceptual antecedents and consequences. *American Behavioral Scientist, 33,* 26–43.

Gold, D. T. (1989b). Sibling relationships in old age: A typology. *International Journal of Aging and Human Development, 28,* 37–54.

Neugarten, B. L. (1969). Continuities and discontinuities of psychological issues into adult life. *Human Development, 12,* 121–130.

Seltzer, M. M. (1989). The three R's of lifecycle sibship: Rivalries, reconstructions, and relationships. *American Behavioral Scientist, 33,* 107–115.

# Comments

## Lillian E. Troll

F̲our issues interest me most in Deborah Gold's chapter on sibling continuities and discontinuities in later life. One is the relevance of her findings for my own interest, modified-extended family systems. Second is that of the persistent gender effects in research in this area. Third is life span and life events effects. And last but not least is the definition of the major variable, *closeness.* I might add a methodological point, that of unit of analysis: individuals or dyads.

The issue of family system dynamics comes up particularly in Gold's findings about the effects of parental death. In the 10 families I am studying, sibling ties seem to be major factors in continuity, although when I originally looked for such effects by focusing on the deaths of the omega generation on the next two generations, I did not find what I expected, the fragmentation of family systems along sibling linkages. Where there was indication of ongoing fragmentation or disintegration, these sibling separations seemed to have been in the works much before the deaths of the parents. Nevertheless, the strongest-linked family systems seem to be characterized by strong sibling ties, particularly in the second generation. Colleen Johnson (1982) noted, also, that Italian families, whose ties remain remarkably strong, have such strong sibling linkages. I think we need to look more closely at this relation between sibling bonds and extended family cohesion.

What is there, we keep asking, about women that makes them more prominent than men in relationship strengths? The findings here are thoroughly consistent with all the others in family and friendship studies. Why are two sisters closer than two brothers? Will future cohorts of women still carry the ball, or load, or burden of kinkeeping? Do cross-cultural studies shed light on this?

The life span and life event changes are interesting. Are they attributable to time and effort availability, to focus of attention, or to something else? Marriage is more important than career in young adulthood, but retirement is important later on. Johnson's (1982) work on the oldest-old adds another dimension. When both siblings are frail, their ties seem to weaken, at least so far as contact and help is concerned. Siblings in Johnson's study of San Franciscans over 85 do not seem to substitute for children in giving care and attention to the very old. This needs further study.

What do we mean by closeness? Is it attachment? Is it behavior or is it affect? Is it a kind of force that keeps people tied together regardless of their feelings for each other?

Finally, would it be possible to study these dyads as dyadic units instead of multiple individuals? If so, how could this be done?

## REFERENCE

Johnson, C. L. (1982). Sibling solidarity: Its origin and functioning in Italian-American families. *Journal of Marriage and the Family, 44,* 155–167.

# CHAPTER 11

# Modified-Extended Families Over Time: Discontinuity in Parts, Continuity in Wholes

## Lillian E. Troll

It has been said that higher level systems have a slower rate of change than lower level ones (Mesarovic, 1970). If that is so, then modified-extended family systems, into which individuals, dyads, and nuclear households are nested, should exhibit less or slower change than the component individuals, dyads, and nuclear units. That is, the whole would not only be greater than the sum of its parts but would also be more continuous than its parts. But is this true? Do family systems persist over time? Do these wholes endure while new component individuals arrive into the system by birth or marriage and leave by death or divorce, developing and changing insistently along the way? Do the systems persist as households wax and wane? This is the issue that I am addressing now by considering the histories of ten modified-extended family systems over a period of twenty years.

Some thirty-five years ago, when Bernice Neugarten encouraged me to return to the Committee on Human Development to finally complete a dissertation, I was introduced to Hess and Handel's *Family Worlds* (1959). This eloquent description of six family systems showed me how one could understand and portray what I had been observing in my clinical work with school children and their parents. It provided me a vehicle for my up-to-then fumbling efforts to counter the prevailing belief that strong family relationships were necessarily manifestations of pathology. This prevailing belief, based on our Western valuation of independence, is that close bonds between adults are symptoms of undesirable dependency. Only ties between spouses and between parents and young children are exceptions. My conclusions about the ubiquity and normality of family systems had evolved not only from my own observations but also from fortuitous contact with the work of Don Jackson and his colleagues in the Palo Alto Mental Research Institute, who were studying the families of schizophrenics. Finally, and just recently, Carlfred Broderick's *Understanding Family Process* (1993) helped me further with conceptual integrations. Unfortunately, both Hess and Handel's and Broderick's conceptions—as well as those of most other family-process students—have been restricted to child-rearing nuclear households. Anyone approaching families from the perspective of older people, as I have done over the past decades, finds such restrictions artificial and limited. Older people are also family members, and studying families as systems that encompass them leads one necessarily to consider systems larger than households or child-rearing units. It leads one to Eugene Litwak's (1960a, 1960b) construct of the *modified-extended family*, to systems that include a number of related households which maintain ties with each other even though they may not be near each other.

Further, after two decades of work on generations in the family, I wanted to expand from studies of dyadic or triadic relationships to larger units. I was struck by the major impact my mother's death had on me, even though she was 93 when she died and by all rules I should have expected and rehearsed for her loss. Considering Gunhild Hagestad's (1982) concept of alpha and omega generations and Victor Marshall's (1975) findings about calculations of mortality based on parental ages of death, I decided to look at the effects of deaths in the oldest (omega) family generation on the surviving generations. It made sense to study this within a framework of modified-extended families. Vern Bengtson graciously invited me to carve out family groups from his ongoing University of Southern California (USC) Longitudinal Study of Generations (LSG). Their data include responses from at least three members of each family, although no one had so far analyzed them by family systems. It is much easier to use statistical techniques with aggregated individuals and dyads than on slippery entities like family systems.

A major challenge in looking at family systems instead of at individuals and dyads is selecting appropriate variables. Broderick's (1993) description of the evolution of family-process theory from Parson's (1951) structural-functional theory lists some universal requirements for maintenance of social systems. I turned to Broderick's (1993) set of requirements necessary for the maintenance of social systems, a list he had derived from Parson's (1951) structural–functional theory. Although most of the requirements mentioned by Broderick as necessary for system continuity could apply to modified-extended family systems, some are more salient to this study than others. For example, the need to meet nutritional and biological needs, while certainly critical to family relations when small children and frail elders are considered, is probably a variable more central to system integrity and continuity of household or parent–child units than modified-extended family systems. On the other hand, the need to provide a sense of group loyalty seems critical. Broderick cites, as contemporary approaches to family systems theory, the requirements of interdependence of parts, boundary maintenance, and equilibrium maintenance. Pauline Boss's (1980) work on system boundaries is a heuristic example of the kind of variable that would be appropriate for measuring system continuity in modified-extended family systems. From Broderick's list, I have selected as variables system integration and shared culture and identity.

Like their component nuclear family systems, some modified-extended family systems are more integrated than others. Also like nuclear family systems, larger family systems tend to share a history and to have common themes and values, which provide a sense of group loyalty, identity, and morale. Broderick points out, however, that real families are idiosyncratic and adapt societal norms to their individual circumstances, varying widely in goals, styles of interaction, and structural anatomies. As I describe the ten modified-extended families in the USC LSG sample, I will touch on some of these requirements and variations.

## SAMPLE: THE TEN FAMILIES

The University of Southern California Longitudinal Study of Generations has surveyed three generations of adults since 1971. The ten families I have analyzed consist of grandparental couples and all their children and grandchildren. Information about spouses and great-grandchildren has not been looked at directly in the present report. Extensive and repeated survey protocols gathered from 1971 to 1988 are available for at least 6 members of each family, often many more. In addition, my assistants and I conducted face-to-face interviews with 18 members of the second and third generations in 1989 and 1990, so that information about each family comes from multiple perspectives.

The families include 112 individuals and, over time, at least 50 household units. As can be seen in Table 11.1, the grandparental couples had a total of 28 children (11 sons and 17 daughters) and 64 grandchildren (32 grandsons and 32 granddaughters). Because my original interest in the study was the effect of the deaths of the omega (oldest) generation on the surviving family members, the families selected in 1989 were those in which both grandparents had died. At that time, only 11 families fulfilled this requirement, and of this 11, only one did not wish to

**TABLE 11.1  Description of Gender-Generation Categories: Ten Families**

|  | G1 | | G2 | | G3 | |
|---|---|---|---|---|---|---|
|  | Men | Women | Men | Women | Men | Women |
| *N* | 10 | 10 | 11 | 17 | 32 | 32 |
| Born[b] | 1903 | 1908 | 1928 | 1930 | 1955 | 1955 |
| Married[b] | 1924 | 1924 | 1950 | 1950 | 1979 | 1977 |
| Age married[b] | 22 | 16 | 22 | 20 | 24 | 22 |
| No. marriages: | | | | | | |
| 0 | 0 | 0 | 0 | 0 | 14 | 5 |
| 1 | 6 | 7 | 5 | 9 | 16 | 18 |
| 2 | 4 | 1 | 4 | 6 | 2 | 5 |
| 3 | | 2 | | 1 | | |
| 4 | | | | 1 | | |
| No. divorces | 2 | 1 | 5 | 12 | 5 | 7 |
| No. children[c] | 29 | | 17 | 53 | 24 | 39 |
| Children per indiv.[b,c,d] | (2.9) | | (1.5) | (3.1) | (0.7) | (1.2) |
| Education[b] | H.S. | H.S. | H.S. | Some coll. | Some coll. | H.S. |
| Death[b] | 81 | 78 | | | | |

[a] Based on all family members about whom there is sufficient information.
[b] Medians.
[c] Men and women same in G-1.
[d] Children per individual.

be involved. As mentioned, the three rounds of survey questionnaires were distributed and returned by mail. Most of the questions were structured, but there were also a number of open-ended ones that produced valuable write-in comments. Most of the respondents in my addition to the study were interviewed at home for an hour or more, a few by telephone. All family members are white and largely of lower-middle-class origin. Relatively little socioeconomic or geographic mobility occurred over the twenty years. My analysis so far is qualitative and primarily impressionistic or inductive, based on the respondents' reports about themselves and their relatives.

Table 11.1 describes these 112 individuals, their median dates of birth and marriage, the numbers of marriages, divorces, children, and years of schooling. The three family generations of grandparent, parent, and child are remarkably synchronous with the three societal cohorts they represent. The grandparents, it can be observed, were born about the turn of the century, their children mostly just before the Depression, and their grandchildren during the "baby boom" of the 1950s. The grandparents died between the ages of 69 and 86, with a median age of 81. Only one of the second- and third-generation members died during the course of the study—a grandchild who was killed in an automobile accident together with her husband and two children—even though almost all the second-generation men had been in the military service during World War II, and many of those in the omega generation had been in World War I.

The demographic characteristics of gender-generation cohorts are consistent with those in the U.S. population. For example, the men are older and have slightly more education than their wives. The women's age of marriage went up from one generation to the next, as did the number of women employed. The number of divorces also went up by generation, and in the third generation there is a large number of never-married—almost half (44%) of the men and 5 (16%) of the women. Many of the grandchildren, both men and women, had experienced drug and alcohol abuse and some were addicted. In fact, one of the grandsons had been a "street person" for many years before his rehabilitation in a 12-step program. Others are still seriously addicted. Many of the third generation, including those originally Jewish and Catholic, had become religious fundamentalists, "born-again Christians." In other words, the experiences of these family members followed the history of their times.

# DISCONTINUITY

The changes in the individuals over the twenty years are largely predictable. The oldest generation expressed concerns in the first survey about health and retirement income. Even before that time, two of the grandmothers had died and their widowers remarried. Interestingly, both dead grandmothers were the only ones that had been foreign-born, one Italian and the other Costa Rican. Most of the grandparents had been closely involved with their children and grandchildren. Five of the grandmothers could be classified as kinkeepers until their health and vigor deteriorated. (I will talk more about kinkeeping later.) One of the widowers and the one grandfather who was divorced and remarried also served to keep their families united, perhaps by default. Two other grandfathers seemed more important kinkeepers than their wives, contrary to the findings of Rosenthal (1985) that kinkeepers are mostly women. The Italian grandfather decamped when his wife died; it was his daughter that took over her mother's role by taking her younger siblings into her home and keeping in close touch with them as they grew up.

Each of the 10 families started out with vigorous kinkeeping (Rosenthal, 1985). That is, there was at least one person in each system who spread the family news, arranged get togethers, and monitored needs for help. As the members of the omega generation eventually grew feeble and died, their children in the next generation seemed to move into their places, not only in family functions but also in developmental status. For one thing, they came to express the concerns about health and retirement income that their parents had earlier. In the first round of questionnaires, the members of this second generation had worried about their parents and their children; now they worried about themselves. Meanwhile, their children, the original third generation, who had initially, as teenagers, been concerned mostly about finding friends and spouses, moved to worrying about their marriages and their own children's behavior and future, just as their parents had expressed these concerns about them in the beginning of the study. As noted, 1 of these grandchildren died and 12 divorced. Seventeen of the original second generation, their parents, had divorced and many remarried. While 19 of the grandchildren had not married by their 30s, 7 were in their second marriages.

Table 11.2 describes some of the dyadic relationships. Change was endemic for the 70 marital couples in the sample. The general trajectory of relations went from honeymoon euphoria to midlife complaints of no communication and lukewarm ratings of mutual feelings, to later life helping, accepting relationships. Only 20% of the G1 couples could be said to have had a high-quality relationship (i.e., close, warm and enjoyable) while most of the G2 and G3 couples—those still together or remarried—seemed to, or said they did.

Dyadic relationships for all five kinds of dyads (marital couples, mother-son, mother-daughter, father-son, and father-daughter) are shown in Table 11.2. Table 11.2 does not include grandparent-grandchild relationships, however, although these were important in many cases.

**TABLE 11.2   Dyadic Relationships in 10 Families**[a]

|  | Quality[b] (%) | Communication[c] (%) | Continuity[d] (%) | Help[e] (%) |
|---|---|---|---|---|
| Couples |  |  |  |  |
| G1 | 20 | 70 | — | 70 |
| G2 | 77 | 62 | — | 100 |
| G3 | 65 | 73 | — | 94 |
| Mother/Daughter |  |  |  |  |
| G1–2 | 88 | 79 | 45 | 86 |
| G2–3 | 92 | 76 | 41 | 56 |
| Mother/Son |  |  |  |  |
| G1–2 | 45 | 37 | 45 | 36 |
| G2–3 | 71 | 82 | 58 | 55 |
| Father/Daughter |  |  |  |  |
| G1–2 | 75 | 31 | 47 | 47 |
| G2–3 | 29 | 43 | 43 | 71 |
| Father/Son |  |  |  |  |
| G1–2 | 44 | 40 | 54 | 54 |
| G2–3 | 50 | 60 | 50 | 50 |

[a] Based on dyads with enough information.
[b] Ratings by investigator based on self-reports and reports of family members: good, poor, can't tell.
[c] Good, poor, can't tell; % rated good by investigator.
[d] Percentage living in same area.
[e] Percentage reporting exchange of service.

The two sets of mother-child dyads show opposite trajectories over time. Most mothers and daughters had stormy relationships during the daughters' adolescence but close and friendly ones once the daughters left home, whether or not they married. In fact, consistent with the family literature, the female-female dyads surpassed others of parents and children in all relationship ratings. The mother-daughter ratings between the grandmothers and their daughters were different from those of the younger two generations only in that the daughters in the older dyads helped their mothers more. After all, older mothers are likely to need more help.

Most mothers and sons, on the other hand, had close, loving relationships in adolescence, as evidenced by the young men saying that the first person they would go to for help or advice was their mother. This is reminiscent of the findings of Kandel and Lesser (1972) about the differences between Danish and American youth in parent versus friend relationships. American high school boys, at least in the early 1970s, were closer to their mother than to their best friend. This relationship, though, became more distant as the youths matured.

As expected, most of the caretakers of the grandparents in their last years were their daughters. In one family, a son who lived closer to his parents than his sister assumed a major part of the role at the end, but his wife did most of the actual work. It should be noted that the father-child relationships showed little commonality. Some were close and some were not.

Changes in household composition went on continuously over the years. By the time of the first survey, few of the second or third generation members lived with the first generation, although the three grandfathers who had remarried—two widowed and one divorced—were living with their second wives' children from their previous marriages. All three of these men had married women about the ages of their own children or younger, so that they were really in child-rearing households.

The family I have called the "Army" family (see Figure 11.1) is an example of changing household composition. The grandfather, Adam, who once lived with his wife Hilda and their two daughters, later lived with his second wife Joan and her three children. After the divorce from Adam, Hilda later lived with her second and then her third husband and at different periods also with her daughter Nora and grandson Stuart. Nora lived successively with her first, second, and third husbands, with

Year
Born

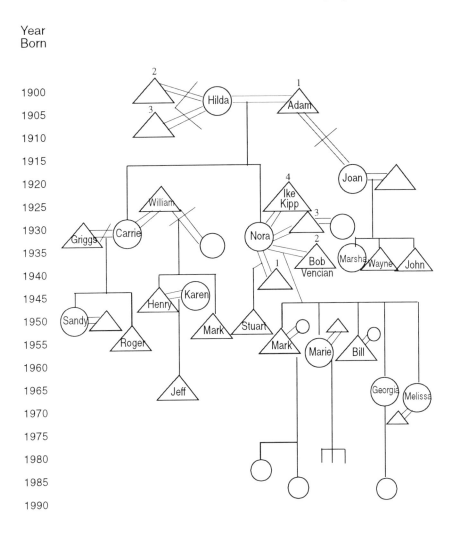

Figure 11.1   The Army family.

her son Stuart by her first husband, and then with her five children by
her second. Later Stuart lived on the street and later still with a girlfriend. His five half-siblings lived either with a friend, a spouse, or
alone, and three with their children, either alone with the children or
together with a friend or spouse.

Meanwhile, Nora's sister Carrie, who once lived with her parents before their divorce, later lived with her first husband and two children, then with her second husband alone, while her children lived with their father, and later alone with her second husband. Her second husband's children were living with their mother.

By the time of the first survey in 1971, Adam, now a grandfather, was living with his second wife, Joan; Hilda, his ex-wife, with her third husband; Nora, with her third husband and her five children from her second marriage; Stuart, alone; and Carrie, with her first husband and children. Twenty years later, Adam and Hilda were dead, Nora was living alone. Stuart was living with his girlfriend. Four of Nora's other children were living with a spouse, two of these also with children, and one daughter, Georgia, lived alone with her little daughter. Carrie was living with her second husband; her daughter, Sandy, with her husband and four children; and her son, Roger, alone. I have not mentioned many of the shifts in the intervening years. In 6 of the 10 families, grandchildren lived for varying periods of time with their grandparents instead of with their parents. This seems to have been true of Nora's children.

In the "Carr" family (Figure 11.2), the one with the most stable households and perhaps the most traditional lifestyles, the grandparents, Gus and Hope, lived together until Hope's death, when Gus lived alone until he moved into a nursing home together with his sister. Joe, Gus and Hope's oldest son, lived with his wife Mary, Mary's child Lois from her first marriage, and their joint children, Patty and Ed, until Lois, Patty, and Ed moved into their own quarters, followed by Lois' moving in with a boyfriend and subsequent husband. Ed was about to get married at the time of the interview.

Hope and Gus' daughter, Jill, lived at home until she married Ezra. They had four children, all of whom lived with them at the time of the first survey. By the time of the 1989 interview, three of their children were married and living with a spouse and children. Their fourth son, Peter, had just moved out from living with his homosexual lover, and now lived alone. Jed, Hope and Gus' third child, lived alone and had never married.

Obviously, in these ten families there were extensive individual and dyadic changes over the twenty years, much of it expectable development and aging, and much of it not. As noted, there was certainly enormous change in nuclear household units, some of it expectable.

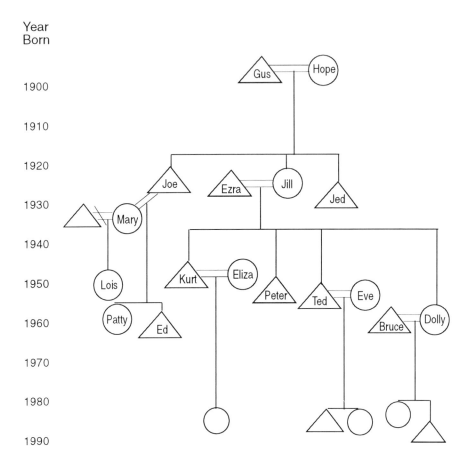

Figure 11.2   The Carr family.

## CONTINUITY

But while individuals, dyads, and households moved along different paths over the years, there was notably less change in the 10 family systems. In part, this continuity is to be expected. The initial selection process had ensured that there would be three generations in contact with each other. But in part, the continuity was unexpected because the premise of selecting families where the grandparents had died recently was that there would be a certain amount of fragmentation of the original structures consequent upon the loss of kinkeepers. I had intended to study the process of falling apart, expecting divisions along sibling lines in the absence of the glue provided by their parents, the omega generation. But I did not find what I expected—disintegration resulting from the loss of kinkeepers. Although some of the grandparents had died as long ago as eight years before our interviews with their children and grandchildren, fragmentation, when it was evident, seemed to have been integral to the systems almost from the beginning of the study. There had been unharmonious structures all along.

The family systems differ greatly in stability or integration. Table 11.3 ranks them in order of their integration at the end of the study, although as noted, this ranking was probably true much earlier. These paired-comparison rankings are my own global impressions based on family members' communications, contacts, and interest in each other. They might be called attachment indices, although "attachment" is generally considered a dyadic term, between individuals, and thus not a system measurement. In other words, I tried to assess the strength of the systems regardless of the strength of any individual or dyadic bonds within the systems.

At one end of the integration continuum is the Carr family (Figure 11.2), the most tightly knit, and at the other end is the Army family (Figure 11.1), the most disjointed. When Hope and Gus Carr were alive, the family was important to all three generations. Since their deaths, Jill Carr, their daughter, keeps in close touch with her two brothers and their children, and they all get together often. The sibling linkage is a principal axis in the Carr family unity, operating at all three generations. Hope and Gus remained in close contact with their siblings. Jill, Joe, and Jed were perhaps even closer. And the four children of Jill and Ezra were the same way, perhaps even the three children of Joe and Mary. Another important axis of linkage in the Carr family system is the parent-child ties, particularly for Gus and Hope and their three children and for Jill and Ezra and their four children. The link between Joe and Mary and their three children seems a little less strong, but only in comparison to the other ties in the family. As noted in Table 11.3, information about their family was given by all 12 primary members; all either had sent in questionnaires over the years or agreed to be interviewed later.

The Carr family culture is rich and detailed. They have family stories, which were recited to the interviewers by most of the respondents.

**TABLE 11.3  Ten Families**

| | Integration[a] (Rank) | Size (G1–3) (Median) | Information[b] (%) | Kinkeeper[c] | Hero[d] |
|---|---|---|---|---|---|
| Carrs | 1 | 12 | 100 | Hope, Jill | Kurt |
| Bergers | 2 | 8 | 100 | Ada, Bonnie | Boris |
| Firemen | 3 | 9 | 100 | Mollie, Mildred, Lucy | Mollie |
| Expatriates | 4 | 13 | 100 | Sheila, Janet | Arthur Jr. |
| Resenters | 5 | 12 | 100 | Lydia, Laura | Vincent |
| Beachboys | 6 | 13 | 77 | Mary, Linda | — |
| Hispanics | 7 | 16 | 56 | Francisco, Louise | Francisco |
| Italians | 8 | 15 | 67 | Valerie | — |
| Separators | 9 | 9 | 67 | Sonia, Helen | — |
| Army | 10 | 12 | 42 | Adam, Stuart | — |

[a] Paired comparisons; investigator's overall judgments based on Table 11.2 information.
[b] Percentage family members who have responded or been described in detail.
[c] Designated by several family members as person who spreads news, arranges get-togethers, and helps when needed.
[d] Designated by other family members in response to interview question.

258

One concerned the character of Hope, the grandmother, who was described by her children and grandchildren as a "dynamo"; some thought this was an admirable trait and others did not. Her career as a civil servant was reported by her in her initial survey questionnaire and repeated by her children and grandchildren in interviews twenty years later. Another was the story of the 100th birthday party of Hope's aunt. Still another was the history of Hope and Gus' siblings, parents, and aunts and the family migration from small towns in the Midwest to a small town in central California. All the homes visited had many photographs of family members, some in albums trotted out for the interviewer and others hung on walls and lined up on tables.

Although Joe had fought a lot with his parents in his youth, he remained in the same small town where he had grown up and where they lived, and was there to take care of them at the end of their lives. The Carr family system had heroes beside Hope. Jill's sons Kurt and Peter were the most notably successful, and this was respected. Kurt is the manager of a large ranch and his wife is a judge. Peter is a noted interior decorator. The family has supported a network of kinkeepers, starting with Hope, who was eventually aided by her daughter Jill, as later Jill was aided by her daughter, Dolly, and daughter-in-law, Eve.

The members' scores on the familism scales in the questionnaires were uniformly pro-family. Almost all believed family was important and all seemed to enjoy their frequent visits and celebratory gatherings. In fact, Jed, the unmarried G2 brother, spoke regretfully of the possibility that they might have to break up into more than one Christmas gathering because there were getting to be too many of them for one house. This family is so familistic that the boundaries are much wider than Hope and Gus' direct descendants. Their concerns and gatherings include the aunts, siblings, and cousins of Hope and Gus as well as Ezra's parents, siblings, nephews, and nieces. On the other hand, the in-laws of Joe, Dolly, Kurt, and Ted do not seem significant. Perhaps the involvement of Jill and Ezra's children in Ezra's family fertilizer business has something to do with the importance of his relatives to the other members of the Carr system.

Even in the Army family (Figure 11.1), however, which by my estimate is the least integrated of the 10, Nora and Carrie, the two G2 sisters, know more or less where the other sister and her children live, even though they seem to have no interest in communicating. Stuart, Nora's oldest son, and the closest to a family kinkeeper at this time, mentions his Aunt Carrie and cousins in his interview. The divorce of the grandparents, Adam and Hilda—before the onset of the study—certainly had to be a significant factor in the low integration of this family, plus Hilda's postdivorce move to the east coast. Actually, geographic instability consequent upon Adam's army career was characteristic of the family from the start. The split between Nora and Carrie happened when the sisters were young adults, probably not too long after their parents' divorce. Nora moved near her mother in the Washington, DC, area and Carrie stayed on the west coast near where her father retired at the end of his army career. It is curious that Carrie's children and stepchildren moved far away from her—her daughter to Hawaii and her son to South Africa—while Nora's children moved no farther than a state or two away from her. Fewer than half (42%) of Adam and Hilda's children and grandchildren were respondents in the study, compared with 100% of the Carr family members.

The function of keeping the family united was performed by the grandfather, Adam, while he was alive. He visited Carrie and her family and Nora and her's regularly, although not frequently. His last visit to Washington, a few months before he died, was very important to his grandson, Stuart, who shortly after joined a 12-step drug rehabilitation program and then worked to bring his mother and half-siblings into a family structure. He started keeping in touch with them and organizing birthday and holiday get togethers. At this point, in fact, he contacted the USC study and asked to be included back in as a respondent. Where one would call Adam the original kinkeeper, one would nominate Stuart as the present kinkeeper, at least of his—Nora's—branch of the family. As can be seen in Table 11.3, where the 6 most integrated families all mention heroes, the last 4 do not. There is no hero for the Army family, at least none its informers recognize. It is possible that I am wrong in calling this group of people a single family, that I should count it as two families, Nora's family and Carrie's family, with both of them low in integration. It is mainly the fact that they all acknowledge their relationship that qualifies them for consideration as a system, albeit a wobbly one.

Each of the families has unique systemic characteristics. The "Bergers," second highest in integration, show fluctuation of family attachment in individuals over time combined with continuity in overall system maintenance. Children moved away from their parents during their adolescence and then came closer again. Marriages were followed by divorces and remarriages. The fact that it is women who have done most of the kin-keeping may be a factor in this family's and in the Carr's overall strength. In fact, the two families where the grandfathers were the original kinkeepers, the Hispanics and the Army family, are in the lower half of the chart on integration. The Berger grandmother, Ada, was a dedicated kinkeeper in her time, close to her own parents and siblings and doing many things for her children when they were young. Family was very important to her. She traveled back and forth between Los Angeles and San Francisco when her daughter, Bonnie, moved there, and lived with her divorced son, Boris, after her husband died. Her granddaughter, Hester, who had, like her mother, rejected her family during her teens by dropping out of high school to marry and have a child, came to a turning point when she moved back from Los Angeles— where she had lived close to her grandparents and uncle—to San Francisco explicitly "to be near family," meaning her mother, stepfather, and sisters. As Ada's health deteriorated, Bonnie assisted her in kinkeeping and then took over the role with her own two older daughters, Hester and Martha, both of whom had followed her own pattern of dropping out of high school, early marriage, children, divorce, remarriage, and return to the family fold.

The family hero was Bonnie's brother Boris, who has a PhD in sociology and, in fact, is the only member of the family with any college education. The grandfather had been a radical hobo and then a taxi driver, the grandmother never worked outside her home, and Bonnie and her daughters were all artists who did not finish high school. Boris had been married briefly, but then divorced. He stayed close to his family throughout the years, living with his mother for a while after his father died and keeping the family house when his mother moved to San Francisco to live with Bonnie. Family boundaries seem to be tight, except for the inclusion of Ada's siblings. No other relatives are mentioned by respondents, neither Bonnie's in-laws nor those of her daughters, although Boris' friends are described as being at family gatherings. The beliefs of this family combine left-wing politics with high familism. Except for Boris, who seems mostly to be a community activist although he teaches at different colleges (but never gets tenure), the younger generations see themselves as artists.

The family I call the "Firemen" because so many of them are, is interesting because it has kept two geographic enclaves for many years, one in Los Angeles and the other in the state of Washington. Most of the family members have lived in both locations at one time or another, have visited back and forth over the years, but have enjoyed closer contact with those who live near them than with those who live in the other enclave even though the individuals at each location change from one year to the next. In other words, the individuals seem to be interchangeable. The Firemen are also interesting because two granddaughters who are cousins took over as kinkeepers from their grandmother toward the end of her life, both having lived with her in their childhood while their mothers were in the process of divorce. Mollie, the grandmother, is the family heroine and is described by her daughters and granddaughters as a saint, devoted to her family and protecting her daughters from the anger of her alcoholic husband. Her deathbed request that her two daughters patch up their quarrels and become friends seems to have been taken seriously. Both women mention this request and say they have tried to abide by it. The grandsons seem to be on the periphery of the family compared with the granddaughters and are seen by them as somehow pathetic. In-laws are also perceived as peripheral. The main axis of family structure is the female cluster of grandmother, daughters, and granddaughters.

The "Expatriates" developed two geographic enclaves (as did the Firemen) but their locations are not quite as interchangeable as the Firemen's locations. Arthur, the G2 brother, moved to Paris to become an artist after World War II and has remained there, but he traveled to Los Angeles regularly, visiting his parents as long as they lived, and his sister, Janet periodically thereafter. Janet and her husband visit Paris about once a year. Arthur's children came to California for their college educations, staying with one or another of their relatives, but none of Janet's children spent much time in Europe. The separation between the European expatriates and the Los Angeles branch does not seem to have affected the family unity, however. They all seem to feel that they are part of one family. There is some boundary stretching here, too, as among the Carrs, because Janet was the caretaker of Arthur's mother-in-law when she got old. Sheila, the grandmother, was the kinkeeper while she was alive, although a much more whimsical and poetic one than Ada in the Berger family, or than Mollie, the grandmother in the Firemen family. When Sheila died, her daughter Janet took over the role easily and seems still to be going strong. She names her youngest son as the kinkeeper because everybody goes to him with their problems, but all her five children seem highly involved with the family and it is uncertain who would take over the kinkeeping role from her. Her brother Arthur, a successful artist and author, is the preeminent family hero.

The "Resenters" is a curious family because its bonds seem to be the members' resentment and jealousy of each other. The grandparents were hostile to their two daughters-in-law because they were not Baptists but Catholics, and ostracized their oldest granddaughter because she had joined a charismatic sect. Their children resented them and each other. Their oldest daughter repeated the story of her mother's neglect of her eye injury when she was three years old that resulted in her blindness in that eye and inability to drive. She also dwelt upon her giving more help to her parents and brothers than any of her siblings had acknowledged or reciprocated. The sons resented their parents' and sisters' treatment of their wives and children. The youngest daughter in G2 was the least resentful, but complained that her brothers wanted to be considered part of the family now but had not done what they should to take care of their parents earlier. Yet, paradoxically, they all want to get closer to the others and be part of the family. The grandmother, Lydia, and her two daughters could all be considered kinkeepers, although William, the older brother, would like to have that role now that his wife is dead. The only grandchildren who seem to want to participate in the family are the two sons of Maisie, the younger daughter. Maisie and her children are all evangelical Christians and put such a high value on family that the sons have broken up with girlfriends who have not fit into their family. Martha, the oldest granddaughter, joined a sect that will not allow her to enter a church of any other denomination and therefore refused to go to her mother's funeral. This was resented by all. Her three children all moved out at a very young age—as had she and her father and uncle—and two of them went to live with her father, their grandfather. They have very little to do with her or their father.

In spite of their negative feelings, once could say that the Resenters have a family hero, Vincent, the younger brother in G2. He lived in exotic places and made more money than the others. They all seem to share the grandparents' values of religiosity and right-wing Republicanism and all wish they were rich, or at least richer.

In some ways, the "Beachboys" have a tighter system than the "Hispanics." Although the Carrs are largely small-towners, the other families are predominately urban, except for the Beachboys, who are almost all clustered in a beach town on the California coast. Many of the grandchildren earned their livings building surfboards. They surf and take copious quantities of drugs and play loud music. The grand-parents had worked for the post office in the same town, as did their daughter. Both sons in the G2 generation were in the navy; one still is. The great-grandmother was the family kinkeeper, and raised her daughter's two older children, Linda and George. Carlos, the grandfather, took over the kinkeeper role as he got older. The grandparents had married in their teens.

The women's movement came along at the right time for their daughter, Linda, because after three marriages and six children, one every year, she went to college and became a civil servant, and eventually mayor. At the time of the interview in 1989, she was uniting her family as much as she was able. Her older sons (from her first marriage), who had previously lived with their father, now either live with her or a house or two away. Her daughter lives with her while she is "pulling herself together" and studying for a master's degree, and one of her sons, who is gay and the only son with a college education, lives in Berkeley, working for the university. Linda has remained close to her younger brother throughout—they united in taking care of their mother after their father died—and they join in family rituals. Her daughter Joan has begun to assist her now in kinkeeping activities. None nominates a family hero. On the other hand, there do seem to be some system boundaries and they share the beach culture.

The remaining three families, the "Hispanics," the "Italians," and the "Separators" illustrate similar processes but each has its own distinctive flavor. Although they are all what might be called "ethnic" families, I am not implying that their characteristics are representative of their various ethnic groups, Hispanic, Italian, and Jewish. I will describe them briefly. Francisco, the grandfather in the "Hispanics" family, believed his family was supposed to cater to him. He said of his second wife at the first round of questionnaires, "What kind of woman could ever make me happy?" His first wife had died before that time, and he felt only a mild amount of responsibility for his four daughters and their families, only one of whom lived in San Diego near him. It was this daughter that the others nominated as the family kinkeeper, but their hesitation was seen in that they all gave as a reason, "because she lived near him." This is the most geographically dispersed family, with one daughter in Illinois and two others in the San Francisco area. Each of the daughters expressed interest in their father while he was alive and in their sisters after he died, but it was a mild interest. They kept in touch with each other, mostly by writing, rarely by visiting. The grandfather was nominated the family hero. "He was our father." In spite of his having been a teacher and something of an intellectual, his children and grandchildren seem determinedly middle-American. The system boundaries are highly permeable. Some of the grandchildren seem close to their parents, but others are drifting away, at least at this time.

The grandmother in the "Italians" family died in her 50s of diabetes, when her children were young. This was before the first round of questionnaires. Valerie, her oldest child, who had recently been married, took over her mothering role and raised her brothers and sister, staying in touch with them through the years. The grandfather, Guido, left Detroit after his wife's death and moved to California where he remarried. He did not seem overly concerned about his children, although his younger son, also named Guido, moved to Los Angeles when he was in his late teens to be near him. Guido Jr. never married. Valerie is also in touch with her six children and one grandchild; her youngest son was still living with her and her husband at the time of the interview. Valerie's older brother, Louis, divorced and then rejected two of his three children, even though they live in the same town. They are unhappy at the way he has rebuffed their efforts to get near him. Gina, Valerie's sister, lives in Germany but keeps in touch with the others, mostly by mail. This family is not very highly organized, but its members do seem to feel some kinship with each other. It would be hard to describe a family culture for them, unless it is one of religion, anger, and a scrabbling economic existence. All the respondents from this family talk a lot about money worries and health worries. None has more than a high school education and few have any marketable skills.

I called the final family the "Separators" because its members seem to go in for separating themselves from particular other relatives. Julius, the grandfather, was the youngest of ten children. He had been selected as a protégé by his one successful brother and brought to California to a job in the movie business. This was the extent of the two brothers' togetherness, and neither seemed to have much to do with the rest of the family in New York. Julius and Sonia had two children who separated from each other during their teens, with Lillian considered the good child because she had married well. Lillian stayed in close contact with her parents but her brother George tried to keep as far away from both his sister (and her children) and their parents as he could. George divorced his first wife and never saw her or their child again. He did not seem to know where his daughter was. His second wife was a widow whose small son, Terry, he adopted. She never had anything to do with her family or her first husband's family again.

The theme of separation was repeated by Terry, who felt much closer to his wife's family than to his own, but otherwise the theme of separation is much weaker in the third generation. Terry does keep in touch with his parents and siblings, Celia and Edwin. Celia and Edwin had both gotten married the year before the interview and these weddings were important family events, that is, in the family of George and his wife and children. In the interviews, both George and his wife emphasized that the family they were talking about did not include their Los Angeles relatives. George had moved to the Bay Area a few years before the interviews. His children were already living there and Celia, in her interview, talked about how her father did not welcome her efforts to "take care of him" before her mother moved up. George was thus separating himself from his children as well. Celia had invited her aunt, Lillian, to her wedding, which angered her father. Lillian did not come, but has been corresponding with Celia since.

It is curious that the efforts of George to separate from family have not been altogether successful. His wife, Helen, is a serious mother and his children are all attached to her and George, and to each other. They do not have much of a family culture, it is true. The grandfather was a skilled technician but George has been striving to make it as a salesman. On the other hand, two of the grandchildren, Celia and Edwin, are skilled technicians, somewhat like their grandfather. Celia, with a degree in art, makes models for detailed machine work and Edwin is an engineer in the Peace Corps. Terry sells musical instruments in Arizona and is an evangelical Christian like the members of his wife's family, even though his own family is Jewish. It is possible that the efforts of Lillian and Celia will bear fruit and pull the Separators together.

## FACTORS FOR CONTINUITY

As observed, while these ten families differ widely in system integration, even the least integrated seems to provide a sense of belonging. There is continuity over time in spite of individual development and generational changes. Two factors seem to me important for maintaining family system continuity. One is the commonality of family themes and values, the family's culture. The other is the active role of the family kinkeepers. The members of the most integrated, continuous families like the Carrs, the Bergers, and the Expatriates share stories, beliefs, and enjoyment of rituals. Members seem to want to maintain the system and tend to share in kinkeeping; they readily nominate family heroes. The members of the least integrated systems like the Italians, the Separators, and the Armys have few joint interests, and there are not a lot of them who participate in saving the structure. They are low on kinkeepers and do not think they have family heroes.

Female kinkeepers seem more effective than male. Seven of the ten kinkeepers in the first generation were the grandmothers, and these were the strongest knit families. When the grandmother became too feeble to carry on the work of spreading family news and arranging get-togethers, her daughter usually took over. In the Carrs, it was Hope, the grandmother, and her daughter Jill, who began to assume kinkeeping functions when Hope's mother started showing symptoms of dementia. The Bergers' kinkeeper was also the grandmother, Ada, who was succeeded by her daughter, Bonnie, when she lost her vision and became crippled with arthritis. Furthermore, in the later interviews, Jill's children were assisting their mother in these functions, just as Bonnie's daughters helped her. What is most intriguing is that in the Army family, Nora's oldest son Stuart, when he became rehabilitated, set to work bringing his mother and half-siblings together into a family group. They have begun to have gatherings at Christmas and Thanksgiving and a few birthdays. Stuart's grandfather, Adam, had been the Army kinkeeper—to some extent—when his ex-wife and daughter had both been too dysfunctional to serve. Restoration can also be seen in the Separators, for whom the granddaughter, Celia, now seems to be initiating communication with her aunt to bring the two separated branches together.

There are undoubtedly family systems that truly disintegrate. Some may just die out for want of new generations. But these ten modified-family systems, which had at least some integrity at the beginning of the study, have survived over more than two decades of USC's Longitudinal Study of Generations.

# REFERENCES

Boss, P. G. (1980). Normative family stress: Family boundary changes across the life-span. *Family Relations, 29,* 445–450.

Broderick, C. B. (1993). *Understanding family process: Basics of family systems theory.* Newbury Park, CA: Sage.

Hagestad, G. O. (1982). Parent and child: Generations in the family. In T. F. Field, A. Huston, H. C. Quay, L. Troll, & G. E. Finley (Eds.), *Review of human development* (pp. 485–499). New York: Wiley.

Hess, R. S., & Handel, G. (1959). *Family worlds: A psychosocial approach to family life.* Chicago: University of Chicago Press.

Kandel, D. B., & Lesser, G. S. (1972). *Youth in two worlds.* San Francisco: Jossey-Bass.

Litwak, E. (1960a). Occupational mobility and extended family cohesion. *American Sociological Review, 25,* 9–21.

Litwak, E. (1960b). Geographic mobility and extended family cohesion. *American Sociological Review, 25,* 385–394.

Marshall, V. (1975). Age and awareness of finitude in developmental gerontology. *Omega, 6*(2), 113–127.

Mesarovic, M. D. (1970). *Theory of hierarchical multi-level systems.* New York: Academic Press.

Parsons, T. (1951). *The social system.* New York: Free Press.

Rosenthal, C. J. (1985). Kinkeeping in the familial division of labor. *Journal of Marriage and the Family, 47,* 965–974.

# Comments

## Margaret H. Huyck

I
t is a pleasure to study this close analysis of a few of the complex family systems in the University of Southern California Longitudinal Study of Generations database. Lillian Troll has succeeded in preserving the family as the unit of analysis, as untidy as that often is. It is more tempting—and certainly more convenient—to aggregate the responses of members of each generation together, and hope that such aggregate analyses accurately reflect the ways that generations relate to each other. Troll has kept her analytic eye keenly on the ambiguities of each family system, relying on graphs and descriptions to help us understand the ways in which various members preserved, redefined, or defied what they construe as family traditions. Unfortunately, there are no reassuring statistics available that can either describe or summarize such patterns of continuity and discontinuity, at least to the satisfaction of qualitative researchers. It is a major challenge to develop such measures, so that we can move beyond marveling at the complexity of a small number of family systems.

It is also well to question how we can relate the construct of *attachment,* used by Troll, to Bengtson's construct of *family solidarity.*

Reading the descriptions of these families, I am reminded of an essay by Matilda White Riley (1983) some years ago, in which she suggested that we think of families not so much as "trees" but "networks of potential kin." Considering the realities of divorces, remarriages, and informal alliances with kin—recognized socially and/or legally—and with "ex-laws," Riley noted that individuals seem to be moving toward a system where kinship bonds can be evoked, left dormant, or even renounced, depending upon the needs and desires of each potential partner. This means that family boundaries may be much more fluid than traditionally assumed in theory, research, or family policy. The data that Troll summarizes suggests that both continuity and discontinuity are important, and that flexible family bonds may ultimately support family solidarity.

## REFERENCE

Riley, M. W. (1983). The family in an aging society: A matrix of latent relationships. *Journal of Family Issues, 4*(3), 439–454.

# CHAPTER 12

# Continuities and Discontinuities in Intergenerational Relationships Over Time

## Vern L. Bengtson

Issues of continuity and contrast between generations have been important to many theories in sociology and developmental psychology during the past half-century. Yet we have had very little empirical data by which to assess these issues, and we have lacked data to examine long-term consequences of generational continuity and contrast for either younger or older generation family members.

Most research on intergenerational relations to date has focused on the early stages of family development and the effects of parenting styles on child outcomes. Recently, however, the worldwide trends of population aging (caused by decreased mortality and decreased fertility during the 20th century) and their consequences for the informal "contract across generations" have created some new issues in the age-old problem of intergenerational relationships (Bengtson, 1993). In response to these trends scholars have emphasized the need for empirical investigations concerning long-term relationships between parents and children over time, and their consequences for the well-being of family members over several generations (Hagestad, 1987a, 1987b, 1988; Hill, Foote, Aldous, Carlson, & MacDonald, 1970; Neugarten, 1968).

In this chapter I want to summarize some results from one research program on long-term intergenerational relationships, the Longitudinal Study of Generations, which has been fielded at the University of Southern California since 1971. Over the past two decades colleagues and I have been examining several issues concerning continuities and contrasts across generations:

1. In what ways do cross-generational family relations change over time, and in what ways do they exhibit continuity? How much of the change is due to the individual development and aging of family members, and how much is due to broad sociohistorical trends?

2. How do individual family members' personal attributes—values, sociopolitical attitudes, marital happiness, health, and well-being—change or remain stable over time? What effect do these changes have on intergenerational relationships?

3. Is there a connection between intergenerational solidarity and family members' well-being? Does this relationship change from adolescence through middle adulthood and later life?

The Longitudinal Study of Generations (LSG) is a study of linked members from some 300 three- and four-generation families as they have grown up and grown old over the last quarter of a century. Based on responses from over 2,000 family members (grandparents, parents, adult grandchildren, and, now, great-grandchildren), the study provides micro-social data concerning effects of earlier family relationships on later patterns of interaction and support, and macro-social trends on family intergenerational relationships.

The first section describes the design, methods, and procedures of the LSG. The remainder of this chapter summarizes findings concerning the three project research questions outlined above. Section two reviews continuities and changes in dimensions of intergenerational family solidarity across two decades of time. Section three presents examples of how attributes of individual family members reflect continuity or contrast since 1971. The fourth section examines consequences we have observed of family change for individual well-being over time.

# METHODS AND PROCEDURES

## Population and Sample

The study began in 1971 with 2,044 respondents, aged 16–91, representing over 300 three-generation family lineages. Eligible sample members were recruited from the families of probable grandfathers randomly selected from the membership of a large (840,000-member) pioneering health maintenance organization (HMO) in the southern California area; the HMO was designed initially for steelworkers and their families following World War II. The sample pool was generally representative of economically stable labor union heads-of-households in the area during the postwar period; in consequence it is about 75% white and of working-class origins (for details see Bengtson, 1975). In 1971 self-administered questionnaires were mailed to the grandparents and their spouses, their adult children, and their adolescent or young adult grandchildren over age 16.

The data collection design is summarized in Figure 12.1. The study became longitudinal when funding was awarded by the National Institute on Aging (NIA) in 1985 to support a follow-up survey of the original respondents 13 years after the original data were collected. The response rate in 1985 for the Time 2 survey was 68%, a high figure after more than a decade of no contact with respondents. Since then, surveys have been repeated every 3 years, in 1988, 1991, and 1994. Thus the study has now followed members of the same families over almost a quarter of a century and over five waves of survey measurement.

Table 12.1 summarizes the number of participants at each survey wave through 1991 (responses from the 1994 wave are at this writing still being received and will not be described in this chapter). At Time 1 (1971) the baseline sample included 516 grandparents (G1, average age 67), 701 parents (G2, 44 years), and 827 grandchildren (G3, 19 years). Of the 2,044 respondents who participated in 1971, 47% ($n$=953) remained as study participants in 1991, of whom 820 participated at all four waves of data collection. Most of the data to be presented in this chapter are from this four-wave longitudinal sample. Sample attrition has been due principally to death or incapacity of older-generation respondents; the 20-year longitudinal response rate is 60% (953/1,584).

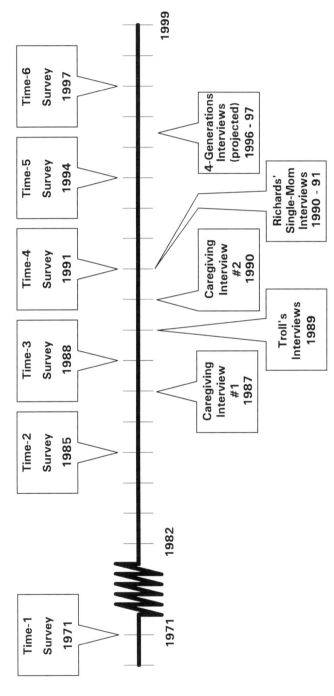

Figure 12.1. Survey and interview data collection in the Longitudinal Study of Generations.

**TABLE 12.1 Number and Average Age for Cross-Secitonal and Longitudinal Respondents in the Longitudinal Study of Generations, 1971–1994 by Gender**

| | Cross-Sectional | | | | | | | | | | Longitudinal | |
| | Time 1 1971 | | Time 2 1985 | | Time 3 1988 | | Time 4 1991 | | Time 5 1994* | | Sample 1971–1991 | |
| | $N$ | $\bar{x}$ Age | $N$ | $\bar{x}$ Age | $N$ | $\bar{x}$ Age | $N$ | $\bar{x}$ Age | $N$ | $\bar{x}$ Age | $N$ | $\bar{x}$ Age |
|---|---|---|---|---|---|---|---|---|---|---|---|---|
| *G1:* | | | | | | | | | | | | |
| Male | 266 | 68 | 91 | 79 | 64 | 81 | 44 | 83 | 27 | 86 | 34 | 84 |
| Female | 250 | 66 | 130 | 77 | 111 | 79 | 93 | 83 | 75 | 86 | 76 | 83 |
| *G2:* | | | | | | | | | | | | |
| Male | 322 | 46 | 243 | 59 | 240 | 61 | 204 | 65 | 213 | 68 | 147 | 65 |
| Female | 379 | 42 | 313 | 56 | 327 | 59 | 291 | 62 | 311 | 64 | 220 | 62 |
| *G3:* | | | | | | | | | | | | |
| Male | 385 | 20 | 226 | 33 | 313 | 36 | 297 | 40 | 280 | 43 | 122 | 40 |
| Female | 442 | 19 | 328 | 33 | 427 | 35 | 401 | 39 | 386 | 41 | 221 | 39 |
| *G4:* | | | | | | | | | | | | |
| Male | — | — | — | — | — | — | 82 | 20 | 111 | 22 | — | — |
| Female | — | — | — | — | — | — | 117 | 20 | 179 | 22 | — | — |
| *Total N:* | 2,044 | | 1,331 | | 1,482 | | 1,529 | | 1,582 | | 820 | |

*Results for 1994 survey are incomplete and are not discussed in this chapter.

The sample has been augmented cross-sectionally by the addition of spouses of the grandchild (G3) respondents as they married, and of their children (the great-grandchildren, G4s) as they turned age 16.

## Attrition Bias and Generalizability

In every longitudinal study it is necessary to assess the extent of non-response bias (Campbell, 1988; Schaie, 1983): whether those remaining in the study over time are different from those who have "dropped out" due to death, incapacity, or refusal, leading to potential problems in interpreting results. When we conducted attrition analyses comparing longitudinal respondents to those who have died or dropped out of the survey, results indicated only two significant differences: (1) for all generations, drop-outs were more likely to be male than female; and (2) drop-outs had a slightly lower level of education than longitudinal respondents.

Because the original sample was not derived from a nationally representative population, it has also been necessary to test whether results from our study are generally similar to those based on national probability samples. We compared distributions on our measures to similar information from three national data sets: the American Association of Retired Persons (AARP) Study of Intergenerational Linkages, a national random probability sample of 1,500 adults (see Bengtson & Harootyan, 1994); the 1986–87 National Survey of Families and Households (NSFH), a national survey of 13,017 randomly selected adults (see Sweet, Bumpass, & Call, 1988); and the nationally representative General Social Survey data from the early 1970s (Roos, 1985).

Results indicated that the distributions on attitudes, contact, and cohesion reported by members of our sample were very similar to those derived from national probability samples, as were occupational distributions (analyses on specific dependent variables are reported in Acock & Bengtson, 1980; Glass, Bengtson, & Dunham, 1986; Roberts & Bengtson, 1993; Silverstein & Bengtson, 1991). Thus, while the study population does not reflect a national probability sample demographically representative of the American population, it does not appear to be atypical when compared to distributions on key variables used in other nationally representative samples.

## Survey Measurement

The LSG surveys from 1971 to 1994 have included a number of measures for examining continuities and discontinuities in intergenerational relationships. The key constructs measured by the survey are summarized in Table 12.2. The reliability and validity of the measures reflecting these constructs have been extensively examined, and the citations in Table 12.2 are relevant for assessment of measurement properties. The most comprehensive analyses have been conducted on the six family solidarity variables, as reported by Mangen, Bengtson, and Landry (1988) and Bengtson and Roberts (1991).

---

**TABLE 12.2   Key Constructs and Their Measurement in the Longitudinal Study of Generations**

1. Six dimensions of intergenerational solidarity: affect, association, consensus, normative, functional, structural (Bengtson & Roberts, 1991; Bengtson & Schrader, 1982; Mangen, Bengtson, & Landry, 1986; Roberts, Richards, & Bengtson, 1991)

2. Family conflict (Clarke, Preston, Raksin, & Bengtson, 1993; Giarrusso, Silverstein, & Bengtson, 1990; Parrott, Giarrusso, & Bengtson, 1994)

3. Family caregiving (Gatz, Bengtson, & Blum, 1990; Mellins, Blum, Boyd-Davis, & Gatz, 1993)

4. Sociopolitical attitudes—conservatism, gender ideology, religiosity (Glass, Bengtson, & Dunham, 1986)

5. Value orientations (Bengtson, 1975; Roberts & Bengtson, 1988, 1994)

6. Psychological well-being (Baker, Cesa, Gatz, & Mellins, 1992; Gatz & Hurwicz, 1990; Gatz & Karel, 1993)

7. Self-esteem (Roberts, 1990; Roberts & Bengtson, 1993)

8. Physical health (Silverstein & Bengtson, 1991)

9. Position in social, occupational, and economic hierarchy (Biblarz, Bengtson, & Bucur, in press)

10. Perceptions of "generation distance" and "generational equity" (Bengtson & Murray, 1993; Bengtson & Parrott, 1994)

11. Life events (Hurwicz, Dunham, Boyd, Gatz, & Bengtson, 1992)

## Qualitative Analyses

The discussion of LSG methods so far has focused on the longitudinal survey design and its quantitative measurement. Equally important are the qualitative analyses from the LSG sample, which only recently have come into publication.

The collection of in-depth interview data from LSG families is indicated in the bottom portion of Figure 12.1. In 1988 Margaret Gatz and her colleagues began collecting extensive interview data from a subsample of 16 multigenerational families who were caregivers of health-dependent G1s, as well as a "control" group of 14 families who were not yet caregivers but, because of the advanced age of the G1s, were likely to become so soon (Gatz, Bengtson, & Blum, 1990). They conducted follow-up interviews with the family members in 1990 (Mellins, Blum, Boyd-Davis, & Gatz, 1993). In 1989 Lillian Troll developed an innovative study to examine effects of the death of the oldest ("omega") generation on surviving members of ten multigeneration families. She started by examining the survey protocols available since 1971 for six or more members of each of the families; then she conducted extensive interviews with members of the second and third generation (Troll, Chapter 11 in this volume). In 1990 Leslie Richards conducted telephone interviews with a subsample of single mothers and fathers from the G3 (grandchild) generation concerning the stresses and satisfactions they experienced in their single-parent role (Richards & Schmiege, 1993).

In 1993, Judith Richlin-Klonsky began an intensive case study of one of the families in our sample, using both quantitative survey responses and data from the 1988–1990 interviews to construct a portrait of multigenerational family change over two decades. Karen Pyke has similarly used both the caregiver and noncaregiver family interview data to identify different family caregiving orientations and their effect on the quality, experience, and meaning of family eldercare (Pyke & Bengtson, 1995). Richards, Bengtson, and Miller (1989) analyzed responses to open-ended questions in terms of the comments of G2s—the generation in the middle—on problems of intergenerational obligations and satisfactions with aging parents on the one hand and young adult children on the other. Clarke, Preston, Raksin, and Bengtson (1993) used open-ended survey responses to examine conflict issues within multigenerational families, developing a promising typology of intergenerational conflict issues.

Thus the combination of quantitative and qualitative methods is an important research agenda in the LSG design strategy, although one on which we are only beginning to capitalize. While most of the results summarized in this chapter focus on quantitative survey data, the qualitative analyses of family processes and conflicts—such as those Lillian Troll describes in Chapter 11 in this volume—may provide the most concrete evidence of intergenerational continuities and discontinuities.

# STABILITY OR CHANGE IN SOLIDARITY

In what ways do family intergenerational relations change over time, and in what ways do they exhibit continuity? This is the first of the three general research questions around which the LSG has been designed. Since the study now represents over two decades of longitudinal data for analysis, we can begin to examine long-term continuities and discontinuities in various aspects of intergenerational family relationships over time. We can also test the adequacy of the conceptualizations we held in 1970 against data collected over twenty years later.

## Dimensions of Intergenerational Solidarity and Conflict

Where does one begin in examining the complexities of intergenerational interaction? One of the concerns we have grappled with since the study began in 1971 is conceptualization of the several dimensions of adult intergenerational relationships, and their adequate measurement in survey research. We use the construct of *intergenerational solidarity* to characterize the dimensions of interaction, cohesion, sentiment, and support between parents and children or grandparents and grandchildren; we use *intergenerational conflict* to describe their negative, conflictual, or nonaffirming dimensions.

When the study began we conceptualized adult intergenerational solidarity as having three components (Bengtson, Olander, & Haddad, 1976). The first we termed *affectual solidarity,* the sentiments or evaluations regarding relations with other family members. The second component was *associational solidarity,* defined as the type and frequency of interactions shared between generations. Third was *consensual soli-*

*darity,* the degree or perception of agreement in opinions, values, and orientations between generations.

We further hypothesized that these theoretical components were interdependent although mutually reinforcing behaviors in intergenerational interaction, following social psychological theories of Homans (1950, 1961), Heider (1958), and Festinger, Schachter, and Back (1950). Atkinson, Kivett, and Campbell (1986) subsequently tested the hypothesized interdependence of these constructs on data from their North Carolina study. They found, however, no evidence that these reflected a unitary, higher-order construct of intergenerational solidarity, as our initial theorizing had indicated. Our own subsequent analysis (Roberts & Bengtson, 1990) of baseline (1971) LSG data confirmed this finding, but suggested an alternate causal model of relationships between variables: that affectual and consensual solidarity were highly correlated, and that affect predicted association.

In the meantime we had concluded that the dimensions of intergenerational solidarity were more complex, requiring at least three more concepts to describe them (Bengtson & Schrader, 1982). The additional dimensions we defined included *functional solidarity* (the giving, receipt, and exchange of tangible assistance and social support between parents and children); *normative solidarity* (expectations regarding social support, familistic values, and filial obligations); and *structural solidarity* (the "opportunity structure" for intergenerational interaction, reflecting the number, gender, and geographic proximity of members in the intergenerational family network). The theoretical rationale for these six dimensions and the adequacy (or limitations) of their measurement in survey research have been described at length in the volume by Mangen et al. (1988) and in subsequent journal publications from the project (Roberts, Richards, & Bengtson, 1991; Silverstein, Parrott, & Bengtson, in press).

From the evidence that is accumulating we conclude that our conceptualization of family intergenerational solidarity in terms of six distinct dimensions—affect, association, consensus, functional support, normative obligations, and opportunity structure—appears to have justification in terms of both theoretical and measurement criteria. These are, to be sure, not the only nor perhaps the best way to characterize the behavioral-emotional interactions between adult children and their parents, but they can be empirically defended and have been proven useful. A number of subsequent analyses using these intergenerational solidarity components with other data sets further suggest the utility of this conceptualization (see, for example, Andersson & Stevens, 1993; Lee, Netzer, & Coward, 1994; Morioka & Aoi, 1987; Rossi & Rossi, 1990; Starrels, Bould, & Nicholas, 1994).

At the same time, a quite different and theoretically orthogonal dimension of intergenerational relationships—conflict—must also be considered. Conflict reflects negative emotions, interactions, and expectations between adult children and parents (Bengtson, Rosenthal, & Burton, in press; Clarke et al., 1993). We are only beginning to explore this dimension. Initial findings suggest that, over the years, some parent–child interactions may reflect what we term "long-term lousy relationships" over many decades. Our estimate is that this is true in about one in eight of the adult intergenerational relationships in our sample. At the same time, other parents and children may consistently reflect very high levels of intergenerational solidarity over decades of time; this is true of perhaps two out of three parent–child relationships in our sample.

## Affectual Solidarity and the Intergenerational Stake Hypothesis

In the pilot testing 25 years ago for the 1971 survey, we were struck by what appeared to be a generational bias in perceptions. Why were parents and children so far apart in their views of their common relationship? Why were descriptions of relationships downward in the generational chain—toward children—consistently more positive than reports of relationships upward toward parents?

With Joe Kuypers, a fellow graduate student and gerontology trainee in the Committee on Human Development under Bernice Neugarten, I began to speculate about this. We came up with what we called the *developmental stake hypothesis* to explain these findings (Bengtson & Kuypers, 1971). Our data indicated that middle-aged parents consistently reported higher levels of closeness, interaction, and consensus in the parent-child relationship, relative to the perceptions of their adolescent and young adult children, who reported lower levels. We suggested that such systematic contrasts may emerge because each of the generations have different developmental concerns, and in consequence a different investment or stake in their mutual relationship. We reasoned that the developmental stake of the older generation centers on continuity and transmission, while the quite different developmental stake of the younger generation focuses on autonomy and innovation. The contrast between these developmental stakes provides the mechanism for differences observed between parents and young adult children in perceptions of their common solidarity.

Twenty years later, we revisited what we now call the *intergenerational stake hypothesis* with longitudinal data (Giarrusso, Stallings, & Bengtson, 1995). Our goal was to examine whether the phenomenon of generational bias persists over time, with the aging of parents and their now middle-aged children. These data, summarized in Figure 12.2, suggest several things about the perceptions of affect between members of family generations over two decades.

First, note that the affectual solidarity average scores—based on a six-item index with high internal reliability—are high, and considerably over the expected midpoint of the scale: Response distributions are skewed in the positive direction. Second, the mean scores are remarkably consistent over the four measurement points. There are no significant differences between 1971, 1985, 1988, and 1991 for any of the intergenerational dyads; correlations over time are between .5 and .8. Third, there is indeed empirical support for the intergenerational stake hypothesis: parents consistently report higher affect than their children, and the magnitude of such difference does not change much from one time of measurement to another. The same is true for grandparent–grandchild dyads, though the grandparents' perceptions of affectual solidarity are considerably higher than grandchildrens' at each point of time. The results reported above have led to a healthy discussion about the measurement of intergenerational relations and the theory used to explain such differences (see Marshall, 1995; Rossi, 1995; and the comments by Gunhild Hagestad that follow this chapter).

Other dimensions of intergenerational solidarity over time show a remarkably similar pattern to those of affectual solidarity across generations. Figure 12.3 summarizes data on consensual solidarity, the perception of similarity between generations in orientations and outlooks. These results indicate three things: a high level of perceived intergenerational agreement, considerably higher than the midpoint of the scale; high stability in scores over time; and parental perceptions of consensus that are significantly higher than those of children at each measurement point, over twenty years of data collection.

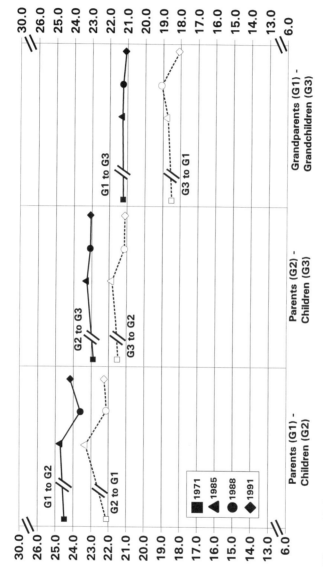

Figure 12.2. Affectual solidarity scores, 1971–1991: G1 (grandparents) and G2 (children); G2 (children) and G3 (grandchildren); G1 (grandparents) and G3 (grandchildren).

283

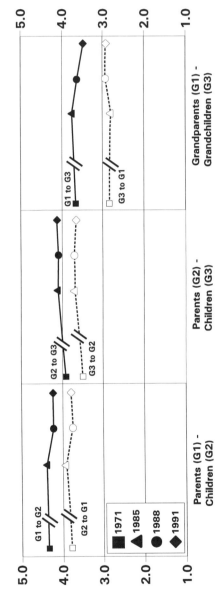

Figure 12.3.   Consensual solidarity scores, 1971–1991: G1 (grandparents) and G2 (children); G2 (children) and G3 (grandchildren); G1 (grandparents) and G3 (grandchildren).

The mirror image of this trend can be seen in the measure of inter-generational conflict, a three-item scale which has been included in LSG surveys since 1988 (see Figure 12.4). While there are relatively low levels of conflict perceived by each of the generational dyads, the younger generation consistently perceives more conflict than do older generation family members.

## Relationships Among Dimensions of Intergenerational Solidarity

Other analyses have explored relationships among the dimensions of par-ent–adult child solidarity, in order to empirically test their antecedents and outcomes. Silverstein et al. (1996) examined factors that predis-pose middle-aged sons and daughters to provide support for older par-ents, looking at longitudinal relationships among affectual, normative, associational, and functional solidarity. The analysis focused on pre-dictors of functional solidarity—the propensity of adult children (G2s and G3s) in the 1991 survey to provide support to their aged parents (G1s and G2s) in household chores, transportation/shopping, financial assistance, information and advice, or help when the parents are sick. We were especially interested in hypothesized differences between adult sons and daughters in providing support to elderly parents.

Figure 12.5 summarizes the results (in order to simplify, we present only mother–daughter and father–son models; the results for mother–son and father–daughter dyads are substantially similar). Results indicate that provision of instrumental support from daughters to mothers is related to previous support to parent, frequency of contact, and levels of affection. Sons appear to provide support based more on perceptions of obligation (normative solidarity) while daughters seem to be moti-vated somewhat more by perceptions of closeness (affectual solidarity). Moreover, the expectation of an inheritance from the mother is nega-tively related to the social support provision for daughters, whereas it is positively related for sons and fathers.

The results of this analysis suggest confirmation of gender differ-ences in adult child support patterns for aging parents: While daughters appear to be influenced by intimacy and altruism, sons are influenced more by normative principles, familism, and the expectation of financial reward implicit in the endorsement of intergenerational inheritance.

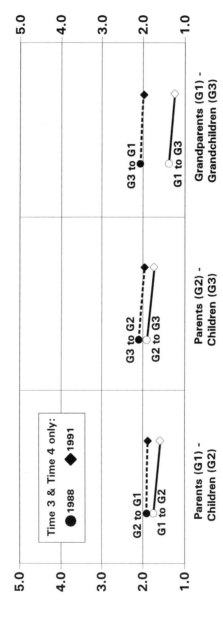

Figure 12.4.   Perceived conflict scores, 1971–1991: G1 (grandparents) and G2 (children); G2 (children) and G3 (grandchildren); G1 (grandparents) and G3 (grandchildren).

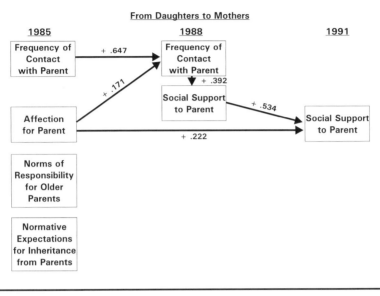

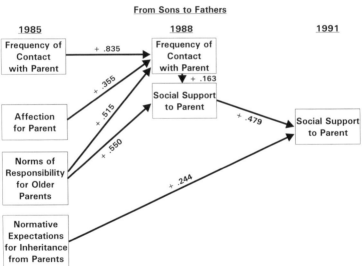

Figure 12.5. Predictors of social support provided by sons and daughters (controlling for parents' gender, health, and marital status).

## CONTINUITIES AND DISCONTINUITIES IN INDIVIDUAL FAMILY MEMBERS

The second general question of this longitudinal research program concerns the life course development of younger and older members of multi-generation families over time: how the personal attributes and well-being of individual family members exhibit continuity or change, and what effects these changes have on family intergenerational relationships. Now that we possess longitudinal data, we can begin to examine these questions. In this section I want to summarize two studies to date: long-term consequences of G3s' political activism in the 1960s, and long-term trends in occupational status transmission during the past half-century.

### Long-Term Family Effects of 1960s Political Activism

The 1960s have been described as the "decade of protest" in 20th century American history, and many of the G3 (grandchild) generation in our sample were involved in the demonstrations and civil disobedience activities of this era. What are the long-term effects of such activism on the lives and subsequent family relationships of these youth? Is youthful activism a temporary rebellious episode from which youth emerge to eventually follow traditional middle-age pursuits? Compared to non-activists, have they experienced a distinctive family "career" in terms of subsequent marriage and parenthood?

Dunham and Bengtson (1992, 1994) explored these questions by identifying 143 G3 former political "activists" and 341 nonactivist "traditionalists" on the basis of their responses to the 1971 LSG survey, when they were about age 20. The activists subsample was defined on the basis of self-reports (having been involved in a demonstration or participating in protest groups during the 1960s). The analysis examined responses of the two groups 13 years later, in the 1986 survey, when they were about age 34 and had achieved many of the social attributes associated with middle adulthood: education completed, career begun, marriage contracted, and parenthood begun. We assessed the effects of activism, gender role attitudes, and education on the subsequent timing of family life course events in mid-adulthood.

Our findings indicate pervasive continuities over the early adult life course for those who engaged in political activism as youth, as well as some enduring contrasts with their nonactivist generational cohorts. First, youthful activists delayed childbearing significantly compared to nonactivists (holding constant factors such as level of education and family background). Second, activist women had fewer children, or delayed having more than one child, compared to nonactivists. Third, there were persistent differences in gender role attitudes for both men and women over time, with activists expressing more nontraditional sex role orientations.

The results of this analysis lend support to two central tenets of the emerging *life course* theoretical perspective on the family (Bengtson & Allen, 1993; Elder, 1975, 1985, 1994; Hagestad & Neugarten, 1985). The first is that there are crucial contextual effects on family decisions that are both sociohistorical and sociostructural, and that these must be considered in modeling or explaining family behaviors across the life course. The second is that there are important within-cohort (as well as between-cohort) differences in family transitions and relationships over time, and some of the within-cohort differences may be caused by contrasting subcultural experiences—such as youthful political activism or conventionality. The next step of this investigation is to examine the consequences of youth protest lifestyles on the next generation of family members (the G4s in our study design) and to see whether the G4 children of G3 activists or traditionalists differ in their own individual and family life course trajectories into adulthood.

## The Transmission of Occupational
## Achievement Across Generations

One of the central concerns of the LSG project has been the transmission of values, statuses, and behaviors from one generation to the next, and the impact of major social changes of the 20th century on family transmission. For example, an analysis of 1971 survey data examined three-generation members down intrafamily lineages, comparing the "generation gap" in values between parents and children in the 1940s and 1950s with the generation gap in values between parents and children in the 1960s and 1970s (Bengtson, 1975). The results indicated considerable value similarity between parents and children in both intergenerational dyads. Generation membership did not seem to condition the impact that parents' values had on their children's values.

Biblarz, Bengtson, and Bucur (1996) have employed a similar conceptual framework to study within-family socioeconomic attainment and the intergenerational transmission of socioeconomic levels over time. We compared the level of inheritance of occupational stratum experienced by three successive generations of offspring in the LSG: grandparents (Generation 1, or G1s), who inherit great-grandparents' (Generation 0, or G0s) socioeconomic positions; parents (Generation 2, or G2s), who inherit G1s socioeconomic positions; and adult children (Generation 3, or G3s), who inherit G2s' socioeconomic positions (the analysis of a fourth generation, the G4s, is currently under way).

We focused on the implications of four 20th century social changes—expanding universalism, a shift in child-rearing values from obedience to autonomy, the growth of alternative family structures, and changing gender role attitudes—for intergenerational social mobility. In our analysis we predicted that (1) generation would be associated with socioeconomic position independent of age (each successive generation would have higher occupational attainments than the one before); and (2) generation would condition the effect of parents' socioeconomic position on children's socioeconomic position (the effect of parents' statuses on children's occupational outcomes would decline with each successive generation). The specific hypotheses of this analysis, and the results, are summarized in Table 12.3.

We found that each successive generation of offspring in the LSG sample had higher occupational attainment than the one before, but the rate of upward mobility slowed across generations. Our findings suggest that future generations (e.g., members of "Generation X," the G4s) may have a more difficult time doing better than their parents. Also, the association between parents' socioeconomic stratum and children's socioeconomic stratum weakened across generations (independent of structural shifts in the distributions of occupations). Members of G3 were less likely than G2s (who, in turn, were less likely than G1s) to stay in or remain near the same socioeconomic stratum they were born into. In the language of Bengtson's (1975) original paper, the generation gap in social class position seems to have widened. This pattern suggests a decline in family transmission of social position to offspring, indicating, perhaps, an increasingly meritocratic opportunity structure. However, our results also suggest that the level of occupational segregation faced by every successive generation of women has remained constant over the past half-century.

**TABLE 12.3  Summary of Hypotheses and Results**

| Hypothesis | Result |
|---|---|
| 1. The association between socioeconomic origins and socioeconomic destinations will decline with each generation. | *Supported.* The odds of ending up in the same socioeconomic stratum as one's parents were strongest for G1s, weaker for G2s, and weakest among G3s. |
| 2. Each successive generation will have higher occupational attainment than its predecessor. | *Supported.* The G2s and G3s were (equally) less likely than the G1s to hold manual occupations, but the G3s were more likely than the G2s (who (were, in turn, more likely than the G1s) to hold upper nonmanual occupations. |
| 3. The effect of gender on occupation will go down with each generation. | *Not supported.* The segregation of women into female-typed occupations remained constant over three generations. |
| 4. Sons will be more likely than daughters to inherit their fathers' occupational stratum. | *Supported.* Holding constant gender differences in the distributions of occupational origins and destinations, the odds of inheriting father's socioeconomic stratum were higher for sons than for daughters. |

# FAMILY SOLIDARITY AND INDIVIDUAL WELL-BEING

The third general question of the LSG program of research concerns the relationship between intergenerational dynamics and individual well-being. With our longitudinal data we are beginning to assess one of the most important but frequently untested premises of life course developmental theory: that there are consequences of family solidarity for physical and psychological health that are important for both younger and older generation members, as each generation develops and ages over time.

## Influence of Intergenerational Social Support on Older Parents

To what extent does the quality of life of aged individuals hinge on the quality of their intergenerational family relationships? Is there any support for the notion that longevity of aged parents is related to the solidarity and support of their adult children? It has been argued that families in postmodern society have become less important for satisfying basic social needs of older relatives because intergenerational families have become less socially and economically interdependent. Does the absence of social forms of assistance from adult children adversely affect the psychological well-being of elderly parents?

Silverstein and Bengtson (1994) used LSG data to compare the change in well-being among older parents who are socially and emotionally supported by their children to that of older parents who are not supported by their children. We then examined whether social support from adult children moderates the decline in psychological well-being that is often associated with physical decline and widowhood.

Our results indicate two things. Instrumental and expressive support were related, although weakly, to short-term (three-year) changes in positive and negative aspects of psychological well-being. More important is the finding that both types of support help to moderate the declines in well-being associated with poor health and widowhood.

We concluded that the psychological benefits of intergenerational support and solidarity are contingent on the vulnerability of the older parent. Vulnerability both raises expectations assistance and predicts their greatest benefits. This finding has important implications for family theory and policy: adult children who are actively involved in supporting vulnerable parents should be encouraged to continue their actions through incentives and services that provide support and relief to their parents.

## Consequences of Family Change for Individuals

That families change over time is obvious. How and why they change, and with what consequences for individual family members, are questions that can be addressed by longitudinal data using the life course theoretical perspective (Bengtson & Allen, 1993). This can be seen in an analysis of one large, multigenerational family in our LSG panel, the "Potters" (Richlin-Klonsky & Bengtson, 1996).

Data about the Potters came from four survey assessments between 1971 and 1991 and from extensive interviews with some family members in 1987 and 1990. This case study suggests what may be an enduring theme of multigenerational family life: "drifting apart" and "pulling together" in response to individual, developmental, and family events (Richlin-Klonsky & Bengtson, 1996).

The Potters' multigenerational family structure in 1971 when the LSG began is depicted in Figure 12.6. The primary subject is G1 Robert Potter Sr., aged 69, a house painter who had divorced his first wife, Leah, the mother of his three children, two decades earlier. The Time 1 survey data came from him, his second wife Elaine, and his three G2 children: Robert Jr. (then aged 45), Roberta (aged 43), and Maria (aged 38). In addition, seven grandchildren (G3s) provided responses to the 1971 survey—including Maria's 19-year-old son, David, who filled out his survey from prison.

Based on their individual responses to our 1971 survey, this was not a family with high intergenerational solidarity. The three G2s reported relatively little contact with their father, and not much affection for either him or his second wife; nor did there seem to be much contact between the G2 siblings. Each family member seems to have drifted apart from Robert Sr. after his divorce from Leah, their mother (and grandmother), though they remained in close contact with her.

Twenty years later in our longitudinal study the Potter family structure is even more complex, as seen in Figure 12.7. In the G1 generation Robert Sr. is still alive at the age of 89, having outlived both Leah and his second wife, Elaine. In the G2 generation Robert Jr. has died, as has Roberta's third husband. In the G3 generation there have been marriages, divorces, remarriages, and one death (David's, at the age of 38, after his release from prison). A G4 generation of young adults has emerged. And there are at least two G5s, great-great-grandchildren in Robert Sr.'s lineage.

What can be summed up about the Potter family's relationships over time, given the many changes in their intergenerational structure and interactions over two decades? From what is by now a voluminous body of survey and interview data about the many Potters, we conclude that one characteristic theme of this family is its "drifting apart":

All in all, as we view them over time, this seems to be a family beset by troubles of various kinds, from both inside and out. Interpersonal antag-

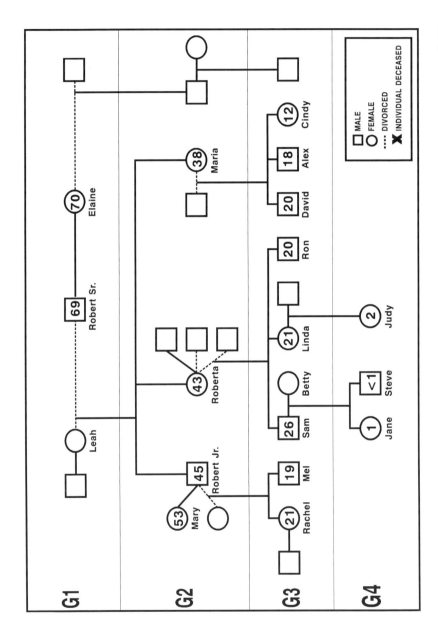

Figure 12.6. The "Potter" multigenerational family at the beginning of the study in 1971. Numbers indicate the age of those who responded to the survey.

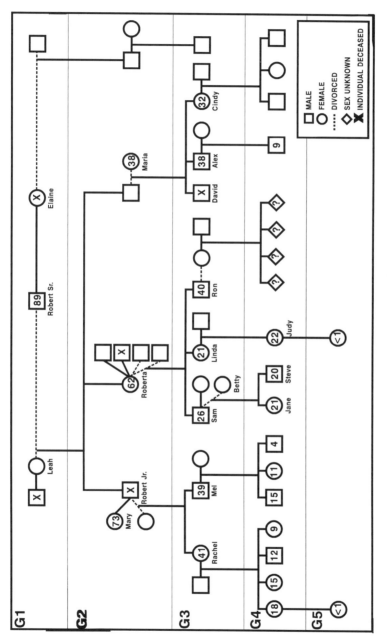

Figure 12.7.  The "Potter" family 20 years later in 1991.

onisms alienate members within and between generations. The G1 divorce (Robert Sr.) generates a split among family factions. Members are distracted by financial worries and disagree over values and lifestyle. These are among the issues which play a role in the family "drifting apart." (Richlin-Klonsky & Bengtson, 1996, p. 402)

On the other hand, an equally prominent theme concerns how family members "pull together" toward each other at times over the past two decades. Despite the emotional distance that characterizes relationships among many of the Potters, there are individuals and family subgroups who express much affection and respect for each other. Reflections of family solidarity connecting members both between and within generations are seen in several contexts: caregiving of ill or dependent family members; "kin-keeping" efforts; a tradition of spending holidays together.

The serious medical problems that have been pervasive in all generations of the Potter family since 1971 are a primary focus of members' coming together: G3 Ron's many surgeries, G2 Ron Jr.'s emphysema and death, and G1 Leah's sickness (it is interesting that G3 David, after his release from prison, was the family member who moved in to undertake full-time care of his biological grandmother). And, over time, the family's "taking turns" in tending for dependent members is evident: when G2 Roberta, who has been the primary caretaker for Leah, moves out of state, her sister Maria takes over—and reconciles with her father, Robert Sr., at Roberta's instigation.

Third, studying the family both vertically and horizontally over time provides significant insight into the remarkable variability of intergenerational relationships, and how they can change over time.

The Potter family demonstrates that levels of interpersonal closeness—of solidarity—are neither consistent across the many relationships which constitute a family or constant over the years they share together. At any given point, some members' lives are closely woven together, as they actively share care-giving alliances or family tradition. Others hang on by a thread, connected to the family by their relationship with just one other member. (Richlin-Klonsky & Bengtson, 1996, p. 409)

This study represents a rare attempt to examine a large multigenerational family as a whole over a longitudinal perspective. Notwithstanding episodes of antagonisms and apathies among the Potters, something members recognize as "family" seems to have been maintained through a variety of elastic bonds as members drift apart and pull together over time.

## SUMMARY AND CONCLUSIONS

The USC Longitudinal Study of Generations now has over two decades of data from some 2000 individuals representing three, four, and now five-generation families. These data suggest the following conclusions about continuities and discontinuities in intergenerational relationships:

1. The "intergenerational stake" phenomenon is consistent over time and across generational dyads: parents' perceptions of intergenerational relationships tend to be more positive than childrens' (and grandchildrens'), reflecting perhaps the elders' greater "investment" in family continuity.

2. The intergenerational solidarity model—affect, association, agreement (consensus), functional (exchange), normative, and structural—has proven a useful conceptual and theoretical framework for understanding multigenerational family relationships over time. For example, what are the factors predicting functional solidarity—the propensity of adult children to provide support for their aged parents? We find that these include previous support for parents, frequency of contact (associational solidarity), and affectual solidarity. But we also find gender differences: sons appear to provide support based more on perceptions of obligation (normative solidarity), whereas daughters seem more motivated by perceptions of closeness (affectual solidarity).

3. Some youthful behaviors—for example, political activism—have important consequences that are maintained over several decades of adulthood. For example, former activists delayed family formation and maintained progressive sex-role attitudes, compared to nonactivists.

4. Intergenerational continuities in occupation and attainment have decreased considerably over the past half-century, though there is still some indications of transmission effects.

5. Emotional and instrumental support from adult children affects both positive and negative well-being of aging parents. This is especially true for elders who are in poor health or are widowed.

6. There is, as seen from the case study of the Potter family since

1971, considerable variability in intergenerational solidary and conflict, and these may change as family members "drift apart" and "pull together" over time.

Many questions remain for future investigation. What are the social structural constraints on intergenerational interaction; how much do they affect parent– child solidarity over time? What is the relationship between conflict and solidarity across generations; is it orthogonal, or bipolar? To what extent are there cross-cultural and cross-societal differences (or similarities) in the multigenerational patterns we have found? And what are the implications of family intergenerational solidarity or conflict in light of the possible breakdown of the state welfare provisions in the early decades of the 21st century? Only long-term longitudinal data can adequately address these questions.

## ACKNOWLEDGMENTS

This chapter reflects the collaborative efforts of the Longitudinal Study of Generations research team at the University of Southern California. Special acknowledgment is due to Roseann Giarrusso, the Project Director, and to Timothy Biblarz, Charlotte Dunham, Du Feng, Richard Miller, Tonya Parrott, Leslie Richards, Judith Richlin-Klonsky, Robert Roberts, Merril Silverstein, and Michael Stallings, whose analyses of project data are reflected in this paper. I want also to recognize the many contributions over the last decade of Linda Hall, Administrative Coordinator for the LSG Project, along with Mar Preston, David Sharp, and Christopher Hilgeman, whose technical assistance have been invaluable. The study has been supported by a MERIT award (Grant #R37 AG07977) from the National Institute on Aging.

## REFERENCES

Acock, A. C., & Bengtson, V. L. (1980). Socialization and attribution processes: Actual versus perceived similarity among parents and youth. *Journal of Marriage and the Family, 42,* 501–515.

Andersson, L., & Stevens, N. (1993). Associations between early experiences with parents and well-being in old age. *Journal of Gerontology: Psychological Sciences, 48,* P109–P116.

Atkinson, M. P., Kivett, V. R., & Campbell, R. T. (1986). Intergenerational solidarity: An examination of a theoretical model. *Journal of Gerontology, 41,* 408–416.

Baker, L. A., Cesa, I. L., Gatz, M., & Mellins, C. (1992). Genetic and environmental influences on positive and negative affect: Support for a two-factor theory. *Psychology and Aging, 7,* 158–163.

Bengtson, V. L. (1975). Generation and family effects in value socialization. *American Sociological Review, 40,* 358–371.

Bengtson, V. L. (1993). Is the "contract across generations" changing? Effects of population aging on obligations and expectations across age groups. In V. L. Bengtson & W. A. Achenbaum (Eds.), *The changing contract across generations* (pp. 3–24). New York: Aldine de Gruyter.

Bengtson, V. L., & Allen, K. R. (1993). The life course perspective applied to families over time. In P. Boss, W. Doherty, R. LaRossa, W. Schumm, & S. Steinmetz (Eds.), *Sourcebook of family theories and methods: A contextual approach* (pp. 469–498). New York: Plenum.

Bengtson, V. L., & Harootyan, R. (Eds.). (1994). *Hidden connections: Intergenerational linkages in American society.* New York: Springer Publishing Co.

Bengtson, V. L., & Kuypers, J. A. (1971). Generational differences and the "developmental stake." *Aging and Human Development, 2,* 249–260.

Bengtson, V. L., & Murray, T. M. (1993). Justice across generations (and cohorts): Sociological perspectives on the life course and reciprocities over time. In L. Cohen (Ed.), *Justice across generations: What does it mean?* (pp. 111–138). Washington, DC: American Association of Retired Persons.

Bengtson, V. L., Olander, E. B., & Haddad, A. A. (1976). The "generation gap" and aging family members: Toward a conceptual model. In J. E. Gubrium (Ed.), *Time, roles and self in old age* (pp. 237–263). New York: Human Sciences.

Bengtson, V. L., & Parrott, T. M. (1994). Intergenerational conflicts about social equity, expectations and obligations: Lessons from the United States. *Southern African Journal of Gerontology, 3*(2), 6–14.

Bengtson, V. L., & Roberts, R. E. L. (1991). Intergenerational solidarity in aging families: An example of formal theory construction. *Journal of Marriage and the Family, 53,* 856–870.

Bengtson, V. L., Rosenthal, C. J., & Burton, L. M. (1996). Paradoxes of families and aging at the turn of the century. In R. Binstock & L. George (Eds.), *Handbook of aging and the social sciences* (4th ed.). New York: Academic Press.

Bengtson, V. L., & Schrader, S. S. (1982). Parent-child relations. In D. Mangen & W. Peterson (Eds.), *Handbook of research instruments in social gerontology* (Vol. 2, pp. 115–185). Minneapolis: University of Minnesota Press.

Biblarz, T. J., Bengtson, V. L., & Bucur, A. (1996). Social mobility across four generations. *Journal of Marriage and the Family.*

Campbell, R. T. (1988). Integrating conceptualization, design and analysis in panel studies of the life course. In K. W. Schaie, R. T. Campbell, W. Meredith, & S. C. Rollins (Eds.), *Methodological issues in aging research.* New York: Springer Publishing Co.

Clarke, E., Preston, M., Raksin, J., & Bengtson, V. L. (1993, November). *Family conflict in older parent-adult child relationships.* Paper presented at the annual meeting of the Gerontological Society of America, New Orleans.

Dunham, C. C., & Bengtson, V. L. (1992). Long-term effects of political activism on intergenerational relations. *Youth and Society, 24*(1), 31–51.

Dunham, C. C., & Bengtson, V. L. (1994). Married with children: Protest and the timing of family life course events. *Journal of Marriage and the Family, 56,* 224–228.

Elder, G. H., Jr. (1975). Age differentiation and the life course. *Annual Review of Sociology, 1,* 165–190.

Elder, G. H., Jr. (1985). Perspectives on the life course. In G. H. Elder, Jr. (Ed.), *Life course dynamics: Trajectories and transitions, 1968–1980* (pp. 23–49). Ithaca, NY: Cornell University Press.

Elder, G. H., Jr. (1994). Adult lives in a changing society. In K. Cook, G. Fine, & J. S. House (Eds.), *Sociological perspectives on social psychology* (pp. 231–244). Boston: Allyn and Bacon.

Festinger, L., Schachter, S., & Back, K. (1950). *Social pressures in informal groups: A study of a housing community.* New York: Harper & Row.

Gatz, M., Bengtson, V. L., & Blum, M. (1990). Caregiving families. In J. E. Birren & K. W. Schaie (Eds.), *Handbook of the psychology of aging* (3rd ed., pp. 404–426). New York: Academic Press.

Gatz, M., & Hurwicz, M. (1990). Are old people more depressed? Cross-sectional data on CES-D factors. *Psychology and Aging, 5,* 284–290.

Gatz, M., & Karel, M. J. (1993). Individual change in perceived control over 20 years. *International Journal of Behavioral Development, 16,* 305–322.

Giarrusso, R., Silverstein, M., & Bengtson, V. L. (1990, November). *Affect and conflict between middle-aged parents and adult children.* Paper presented at the annual meeting of the Gerontological Society of America, Boston.

Giarrusso, R., Stallings, M., & Bengtson, V. L. (1995). The "intergenerational stake" hypothesis revisited: Parent-child differences in perceptions of relationships 20 years later. In V. L. Bengtson, K. W. Schaie, & L. M. Burton (Eds.), *Intergenerational issues in aging: Effects of societal change* (pp. 227–263). New York: Springer Publishing Co.

Glass, J., Bengtson, V. L., & Dunham, C. C. (1986). Attitude similarity in three-generation families: Socialization, status inheritance, or reciprocal influence. *American Sociological Review, 51,* 685–698.

Hagestad, G. 0. (1987a). Parent-child relations in later life: Trends and gaps in past research. In J. B. Lancaster, J. Altmann, A. S. Rossi, & L. R. Sherrod (Eds.), *Parenting across the life span* (pp. 405–434). New York: Aldine de Gruyter.

Hagestad, G. O. (1987b). Problems and promises in the social psychology of intergenerational relations. In R. Rogel, E. Hatfield, S. Kiesler, & J. March (Eds.), *Stability and change in the family* (pp. 11–46). New York: Academic Press.

Hagestad, G. O. (1988). Demographic change and the life course: Some emerging trends in the family realm. *Family Relations, 37,* 405–410.

Hagestad, G. O., & Neugarten, B. L. (1985). Age and the life course. In E. Shanas & R. Binstock (Eds.), *Handbook of aging and the social sciences* (2nd ed., pp. 35–55). New York: Van Nostrand Reinhold.

Heider, F. (1958). *The psychology of interpersonal relations.* New York: Wiley.

Hill, R., Foote, N., Aldous, J., Carlson, R., & MacDonald, R. (1970). *Family development in three generations.* Cambridge, MA: Schenkman.

Homans, G. C. (1950). *The human group.* New York: Harcourt, Brace & World.

Homans, G. C. (1961). *Social behavior: Its elementary forms.* New York: Harcourt Brace Jovanovich.

Hurwicz, M., Dunham, C., Boyd, S., Gatz, M., & Bengtson, V. L. (1992). Salient life events in three-generational families. *Journal of Gerontology: Psychological Sciences, 47,* P11–P13.

Lee, G. R., Netzer, J. K., & Coward, R. T. (1994). Filial responsibility expectations and patterns of intergenerational assistance. *Journal of Marriage and the Family, 56,* 559–565.

Mangen, D. J., Bengtson, V. L., & Landry, P. H., Jr. (Eds.) (1988). *The measurement of intergenerational relations.* Beverly Hills, CA: Sage.

Marshall, V. (1995). Commentary: A finding in search of an interpretation: Discussion of "the intergenerational stake" hypothesis revisited. In V. L. Bengtson, K. W. Schaie, & L. Burton (Eds.), *Intergenerational issues in aging* (pp. 277–288). New York: Plenum.

Mellins, C. A., Blum, M. J., Boyd-Davis, S. L., & Gatz, M. (1993). Family network perspectives on caregiving. *Generations, 17*(1), 21–24.

Morioka, K., & Aoi, K. (1987). *Life course patterns of middle-aged men in contemporary Japan: The Shizuoka case.* Tokyo: Japan Society for the Promotion of Science.

Neugarten, B. L. (1968). *Middle age and aging: A reader in social psychology.* Chicago: University of Chicago Press.

Parrott, T. M., Giarrusso, R., & Bengtson, V. L. (1994, August). *What predicts conflict and conflict tactic use in parent-adult child relationships?* Paper presented at the meeting of the American Sociological Association, Los Angeles.

Pyke, K., & Bengtson, V. L. (1995, April). *Caring for elderly family members: The construction of family ties in three-generational families.* Paper presented at the annual meeting of the Pacific Sociological Association, San Francisco.

Richards, L. N., Bengtson, V. L., & Miller, R. B. (1989). The "generation in the middle": Perceptions of adults' intergenerational relationships. In K. Kreppner & R. M. Lerner (Eds.), *Family systems and life-span development.* Hillsdale, NJ: Erlbaum.

Richards, L., & Schmiege, C. (1993). Problems and strengths of single parent families: Implications for practice and policy. *Family Relations, 42,* 277–285.

Richlin-Klonsky, J., & Bengtson, V. L. (in press). Pulling together, drifting apart: A longitudinal case study of a four-generation family. *Journal of Aging Studies.*

Roberts, R. E. L. (1990). *Intergenerational affection and psychological well-being: Implications of the changing salience of work and family over the adult life course.* Unpublished doctoral dissertation, University of Southern California, Los Angeles.

Roberts, R. E. L., & Bengtson, V. L. (1988, April). *Value similarity in adults: Family ties, generational co-membership, or shared social status?* Paper presented at the annual meeting of the Pacific Sociological Association, Las Vegas.

Roberts, R. E. L., & Bengtson, V. L. (1990). Is intergenerational solidarity a unidimensional construct? A second test of a formal model. *Journal of Gerontology: Social Sciences, 45,* S12–S20.

Roberts, R. E. L., & Bengtson, V. L. (1993). Relationships with parents, self-esteem, and psychological well-being in young adulthood: A further examination of identity theory. *Social Psychological Quarterly, 56,* 263–277.

Roberts, R. E. L., & Bengtson, V. L. (1994, November). *Intergenerational stability and change in value orientations: A 20-year study of aging families.* Paper presented at the annual meeting of the Gerontological Society of America, Atlanta.

Roberts, R. E. L., Richards, L. N., & Bengtson, V. L. (1991). Intergenerational solidarity in families: Untangling the ties that bind. In S. K. Pfeifer & M. B. Sussman (Eds.), *Marriage and family review. Families: Intergenerational and generational connections, Part One* (Vol. 16(1/2), pp. 11–46). Binghamton, NY: Haworth.

Roos, P. A. (1985). *Gender and work: A comparative analysis of industrial societies.* Albany: State University of New York.

Rossi, A. S. (1995). Commentary. A finding in search of an interpretation: Discussion of "the intergenerational stake" hypothesis revisited. In V. L. Bengtson, K. W. Schaie, & L. M. Burton (Eds.), *Adult intergenerational relations* (pp. 277–288). New York: Springer Publishing Co.

Rossi, A. S., & Rossi, P. H. (1990). *Of human bonding: Parent-child relationships across the life course.* New York: Aldine de Gruyter.

Schaie, K. W. (1983). What can we learn from the longitudinal study of adult psychological development? In K. W. Schaie (Ed.), *Longitudinal studies of adult psychological development* (pp. 1–19). New York: Guilford.

Silverstein, M., & Bengtson, V. L. (1991). Do close parent-child relations reduce the mortality risk of older parents? A test of the direct and buffering effects of intergenerational affection. *The Journal of Health and Social Behavior, 32,* 382–395.

Silverstein, M., & Bengtson, V. L. (1994). Does intergenerational social support influence the psychological well-being of older parents? The contingencies of declining health and widowhood. *Social Science and Medicine, 38,* 943–957.

Silverstein, M., Parrott, T. M., & Bengtson, V. L. (1996). Factors that predispose middle-aged sons and daughters to provide social support to older parents. *Journal of Marriage and the Family.*

Starrels, M. E., Bould, S., & Nicholas, L. (1994). The feminization of poverty in the U.S.: Gender, race, ethnicity, and family factors. *Journal of Family Issues, 15,* 590–607.

Sweet, J., Bumpass, L., & Call, V. (1988). *Design and content of the National Survey of Families and Households.* NSFH Working Paper No. 1. Madison: University of Wisconsin, Center for Population Studies.

# Comments

## Gunhild O. Hagestad

This volume would have been incomplete without a chapter on intergenerational relations. For years, Bernice had students in her basic course on adult development do interviews with a three-generational family. I suspect that she had multiple reasons for this assignment. To begin with, it introduced the students to a common situation in research: having more data than you know what to do with. Although the exercise allowed for the joys of what Geertz (1973) calls "thick description," it also presented the challenge of managing and reducing data without losing sight of *the person* and *the family*. It illustrated the complex interplay of developing persons, a dynamic social group, and a changing societal context. Finally, the assignment opened up for class discussion the question of how data can be explored with two quite different strategies in mind: searching for common patterns or looking for individual differences and family uniqueness.

Maybe more than any other former Human Development student, Vern Bengtson has continually confronted these issues in his program of research on intergenerational relations. The University of Southern California (USC) Longitudinal Study of Generations (LSG) has produced a data set that is the only one of its kind in the world. Not only are four generations involved, but family units have been followed for nearly a quarter of a century. The multifaceted nature of family solidarity as a construct has been systematically explored, measured, and evaluated. Other researchers have applied LSG measures in different countries, among them Germany, Sweden, and Japan. The California study has stimulated debates over such crucial substantive questions as: What makes family members stay in touch and help one another, and how is contact and support related to emotional dimensions of relationships? To what extent do young and old members of intergenerational dyads perceive their common ties similarly? How much of a difference do the contrasting historical anchorings of individual members make?

The enormously complex data set from the longitudinal study presents a dizzying array of analytic possibilities and challenges, and data that researchers are ill-equipped to handle with available analytic tools. We sense the tension of multiple possibilities already in reading the paper's title, which speaks of *intergenerational relations;* this could mean relations between generational units or aggregates, but the body of the paper repeatedly mentions families. When we turn to the data presented on relationships, we find that the main analytic approach is to present central tendencies in the views of generational aggregates (grandparents, parents, and grandchildren) on intergenerational relationships. Group means are compared across four times of measurement, and it is concluded that there is substantial stability in dimensions of solidarity between the generations across time.

Such an approach leaves the reader wondering about some key, interrelated issues. First, there is the question of *variability.* How much variance is there around the central tendencies? Does it differ across generational groups, dyad types, developmental phases, and time of measurement? Questions of variability lead to the issue of units and levels. How do we disaggregate variance? Let me illustrate by using one of the most compelling concepts to come out of this research program, that of *developmental stake.* Since Bengtson and Kuypers' (1971) initial discussion, the concept has been validated in a number of other studies, including my own work. It appears to be a robust finding, replicated on different samples and with different measurements, that one typically gets more positive reports on intergenerational ties from the older member of an intergenerational dyad. The robustness of the finding also presents a challenge to do true dyadic and family analyses. When we observe that the older generational aggregate has higher mean solidarity scores than the means from the younger generation, what proportion of dyads do *not* demonstrate such a pattern? What can we know about dyads in which the *youngest* member gives the most positive report? Are there families in which the "normal" pattern is reversed in all dyadic combinations? What characterizes such families?

The issue of variability around central tendencies becomes more complex when we have longitudinal data on individuals, dyads, and families. We know that stable averages across times of measurement can hide a good deal of "jumping back and forth in the distribution," both by individuals and families. How much such "unrest" is there? What distinguishes stable families from those that fluctuate a great deal? Does variability across time reflect individuals who change their minds, dyads who go through volatile periods, families who change ways of relating, or historical generations with less stable perceptions than others?

Like psychologists studying personality or cognitive abilities across time, we can ponder issues of intra-versus inter-unit stability and come up with such mind twisters as: Do we observe interfamilial variability in intrafamily stability? (Are some families more stable than others? Are unstable families characterized by shifting patterns of solidarity across all dyads?) Do we appear to find interfamilial continuity when there is a good deal of intrafamilial discontinuity? (For example, are mean scores stable across time, but with families "trading places" in the distribution from one time of measurement to another?)

Issues of variability and units can be boiled down to a final, concrete question: How do we put data produced by a longitudinal, multigenerational design to the best use? The greatest scholarly challenge presented by the wealth of data from the Longitudinal Study of Generations is that of maintaining dyads and families as the units of analysis. All too often in intergenerational research, the family gets lost in the computer, and the California study is no exception in this regard. As long as the analysis compares central tendencies in the aggregated reports from generational groups, it would have been sufficient to sample unrelated "grandparents," "parents," and "grandchildren." Those of us who think that multigenerational designs are worth the costs do so because we believe that families constitute their own unique generational and developmental agoras. Unfortunately, our current methodological tool chest is not of much help when we seek to analyze family units over time. It is strong testimony to the limitations of our tools that a seasoned researcher, backed by a highly skilled, multidisciplinary team, still has trouble addressing dyads and families.

The issues raised by Bernice's course assignment also confront the USC researchers. To what extent should the analysis focus on individuals, families, or generational units? To what degree should the emphasis be on commonalities or on variability and differences? I hope that the team will actively work on developing conceptual frameworks and statistical tools that can help future generations of researchers explore multifaceted questions regarding stability and change in multigenerational families.

## REFERENCES

Bengtson, V. L., & Kuypers , J. A. (1971). Generational differences and the "developmental stake." *Aging and Human Development, 2,* 249–260.
Geertz, C. (1973). *The interpretation of cultures.* New York: Basic Books.

# CHAPTER 13

# Continuities and Discontinuities in Public Policy on Aging

## Robert H. Binstock

S tarting with the New Deal of the 1930s and on through the 1970s, most United States public policies providing benefits and protection to older people had a distinct continuity of approach. They were primarily structured on the basis of old age criteria, without much reference to substantial differences in economic status, health status, and social conditions to be found within the older population.

This age-based policy approach was buttressed by popular stereotypes of older Americans as poor, frail, dependent, and above all, deserving. The American polity implemented this compassionate construct through the New Deal's Social Security, the Great Society's Medicare and the Older Americans Act, special tax exemptions and credits for being age 65 and older, and a variety of other measures enacted during President Nixon's New Federalism. Through the 1960s and 1970s many issues and problems affecting older persons identified by advocates for the elderly became at least nominally recognized through a government old age program.

Bernice Neugarten was perhaps the first voice in American society to suggest that the age-based approach in public policy should be discontinued. By the early 1980s, discontinuities did begin to emerge in the form of policies that were more sensitive than those of the past to the different statuses and needs to be found within the older population.

These discontinuities began an incremental trend that has established a new approach in policies on aging for more than a dozen years. It is characterized by sensitivity to variations in economic status among older people, and proposals to lump together the disabled elderly with disabled persons of all ages on the basis of need for long-term care services. There may be limits, however, to how far the new need-based trend can go without seriously threatening political and economic support for policies that aid those aged persons who are substantially in need of help from government.

This chapter begins by reviewing the intellectual challenge that Neugarten presented to the traditional old-age-based approach to policies. Next it traces the transition to discontinuities with the traditional approach, which have, by now, established a new framework for continuity that is more focused on need than on age. Then it points up issues that may challenge the continuity of the present need-based approach as we move into the 21st century. And finally, it considers possible discontinuities in future policies on aging.

## CHALLENGING THE TRADITIONAL APPROACH

In the 1970s Bernice Neugarten began to challenge the traditional, age-based approach by calling attention to the diversity of older people, and suggesting that public policy ought to shift from an old-age-based approach to a need-based approach. In an article entitled "Age Groups in American Society and the Rise of the Young Old" (1974) she attempted to break down age-based stereotypes regarding the economic and health status of older people and social factors in their lives (see also Neugarten, 1970).

Ironically, Bernice's basic message became distorted by others in the field of aging who used her article to engender an age-based stratification of old age stereotypes. It soon became a widespread practice to label persons aged 65 to 74 as the *young-old,* and to perceive all persons in this age group as healthy and capable of earning income. If retired, they have been seen as a rich reservoir of resources to be drawn upon for providing unpaid social and health services and fulfilling a variety of other community roles (e.g., Bass, Caro, & Chen, 1993; Kieffer, 1986). In contrast, persons aged 75 and older became commonly termed the *old-old* and have tended to be saddled with the traditional compassionate stereotypes of older persons as poor and frail.

In the mid-1980s the seeds for an additional level of stratification in old age stereotypes were planted when the National Institute on Aging launched a research initiative focused on the "oldest-old," persons aged 85 and older (U.S. Department of Health and Human Services, 1984; also see Suzman, Willis, & Manton, 1992). With this age category delineated it was not difficult to foresee that policy proposals would soon emerge that would single out very old people for different treatment (Binstock, 1985), such as in the subsequent proposal by Daniel Callahan (1987) that lifesaving care be categorically denied to people in their 80s and older.

Toward the end of the 1970s Neugarten renewed her challenge to public policies primarily structured on the basis of age, rather than need. Building on her earlier observations that societal age norms and the characteristics of older persons were changing, she argued:

> In a society in which age is becoming increasingly irrelevant as a predictor of lifestyle or as a predictor of need, policies and programs formulated on the basis of age are falling increasingly wide of the mark . . . income and health care and housing and other goods and services should be provided, not according to age, but according to relative need. (Neugarten, 1979, pp. 50–51)

Bernice recognized the political complexities of designing, shifting to, administering, and sustaining massive public transfer programs based on the relative needs of individual citizens. So, in a subsequent book (Neugarten, 1982), she assembled a number of policy analysts and scholars to address these complexities. Among their efforts was a particularly intriguing analysis laid out by Nelson (1982), employing three alternative models of policy towards aging: one based on age irrelevance, or the concept of *unitary adulthood;* a second based on attaining age 75 as the eligibility requirement for old age benefit programs; and a third based on the idea of "veteranship," in which old age is conceived of as an "earned status."

# THE CHANGED POLITICAL CONTEXT

Also starting in the late 1970s (see Binstock, 1983) and continuing to the present, the long-standing compassionate stereotypes of older persons have undergone a substantial reversal in the media. And by the early 1980s a shift began toward a need-based approach policy. In contrast to Neugarten's focus on the diversity of older people, however, this movement toward need-based approaches in policy has been driven by federal budgetary concerns.

For nearly twenty years new stereotypes of older people have gained ascendence in popular culture, depicting older persons as prosperous, hedonistic, selfish, and politically powerful. In 1992, for instance, the cover story of Fortune declaimed that "The tyranny of America's old . . . is one of the most crucial issues facing U.S. society" (Smith, 1992). For some years the epithet "greedy geezers" has been commonly used in journalistic accounts of federal budget politics (e.g., Salholz, 1990).

Among the factors that appear to have contributed to this reversal of stereotypes, perhaps the most important has been the "graying" of the federal budget. In the late 1970s academicians (e.g., Hudson, 1978) and journalists (e.g., Samuelson, 1978) began to recognize a tremendous growth in the amount of federal dollars expended on benefits to older Americans; those outlays had come to be more than one quarter of the federal budget and comparable in size to expenditures on national defense. Today, expenditures on aging are well over one third of the budget, and defense has fallen to about 18% (U.S. Congress, 1995a).

As the proportion of the budget devoted to benefits for older people has become increasingly recognized, curtailing the costs of Social Security, Medicare, and a large proportion of Medicaid spent on long-term care is viewed by many as essential for reducing the federal deficit and maintaining the health of the economy (e.g., Concord Coalition, 1993; Peterson, 1993).

In this context various public figures, academicians, and policy analysts have focused on programs for the elderly as an important trade-off element in any attempt to deal with American economic and social problems—such as the welfare of children, health care costs, combatting crime and drug abuse, housing the homeless, rebuilding the infrastructure, and so on. For instance, a distinguished panel convened by the Ford Foundation proposed a series of social policies for the American future costing $29 billion in the first year; the only options it addressed for financing this sum were reductions in, or taxes on, Social Security benefits (Ford Foundation, 1989). The panel did not even feel it was necessary to explain why these were the only financing options it considered.

Such trade-offs between expenditures on older people and other social and economic causes have been thematically unified and publicized as issues of so-called *intergenerational equity* by organizations such as Americans for Generational Equity, active in the 1980s (see Quadagno,

1989), and the Concord Coalition, founded by former U.S. Senators Paul Tsongas and Warren Rudman in 1992. Proponents of the generational equity paradigm have managed to frame policy issues in terms of justice between young and old, as opposed to justice between rich and poor, or between racial and ethnic groups, or along other axes. In addition, on college campuses and elsewhere, their leaders have been highly inflammatory in speeches and discussions, engaging vigorously in "elder bashing." However, the technical analyses they use to support their paradigm are often spuriously constructed and analytically flawed (e.g., see Binstock, 1992b; Christensen, 1992).

Despite such practices, or perhaps because of them, the themes of intergenerational equity and conflict have been adopted by the media and academics as routine perspectives for describing many social policy issues (Cook, Marshall, Marshall, & Kaufman, 1994). During the 1990 budget negotiations between the President and Congress, for example, a headline in the *Washington Post* proclaimed: "Older Voters Drive Budget; Generational Divide Marks Budget Battle" (1990, p. 1). The intergenerational themes have gained currency in elite sectors of American society as well as among journalist and politicians. A president of the prestigious American Association of Universities, for instance, has asserted: "The shape of the domestic federal budget inescapably pits programs for the retired against every other social purpose dependent on federal funds, in the present and the future" (Rosenzweig, 1990, p. 6).

Another factor that has contributed to the reversal of old age stereotypes and fueled the intergenerational equity movement is the dramatic improvements that have taken place in the aggregate economic status of older people, in large measure due to the impact of federal benefit programs. Social Security, for example, has helped to reduce the proportion of elderly persons in poverty from about 35% three decades ago (Clark, 1990) to 12.2% today (Radner, 1993). And statistics on average incomes make it seem that older people, generally, are far better off than other age groups in American society, even though about one third of the older population is just a few thousand dollars above the poverty line or below it.

Still another factor has been the rise of what Robertson (1991) has called "apocalyptic demography," a practice through which foreboding scenarios have been generated for the fiscal implications of population aging in the decades ahead. Apostles of apocalyptic demography (e.g., Schneider & Guralnik, 1990; Wattenberg, 1987) start by assuming that existing policies, institutional arrangements, and social conditions will remain the same over many years to come. Then they generate predictions by plugging into these assumptions the familiar demographic projections regarding greater numbers and proportions of older Americans when the baby boom—a cohort of 76 million persons born between 1946 and 1964—joins the ranks of those eligible for old age benefit programs in the early decades of the 21st century, and when the growing ranks of the oldest-old will substantially swell the demand for health care and social services.

The practice of apocalyptic demography has fomented concerns regarding the economic implications of supporting an aging population, accompanied by discussions of ways to limit governmental obligations for old age benefits in the decades ahead. A principal anxiety that has been expressed for some years is that a projected decline in the number of workers relative to the size of the retired "dependent" population will make it extraordinarily difficult, economically, for our nation to sustain old age retirement benefits through the first half of the 21st century (see President's Commission on Pension Policy, 1980). Another major worry is that when the baby boom cohort reaches old age, health care costs of older people will be an enormous economic burden or, as one observer has put it, "a great fiscal black hole" that will absorb an unlimited amount of national resources (Callahan, 1987, p. 17).

Although these scenarios have fostered concerns, they are exaggerated. For instance, likely declines in child dependency expenditures will probably offset increases in elderly dependency expenditures in the decades ahead (see Crown, 1993; Easterlin, 1996). The total dependency burden will never be as high as it was in the mid-1960s, unless we experience a second baby boom that is comparable to the first in its overall impact.

Moreover, the productivity of an economy and, hence, its capacity to support dependents within it, is a function of a variety of factors—including capital investment, natural resources, balance of trade, and technological innovation—as well as number of workers (Committee on an Aging Society, 1986). Future benefits to the aging will not depend on the proportion of workers to retirees, but on whether the American economy generates sufficient resources to be transferred, and whether the political will to transfer them to older persons will be present.

Similarly, cross-national comparisons of health care expenditures and population aging provide no evidence that substantial or rapid population aging causes high levels of national economic burden from expenditures on health care (Binstock, 1993). Health care costs are far from "out of control" or even "high" in many nations that have comparatively large proportions of older persons or have experienced rapid rates of population aging. The evidence suggests that the public and private structural features of health care systems—health system budgetary and administrative centralization, system capacity, and system use—along with per capita gross domestic product, are far more important determinants of a nation's health care expenditures than population aging and other demographic trends (see Chollet, 1992).

In short, demography is not destiny. Despite the scenarios generated through apocalyptic demography, issues of whether benefits to the aging will be maintained in the decades ahead and how benefits are structured will primarily be resolved through politics, and not through the combined effects of demography and economics.

Nonetheless, in this contemporary political climate some of the long-standing features for structuring old age programs have already been undergoing significant change. For a dozen years a trend has been established through which Congress has reformed policies on aging to reflect the diverse economic situations of older persons.

# EROSION OF THE OLD-AGE APPROACH

## Combining Old Age and Economic Status as Criteria

The Social Security Reform Act of 1983 began this trend by taxing Social Security benefits for the first time, making 50% of benefits subject to taxation for individuals with incomes exceeding $25,000 and married couples over $32,000. The Tax Reform Act of 1986, even as it eliminated the extra personal exemption that had been available to all persons 65 years and older when filing their federal income tax returns, provided new tax credits for very-low-income older persons on a sliding scale. The Older Americans Act programs of supportive and social services, for which all persons aged 60 and older are eligible, have been gradually targeted by Congress to low-income older persons.

The Medicare Catastrophic Coverage Act (MCCA) of 1988 followed this pattern of sensitivity to economic status by establishing the Qualified

Medicare Beneficiary program, which requires that Medicaid pay deductibles, copayments, and Part B premiums for Medicare enrollees who have incomes that are below specific poverty guidelines.

Legislation in the 1990s has continued to apply the principle of sensitivity to economic status in setting standards for responsibilities and benefits in old age programs. The payroll income ceiling on the Medicare portion of the Federal Insurance Contributions Act (FICA) payroll tax has been eliminated. And the Omnibus Budget Reconciliation Act (OBRA) of 1993 continued this tendency by subjecting 85% of Social Security benefits to taxation for individuals with incomes over $34,000 and couples over $44,000.

In sum, a substantial trend of incremental changes has firmly established the practice of combining age and economic status as policy criteria in old age benefit programs.

## Discarding Age as a Criterion: Long-Term Care

Neugarten's notion that governmental benefits should be provided on the basis of need rather than age has been clearly manifest in a number of proposals to establish public insurance for long-term care. Unlike the policy changes that have combined criteria of old age and economic status, these long-term care proposals have been generated by a focus on providing a new set of benefits rather than reducing the deficit.

Although the long-term care needs of disabled persons of all ages are inveterate, the major initial impetus for public long-term care insurance was successful advocacy efforts on behalf of older people. Particularly noteworthy in this regard were the efforts undertaken by a political coalition concerned about Alzheimer's disease, which began to form in the mid-1970s (Fox, 1989). By the mid-1980s, advocates for older and younger disabled people began meeting to explore their common ground of interests (see Brody & Ruff, 1986; Mahoney, Estes, & Heumann, 1986). In 1989 a broad coalition named the Long-Term Care Campaign was formed. A Washington-based interest group claiming to represent 140 national organizations with more than 60 million members, it had as one of its key legislative goals that "long-term care services should be available to all who need them, regardless of age" (Long-Term Care Campaign, 1990).

A specific policy link was forged between younger and older disabled people in 1989 when Representative Claude Pepper introduced a bill to provide comprehensive long-term home care insurance coverage for persons of any age who were dependent in at least two activities of daily living (ADLs) (Long-Term Care Act of 1989). Since then a number of such long-term care bills have been introduced, with projected expenditures ranging from $20 billion to $50 billion, depending upon provisions regarding specific populations eligible, and details regarding the timing, nature, and extent of insurance coverage.

In 1993 President Clinton proposed a new long-term care program for persons of all ages. It posited that to be eligible for publicly financed services, an individual must meet one of the following conditions: (1) requires personal assistance, stand-by assistance, supervision, or cues to perform three or more of five ADLs—eating, dressing, bathing, toileting, and transferring in and out of bed; (2) presents evidence of severe cognitive or mental impairment as indicated by a specified score on a standard mental status protocol; (3) has severe or profound mental retardation; or (4) for a child under the age of six, he or she is dependent on technology and otherwise requires hospital or institutional care (White House Domestic Policy Council, 1993, pp. 171–172).

Largely because of anticipated costs, no federal long-term care program has been enacted as yet. Nonetheless, the principle now seems firmly established that any long-term care policy that may emerge will rely on criteria involving need for services rather than on an age-categorical approach.

## ISSUES IN THE NEW APPROACHES

### Political Viability of Combining Age and Economic Status

Ever since attention began to focus on the economic implications of population aging in the United States nearly two decades ago, various commentators have warned that it would not be viable politically to combine old age and economic status as criteria for distributing benefits and burdens in nonwelfare old age policies. For example, levying taxes on Social Security benefits would be too risky for elected officials (e.g., see Hubbard, 1979, especially pp. 20–23). Yet for more than a decade, Congress has enacted such changes by introducing measures that blend age and economic status as policy criteria. Such policy shifts

have been politically viable even though few of them have been regarded favorably by the American Association for Retired Persons (AARP)
and other old age interest groups (see Binstock & Day, 1996). Ironically,
the one such change that was repealed, the progressive surtax for catastrophic coverage in the MCCA, had been favored by AARP, and that
organization was unsuccessful opposing its repeal (Binstock, 1994).

Further policy changes of this kind are highly likely in the years
immediately ahead, in accordance with the incremental paradigm of policy processes in the American political system (Dye, 1972). Within the
past few years proposals have been made for more such changes, including several in President Clinton's plan for health care reform (White
House Domestic Policy Council, 1993). Reports by the Congressional
Budget Office (U.S. Congress, 1994, 1995b) continue to present and
analyze the implications of a number of additional means-tested policy
options in Social Security, Medicare, and other old age programs.

How far can this trend continue, and what are its long-term implications? The experiences of the enactment of the Medicare Catastrophic
Coverage Act and its partial repeal the next year suggest that some such
measures may not be politically feasible. Two thirds of the principal
portion of the act, a substantial expansion of benefits, were to be
financed through a progressive, sharply escalating surtax on 40% of
Medicare participants in middle and higher income brackets. Despite
AARP's support for the act, there were distinct and highly visible
protests from middle-income elders in virtually every Congressional
district. Although they comprised only a minority of the elderly, no
countervailing popular constituency supported this program, and
Congress gave in to the protesters. This might not have been the outcome, however, if the progressive tax had been more finely tuned, and
Medicare beneficiaries had been more effectively educated as to what
the new benefits would have provided (see Binstock, 1994).

Most contemporary proposals, however, involve reductions in and
taxation of benefits, driven by fiscal concerns, rather than major expansion of benefits, financed by older people. The political difficulties in
carrying forward the means-testing approach may not be substantial in
the years immediately ahead. Yet, in the long run, this trend may not
remain viable. As many have argued (e.g., National Academy on Aging,
1994), reductions in the benefits that middle- and upper-income people
receive from old age programs pose substantial risks. Among the middle-
income elderly—as well as the near elderly, and younger age cohorts—

political support for Social Security, Medicare, and other old age policies may weaken, leaving these programs without a middle-class constituency, as is and has been the case with what are generally thought of as welfare programs. As we know, such programs do not fare well, generally, in our system. Indeed, they were under vigorous political attack during the 104th Congress.

If old age policies become dominated over time by a welfare approach to benefits, the issue of income adequacy will become far more important than the issues of equity. Questions may be raised about the magnitude and largesse of old age "welfare." And the political will to use policy to address income adequacy may not be present. Some old age groups such as the National Council of Senior Citizens, and a few others, have addressed the issue of income inadequacy over the years. But most, including AARP, have never addressed it seriously, and, given their constituencies, are not likely to (Binstock, 1972; Binstock & Day, 1996).

Ultimately, the dominant policy framework for addressing old age policy issues may—as a societal necessity—need to move away from the generational equity paradigm to a more direct examination of the consequences of poverty and near poverty in old age. If the social insurance principle erodes severely, the ensuing focus and pressure on old age "welfare" may force us to confront head-on such issues as a growing number of homeless and frail elderly, and whether we really want to reestablish almshouses for the elderly poor, to institutionalize them as a matter of social policy.

## Aging and Disability: A Politics of Common Ground?

Although congressional and administrative policy leaders seem committed to the principle of a need-based approach in any long-term care insurance program that may be enacted, it remains to be seen whether this tack will prove to be politically viable. Even if the fiscal costs of such a program come to be perceived as manageable, it is far from certain that younger and older disabled people will emerge as a powerful constituent coalition to back such legislation.

Traditionally, advocates for the aged and for younger disabled populations have not been united as a constituency supporting long-term care (see Binstock, 1992a; Torres-Gil & Pynoos, 1986). Organized interests for disabled people have tended to eschew symbolic and political identification with elderly people, in part because of traditional stereotypes of older people as frail, chronically ill, declining, and marginal to society. Younger disabled persons and their advocates reject the medical model that emphasizes long-term care as an essential component of health services. To them, access to services—as well as to certain technologies and environments—is a matter of making it feasible to carry forward an active "normal" life, doing much of what they would be able to do if they were not disabled.

Beyond issues of disparate philosophy lie specific divergences in service needs. Persons disabled through spinal cord injuries, for example, tend to remain in stable medical and functional condition for many years. Persons with AIDS have a trajectory of decline, punctuated by intermittent and continual episodes of acute illness. Although the trajectory for many elderly persons in long-term care is gradual decline, on average their need for acute care is not as frequent (see Benjamin, 1996).

Despite such differences in philosophy and service needs, advocates for the aged and the disabled did work together in the planning process for President Clinton's 1993 initiative on long-term care. Their cooperation is reflected in the fact that the President's proposal incorporated many specific concerns that have been put forward by advocates for the younger disabled population over the years (e.g., the principle that clients should be able at their own discretion to hire and fire services providers). But since the President presented his Health Security Act to Congress in the fall of 1993 there have been many indications that the unity that was achieved is eroding (see Binstock, 1994). Whether sufficient cohesion among these groups can be developed to provide strong political support for a need-based long-term care insurance program remains to be seen.

## DO NEW DISCONTINUITIES LIE AHEAD?

Although the enactment of long-term care policy based on need still remains problematic, a new continuity has been established in policies on aging. The policy trend that combines old age with economic status as criteria for distributing program benefits and burdens has been rather consistent for a dozen years. Policy makers and analysts are still thinking in terms of this approach. How long will it last? Are there signs of any discontinuities that may emerge in the future?

As suggested above, this trend could continue to the point where only the poorest among older people are receiving benefits. Somewhere along a continuum to that point, Social Security, Medicare, and other programs benefiting older persons may in effect become welfare programs with respect to their economics, politics, administration, and social stigma. In short, we may cease to see them as old age programs at all. They will then share the fates of other welfare programs at that time.

Still another distinct possibility for further discontinuity is policy changes that will establish new old age markers, at higher ages than presently used—say, 67, 70, or 75—to determine eligibility for old age program benefits. Many arguments and rationales as well as technical proposals for this new old age approach have already been set forth (e.g., Chen, 1994; Torres-Gil, 1992).

One step in this direction was taken in the 1983 Social Security amendments, which provide for the minimum age of retirement with full benefits to be increased gradually from age 65, beginning in 2003, until it reaches age 67 in 2027. But a more recent proposal for reforming Social Security included a provision that would accelerate the timetable for this transition by 11 years (Pear, 1994). Various members of Congress and federal administrative officials have favored acceleration; some propose that age changes take effect almost immediately. Proposals to raise the age of eligibility for Medicare are just beginning to emerge.

The political feasibility of shifts to higher old age criteria is questionable. The 1983 provision for raising the retirement age was but one, seemingly minor, part of a comprehensive package of reforms that were politically marketed at the time as "saving Social Security." Moreover, it was a far-distant provision that would not even begin to be implemented for 20 years, and was not scheduled to be fully implemented for nearly a quarter of a century after that. If proposals to raise the age for benefit eligibility within a relatively short time frame are placed on the legislative agenda, they may well evoke strong and effective political opposition from old age interest groups.

Ironically, if this older old age approach comes into vogue—as a new discontinuity in the cyclical trends of public policy—it will mirror the intellectual distortions that took place after Bernice Neugarten pointed up the divergent characteristics within the older population in the

1970s. The policy pendulum may swing back from the present trend, which focuses on need-based approaches, and reinvigorate the age-based approach—newly focused on the old-old and, perhaps, the oldest-old.

In so doing it might provide what March and Simon (1958) called a "satisficing" resolution to the long-term tensions between age and need in public policy on aging, which have been so presciently and effectively articulated by Neugarten in the course of her distinguished career. Age will certainly be relevant for those at older old ages; and need will be very relevant for some persons at younger old ages, who will be redefined by public policy as middle aged rather than old.

## REFERENCES

Bass, S. A., Caro, F. G., & Chen, Y.-P. (Eds.). (1993). *Achieving a productive aging society.* Westport, CT: Auburn House.

Benjamin, A. E. (1996). Trends among younger persons with disabilities and chronic diseases. In R. H. Binstock, L. E. Cluff, & O. von Mering (Eds.), *The future of long-term care: Social and policy issues* (pp. 75–95). Baltimore: Johns Hopkins University Press.

Binstock, R. H. (1972). Interest-group liberalism and the politics of aging. *The Gerontologist, 12*(3, Part I), 265–280.

Binstock, R. H. (1983). The aged as scapegoat. *The Gerontologist, 23,* 136–143.

Binstock, R. H. (1985). The oldest old: A fresh perspective or compassionate ageism revisited? *Milbank Memorial Fund Quarterly/Health and Society, 63,* 420–451.

Binstock, R. H. (1992a). Aging, disability, and long-term care: The politics of common ground. *Generations, 16*(1), 83–88.

Binstock, R. H. (1992b). Another form of "elderly bashing." *Journal of Health Politics, Policy and Law, 17,* 269–272.

Binstock, R. H. (1993). Healthcare costs around the world: Is aging a fiscal "black hole"? *Generations, 17*(4), 37–42.

Binstock, R. H. (1994). Older Americans and health care reform in the nineties. In P. V. Rosenau (Ed.), *Health care reform in the nineties* (pp. 213–235). Thousand Oaks, CA: Sage.

Binstock, R. H., & Day, C. L. (1996). Aging and politics. In R. H. Binstock & L. K. George (Eds.), *Handbook of aging and the social sciences* (4th ed., pp. 362–387). San Diego: Academic Press.

Brody, S. J., & Ruff, G. E. (Eds.). (1986). *Aging and rehabilitation: Advances in the state of the art.* New York: Springer Publishing Co.

Callahan, D. (1987). *Setting limits: Medical goals in an aging society.* New York: Simon and Schuster.

Chen, P. (1994). "Equivalent retirement ages" and their implications for Social Security and Medicare financing. *The Gerontologist, 34,* 731–735.

Chollet, D. J. (1992, August). *The impact of aging on national health care spending: Cross-national estimates for selected countries.* Paper presented at the annual meeting of the American Risk and Insurance Association, Washington, DC.

Christensen, S. (1992). The subsidy provided under Medicare to current enrollees. *Journal of Health Politics, Policy and Law, 17,* 255–264.

Clark, R. L. (1990). Income maintenance policies in the United States. In R. H. Binstock & L. K. George (Eds.), *Handbook of aging and the social sciences* (3rd ed., pp. 382–397). San Diego: Academic Press.

Committee on an Aging Society, Institute of Medicine and National Research Council. (1986). *America's aging: Productive roles in an older society.* Washington, DC: National Academy Press.

Concord Coalition. (1993). *The zero deficit plan: A plan for eliminating the federal budget deficit by the year 2000.* Washington, DC: The Concord Coalition.

Cook, F. L., Marshall, V. W., Marshall, J. G., & Kaufman, J. E. (1994). The salience of intergenerational equity in Canada and the United States. In T. R. Marmor, T. M. Smeeding, & V. L. Greene (Eds.), *Economic security and intergenerational justice: A look at North America* (pp. 91–129). Washington, DC: Urban Institute Press.

Crown, W. H. (1993). Projecting the costs of aging populations. *Generations, 17*(4), 32–36.

Dye, T. R. (1972). *Understanding public policy.* Englewood Cliffs, NJ: Prentice-Hall.

Easterlin, R. A. (1996). Economic and social implications of demographic patterns. In R. H. Binstock & L. K. George (Eds.), *Handbook of aging and the social sciences* (4th ed., pp. 73–93). San Diego: Academic Press.

Ford Foundation, Project on Social Welfare and the American Future, Executive Panel. (1989). *The common good: Social welfare and the American future.* New York: Ford Foundation.

Fox, P. (1989). From senility to Alzheimer's disease: The rise of the Alzheimer's disease movement. *The Milbank Quarterly, 67,* 58–102.

Hubbard, J. P. (Ed.). (1979). *The economics of aging: The economic, political and social implications of growing old in America.* Washington, DC: The Government Research Corporation.

Hudson, R. B. (1978). The "graying" of the federal budget and its consequences for old age policy. *The Gerontologist, 18,* 428–440.

Kieffer, J. A. (1986). The older volunteer resource. In Committee on an Aging

Society, Institute of Medicine and National Research Council (Ed.), *America's aging: Productive roles in an older society* (pp. 51–72). Washington, DC: National Academy Press.

Long-Term Care Act of 1989. U.S. House of Representatives, 101st Congress, House of Representatives 2263.

Long-Term Care Campaign. (1990, January/February). Pepper Commission recommendations released March 2nd. *Insiders' Update,* p. 1.

Mahoney, C. W., Estes, C. J., & Heumann, J. E. (Eds.). (1986). *Synthesis and recommendations. Toward a unified agenda: Proceedings of a national conference on disability and aging.* San Francisco: Institute for Health and Aging, University of California.

March, J. G., & Simon, H. A. (1958). *Organizations.* New York: Wiley.

National Academy on Aging. (1994). *Old age in the 21st century.* Washington, DC: Maxwell School, Syracuse University.

Nelson, D. W. (1982). Alternative images of old age as the bases for policy. In B. L. Neugarten (Ed.), *Age or need? Public policies for older people* (pp. 131–169). Beverly Hills, CA: Sage.

Neugarten, B. L. (1970.) The old and the young in modern societies. *American Behavioral Scientist, 14,* 13–24.

Neugarten, B. L. (1974). Age groups in American society and the rise of the young old. *Annals of the American Academy of Political and Social Science, 415,* 187–198.

Neugarten, B. L. (1979). Policy for the 1980s: Age or need entitlement? In J. P. Hubbard (Ed.), *Aging: Agenda for the eighties* (pp. 48–52). Washington, DC: Government Research Corporation.

Neugarten, B. L. (Ed.). (1982). *Age or need? Public policies for older people.* Beverly Hills, CA: Sage.

Older voters drive budget: Generational divide marks budget battle. (1990, October 15). *Washington Post,* p. 1.

Pear, R. (1994, April 19). To shore up social security, cuts and tax rises are urged: Rostenkowski plan is given good chance. *New York Times,* p. A7.

Peterson, P. G. (1993). *Facing up: How to rescue the economy from crushing debt & restore the American dream.* New York: Simon and Schuster.

President's Commission on Pension Policy. (1980). *Demographic shifts and projections: Implications for pension systems* (working paper). Washington, DC: U.S. Government Printing Office.

Quadagno, J. (1989). Generational equity and the politics of the welfare state. *Politics and Society,* 353–376.

Radner, D. B. (1993). Economic well-being of the old-old: Family unit income and household wealth. *Social Security Bulletin, 56*(1), 3–19.

Robertson, A. (1991). The politics of Alzheimer's disease: A case study in apocalyptic demography. In M. Minkler & C. L. Estes (Eds.), *Critical per-*

*spectives on aging: The political and moral economy of growing old* (pp. 135–150). Amityville, NY: Baywood.

Rosenzweig, R. M. (1990, November). *Address to the president's opening session,* presented at the annual meeting of the Gerontological Society of America, Boston.

Salholz, E. (1990, October 29). Blaming the voters: Hapless budgeteers single out "greedy geezers." *Newsweek,* p. 36.

Samuelson, R. J. (1978). Aging America: Who will shoulder the growing burden? *National Journal, 10,* 1712–1717.

Schneider, E. L., & Guralnik, J. M. (1990). The aging of America: Impact on health care costs. *Journal of the American Medical Association, 263,* 2335–2340.

Smith, L. (1992, January 13). The tyranny of America's old. *Fortune,* pp. 68–72.

Suzman, R., Willis, D., and Manton, K. (Eds.). (1992). *The oldest old.* New York: Oxford University Press.

Torres-Gil, F. M. (1992). *The new aging: Politics and change in America.* New York: Auburn House.

Torres-Gil, F. M., & Pynoos, J. (1986). Long-term care policy and interest group struggles. *The Gerontologist, 26,* 488–495.

U.S. Congress, Congressional Budget Office. (1994). *Reducing entitlement spending.* Washington, DC: U.S. Government Printing Office.

U.S. Congress, Congressional Budget Office. (1995a). *The economic and budget outlook: Fiscal years 1996–2000.* Washington, DC: U.S. Government Printing Office.

U.S. Congress, Congressional Budget Office. (1995b). *Reducing the deficit: Spending and revenue options.* Washington, DC: U.S. Government Printing Office.

U.S. Department of Health and Human Services. (1984, November 9). Announcement: The oldest old. *National Institutes of Health guide for grants and contracts, 13*(12), 29–32.

Wattenberg, B. J. (1987). *The birth dearth.* New York: Pharos.

White House Domestic Policy Council. (1993). *The President's health security plan.* New York: Random House.

# Comments

## W. Andrew Achenbaum

Robert Binstock's analysis of certain continuities and discontinuities in old age policy making in the United States since the 1930s nicely fits two themes of this *festschrift*. He shows how dramatic shifts in the political economy rechanneled the incremental manner in which policies usually evolve. Furthermore, he rightly extols Bernice Neugarten's role during the past two decades in challenging conventional wisdom. Neugarten's distinction between the "young-old" and "old-old," he shows, was both used and misused by experts in academic as well as political circles.

Binstock's primary claim—that a major discontinuity has occurred in United States old age policy since the Great Depression—is incontestable. Members of Congress, presidents, and ordinary Americans have become less and less willing to cater to senior citizens' demands. A new form of ageism grew quite evident in the Reagan years; it animates the so-called "Contract for America." Binstock indicates that at least four factors are at play: (1) the diffusion of apocalyptic interpretations of population aging; (2) growing concern over the costs of supporting the nation's elderly, at a time when the aged as a group were healthier and more financially secure than before; (3) the rise of new stereotypes portraying the aged as scapegoats, needy, and greedy; and (4) the rhetoric of conflict concerning intergenerational inequities in security and access to other public goods.

"Continuities and Discontinuities in Public Policy on Aging" is very good as far as it goes. The chapter would have been even better had Binstock done two things. First, he should have extended his timeline. Second, he could have acknowledged that there is greater ambiguity embedded within the "traditional" approaches than he suggests.

Consider, for instance, how a historical perspective might enrich Binstock's analysis of three strategies for policy making. Recognizing that conflicts over "equity" and "adequacy" evident in the Progressive era have never really been resolved in Social Security legislation helps to explain the conundra in "combining old age and economic status" today. Similarly, examining the sordid history of North American almshouses might show "hidden" costs of discarding age as a policy criterion. The poorhouse was designed as a humanitarian institution. Over time it became dreaded as a place to abandon the aged, because the deaf, juveniles, the mentally ill, and paupers were transferred to their own special facilities. And although I agree that the aged and the disabled should join forces on fighting some policies and advocating others, the history of this country's veterans' homes surely suggests that good logic does not always lead to easy solutions.

Let me anticipate Professor Neugarten's query, "So what? Does a historical approach add anything here?" The answer is yes, in two Neugartenian ways. First, history reminds us that the elderly have always been a heterogeneous group. They have diverse needs. Special attention must be paid to racial, gender, and ethnic differences. Second, extending our baseline back to the founding fathers alerts us to the messiness of the policy-making process in the United States. States have long exercised considerable discretionary power over allocating funds for the elderly. Factions, as James Madison wrote in *Federalist 10* (Gabriel, 1904), play a critical role in a democracy. Elderly Americans must show that it is in nearly everyone's best interest to give priority to remedying problems occurring in later years and unleashing the potentials of age.

# REFERENCE

Gabriel, R. (Ed.). (1954). *Hamilton, Madison and Jay on the Constitution: Selections from the Federalist Papers.* New York: Liberal Arts Press.

# CHAPTER 14

# Public Support for Programs for Older Americans: Continuities Amidst Threats of Discontinuities

## Fay Lomax Cook

In "Interpretive Social Science and Research on Aging" (1985), Bernice Neugarten reminds us that aging has multiple biological, psychological, and sociological components and that neither the behavior of older persons nor the status of older persons can be understood otherwise. Further, she argues that attention to change over time is fundamental in all our disciplinary approaches. It is this understanding of, and attention to, continuity and change over time in the lives of individuals, family, and society that is one of Neugarten's most important contributions. In relation to policy and change, she was one of the first to see the profound implications of the growing proportion of elderly persons in the population and, as far as I can tell, perhaps the very first to use the phrase "the aging society" to describe the United States with its increasing proportions of persons over age 50 (Neugarten, 1979). She saw, again perhaps before others, that one implication of the growing numbers of elders might be a backlash against the old. In the very early 1970s, she wrote that:

> Anger toward the old may also be on the rise. In some instances, because a growing proportion of power positions in the judiciary, legislative, business, and professional arenas are occupied by older people, and because

of seniority privileges among workers, the young and middle-aged may become resentful. In other instances, as the number of retired increases, the economic burden is perceived as falling more and more upon the middle-aged as taxpayer. (1973, p. 578)

The purpose of this chapter is to examine the extent to which one accompaniment of the aging society has been growing resentment and anger directed against the old. I do this by looking at portrayals in the mass media and at survey descriptions of the public's and policy makers' support for programs for older Americans. I find that, in fact, if we look at the media and the views of certain policy elites, Neugarten was quite right in her warnings regarding the possible development of resentment and anger against the old. However, I find that these media portrayals have not resulted in a loss of public support for social programs for the old. Instead, the public's support for programs that target elderly people is strong and has shown a remarkable degree of continuity over time. In reaching these conclusions, I draw on research that I have done with Victor and Joanne Gard Marshall at the University of Toronto on the salience of the intergenerational equity debate (Cook, Marshall, Marshall, & Kaufman, 1994; Marshall, Cook, & Marshall, 1993); on two public opinion surveys I conducted—one in 1976 (Cook, 1979) and another in 1986 (Cook & Barrett, 1988, 1992); on a survey I conducted of members of the U.S. Congress (Cook, 1990; Cook & Barrett, 1992); and on surveys conducted by others (National Opinion Research Center, 1993; Rosenstone, Miller, Kinder, & the National Election Studies, 1995).

## HOW PERCEIVED SCARCITY AND CONFLICT AFFECT PROGRAMS FOR THE OLD

To understand the way that resentment has grown against the old, the long view can help us to see where we are. Beginning in the 1970s, the United States entered a period of relative scarcity. Productivity increased at a slower rate in the 1970s than in the two previous decades; the cost of raw materials rose at a dramatically faster rate than inflation; and the percentage of adults in the work force decreased, in part because of the increasing numbers of retired persons. These and other pressures such as the costs of meeting environmental, occupational safety, and health requirements led to a slowdown of economic growth. Since the pie of goods and services was not enlarging at the rates that held in the 1940s, 1950s, and 1960s, policy makers acknowledged more than previously the difficult decisions that had to be made about budget allocations when the overall allocations were "austere and lean," as President Carter characterized his budget for fiscal year 1980. According to Charles Schultz, Chairman of President Carter's Council of Economic Advisors (Council of Economic Advisors, 1979), "the pie is growing less rapidly, and both government and private demand are going to have to be scaled down accordingly" (p. 4). When policy makers and interest groups are confronted with a smaller pie—or one that is not growing at its former rate—there is likely to be a heightened sense of competition among those who want to partake of the pie.

Of course, policy makers at any time are inevitably confronted with the need to make decisions about the allocation of funds for various programs and societal needs. However, in a period of relative scarcity, the task is all the more difficult because it is likely to be carried out in a politicized atmosphere in which groups with competing interests are vying with each other to protect their share of the pie. The 1980s and 1990s have become just such a time. The rapidly mounting budget deficit adds to the sense of crisis about who gets what. The young and the old have been pitted against each other, but the adversarial stance has not been taken by the young or by advocacy groups representing the young.

Pitting of young against old became salient in the 1980s with the rise of what has become known as "the intergenerational equity debate." *Intergenerational equity* refers to the concept that different generations should be treated in similar ways and should have similar opportunities. The debate is about whether the young are being deprived of opportunities for economic and social well-being because of excessive allocations of resources to the old. In 1984, two independent events pushed the issue of intergenerational equity onto the agendas of both the policy and academic communities. In the policy community, Senator Dave Durenberger (R-MN) founded Americans for Generational Equity (AGE). In the academic community, Professor Samuel H. Preston gave the Presidential Address to the Annual Meeting of the Population Association of America, entitled "Children and the Elderly: Divergent Paths for America's Dependents." The address was later reprinted in the journal *Demography* (Preston, 1984a) and published in revised form in *Scientific American* (Preston, 1984b).

According to Durenberger, AGE's goal was "to promote the concept of generational equity among America's political, intellectual, and financial leaders" (as quoted in Quadagno, 1989, p. 360). The AGE 1990 *Annual Report* claims credit for calling "into question the prudence, sustainability, and fairness to future generations of federal old age benefit programs" (Americans for Generational Action, 1990, p. 2). Although AGE no longer exists due to some politically damaging financial problems of Durenberger, its effects were important. According to sociologist Jill Quadagno (1989), it reshaped the parameters of the policy debate about programs for the elderly "so that all future policy choices will have to take generational equity into account" (p. 364).

Although demographer Samuel H. Preston never mentioned the term *generational equity* in his presidential address or subsequent articles, it was clearly his theme. He amassed and integrated large bodies of data on changes for children and the elderly in three domains: economic well-being, the family, and politics. His data made a strong case that conditions have deteriorated for children and improved dramatically for the elderly and that "in the public sphere at least, *gains for one group come partly at the expense of another*" (Preston 1984a, p. 450, my italics). He argued that policy makers in the United States have made a set of choices that have dramatically altered the age profile of well-being: "Let's be clear that the transfers from the working-age population to the elderly are also transfers away from children . . . and let's also recognize that the sums involved are huge" (pp. 451–452).

Preston's argument was clearly a zero-sum one: the elderly are doing well because children are being shortchanged. His arguments piqued the interests of both journalists and scholars, who cited his work heavily. Although, as noted above, Preston did not use the term *intergenerational equity,* the many scholars who cited his work used the term frequently, and their research, along with Preston's, helped to legitimize the general concept of generational equity by providing empirical data to underpin the debate in the policy community.

Elsewhere, colleagues and I examined the salience of the issue of intergenerational equity in the print media, using several publicly available on-line databases (Cook et al., 1994). Between 1984 and 1992, we find 39 articles that prominently mention intergenerational equity. Although not dramatically large in number, they are dramatically inflammatory in content in their portrayal of conflict. They have titles such as these: "Older Voters Drive Budget" (Mufson, 1990), "U.S. Coddles Elderly but Ignores Plight of Children" (Tucker, 1990), "America Is at War with Its Children" (Reeves, 1989), "Robbing Baby Peter to Pay Aging Paul" (1991), and "The Tyranny of America's Old" (Smith, 1992).

Binstock documented the beginnings of this changing portrayal of the elderly as early as 1983. According to him, the compassionate stereotype of the elderly as poor, frail, and impotent as a political force started shifting in 1978, when the media, political speeches, public policy studies, and scholars began to characterize the elderly as well-off, active, and politically powerful. Further, he showed how these new "axioms" regarding older persons provided the foundation for the "aged as scapegoat," bearing the blame for a variety of economic and political problems (Binstock, 1983, p. 136). Binstock was quite right in his predictions that this scapegoating had the potential to engender intergenerational conflict, which could have serious implications.

Conservatives (e.g., Peterson, 1987; Peterson & Howe, 1988) have clearly tried to use the generational equity theme to undermine public support for programs targeted at the old, especially social insurance. As noted, the theme has been defined and widely disseminated to the public by the media. Further, the Concord Coalition, funded by Pete Peterson, has taken up where AGE left off to promote the view that the elderly are to blame for the deficit, skyrocketing health care costs, the crushing fiscal burden on taxpayers of entitlements such as Social Security and Medicare, and the economic plight of children.

From these descriptions of media portrayals and AGE activities, it is clear that Neugarten was right in her warnings of a possible rise in resentment and anger against the old. The question is: To what extent has public support for programs for the old been undermined by this siege? To answer that question, I report on two of my own studies—one in 1976 and one in 1986—as well as on a number of studies by others.

## PUBLIC SUPPORT FOR PROGRAMS FOR OLDER AMERICANS

### The Second Half of the 1970s

Over the years, many contradictory perspectives have been proffered about opinions toward the elderly. In 1975, Robert Butler wrote in his

Pulitzer Prize-winning *Why Survive? Being Old in America* that there is little support for the elderly. According to him, "Society seems to be saying, 'They're old—they don't need much in the way of services. Don't waste resources on them'" (p. 140). At about the same time, another author claimed that public opinion reserves its most unstinting compassion for the nation's children (Carter, Fifield, & Shields, 1973). Another referred to the disabled as the most supported group. (See Cook, 1979, for a detailed description of the conflicting perspectives on opinions about support for different groups.) To detect differences in support for several groups, survey respondents must be asked about all groups in the context of the same interview. In the mid-1970s, there had been no study that compared support for one group to support for another group.

The study I conducted to fill this gap had two parts in order to probe the claims about differences in support for social groups. In one part, respondents were presented with vignettes—brief stories about people who needed assistance—and asked how willing they would be to provide tax-financed assistance to them. Respondents' support was measured by their answers to questions about whether they thought it was important to have services financed by the federal government to help people in situations like that of the vignette character and about the extent to which they would be willing to go to demonstrate their support by

1. signing petitions and writing letters
2. attending local public meetings
3. paying higher taxes

These vignettes varied four characteristics of the person described:

1. age—either a young adult under age 35 or an older adult over age 65
2. responsibility for plight—either the needy individual himself or herself or some circumstance external to the person and outside his or her control
3. level of poverty—none, marginal, acute, or chronic
4. level of disability—none, marginal, acute, or chronic

The results showed that the age of the vignette character made a very significant difference in respondents' willingness to provide tax-financed assistance. That is, when respondents were presented with vignette characters whose characteristics were exactly alike in all respects except age, respondents were much more likely to support assistance for the older person than for the younger person. From this finding, I concluded that elderly persons evoked high support, not low, as some commentators such as Butler (1975) had asserted.

The question remained: Was support high regardless of which social service for the old was in question, or was support linked to particular services? To learn the answer, respondents were presented with four service areas—nutrition, transportation, education, and guaranteed minimum income—and asked to rank order which social groups should get each program. The social groups were the poor elderly, the disabled elderly, poor children, disabled children, poor adults under 65, and disabled adults under 65. Some commentators argue that the public is undiscerning and thus predict that members of the public would rank support for groups for services in the same way, regardless of service area in question (Converse, 1964). That is not what I found. Respondents were very discerning and linked the need they perceived for the group to the service in question. For example, both the disabled elderly and the poor elderly received a lot of support for nutrition programs and for income programs, but not for education programs. For transportation programs, respondents were not concerned about age so much as disability—all the disabled groups received high ranks for transportation. Further, not only were respondents discerning, but also they were homogeneously discerning; that is, regardless of race, gender, income, and education, respondents ranked groups for services in the same way.

In short, the two parts of the study, taken together, show us that there was high support for the elderly in comparison to younger persons in the latter half of the 1970s. Also, support was discriminating—that is, it was contingent on the nature of the service in question.

The study I conducted in the latter half of the 1970s answered questions about generalized support for the elderly, but it did not reveal much about public support for particular programs for older people, such as the largest public programs—the social insurance programs of Social Security and Medicare and the public assistance program of Supplemental Security Income. Further, given the scapegoating of the elderly described by Binstock (1983) as beginning in 1978, and the intergenerational equity debate that began in 1984, it is impossible to know the extent to which we can generalize from 1976 to the 1980s and 1990s.

## The Second Half of the 1980s

In 1986, I conducted two surveys (Cook & Barrett, 1992). The first was a national random sample of 1,209 United States citizens interviewed by telephone for approximately 45 minutes. The response rate was 71%. The second was a random sample of 58 members of the U.S. House of Representatives whom I interviewed in person in Washington, D.C. The response rate was 60%. For a survey of elites, this response rate is excellent (Verba & Orreu, 1995).

In both surveys, respondents answered a series of questions about their support for seven of the largest programs that make up the American welfare state—the social insurance programs of Social Security, Unemployment Insurance, and Medicare, and the public assistance programs of Aid to Families with Dependent Children (AFDC), Food Stamps, Medicaid, and Supplemental Security Income (SSI). Using the answers to these questions, we can examine the extent to which the American public supports the major programs targeted at the elderly, namely, Social Security, Medicare, and SSI (although of course the elderly also benefit from Medicaid and Food Stamps); whether some programs receive more support than others; and, if that is the case, which programs are most and least supported. In so doing, we can assess just how much support exists for programs for the old and the extent to which there appears to be anger and resentment against the old. Anger and resentment might be said to exist (1) if most members of the public and Congress want cuts in programs targeted to older persons, (2) if the public is not willing to make active commitments to support programs through either contacting their congressional representatives or paying higher taxes to prevent cuts, or (3) if representatives consistently fail to vote for measures designed to maintain or increase programs for the elderly.

Table 14.1 presents the public's preferences for increasing, maintaining, or decreasing benefits for the seven major social welfare programs. Clearly, members of the public overwhelmingly favor maintaining or increasing benefits for the three programs that most obviously target the old—Social Security, Medicare, and Supplemental Security Income. Sixty-eight percent want to see Medicare benefits increased, 30% want to see benefits maintained, and only 2% want to see benefits cut. For both Social Security and SSI, an astounding 97% want benefits to be maintained or increased and just 3% want to see cuts.

**TABLE 14.1    Public Support for Increasing, Maintaining, or Decreasing Benefits for Seven Social Welfare Programs**

| | Respondents saying programs should be: | | | |
|---|---|---|---|---|
| | Increased % | Maintained % | Decreased % | Support Score Mean |
| Medicare (N=1198) | 67.6 | 29.9 | 2.5 | 2.65 |
| Supplemental Security income (N=1167) | 57.3 | 40.0 | 2.7 | 2.55 |
| Social Security (N=1200) | 56.7 | 40.0 | 3.3 | 2.53 |
| Medicaid (N=1170) | 47.1 | 46.3 | 6.6 | 2.40 |
| Unemployment insurance (N=1155) | 31.5 | 55.5 | 13.0 | 2.18 |
| Aid to Families with Dependent Children (N=1170) | 32.6 | 51.9 | 15.5 | 2.17 |
| Food stamps (N=1132) | 24.6 | 51.0 | 24.4 | 2.0 |

One of the most striking results is how few respondents believe benefits should be decreased for any of the seven programs. For no program does a majority favor a decrease. Of the seven programs, food stamps is clearly the loser in terms of support. But even here, only about one in four respondents wants to see it cut. Unemployment insurance and AFDC run a distant second with about one in six wanting cuts.

The picture painted by these data is hardly what one would have expected given the barrage of scapegoating-the-elderly rhetoric and intergenerational equity debate that the public have been subjected to since the late 1970s. Indeed, Table 14.1 shows that programs targeting the elderly receive more support than other programs.

It is important to learn that the public wants to maintain or increase benefits for the three principal social welfare programs that assist the elderly, but it is even more important to learn the strength of the commitment behind these preferences. Policy makers are not apt to act on public support unless it is committed and active. To understand the degree of commitment behind statements of support, we asked a series of in-depth questions about actions that respondents would be willing to take to demonstrate support.

To assess behavioral support, we asked questions about three of the seven programs, each question probing a deeper commitment from the respondents. First, are they satisfied that a portion of their tax dollars goes to support the program? Second, how opposed would they be to cuts in the program? Third, if they are opposed, would they sign a petition or write their representatives in Congress to express their opposition? Further, we asked them whether they would be willing to pay higher taxes to prevent such cuts. Given all the discussion about intergenerational equity, programs for the elderly driving the deficit, "greedy geezers," and the crisis of public support for the welfare state in general, we expected to find only a minority of respondents satisfied that a portion of their tax dollars funds programs for the old and even fewer willing to go beyond attitudinal support with actions.

As the data in Table 14.2 show, however, we were wrong in our predictions. Over two thirds of the respondents report satisfaction that taxes help fund these social programs. Social Security receives the largest proportion of supporters (81%), and Medicaid the next largest proportion (78%). Sixty-five percent are satisfied with paying taxes for AFDC. However, when the questions require further behavioral commitments, levels of support decrease, especially among the programs that originally receive lower support. Nonetheless, a majority of respondents continue to support Social Security. Roughly two thirds are willing to write a letter or sign a petition protesting cuts in Social Security benefits, whereas about half are willing to take such action for Medicaid and only a third report being willing to do so for AFDC. Similarly, three in five respondents say they are willing to have their taxes raised to avoid cuts in Social Security benefits, but only one in three say they would pay higher taxes to avoid cuts in AFDC.

We can now address the question of the extent to which there appears to be anger and resentment against the elderly as expressed through unwillingness to support programs for the old. We see clearly that most members of the public do not want cuts in any of the major social welfare programs. Instead, the vast majority of the public believe programs should be maintained or expanded. For programs that target the elderly—Social Security, Medicare, and SSI—especially high levels of support exist.

TABLE 14.2  Respondents Willing to Perform Actions as Proportion of Total Sample and as Proportion of Satisfied and Dissatisfied Respondents

| | AFDC | | Medicaid | | Social Security | |
|---|---|---|---|---|---|---|
| | Percentage of total | Percentage of satis. | Percentage of total | Percentage of satis. | Percentage of total | Percentage of satis. |
| *Satisfied respondents who are:* | | | | | | |
| Satisfied with paying taxes for program | 64.5 | 100.0 | 78.4 | 100.0 | 81.4 | 100.0 |
| Opposing spending cuts | 50.8 | 77.6 | 63.4 | 80.8 | 73.1 | 89.8 |
| Willing to write a letter or sign a petition against spending cuts | 35.4 | 54.8 | 49.2 | 62.7 | 62.8 | 77.3 |
| Willing to pay more taxes to avoid cuts | 36.2 | 56.1 | 47.5 | 60.6 | 58.0 | 71.2 |

| | AFDC | | Medicaid | | Social Security | |
|---|---|---|---|---|---|---|
| | Percentage of total | Percentage of dissatis. | Percentage of total | Percentage of dissatis. | Percentage of total | Percentage of dissatis. |
| *Dissatisfied respondents who are:* | | | | | | |
| Dissatisfied with paying taxes for program | 33.6 | 100.0 | 21.6 | 100.0 | 18.6 | 100.0 |
| Opposing spending increases | 24.9 | 74.4 | 13.2 | 66.0 | 10.9 | 60.6 |
| Willing to write a letter or sign a petition against spending increases | 19.0 | 56.7 | 9.1 | 45.4 | 7.9 | 43.8 |
| Willing to decrease taxes spent on program | 15.0 | 44.7 | 9.3 | 46.4 | 4.8 | 26.9 |

*Note.* From SUPPORT FOR THE AMERICAN WELFARE STATE, by Fay Lomax Cook and Edith J. Barrett. Copyright© 1992. Reprinted with permission of the publisher.

VIEWS OF THE U.S. CONGRESS.   Fifty-eight members of the U.S. House of Representatives also answered questions about whether benefits should be maintained, increased, or cut for the same seven major programs about which we asked the public. Table 14.3 reports the responses to the set of questions about benefit levels. If we define support as wanting to maintain or increase benefits for the major programs, a tremendous amount of support exists among members of Congress. At least three out of four say they believe benefits should be maintained or increased for each program. In no case does a majority favor decreasing benefits. Separating supportive representatives into those who want to maintain and those who want to increase benefits, we see that for no program does a majority favor increasing benefits. Medicaid receives the highest percentage of advocates for increases (42%), followed closely by Medicare (32% favoring increases). Although no representative favors decreasing Social Security, neither do many elect to increase benefits. The overwhelming feeling appears to be that Social Security benefits are adequate at their current level and need not be changed.

How do the privately expressed views of representatives compare to their public actions? In regard to Social Security, the most relevant indicator is the vote made in the preceding year on an amendment offered by Representative Marvin Leath (D-Texas) to the budget resolution to eliminate cost of living adjustments (COLAs) for Social Security in order to produce additional deficit reductions. Eighty-seven percent of the representatives voted against this amendment, thus voting the same way they answered the survey question—that is, against any cuts in benefits.

We also compared the level of support that representatives express for programs targeted at the elderly with the 10 major votes they cast for legislation affecting the elderly, as tallied by the National Council on Senior Citizens (NCSC). Those representatives who favor increases in benefits for the three programs aimed toward the elderly have an NCSC voting record of 8.2 (i.e., they voted for 8 of the 10 bills), whereas those who favor decreases in benefits have a voting rating of 3.1 (i.e., they voted for an average of 3 of the 10 bills). These results show that their reported beliefs about programs are consistent with their actions.

CONGRESS AND THE PUBLIC.   How do the beliefs of the public and their representatives compare? The most important conclusion is that support for programs for the old is high when we define support as a desire to maintain or increase benefits. An overwhelming majority among both

**TABLE 14.3 Congressional Support for Increasing, Maintaining, or Decreasing Benefits for Seven Social Welfare Programs**

| | All Congress[a] % | Nonleaders % | Leaders % |
|---|---|---|---|
| Medicaid | | | |
| Increase | 41.8 | 41.2 | 54.5 |
| Maintain | 52.8 | 52.9 | 45.5 |
| Decrease | 5.4 | 5.9 | — |
| AFDC | | | |
| Increase | 32.7 | 32.4 | 40.9 |
| Maintain | 58.7 | 58.8 | 54.5 |
| Decrease | 8.2 | 8.8 | — |
| Means tested | 0.4 | — | 4.5 |
| Medicare | | | |
| Increase | 32.4 | 32.4 | 36.4 |
| Maintain | 55.6 | 55.9 | 50.0 |
| Decrease | 10.9 | 11.8 | — |
| Means tested | 1.2 | — | 13.6 |
| SSI | | | |
| Increase | 23.8 | 23.5 | 31.8 |
| Maintain | 68.0 | 67.6 | 68.2 |
| Decrease | 8.2 | 8.8 | — |
| Social Security | | | |
| Increase | 11.7 | 11.8 | 13.6 |
| Maintain | 85.5 | 85.3 | 86.4 |
| Decrease | — | — | — |
| Means tested | 2.7 | 2.9 | — |
| Unemployment compensation | | | |
| Increase | 12.3 | 11.8 | 22.7 |
| Maintain | 76.5 | 76.5 | 72.7 |
| Decrease | 11.2 | 11.8 | 4.5 |
| Food stamps | | | |
| Increase | 15.7 | 14.7 | 31.8 |
| Maintain | 59.4 | 58.8 | 63.6 |
| Decrease | 24.9 | 26.5 | 4.5 |

[a] Weighted sample
*Note.* From *SUPPORT FOR THE AMERICAN WELFARE STATE,* by Fay Lomax Cook and Edith J. Barrett. Copyright© 1992. Reprinted with permission of the publisher.

the public and Congress favor maintaining or increasing benefits for the major programs that target the old; only a small minority favor cuts.

Other conclusions point to differences between Congress and the public. The most noticeable difference is that members of the public are more likely than representatives to favor increases in program benefits. Were we to define support for Social Security, Medicare, and SSI based solely upon a willingness to increase benefits, we would see representatives holding less favorable views towards programs than the general public. However, the representatives interviewed explain quite clearly why they are hesitant to say "increase." They are concerned about the cost of adding more benefits to a system they see as already overburdened. As one representative said:

> I'm going to sound like I'm just for the status quo, but the reason I favor maintaining the current levels . . . is not that I don't think we should do more, but just taking into account the economic realities, I think that's about all we can do.

A second difference between representatives and the general public can be seen in the choice of program favored most by the two groups. The three programs favored most by the public generally target the elderly, but among Congress higher support is given to programs principally seen to help poor children and their parents—AFDC and Medicaid. The proportion of representatives favoring increases in Social Security benefits is much smaller than that of the general public, 12% of representatives versus 57% of the public.

A third difference between the views of the public and members of Congress is in the target groups that respondents rank highest for social services. In a part of the survey not discussed earlier, respondents ranked which groups should be given highest priority for services. Representatives are most likely to give children top priority for services, whereas the general public is most likely to give the elderly top priority. Representatives who rank children first say that they are aware of statistics that show children to be more likely than other age groups to be living in poverty and that additional help is needed. They rank children above the elderly, they say, because the problem of poverty among the elderly is diminishing while the problem of poverty among children is increasing. In the interviews, they described data showing the elderly, as a group, to be much better off than they were in the early 1960s before the introduction of such programs as Medicare, Medicaid,

SSI, the Older Americans Act, and Social Security cost of living adjustments (COLAs). For example, one representative said:

> We are pretty well taking care of the elderly through various programs that we have. I think the statistics bear that out in the last year. But for the same period of time I've seen children drop through the net, so to speak.

Representatives do not seem to be saying that federal resource distribution between the young and old is a zero-sum game such that giving to the young entails taking from the old. Rather, they are simply saying that federal efforts since the 1950s have had the effect of reducing poverty among elderly Americans and that the need now is to give a higher priority to children, the age group most likely to live in poor families.

## CONTINUITY OF SUPPORT OVER TIME: RESULTS FROM OTHER SURVEYS

A final piece of information useful in assessing the extent to which there may be a shift in attitudes toward the elderly can be found in public opinion data over time, especially data since 1986. For this, we have turned to three sources—a 1994 Gallup Opinion Poll survey for the Employee Benefit Research Institute (EBRI), the National Election Surveys conducted every other year by the University of Michigan Institute for Social Research, and the General Social Surveys conducted every year by the National Opinion Research Center.

In 1994, in consultation with me, Gallup asked an almost identical question to one that I asked respondents in 1986—the extent to which respondents favored the fact that a part of every working person's income goes to support the Social Security program. Eighty-one percent of the public in 1994 were in support—the exact same proportion as in 1986 (Friedland, 1994).

In 1982, 1986, 1990, and 1992, the National Election Survey asked a large nationally representative sample of respondents whether they thought the government was "spending too much, too little, or about the right amount on Social Security." The results are reported in Table 14.4. As can be seen, an overwhelming majority in each of the years said that spending should stay the same or be increased.

**TABLE 14.4   Public Support Over Time for Increasing, Maintaining, or Decreasing Spending for Social Security, by Year**

|            | 1982 % | 1984 % | 1986 % | 1988 % | 1990 % | 1992 % |
|------------|------|------|------|------|------|------|
| Increase   | 46   | 52   | 63   | 59   | 63   | 49   |
| Stay same  | 33   | 44   | 31   | 38   | 34   | 47   |
| Decrease   | 12   | 4    | 3    | 3    | 3    | 4    |

*Note:* Data compiled from National Election Surveys (Rosenstone, Miller, Kinder, and the National Election Studies, 1995). The question was: "Should federal spending on Social Security be increased, decreased, or kept about the same?"

In 1984–1986, 1988–1991, and 1993, the National Opinion Research Center's General Social Survey asked respondents whether they thought the United States was spending too little money, about the right amount of money, or too much money on Social Security. As Table 14.5 shows, the vast majority said we are spending too little or about the right amount. Only a small percentage (4–9%) said we are spending too much money.

The results from these surveys lead to the conclusion that support has not declined since the time of the in-depth interviews in 1986. This stability in opinion of the American public is consistent with the stability over time on a range of domestic and foreign issues that Page and Shapiro (1992) describe in *The Rational Public*. However, although Page and Shapiro show that for the most part Americans' opinions are stable and consistent, opinions can and do shift under certain conditions—for example, when there is war, when there are shifts in the economy, or when new information becomes available about social problems. From the available data, it appears that support among the public for programs for the old remains high. However, the political landscape of the United States has undergone significant changes since the late 1980s, some of which might provide a fertile environment for changing opinions.

## CONCLUSION

In the early 1970s, Neugarten wrote about the aging society and saw—before most others—that one implication of the growing numbers of

**TABLE 14.5    Public Support for Social Security: Public Beliefs Over Time Regarding the Amount of Money the U.S. Spends on Social Security**

|  | 1984 % | 1985 % | 1986 % | 1988 % | 1989 % | 1990 % | 1991 % | 1993 % |
|---|---|---|---|---|---|---|---|---|
| Too little | 48 | 43 | 37 | 55 | 57 | 52 | 55 | 46 |
| About right | 45 | 49 | 55 | 40 | 39 | 42 | 41 | 46 |
| Too much | 7 | 8 | 9 | 6 | 5 | 6 | 4 | 8 |

*Note.* Data compiled from General Social Surveys (National Opinion Research Center, 1993). The question was: "We are faced with many problems in this country, none of which can be solved easily or inexpensively. I'm going to name some of these problems and for each one I'd like you to tell me whether you think we're spending too much money on it, too little money, or the right amount . . . Social Security." Percentages may not add to 100 due to rounding. The question about Social Security was not asked of all respondents in 1987 and 1992.

older persons might be increased levels of resentment and anger against the old. A possible backlash against the old could occur that would undermine support. In this chapter, I have shown that Neugarten was quite right in her warnings regarding the possible change in anger and resentment against the old; this is clear if we look at the media and views of certain policy elites, such as those who belonged to Americans for Generational Equity, many of whom now support the Concord Coalition. However, these media portrayals have not resulted in a loss of public support for social programs for the old. Instead, the public's support for social programs that target elderly people is strong and has shown a remarkable degree of continuity over time.

Despite the current levels of support, we cannot be sanguine about the future. Since the late 1980s, the political landscape has changed dramatically. Congress is controlled by Republicans, public concern over the deficit has grown more widespread, and programs for the elderly are being challenged as never before. The current political climate for the elderly is decidedly hostile. As Binstock (1994) has noted, "Contemporary public rhetoric is laced with proclamations that entitlement programs (read Social Security, Medicare, and Medicaid) must be drastically curtailed if significant progress is to be made toward eliminating the large annual federal deficits that began to emerge during President Reagan's administration" (p. 726).

What lies ahead? Will public anger and resentment grow, as presaged by the media portrayals we have seen and as predicted by Dychtwald and Flowers (1989), who see crushing "age wars" ahead? Or will public support remain as strong as we have seen it to be in this chapter? To date, public support has been remarkably resistant to negative media portrayals, the generational equity rhetoric, and the politics of blame that accuse the elderly of exacerbating problems from the deficit to soaring health care costs. It is difficult to predict how long such support can be maintained.

## ACKNOWLEDGMENTS

I am grateful to my colleagues with whom I collaborated in conducting some of the research described in this chapter: Edith J. Barrett of Brown University, Victor Marshall and Joanne Gard Marshall of the University of Toronto, and Julie Kaufman of the University of Illinois-Chicago. I am also grateful to Richard A. Settersten, Case Western University, who was a good friend, sounding board, advisor, and research assistant when large parts of the research described in the chapter were being conducted. His assistance was invaluable. Finally, I thank the University of Toronto for the invitation in 1994 to give the 12th Annual Wilson Abernathy Distinguished Lecture, which was an important opportunity to begin to pull together some of the ideas presented in this chapter.

## REFERENCES

Americans for Generational Equity. (1990). Annual report. Washington, DC: Author.

Binstock, R. H. (1983). The aged as scapegoat. *The Gerontologist, 23,* 136–143.

Binstock, R. H. (1994). Changing criteria in old-age programs: The introduction of economic status and need for services. *The Gerontologist, 34,* 726–730.

Butler, R. R. (1975). *Why survive? Being old in America.* New York: Harper & Row.

Carter, G. L., Fifield, H., & Shields, H. (1973). *Public attitudes toward welfare: An opinion poll.* Los Angeles: Regional Research Institute in Social Welfare, University of Southern California.

Converse, P. E. (1964). The nature of belief systems in mass publics. In D. E. Apter (Ed.), *Ideology and discontent* (pp. 219– 227). New York: Free Press.

Cook, F. L. (1979). *Who should be helped? Public support for social services.* Beverly Hills, CA: Sage.

Cook, F. L. (1990). Congress and the divergent opinions on Social Security. In H. Aaron (Ed.), *Social Security and the budget* (pp. 79–107). Lanham, MD: University Press.

Cook, F. L., & Barrett, E. J. (1988). Public support for social security. *Journal of Aging Studies, 2,* 339–356.

Cook, F. L., & Barrett, E. J. (1992). *Support for the American welfare state: The views of congress and the public.* New York: Columbia University Press.

Cook, F. L., Marshall, V. W., Marshall, J. G., & Kaufman, J. K. (1994). The salience of intergenerational equity in Canada and the United States. In T. R. Marmor, T. M. Smeeding, & V. L. Greene (Eds.), *Economic security and intergenerational justice: A look at North America* (pp. 91–129). Washington, DC: Urban Institute Press.

Council of Economic Advisors. (1979). *Economic report to Congress.* Washington, DC: U.S. Government Printing Office.

Dychtwald, K., & Flowers, J. (1989). *Age wave: The challenge and opportunities of an aging America.* New York: Tarcher.

Friedland, R. B. (1994). *Social Security: Public support and public confidence* (Working Report, National Academy of Social Insurance). Washington, DC: National Academy of Social Insurance.

Garfield, E. (1984). The 100 most-cited papers ever and how we select "citation classics." *Current Contents, 23,* 3–9.

Marshall, V. W., Cook, F. L., & Marshall, J. G. (1993). Conflict over intergenerational equity: Rhetoric and reality in a comparative context. In V. L. Bengtson & W. A. Achenbaum (Eds.), *The changing contract across generations* (pp. 119–140). New York: Aldine de Gruyter.

Mufson, S. (1990, October 15). Older voters drive budget. *The Washington Post,* p. 1.

National Opinion Research Center (1993). *General social surveys, 1972–1993: Cumulative codebook.* Storrs, CT: Roper Center for Public Opinion Research.

Neugarten, B. L. (1973). Patterns of aging: Past, present, and future. *Social Science Review, 47,* 571–580.

Neugarten, B. L. (1979). Time, age, and the life cycle. *American Journal of Psychiatry, 136,* 887–894.

Neugarten, B. L. (1985). Interpretive social science and research on aging. In A. S. Rossi (Ed.), *Gender and the life course* (pp. 291–300). New York: Aldine de Gruyter.

Page, B., & Shapiro, R. (1992). *The rational public.* Chicago: University of Chicago Press.

Peterson, P. G. (1987, October). The morning after. *The Atlantic Monthly,* pp. 43–69.

Peterson, P. G., & Howe, N. (1988). *On borrowed time: How the growth in entitlement spending threatens America's future.* San Francisco: ICS Press.

Preston, S. H. (1984a). Children and the elderly: Divergent paths for America's dependents. *Demography, 21,* 435–457.

Preston, S. H. (1984b). Children and the elderly in the U.S. *Scientific American, 25*(6), 44–49.

Reeves, R. (1989, October 12). America is at war with its children. *San Francisco Chronicle,* p. 35.

Robbing baby Peter to pay aging Paul. (1991, February 10). *Boston Globe,* p. 1.

Rosenstone, S. J., Miller, W. E., Kinder, D. R., & the National Election Studies. (1995). *American national election study: Post election survey* [machine-readable codebook file]. Ann Arbor, MI: University of Michigan Center for Political Studies, Inter-university Consortium for Political and Social Research [Producer and Distributor].

Quadagno, J. (1989). Generational equity and the politics of the welfare state. *Politics and Society, 17,* 353–376.

Smith, L. (1992, January 13). The tyranny of America's old. *Fortune,* pp. 68–74.

Tucker, C. (1990, October 10). U.S. coddles elderly but ignores plight of children. *Atlanta Constitution,* p. A9.

Verba, S., & Orreu, G. R. (1985). *Equality in America: The views from the top.* Cambridge, MA: Harvard University Press.

# Comments

## Robert H. Binstock

I can hardly take a generally critical stance regarding Fay Cook's chapter. My own chapter in this volume is in harmony with her view that policies benefiting older persons will be continuously under attack in Washington in the years immediately ahead. Moreover, Fay Cook has been kind enough to cite, incorporate, and quote from some of my work. Consequently, I am impelled to state that her analysis is outstanding.

In addition, Cook's survey work is impeccable. I say this even though for many years I have been highly skeptical of surveys and their interpretations when applied to political and public policy matters.

A number of recent surveys, for example, have reported that from 75% to 85% of older persons have negative opinions about programs run by the government. Yet, comparable proportions of respondents in these same surveys say that Medicare and Social Security are wonderful programs. Such gaps in the general public's knowledge about political and policy matters is reflected in recurring polls in which adults of all ages are asked, during election campaigns, if they know the name of their representative in the U.S. Congress. Usually, just under half of the people say they know the name; and of these, about half are not able to name their representative.

I am not skeptical, however, with respect to Fay Cook's work. She takes great care in designing, implementing, analyzing, and interpreting her survey data. Specifically, note that she found a high level of correspondence between how members of the House of Representatives responded to her survey and how they voted on the issue of eliminating the cost-of-living adjustment (COLA) for Social Security benefits. (Parenthetically, Fay Cook did find higher support for Aid to Families with Dependent Children (AFDC) in Congress than within the public at large. One doubts if the same result would have been found in the first hundred days of the 104th Congress when the House, under the leadership of Newt Gingrich, was attacking AFDC head on.)

All this having been said I do, however, have two areas of slight disagreement with Fay Cook's analysis. They would be apparent from a careful comparison of her chapter and mine on "Continuities and Discontinuities in Public Policy on Aging."

First, as indicated in my chapter, and in contrast with Cook's chapter, I believe that cutbacks in old age benefits have been taking place for some time. I share her view that there will be more to come. Cook points out that during the 1980s public support for old age programs did not decline. Yet, cutbacks in old age policies were enacted during the 1980s. This suggests that common assumptions regarding the linkage between public attitudes and governmental actions ought to be reconsidered.

Second, I do not think as Cook does that a shrinking federal "budgetary pie" was responsible for an artificially homogenized group termed "the aged" becoming scapegoat for a wide variety of problems from the late 1970s until today. Actually, the budgetary pie has enlarged a great deal. Federal outlays have more than tripled since 1978, from $458 billion then to $1,461 billion in 1994 (U.S. Congress, 1995, p. 96). As indicated in my chapter in this volume, I believe that the prime factor for the focus on older people and old age programs can be attributed to the growing proportion of the federal budget spent on benefits to older persons. An additional factor was the so-called crisis in Social Security in the late 1970s and early 1980s. It was fueled by exceptionally high rates of inflation (which substantially increased Social Security benefits through cost-of-living adjustments) and by high unemployment rates (which simultaneously reduced the tax base on which the Federal Insurance Contributions Act is levied).

But these are minor quibbles with her excellent chapter, which reflects a major area of research that she has developed superbly. Notable as well in Cook's chapter is the effective fashion in which she has pointed up Bernice Neugarten's extraordinary prescience over the years in generating ideas and dialogue concerning public policies on aging.

# REFERENCE

U.S. Congress. (1995). *The economic and budget outlook: Fiscal years 1996–2000.* Washington, DC: U.S. Government Printing Office.

# CHAPTER 15

# Looking at Our Future Selves: Neugarten as Gerontology's Seer

## W. Andrew Achenbaum and Celia Berdes

W hen trying to understand and interpret the body of work of a prolific and influential intellectual, it is sometimes useful to appropriate that scholar's own modus operandi. A life course approach suggests that Bernice Neugarten's work evolved in overlapping phases. Her earliest research focused on children and class. Neugarten's major contributions for the past three decades have been in the domain of adult development and aging—although, since returning to the University of Chicago, she has been interested in welfare issues at both ends of life. In this collection, we see the fruits of Neugarten's ability to instill into her students a commitment to scholarly excellence and high professional standards. Yet we should not lose sight of the fact that Neugarten's extraordinary success as a role model, mentor, and builder of organizations in Chicago and elsewhere all were animated by her own intellectual curiosity, critical acumen, and ability to anticipate emerging trends.

Bernice Neugarten was at the cutting edge of research most of her career. She was greatly influenced by her mentor, Robert Havighurst, himself a polymath who distinguished himself in the natural sciences

and in the foundation world before establishing himself as a major fig-
ure among the first wave of social science investigators from the United
States in the field of aging during the 1940s. First in collaboration with
Havighurst, and then with her students and with other members of the
Committee on Human Development, Neugarten rightly can be viewed
as one of the leading figures in the second generation of gerontologists.
As she herself noted in 1987, "I think my research has not been unified
around a single theme, except that it has all been concerned with issues
of change and stability in the second half of life" (COA Interviews,
1987/1988, p. 3). Neugarten has revisited critical "problems" as her
interests have expanded, affording her new frames of reference. There
have been certain continuities in themes. She has long urged fellow
gerontologists, for instance, to take account of the diversity in late-life
personalities and the heterogeneity of older people's needs and capacities. Furthermore, Neugarten has always been fascinated with the ways
that continuities and changes in adult development manifest themselves
over the course of individuals' lives, and how they vary from generation
to generation. "My pattern of research has been to open up new topic
areas rather than to follow a single line of inquiry; to use sometimes
qualitative, sometimes quantitative methods; to prefer exploration to
replication," Neugarten reflected a year later, "in short, to map out
some of the landscape of what had earlier been the neglected territory
of the second half of life" (Neugarten, 1988, pp. 100–101).

In this essay, we take Neugarten at her word, and examine how she,
a self-acknowledged explorer, sought to anticipate trends in gerontology in the academy, in public policy, and in society at large. We
acknowledge at the outset that her work in "future studies" is not her
most important intellectual contribution: Neugarten is far more likely to
be remembered for her analyses of continuities and discontinuities in
age norms, in family structures, and in social-psychological processes.
She has enriched the gerontologic literature with phrases such as
*young-old, old-old* and *on-time, off-time.* Yet by choosing to delve into
a relatively minor area of Neugarten's concern, we are able to trace how
this mature, respected scholar ventured into new domains. Few researchers
on aging are willing to cross disciplinary boundaries, and fewer still
have been as effective as Neugarten in reframing public policy debates.
As we shall see, she succeeded by dint of her steadfast insistence that
ideas be critically examined with solid data. Neugarten became a pioneer in the field of *gero-futures* by expanding her intellectual repertoire

when most scholars at a comparable stage in their careers would have been content to rest on their accomplishments.

## EARLY VENTURES INTO SOCIAL FORECASTING

In her empirical and conceptual studies of age norms, conducted primarily with Robert Havighurst and other members of the University of Chicago's Committee on Human Development beginning in the late 1950s, Neugarten was already beginning to map out the landscape of the individual consequences and the societal effects of increased life expectancy. See, for instance, her essay with Joan W. Moore on "The Changing Age-Status System," published in *Middle Age and Aging* (Neugarten & Moore, 1968). This essay surveyed postwar changes in the family cycle, economic system, and political institutions in the United States. At the end of the article, however, Neugarten took a risk that social scientists typically eschew: She tested the robustness of her analysis by offering predictions grounded in scant theory. Rather than pretend to be expostulating grand hypotheses, Neugarten set forth a reasonable strategy for gauging continuities and changes over time:

> The foregoing analysis of changes in the American age-status system refers to the period through the mid-1960s. This picture is likely to change more within the next decade because, due to the birth rates of the 1940's, there will be dramatic shifts in the age distribution of persons on the labor market. . . . . At the same time, the number of the aged will increase in the decade of the 1970s with increases in longevity. . . . . Without reference to the state of the economy, nor to the various other factors of social change which will influence the general picture, these alterations in the age distribution of the society will lead to new relationships between the young, the middle-aged, and the old, and, in turn, to new changes in the age-status systems of American society. (Neugarten & Moore, 1968, p. 21)

At a time of great upheaval in the United States, when pop sociologists—on the basis of scant empirical evidence—were outdoing one another in predicting the end of an era, Neugarten eyed the future cautiously.

Neugarten took prevailing conditions as her temporal baseline. This tack for limning the future had advantages and disadvantages. Methodologically conservative, Neugarten's forecast did not rest on unexamined assumptions or trendy hypotheses about the future. Unless she came across data that indicated developments to the contrary, Neugarten assumed that the future would be the present writ large. So in discussing "The Changing Age-Status System," Neugarten and Moore were willing to make certain inferences concerning how recent demographic shifts would affect the relative numbers of older, younger, and middle-aged Americans. It seemed reasonable, though hardly controversial, to hypothesize that a quarter century after the baby boom began there would be a surge in young workers seeking employment. But at this stage of her career as a future gazer, Neugarten was not prepared to be too bold a risk taker. Thus she chose not to extend her timeline beyond the 1980s because she did not feel that she yet had a clear enough sense of how these known demographic trends would affect the economy.

This same conservative approach characterized Neugarten's analysis of the future of the aged as a subculture, which, she concluded in the late 1960s, was a "debatable phenomenon." Although she included Arnold M. Rose's "The Subculture of the Aging: A Topic for Sociological Research" as Chapter 3 in *Middle Age and Aging* (Rose, 1968), Neugarten was not wholly persuaded by Rose's provocative thesis. In her chapter with Moore, she noted that there was no clear analog among the current cohort of older Americans to the middle-class teen world, fueled by the consumption of goods and services. Compared to the numbers of adolescents creating for themselves a collective identity in high schools, the numbers of senior citizens then migrating to retirement communities in California, the southwest, and Florida were still small. "The next generation of pensioners will be different from the present one insofar as they will be less differentiated from other age groups in respect to income, education and ethnicity," Neugarten and Moore stipulated. "Whether or not they will become more segregated, by choice or by assignation, cannot be determined."[1] Neugarten knew that the difference between possibilities and probabilities affected future scenarios. Her increasing confidence in her ability to state what trends did not interest her, that is, to state what was not plausible, was an important step in her willingness to enunciate that range of future scenarios which seemed likely to occur.

Neugarten's long and multifaceted intellectual odyssey, as it appears in retrospect, took a new direction in the mid-1970s: She began to devote more scholarly energy to forecasting the reciprocal impact of societal change and aging populations on each other. As she began to explore this new topic area, Neugarten realized that speculating about complex issues with obvious policy relevance would require a different kind of knowledge than gerontologists typically produced: "Our intention has been to develop a research needs assessment program," Neugarten declared. "By needed research, we mean not only new types of data, but new ways of organizing existing data, and new social experiments" (Neugarten, 1975, p. 3).

Note here the link between research and curricular matters that Neugarten consistently made such a high priority in her mentoring. Always observing how ideas were formulated and disseminated, she was very concerned that researchers' methods be appropriate to the task at hand. In the domain of forecasting aging trends, Neugarten saw an opportunity to develop new ways of seeing and assessing ideas.

In a few years, without compromising her standards of intellectual rigor, Neugarten was collaborating with colleagues at the University of Chicago on several interdisciplinary projects that aimed to delineate likely scenarios for future cohorts of senior citizens. She was well prepared for the task. Neugarten's interdisciplinary credentials were established in her undergraduate years at the University of Chicago, when she concentrated in English and in French; her cross-disciplinary orientation surely was refined in the Committee on Human Development, where psychologists, psychiatrists, education professors, sociologists, anthropologists, and an occasional biomedical researcher interacted.

So the point to be underscored is not that Neugarten was somehow becoming more of a multidisciplinary maven. Rather, in blazing a new frontier, she relied on the perspectives afforded through several academic disciplines in order to get a sense of the big picture. If there is anything new in her approach, it may be that Neugarten evinced more interest in cross-national data sets. Early in her career she had worked with Havighurst on some of his research into the educational needs of Native American children and youth. Now, Neugarten became more willing to speculate about how advanced industrial societies such as the United States were undergoing profound transformation. (Some of this cosmopolitanism, of course, may simply reflect the increasing opportunities Neugarten had to travel around the world as a consultant and speaker.) Nevertheless, by the late 1960s, Neugarten seems well positioned and appears to have been more comfortable writing as a "seer." Increasing visibility and participation in the federal policy arena, moreover, reinforced this new direction in Neugarten's work.

## SOCIAL POLICY, SOCIAL ETHICS,
## AND THE AGING SOCIETY

In the 1970s, Neugarten's interest in social policy was fueled by her appointment to the Federal Council on Aging:

> I became convinced that social sciences training was deficient in neglecting the importance of policy decisions in altering the course of human lives. . . . I saw how the lives of adults are altered dramatically by what Congress decided to do yesterday. (COA, 1987/1988, p. 6)

Her interest in policy blossomed in her work on a number of reports for national bodies published between 1976 and 1982. Dr. Neugarten was the editor (with Robert J. Havighurst) of two National Science Foundation publications, *Social Policy, Social Ethics, and the Aging Society* (1976), which sought to make explicit the relations between social ethics and social policy regarding older persons, and *Extending the Human Life Span: Social Policy and Social Ethics* (1977). She was the editor (with George L. Maddox) of a blueprint for the newly created National Institute on Aging: *Our Future Selves: A Research Plan Toward Understanding Aging* (National Institutes of Health, 1978), specifically the report of the panel on behavioral and social science research. She authored a chapter in *Aging: Agenda for the Eighties* (Neugarten, 1979a) entitled "Policy for the 1980s, Age or Need Entitlement?" Finally, she was the editor of "Aging Society: Policy Agenda for the 1980s," a special issue of the *Phi Kappa Phi Journal* (Neugarten, 1982b).

To cite this long and impressive list of publications implies a certain inevitability to Neugarten's forays into gero-futures, wherein success predictably follows upon success. Yet the seeming linearity of the story line is deceptive. Retracing the process that led Neugarten to edit *Social Policy, Social Ethics, and the Aging Society* illustrates how even established scholars sometimes fall into new ways of looking at things.

In early 1973, Bernice Neugarten and two other University of Chicago faculty members, supported by a small grant from the Alfred P. Sloan Foundation, began to guide a student task force charged with exploring future policy issues for the aged. Interest quickly grew. Eventually, 18 professors from a variety of disciplines (including such luminaries as health administration specialist Odin Anderson, educa-

tional ombudsman Robert Havighurst, biogerontologists Leonard Hay-
flick and George Sacher, anthropologist Sol Tax, economist George S.
Tolley, and philosopher Warner A. Wick) and 30 students joined the
project. With a three-year grant from the National Science Foundation's
Division on Research Applied to National Needs (RANN), the group
endeavored to identify research questions that clustered around three
topics: (1) the economic welfare of older persons, (2) health services
for older persons, and (3) the extension of the human life span.

Given the intellectual breadth and the political implications of the
agenda, a longer time frame was necessary than the circumscribed 10-
year horizon that Neugarten and Moore had set forth in their 1968 article in *Middle Age and Aging*. "There has been no major analysis of
what future populations of older persons will require or what they will
want, even though we know that older persons in 1990 and 2000 will be
very different from the present population of older persons," Neugarten
noted. "Nor have there been systematic analyses of the effects of their
increased numbers on the larger society" (Neugarten, 1975, p. 3). A
seminar met regularly during the 1973–1974 academic year, and various memoranda and working papers were drafted.

Convinced that "cultural lag" caused many of the problems besetting
the country's current cohort of senior citizens, Neugarten thought it was
essential to prepare social institutions to accommodate the needs and
demands of increasing numbers of older men and women:

> It is increasingly evident that policy formulation requires the ability to
> predict future contingencies as well as to develop appropriate responses
> to current problems. Although there has been an enormous growth of
> research on aging in the past two decades that has relevance for social
> policy, and although excellent reviews and reports suggesting areas of
> research priorities have appeared, they have been phrased in terms of the
> 1970s. (Neugarten, 1975, p. 3)

Note the contrast in tone and focus to the more tentative position that
Neugarten and Joan Moore took in their essay on "Changing Age Norms"
in *Middle Age and Aging* (1968). Now, she and her colleagues were
willing to make policy-relevant forecasts for the next quarter-century.
The extended time frame was made possible by advances in the field as
well as by Neugarten's greater confidence in this domain. (The reference to "future contingencies" seems to anticipate the work of philoso-

pher Richard Rorty, 1989.) In any case, Neugarten's choice of words signals a more speculative mode of discourse.

Nonetheless, keenly aware of the risks of predicting developments beyond the proximate future, Neugarten remained cautious. Visionaries since Plato's day, after all, had imagined both utopian and apocalyptic visions that were inspired by mystic, religious, ethical, and pseudoscientific images of humankind. Science fiction writers, moreover, envisioned brave new worlds utterly redesigned by technology. Eschewing both fantasy and fiction, Neugarten sought to align her "futures research" with inquiries underway in recently emerging specialties in the biological and social sciences. Her survey of the work of that seemingly more respectable scholarly group revealed a niche in which Neugarten felt comfortable making contributions: "Although there are notable exceptions, few of the persons engaged in futures research have looked at changing age distributions and at the social, economic, political, and ethical implications for individuals or for societies at large. This fact is even more noteworthy because many of these investigators have been concerned with issues of social policy" (1975, p. 3).

Accordingly, Neugarten and her chief collaborator, Robert Havighurst, convened the important Conference on Social Policy, Social Ethics, and the Aging Society in 1974. The agenda and participants were notable in at least three regards. First, state and federal officials—people who knew policy firsthand—were invited to write papers and to participate in the conference. Former Social Security Commissioner Robert M. Ball wrote a paper on the income needs of older Americans. Rep. James Cornman of California drafted a position paper on health services. Byron Gold, on leave from the U.S. Administration on Aging, helped to plan the conference. Second, long before a critical mass of experts in the humanities had done significant research on any aspect of aging, Neugarten and her colleagues on the Midway were stressing the ethical dimensions of policy making: "As a nation we are accustomed to moving from the acquisition of knowledge to its application in policy making, but without a careful consideration of the grounds we *ought* to be seeking" (Neugarten & Havighurst, 1976, p. iii). Third, although Chicago social scientists such as demographer Philip Hauser (1942) had written during the 1940s and 1950s about the likely effects of population aging, Neugarten was arguably the first gerontologist to write about an "aging society" in more than demographic terms.

Neugarten during the 1980s would make several strategic efforts (first in planning the 1981 White House Conference on Aging and then in her work on the Aging Society Project, underwritten by the Carnegie Corporation of New York) to persuade researchers on aging to get beyond their interests in patterns of individual growth and development and to consider the ramifications of societal aging. Researchers, Neugarten asserted, had to embrace the broad issues posed by the concatenation of demographic, cultural, social, economic, and political factors of a heterogeneous population. New values, norms, and institutions might be necessary as more and more men and women could expect to live longer than their grandparents. Neugarten's writings increasingly reflected her sensitivity to these societal shifts.

The initial results of the National Science Foundation project appeared in two major reports: a special issue of *The Gerontologist* published in February 1975, "Aging in the Year 2000: A Look at the Future" (Neugarten, 1975b), and a report a year later to the National Science Foundation and the RANN—Research Applications Directorate, *Social Policy, Social Ethics, and the Aging Society* (Neugarten & Havighurst, 1976).[2] In their background paper for that report, "Aging and the Future," Neugarten and Havighurst took "a conservatively optimistic position" concerning developments during the next twenty-five years. In assessing likely changes in future cohorts of older people, the pair's predictions have proved fairly accurate:

- They anticipated no dramatic changes in the length of the human life span, but they did expect average life expectancy to continue to increase. They were confident about this forecast because they knew that everyone who would be old in the year 2000 was already alive; variations would occur due to alterations in mortality rates, not fertility rates. Even so, Neugarten and her associates hedged their bets. In *Social Policy, Social Ethics, and the Aging Society,* the group acknowledged that if, as some gerontologists thought likely, the human life span were to be extended another 5 years by the year 2000, this reality would necessitate a reconsideration of "a wide range of social and economic politics at both the national and local levels" (p. 5).
- Neugarten and Havighurst presumed "better levels of health for older persons because poverty is diminishing over the life-cycles of successive cohorts of older persons, because educational levels are rising, and because we predict more effective forms of public health and

improved systems of health care" (Neugarten & Havighurst, 1976, pp. 4–5).

- Due to increasing longevity and the shortening in the lengths of generations, they predicted four- and five-generation families would become "the norm." Expectations about intergenerational exchanges, they felt, might change by 2000, but the changes were likely to be slow. Of particular interest were the dynamics between very old parents and their aged children.
- The young-old were expected to remain "disproportionately influential" in the electorate. The growth of the old-old subset of the population, which would occur simultaneously, would raise "new and difficult questions . . . regarding what share of the national budget should go to meeting the economic needs of the old, and what share of health and social services should go [to] the old-old" (Neugarten & Havighurst, 1976, p. 11).

In effect, Neugarten's prognostication combatted the doomsday scenario of aging then coming into vogue (see Binstock, Chapter 13 in this volume). The effort has been so successful that older people now frequently name themselves as young-old in an effort to communicate their vitality. This has been a valuable distinction, since vitality can be a self-fulfilling prophecy. In discerning the distinction between the young-old and the old- old, Neugarten was prophesying the existence of the young-old, and it is arguable that the young-old, defined by self and social conditions reciprocally, took strength from this prophecy.

Neugarten and her associates were not right on all counts, of course. It suffices to cite two examples. First, the Chicago group had no way of knowing that the election of Ronald Reagan to the presidency in 1980 would presage the rise of neoconservative values in public policy making. With New Deal liberalism in retreat, the New Federalism has become the prevailing ideological basis for allocating resources and thinking about human rights. Second, questions of race and ethnicity were not much addressed in the Chicago documents. Since the mid-1970s, of course, dramatic changes in the household structure, educational attainments, and economic opportunities within African American communities and among various Spanish-speaking, Native American, and Asian groups have forced social scientists and gerontologists to take greater account of the challenges of multiculturalism.[3]

Such matters have become an increasingly prominent theme in subsequent research on aging.

Such oversights notwithstanding, Neugarten during the 1970s managed in her studies of the future to identify major issues that would become very controversial two decades later. To wit: Gerontologists in the 1960s and 1970s preferred not to explore, lest they confound, conventional wisdom about the relationships between aging, mortality, and morbidity. Neugarten, on the other hand, anticipated the possible convergence of aging policies and disability programs. Having reviewed the health status of older people, Neugarten wrote: "All this says little, however, regarding the period of disability that can be expected to occur for many people in the very last phase of life; and for the moment, we have little basis for predicting that this period will become shorter" (Neugarten & Havighurst, 1976, p. 5). Before James Fries (1980) articulated his "compression of morbidity" thesis and Lois Verbrugge (1982) showed that women as a group lived longer yet were sicker than men, Neugarten understood that scholars had to integrate research on aging and on disability.

## OUR FUTURE SELVES

*Our Future Selves* (National Institutes of Health, 1978) was a cogent analysis of the themes that social and behavioral researchers would pursue in coming years. It was organized under three broad headings: the aging individual, the societal context, and social institutions and the aging. More than most researchers at the time, Neugarten and her associates took care to disaggregate issues at the individual, institutional, and societal levels. Roughly two decades later, social theorists have yet to design a model that makes the necessary conceptual and substantive links across these three dimensions.

Although Neugarten did not offer a synthetic model for subsequent investigations, *Our Future Selves* contained many insights that are still being played out in research today. Many ideas that Neugarten and her colleagues set forth, in fact, sound so familiar to us that it is easy to forget that in the mid-1970s they were bold pronouncements. To have discerned them, we contend, required both a disciplined way of describing reality and mature insights. Neugarten clearly had reached a stage in her distinguished career where it was possible to extend beyond her own research base and incorporate quite disparate veins of inquiry. The following research recommendations illustrate the point. Neugarten stressed:

- The importance of biological substrates—genetic, neurological, and psychophysiological—in understanding psychosocial outcomes in old age. Biomarkers of aging more useful than chronological age are still to be discovered.
- The role of death research. Gerontologists are still reluctant to cross the border of death research, resisting the equation between aging and death. But, as Elie Metchnikoff noted in *The Nature of Man* (1907), gerontology and thanatology are clearly related. Old age inevitably ends in death, and the study of death may have much to offer the study of old age.
- Research into the improvement and maintenance of memory in the fight against the major thief of memory, Alzheimer's disease.
- The social cost of caring for the old, which has only in recent years become clear, as state Medicaid bills for nursing home care have mushroomed and state officials have scrambled to find ways to pay them—or not pay them.
- Research into noninstitutional ways of caring for the old. Recently, these alternatives have been increasingly developed as "continuum of care" and "aging in place" become the bywords, and older people insist that they should not have to leave their homes to get the care they need.

## VARIATIONS ON A THEME

Bernice Neugarten's interest in the future became even more grounded in policy in one of her best-known works, *Age or Need? Public Policies for Older People* (1982a). As chapters by Robert H. Binstock and Fay Lomax Cook in this *festschrift* indicate, it became clear by the mid-1970s that the politics of incrementalism, whereby more and more benefits for older Americans could be negotiated, were giving way to apocalyptic fears about the impact of population aging on national resources, new stereotypes of senior citizens as "greedy geezers," and increasing talk of intergenerational inequities, especially in the areas of income security and health care. Neugarten became greatly concerned with academic and popular reactions to the gloomy forecasts about "the graying of the budget." In response, she took cues from scenarios about the future in an effort to prevent dire predictions from becoming reality.

Rather than evade tough issues, Neugarten and her associates examined the engine of the welfare system: entitlements. She entertained the possibility that the needs of the disabled should be linked to those of older Americans as part of her argument for advancing needs-based programs. Ironically, systems conceived to aid the elderly—Social Security and Medicare—are now held against them because of exclusivity. People wonder, with justification, why old people are entitled to health care when others are not. As she had done in distinguishing between the young-old and old-old, Neugarten opened Pandora's box. Her analysis fuelled policy debates over who among those in need are entitled to help, and which old people are not. In so doing, Neugarten helped to bring American researchers into line with the dialogue over welfare reform taking shape in other developed countries. And that step, in turn, made her more willing to consider developments in other advanced industrial countries.

In the 1980s, Neugarten reprised and updated her earlier predictions, which had proven remarkably prescient. An examination of her curriculum vitae indicates that her insights into the future during this decade were likely to be found in works that fell under the rubric of the "aging society." In recent years, Neugarten wrote a chapter (with her daughter, Dail Neugarten) in Alan Pifer and Lydia Bronte's *Our Aging Society* called "Changing Meanings of Age in the Aging Society" (Neugarten & Neugarten, 1986). Another version of the Neugartens' argument appeared in *Psychology Today* in 1987. She collaborated with Stephen Golant, David Gutmann, and Sheldon Tobin in a report of Chicago's Center for Applied Gerontology, *Aging Society* (Neugarten, 1982b). And there is a chapter (with Dail Neugarten) in Storandt and VandenBos' *Adult Years: Continuity and Change* (Neugarten & Neugarten, 1989), "Policy Issues in an Aging Society," based on a master lecture given at the annual convention of the American Psychological Association in 1988.

As important as her contributions in gero-futures have been for social psychology and social policy, one can not leave a discussion of Bernice Neugarten's role as a seer of future trends without mentioning a third theme: the prospects for continuities and changes over the human life course. This theme of Dr. Neugarten's was set out in an article, "Time, Age and the Life Cycle," presented as a special lecture at the 31st annual meeting of the American Psychiatric Association and published in the *American Journal of Psychiatry* (Neugarten, 1979b). She pointed out that as the timing of life events became less regular, reaching the frontiers of certain ages was losing its former meaning, and that an increasingly fluid life cycle meant an increasingly age-irrelevant society. At the individual level, psychological themes, previously believed to correspond with age groups, are now seen as evolving and transmuting across the life cycle. For these reasons, the life course, rather than the age group, is the proper unit of analysis.

In her chapter on interpretive social science in Alice S. Rossi's *Gender and the Life Course* (Neugarten, 1985), Neugarten pointed out that most research on role transitions across time have been explored through intercohort comparisons, the central tendencies of age groups. Neugarten called, instead, for the study of individual "life pathways," the "timing, sequencing, or spacing transitions" in lives. Out of this work came the idea that people perceive their own lives as "on-time" or "off-time," and that the rise of the age-irrelevant American society has in turn rendered timing more flexible. Neugarten saw that middle age, if not yet old age, is being delayed, with untold consequences for the future.

Ironically, Neugarten's vision of our future selves and her critical, provocative thinking often led her to anticipate future scenarios that did not altogether please her admirers. Nor have some of her more recent judgments corroborated hopes she once expressed for gerontology as an interdisciplinary enterprise. For instance, she recently predicted the "end of gerontology" in favor of a life course approach (Neugarten, 1994). One of the people who gave birth to gerontology now foresees its demise! Neugarten sees the field as fatally flawed by a preoccupation with an arbitrarily defined, unduly circumscribed segment of the life course.

## CONCLUSION

For the past two decades, Bernice Neugarten has been trying to envision the future. The continuities in her work outweigh the discontinuities. From the start, her writings usually have tried to gauge the public policy implications of current laws and social norms as they interact with prevailing patterns and likely developments over the life courses of successive generations of Americans. Neugarten's initial forays as a seer were quite cautious. As she became more confident in the necessity of confronting the future and felt more comfortable moving beyond the theories and methods of social psychology, Neugarten extended her timeline and widened her geographic and cultural horizons. Nonetheless, she does not indulge in political rhetoric. Her predictions have consistently been based on her own research as well as that of her students, colleagues, and other astute commentators whose ideas she respects. Finally, rather than claim any omniscient powers, Neugarten has been inclined to distinguish her speculative hunches from thoughts that are firmly grounded in premises derived from her own analyses and the work of other gerontologists.

Yet, to delineate the evolution of Neugarten's thinking about the future in this way is to miss the fundamental discontinuity in the story. Social psychologists do not invariably become seers. They are not required to assume leadership positions on the Federal Council on Aging or serve as major planners of a White House Conference on Aging. Neugarten's own intellectual odyssey, which increasingly forced her to confront the future capacities and needs of successive cohorts of aging Americans, predisposed her to take the risk and to move into a new domain. Once there, she did what she had always done, but in new ways. Neugarten sought methods appropriate to her research agenda. She encouraged students to follow her lead. As new opportunities presented themselves, as was the case with the National Science Foundation project, Neugarten attempted to lay the intellectual foundation for a paradigm shift. She demanded that researchers on aging try to see things in a new way. By brilliantly encapsulating dense, jargon-laden clusters of ideas into snappy phrases (such as "the aging society"), Neugarten has won adherents, not least among gerontologists, who have pursued research leads of their own utilizing her seminal concepts. The gerontological community is much in her debt, and so are the citizens of this aging society.

Professor Neugarten would want rising generations of scholars to build on her risk taking, in ways they see fit. In retrospect, it is easy to see certain parallels between Neugarten's sense of the future and the metaphor of "time as a messenger of the gods" elaborated in verse by James Birren (1992), or the concern for structural and cultural lags described by Matilda White Riley and John W. Riley, Jr. (1994; see also Riley, Kahn, & Foner, 1995). All are concerned about points of convergence and of divergence between individual development and societal aging, both of which are often mediated through the maturation of institutional networks. In each instance, an historical sensibility is necessary—an ability to appreciate the value of tradition balanced by the inevitable need to exercise some choice in adapting to unexpected contingencies, to new possibilities. So future gerontologists must take the subject of time seriously.

Honoring two other Neugartenian strengths will also serve the research community. First, interdisciplinarity was so central to Bernice Neugarten's way of thinking that she rarely spoke in its defense. Yet it was precisely because she was initially versed in the humanities, and then became expert in the behavioral and social sciences that it was possible for Neugarten to make contributions in the policy domain. The longer Neugarten lives, the more concretely she grasps the big picture. This is why she returned to major themes throughout her career—the importance of class, the importance of diversity.

Second, Neugarten never was loathe to criticize ideas, including her own. Despite her busy schedule, she was self-reflective, ever questioning whether ideas neatly expressed still corresponded to reality. Access to new data sometimes forced her to abandon ideas that now seemed shaky—and she did not hesitate to do so. And if she could fashion a better way to express an idea more clearly and directly, she did so. Here was an intellectual not only ready to defend her ideas in the august company of her academic peers, but also one who so believed in the power of ideas as to share them with ordinary citizens.

Bernice Neugarten, in sum, is that rare person who saw presciently into the future because she was deeply rooted in venerable academic traditions. Teaching was her profession, research her vocation. And she took her talents as a scholar into public service. This is why Neugarten is one of the giants of gerontology.

# NOTES

[1] It is worth noting that Neugarten went on to anticipate an argument that she would elaborate in "Age Groups in American Society and the Rise of the

Young-Old," her justly famous article in the *Annals of the American Academy of Political and Social Science* (1974): "Higher incomes, better health, and more years of retirement may well stimulate the further development of a subculture of leisure for the aged—a development which may, by making old age a less unattractive period of life, raise the prestige of this age group."

[2] Since there are no jarring differences in the findings or interpretations presented in these volumes, we shall focus on the latter study. It should also be noted that Neugarten in both places cited her 1974 analysis of the "young-old."

[3] See her apologia for this failure in "The Aging Society and My Academic Life" (1988, pp. 104–5).

# REFERENCES

Birren, J. E. (1992). Time is the messenger. *The Gerontologist, 32,* 326.

COA interviews: Bernice Neugarten. (1987/1988). *Center on Aging, Northwestern University, 3*(4), 3–4.

Fries, J. (1980). Aging, natural death, and the compression of morbidity. *New England Journal of Medicine, 303,* 130–135.

Hauser, P. (1942). Changes in the labor force participation of the older worker. *American Journal of Sociology, 89,* 312– 329.

Metchnikoff, E. (1907). *The nature of man.* New York: Putnam.

National Institutes of Health. (1978). *Our future selves: A research plan toward understanding aging.* Report of the Panel on Behavioral and Social Sciences Research, National Advisory Council on Aging (Publication No. NIH 78–1444). Bethesda, MD: National Institute on Aging.

Neugarten, B. L. (1974). Age groups in American society and the rise of the young-old. *Annals of the American Academy of Political and Social Science, 415,* 189–198.

Neugarten, B. L. (1975). Introduction: Aging in the year 2000: A look at the future. *The Gerontologist, 15*(Suppl. 3), 3.

Neugarten, B. L. (1979a). Policy for the 1980s: Age or need entitlement? In Government Research Corporation (Ed.), *Aging: Agenda for the eighties* (pp. 48–52). Washington, DC: Government Research Corporation.

Neugarten, B. L. (1979b). Time, age and the life cycle. *American Journal of Psychiatry, 136,* 887–894.

Neugarten, B. L. (Ed.). (1982a). *Age or need? Public policies for older people.* Beverly Hills, CA: Sage.

Neugarten, B. L. (Ed.). (1982b). Aging society: Policy agenda for the 80s. *National Forum: The Phi Kappa Phi Journal, 62*(4).

Neugarten, B. L. (1985). Interpretive social science and research on aging. In A. S. Rossi (Ed.), *Gender and the life course* (pp. 291–300). New York: Aldine de Gruyter.

Neugarten, B. L. (1988). The aging society and my academic life. In M. W. Riley (Ed.), *Sociological lives* (pp. 91–106). Newbury Park, CA: Sage.

Neugarten, B. L. (1994). The end of gerontology. *Center on Aging, Northwestern University, 10*(1), 1.

Neugarten, B. L., & Havighurst, R. J. (Eds.). (1976). *Social policy, social ethics, and the aging society.* Washington, DC: National Science Foundation.

Neugarten, B. L., & Havighurst, R. J. (Eds.) (1977). *Extending human life: Social policy and social ethics.* Washington, DC: National Science Foundation.

Neugarten, B. L., & Moore, J. W. (1968). The changing age-status system. In B. L. Neugarten (Ed.), *Middle age and aging: A reader in social psychology.* Chicago: University of Chicago Press.

Neugarten, B. L., & Neugarten, D. A. (1986). Changing meanings of age in the aging society. In A. Pifer & L. Bronte (Eds.), *Our aging society: Paradox and promise.* New York: Norton.

Neugarten, B. L., & Neugarten, D. A. (1987, May). Changing meanings of age. *Psychology Today,* pp. 28–30.

Neugarten, B. L., & Neugarten, D. A. (1989). Policy issues in an aging society. In M. Storandt & G. R. VandenBos (Eds.), *Adult years: Continuity and change* (pp. 147–167). Washington, DC: American Psychological Association.

Riley, M. W., Kahn, R. L., & Foner, A. (1995). *Age and structural lag.* New York: Wiley Data Science.

Riley, M. W., & Riley, J. (1994). The Kent lecture. *The Gerontologist, 34,* 436–446.

Rose, A. M. (1968). The subculture of the aging: A topic for sociological research. In B. L. Neugarten (Ed.), *Middle age and aging: A reader in social psychology* (pp. 184–193). Chicago: University of Chicago Press.

Rorty, R. (1989). *Contingency, irony, and solidarity.* New York: Cambridge University Press.

Verbrugge, L. (1982). Longer life but worsening health. *Milbank Memorial Fund Quarterly/Health and Society, 62,* 475–519.

# Comments

## Sheldon S. Tobin

When I first read the title of this chapter, I was intrigued, if not mystified. I never considered Bernice Neugarten to be a seer; that is, a prophet who can foresee the future, usually from divine inspiration. Maybe Neugarten can foresee our future selves, but certainly not from divine inspiration. Rather, any telling of our future selves, as discussed by Achenbaum and Berdes, has been from her use of data. These insightful authors provide an understanding for why Neugarten's writings make her gerontology's seer. It is, however, less from foreseeing the future than from setting new agendas for the field.

At the end of the chapter, they begin to answer why she has been able to transcend current considerations to set new agendas. She has always been mindful that gerontology is interdisciplinary and that heterogeneity is ubiquitous. But this mindfulness is not only Neugarten's. Rather, it is intrinsic to the Committee on Human Development. The Committee was formed to focus on issues in human development from many perspectives and from the approaches of many disciplines. With the presence of Lloyd Warner, the progenitor of "socioeconomic status," and of Robert J. Havighurst, who always assumed differences by social class, heterogeneity was a guiding principle in understanding social and psychological phenomena. It was, therefore, natural for Neugarten to ask about heterogeneity when we were developing a scenario for normative events in the latter half of life. This time the heterogeneity was within age cohorts as she began to organize the data that emerged as the foundation for her writings on the rise of the young-old. Her appreciation of heterogeneity, however, went beyond usual distinctions set by age, by social class, and by gender. When I was editing *The Gerontologist,* she told me never to use "the elderly" but always "elderly people" or "elderly persons" or "elderly individuals." The uniqueness of the individual was never to be ignored!

Whereas members of the Committee understood that phenomena in human development could best, or only, be approached from many perspectives, Neugarten always seemed to go further than others in seeking the alternate views. She characteristically not only viewed phenomena from diverse perspectives, but also reached out to others for their approaches and counsel. I recall when she called me to discuss initial ideas for her eventual book on age-based versus need-based policies. One outcome of our conversation was her decision to telephone her friend of many years, Martin Loeb, then the Dean of the School of Social Work at the University of Wisconsin. Later she told me what she had learned from Loeb; indeed, he contributed an important chapter to her book.

Neugarten's interactional style of generating knowledge assisted in developing her excursion into social policy and ethics. When George Brosseau came to see her about research ideas for the new Research Applied to National Needs (RANN) initiative of the National Science Foundation, she had to educate this biologist and dispel his many myths before identifying gaps in our knowledge. After he commented that a broad multidisciplinary project would be welcomed and that support for students as well as faculty could be obtained, the conversation turned to likely studies. With eagerness she envisioned gathering together a diverse array of faculty members, students, and experts from elsewhere. Only a few who participated in studies and conferences are singled out by Achenbaum and Berdes in their chapter. There were many, many more.

Yet it is insufficient to use her multidisciplinary style and her focus on heterogeneity to account for contributions that have made her gerontology's seer. Although missing ingredients may be elusive, one ingredient is certainly manifested in the "So what?" with which she has challenged all she has mentored, students and colleagues alike, and most importantly, with which she has challenged herself. Achenbaum and Berdes refer to her as "self-reflective, ever questioning whether ideas neatly expressed still corresponded to reality."

Some observers, however, glibly suggest that she became gerontology's seer because "She could see the whole field." It is not seeing the "whole field," even if it were possible to do so, that matters. What matters is that she asked herself "So what?" and told herself "Say what you mean." Because Neugarten has been able to question current ideas, examine the data, ask "So what?," and then say what she means, she has been able to set new agendas for the field. Becoming gerontology's seer took a unique combination of inquisitiveness and perceptiveness, qualities that are all too rare but, indeed, are characteristic of Bernice Neugarten.

# CHAPTER 16

# Profile of Bernice L. Neugarten*

Developmental psychologist and sociologist of the life course, Bernice L. Neugarten has pioneered the study of age, the social clock, and social timing. Her studies of personality, aging, the competencies of middle-aged and older people, and generational relations have changed previous negative stereotypes regarding aging. In the arena of public policy, her forward-looking approach to the provision of benefits and services based on need rather than on age have had wide influence. Her generativity as a teacher and her concern with the careers of academic women and men are reflected in the achievements of her students, many of whom have attained international recognition for their studies of adult lives.

## BIOGRAPHY

Bernice L. Neugarten has often been credited with creating the academic field of adult development and aging.

Born in the small town of Norfolk, Nebraska, in 1916, Neugarten entered the University of Chicago as an undergraduate in 1933. She vividly recalls the intellectual excitement and the sometimes buzzing

---

* This biography originally appeared as "APF Gold Medal Awards, Bernice L. Neugarten" in the *American Psychologist,* 1994, *49,* 553–555. Copyright ©1994 by the American Psychological Association. Adapted with permission.

confusion that marked the "Hutchins' college" of the 1930s. The atmosphere was apparently to her liking. Except for an eight-year period during the 1980s, she has been at the University of Chicago ever since. She took an undergraduate degree in English and French literatures in 1936, a master's degree in educational psychology in 1937, and one of the first PhDs given by the interdisciplinary Committee on Human Development in 1943.

Human Development, a newly created academic unit in the Division of Social Sciences, was to become Neugarten's academic home. The program, based primarily on anthropology, psychology, and sociology, concentrated on the course of human lives and on change and continuity from infancy to old age.

After completing her PhD, Neugarten spent eight years raising two children, working part-time at writing and research jobs, and volunteering with her husband in efforts aimed at building a racially integrated community.

She returned to the University in 1951 and joined the Human Development faculty. It was an accident that led her to concentrate on the study of adult development and aging. She was invited to teach the course, "Maturity and Old Age," developed by Robert J. Havighurst, which was apparently the first of its kind. She renamed the course "Adult Development and Aging" and offered ever-changing versions of that course for some 40 years.

In 1956, Neugarten published her first paper on the psychology of aging and a year later her first paper on social change and the aging population. Her research has been concentrated in these general areas ever since.

In her 40s, Neugarten published mostly reports and analyses of empirical studies, often carried out with colleagues and graduate students. In her 50s, she more often published conceptual works that took the form of essays and review chapters. During this period, she spent much of her time in administrative roles and in one-to-one teaching and dissertation supervision. She recalls two occurrences of special significance from this decade: First, in a single year four of her students authored textbooks on middle age and aging, and, second, she received the Distinguished Teaching Award of the American Psychological Foundation in 1975.

By her 60s, Neugarten was involved in the policy field. In 1978, President Carter appointed her to the Federal Council on the Aging, a group mandated to report each year to the president and to Congress on the situation of older people and to make recommendations regarding legislative and executive initiatives. A year later she was appointed deputy chair of the 1981 White House Conference on Aging. She was then of the opinion—as she is today—that such a conference was unnecessary, but she decided that, because it was to occur, she would help shape its agenda. For the next two years, she experienced the vagaries of political life that accompanied the change in the federal administration from one political party to the other.

Between the Federal Council and the White House Conference, Neugarten had learned a good bit about policy making and politics. She had also become convinced that it was important that students in the social sciences understand how policy decisions are formed and how they influence the course of lives. In 1980 she organized a new doctoral program that bridges social science and policy making. She took an early retirement from Chicago to develop that program at Northwestern University. The program, "Human Development and Social Policy," continues to thrive.

After eight years at Northwestern, Neugarten returned to the University of Chicago as Rothschild Distinguished Scholar, where she worked as a consultant to the Center on Aging, Health and Society and the Chapin Hall Center for Children, a policy research center. Neugarten retired again in 1992 and now continues her academic pursuits on a part-time, voluntary basis.

Neugarten has long been recognized as an advocate for women. She takes special pride in having brought many women, some of them middle-aged, into the academic world. One half of her many PhD students have been women. She also chaired the University of Chicago's first Committee on Women. In 1970, that committee issued a report on gender discrimination in faculty appointments and promotions that was widely circulated, then republished in the Hearings Before the Special Committee on Education of the U.S. House of Representatives, 91st Congress.

Neugarten has always been committed to her role as a teacher. Over the years, she has taught and mentored successive generations of graduate students, who are now themselves practitioners, teachers, and scholars conducting research across the world.

As a researcher, Neugarten's pattern has been to open up new topic areas rather than to follow a single line of inquiry—to explore rather than replicate. In short, she has sought to map out some of the neglected psychological and social territory of the second half of life. She has been a prolific author who has coauthored or edited eight books and more than 150 research papers, book chapters, and reviews.

Her studies have been of two general types. The first relates to aging persons and includes changes in personality and in age-sex roles, the diversity of patterns of aging, middle-aged parenting and grandparenting, adjustment to retirement, the changing meanings of age to the individual, and the internalized social clock that tells persons if they are "on time" in following social timetables. The second category includes studies that deal with the sociology of age, changes in the age-status system, age norms as social controls (many of them embodied in the law), societal implications of the longer life span, relations among age groups, and other policy issues related to the aging society.

Neugarten has persistently challenged stereotyped views about aging. In the 1960s she began to study the life events that were touted as the critical transitions of middle age: menopause, the "empty nest," and the "midlife crisis." She found, contrary to widely held views, that these events were rarely regarded as critical events by the persons experiencing them. Instead, they are normal, expectable life events, mentally rehearsed in advance and met with relative equanimity. She learned that retirement is welcomed if it is accompanied by adequate income; that health improves rather than deteriorates after retirement; that most old people are vigorous and competent and have high levels of life satisfaction; and that in the second half of life, the level of life satisfaction is not related to age. It thus became clear that many of the myths about middle and old age did not fit the realities. She found, also, that there are no simple, predictable patterns of aging. Not only do persons grow old in very different ways, but the range of individual differences becomes greater with increasing age. Age therefore becomes a poor predictor of the adult's needs or capacities.

Neugarten also coined the terms *young-old* and *old-old,* with the young-old representing the majority of older persons who are competent, but who are generally underutilized in our aging society. The old-old are that minority of frail older people who need special care and support. The distinction between the two groups is of central importance in policy making, for the needs and desires of the two groups are very different.

Neugarten has repeatedly questioned the proliferation of policy decisions and benefit programs in which target groups are delineated solely on the basis of age. Her view that age-entitlement programs should be reexamined from the perspective of need entitlement, set forth in her 1982 book *Age or Need?*, has made her a controversial figure to special interest groups in aging. That issue has today become central among policy makers, and Neugarten is pleased to note that an increasing number of public and private benefit programs are now being administered more on the basis of need than age.

Neugarten has received several honorary degrees and many awards and prizes from national and international organizations. She was one of the first women, and the first social scientist in the field of aging, to be elected a fellow of the American Academy of Arts and Sciences, and she is a senior member of the Institute of Medicine of the National Academy of Sciences.

A colleague once asked Neugarten what her personal goal was in studying aging. She laughed and said, "To return old people to the human race—to make clear that they are not a special species, not creatures from another planet. Although we social science researchers, as a group, have not accomplished that task, we have come to realize that the same theories regarding human nature will serve as well, or as poorly, for older people as for younger."

## SELECTED BIBLIOGRAPHY

Neugarten, B. L., & Gutmann, D. L. (1958). Age-sex roles and personality in middle age: A thematic apperception study. *Psychological Monographs, 72* (17, Whole No. 470), 1–33.

Neugarten, B. L., Havighurst, R. J., & Tobin, S. S. (1961). The measurement of life satisfaction. *Journal of Gerontology, 16,* 134–143.

Neugarten, B. L., Wood, V., Kraines, R. J., & Loomis, B. (1963). Women's attitudes toward the menopause. *Human Development: An International Research Journal, 6,* 140–151.

Neugarten, B. L., & Associates. (1964). *Personality in middle and late life— Empirical studies.* New York: Atherton.

Neugarten, B. L., Moore, J., & Lowe, J. C. (1965). Age norms, age constraints, and adult socialization. *American Journal of Sociology, 70,* 710–717.

Neugarten, B. L. (Ed.). (1968). *Middle age and aging: A reader in social psychology.* Chicago: University of Chicago Press.

Neugarten, B. L. (1969). Continuities and discontinuities of psychological issues into adult life. *Human Development, 12,* 121–130.

Neugarten, B. L., & Datan, N. (1973). Sociological perspectives on the life cycle. In P. B. Baltes & K. W. Schaie (Eds.), *Life-span developmental psychology: Personality and socialization* (pp. 53–69). New York: Academic Press.

Neugarten, B. L. (1974, September). Age groups in American society and the rise of the young-old. *Annals of Political and Social Sciences, 415,* 187–198.

Neugarten, B. L., & Datan, N. (1974). The middle years. In S. Arieti (Ed.), *American handbook of psychiatry* (Vol. 1, pp. 592–608). New York: BasicBooks.

Neugarten, B. L., & Hagestad, G. (1976). Age and the life course. In R. H. Binstock & E. Shanas (Eds.), *Handbook of aging and the social sciences* (pp. 35–55). New York: Van Nostrand Reinhold.

Neugarten, B. L., & Havighurst, R. J. (Eds.). (1976). *Social policy, social ethics, and the aging society* (Publication No. NSF/RA 7600247). Washington, DC: National Science Foundation, RANN—Research Application Directorate, U. S. Government Printing Office.

Neugarten, B. L. (1979, July). Time, age, and the life cycle. *American Journal of Psychiatry, 136,* 887–894.

Neugarten, B. L. (1981). Age distinctions and their social functions. *Chicago Kent Law Review, 57,* 809–825.

Neugarten, B. L. (Ed.). (1982). *Age or need? Public policies for older people.* Beverly Hills, CA: Sage.

Neugarten, B. L. (1985). Interpretive social science and research on aging. In A. S. Rossi (Ed.), *Gender and the life course* (pp. 291–300). New York: Aldine de Gruyten.

Neugarten, B. L., & Neugarten, D. A. (1986, Winter). Age in the aging society. *Daedalus,* pp. 31–49.

Neugarten, B. L., & Neugarten, D. A. (1989). Policy issues in an aging society. In M. Storandt & G. R. VandenBos (Eds.), *The adult years: Continuity and change* (pp. 147–167). Washington, DC: American Psychological Association.

Neugarten, B. L., & Cassel, C. K. (1991). The goals of medicine in an aging society. In R. H. Binstock & S. G. Post (Eds.), *Too old for health care?* (pp. 75–90). Baltimore: Johns Hopkins University Press.

Neugarten, B. L. (in press). *The meanings of age: Selected papers of Bernice L. Neugarten.* Chicago: University of Chicago Press.

# Index

Acceptance, coping mechanism of, 29
Acceptance of death. *see* Death
  acceptance
Adult life crises
  comments regarding
    post parental years development
      and, 171
    social time and, 170
    widows-in-waiting and, 169–170
  conclusions regarding, 166–167
  introduction to
    definitions regarding, 146–147
    developmental perspective on, 147,
      169
    grief and mourning, 148
    life course vs. illness model and,
      148–149, 166
    life crises vs. psychiatric crises and,
      146
    parent caring and, 147
    phenomenological perspective on, 147
  of widows
    existential confrontation, 151
    new identity: single, 150
    self-revisions, 149–150
    "we" from "I" separation, 150–151
  of widows: studies of
    adaptation measures of, 152–153
    existential awareness case study,
      157–160, 166–167
    findings of, 154–156
    grief pattern measures of, 153,
      154–155, 156
    growth measures of, 153, 155, 157

    liberation through growth case
      study, 160–163
    methods used in, 152
    no pain, no growth case study,
      163–166
    personal growth and, 157, 171
    recovery measures of, 142
    sample used in, 152
    self-change measures of, 153–154, 171
AFDC (Aid to Families with Dependent
    Children)
  Congressional support of, 339, 340,
    347–348
  public support of, 334–337, 347–348
Affectual solidarity, 279, 280, 281–285,
    297
AGE (Americans for Generational
    Equity), 311–312, 329–330, 343
Aging
  biopsychosocial models of, 20
  dependency models of, 18, 24
  medical model of, 41–42
  successful aging definition and, 19–20
  *see also* Adult life crises; Gender
    identity; Life course and psychiatric
    illness; Non-normative old age:
    parents of mentally retarded off-
    spring; Preventive and corrective
    proactivity (PCP) model of aging;
    Psychopathology; Public policy
    continuities and discontinuities:
    *specific subject;* Time continuities
    and discontinuities: *specific subject;*
    Very late life: study of

Aid to Families with Dependent Children (AFDC)
  Congressional support of, 339, 340, 347–348
  public support for, 334–337, 347–348
Alloplastic extroverts, 6–8, 9, 14
Alpha generation, 247
Altruism, 26, 29, 35
Alzheimer's disease
  caregiver study of, 190–194
  lack of control factor and, 85–86
  long-term care insurance for, 315
  sibling caregiving and, 84, 88
American Association of Retired Persons (AARP)
  benefit taxation and, 317
  Study of Intergenerational Linkages of, 276
Americans for Generational Equity (AGE), 311–312, 329–330, 343
*Anatomy of Melancholy, The* (Burton), 148
Androgyny
  in 1970s and 1980s, 100
  vs. gender expansion, 117–118
  inner vs. activity androgyny, 105
  in later life, 108
  measurement of, 102, 107
Anxiety, bereavement grief and, 153, 156
Apocalyptic demography, 312–314
Assertiveness
  non-normative transition study of: divorce, 183, 184, 186, 187
  normative transition study of, 179, 180, 181
Associational solidarity, 279, 297
Autoplastic introverts, 8–9, 10, 14

BABS (Bradburn Affect Balance Scale), 128
Baby boomers generation, 313, 353
Bereavement. *see* Adult life crises
Berkeley Growth Study, of personality development, 175
Birth year. *see* Cohort
Bradburn Affect Balance Scale (BABS), 128

Bradburn Morale Scale, 192
Burton, Robert, 148

Career path, psychiatric illness affecting, 78, 79
Carter administration, economic downturn during, 329
Center for Epidemiological Studies Depression Scale (CES-D), 53, 58, 189–190
CES-D (Center for Epidemiological Studies Depression Scale), 53, 58, 189–190
*Childhood and Society* (Erikson), 126
Clinton administration
  health care reform program of, 317
  long-term care policy of, 316, 319
Clock test, oldest-old study of, 52, 57
Cognitive functioning
  cognitive reframing, 26, 29
  oldest-old study of, 51–53, 57, 60
Cognitive life satisfaction disposition factor, 26, 29, 35
Cognitive theory of gender identity, 100
Coherence, stress invulnerability and, 23
Cohort concept, of life course perspective, 70–71, 73, 75–76
Concord Coalition, 312, 343
Consensual solidarity, 279–280, 282, 284
Consociates, 214
Continuities. *see* Adult life crises; Life course and psychiatric illness; Non-normative old age: parents of mentally retarded offspring; Public policy continuities and discontinuities: *specific subject;* Time continuities and discontinuities: *specific subject*
Contract for America, 325
Control, of normative old age, 127–128
Coping mechanisms
  acceptance/reframing, 26, 29
  altruism, 26, 29, 35
  of Alzheimer's caregivers, 191–194
  hopefulness, 26, 28–29, 34, 36
  life satisfaction, 26, 29, 35, 74
  self-esteem, 26, 29, 35

Counting money, oldest-old study of, 52, 57
Cross-cultural factors
  Italian sibling relationships and, 244
  PCP model of aging and, 35
  personality trait development and, 186
  social relationships and, 28, 359–360
Cultural factors. *see* Cross-cultural factors; Mexican American study

Dante (*Divine Comedy, The,* from), 204
Death acceptance
  by non-normative aged, 136–138
  by normative aged, 131–132
  *see also* Time continuities and discontinuities: illness process
Delayed grievers, 153, 154, 155–156
Dementia, oldest-old study of, 57–58, 60
Dependency models of aging, 18, 24
Depression
  of bereavement grief, 153, 156, 161–163, 166
  of caregivers of Alzheimer's patients, 191
  cultural factors of, 188–190
  oldest-old study of, 53, 58, 59
  T-cell attrition and, 3, 11n. 1
Developmental stability model, of personality development, 175–176
Developmental stake hypothesis, 281–282, 305
Discontinuities. *see* Adult life crises; Life course and psychiatric illness; Non-normative old age: parents of mentally retarded offspring; Public policy continuities and discontinuities: *specific subject;* Time continuities and discontinuities: *specific subject*
Dispositional qualities, 26–27
  as continuities, 34, 35
*Divine Comedy, The, Inferno,* from (Dante), 204
*DSM-III-R,* 51, 52–53, 57

EBRI (Employee Benefit Research Institute), 341

*Elementary Forms of Religious Life* (Durkheim), 204
Employee Benefit Research Institute (EBRI), 341
Environment
  crime rate and, 28
  housing needs and, 28
  mastery of, 127–129, 134–135
  person-environment congruence and, 23, 28, 31, 35
  self-initiated change to, 19, 31–32, 61
Erikson, Erik, 99, 126, 130, 144, 215, 216
Ethnic factors
  schizophrenic caregiving and, 84
  *see also* Cross-cultural factors
Existential awareness bereavement case study, 157–160, 166–167
Extended families. *see* Time continuities and discontinuities: modified-extended families study

Family
  illness interconnected timetables and, 214–217
  *see also* Life course and psychiatric illness; Non-normative old age: parents of mentally retarded offspring; Time continuities and discontinuities: modified-extended families study; Time continuities and discontinuities: *specific subject*
*Family Worlds* (Hess and Handel), 246
Federal Insurance Contributions Act (FICA), 315
Financial resources, external resource of, 32
Food Stamp program
  Congressional support of, 339
  public support of, 334–335
Ford Foundation, 311
Freud, Sigmund
  on grief, 148, 170
  on stability of adult personality development, 175–176

Functional health. *see* Instrumental
activities of daily living (IADL);
Mobility; Personal activities of daily
living (PADL)
Functional solidarity, 280

Gallup Opinion Poll (1994), 341
Gender differences
in elderly parents support, 285, 287,
297
as kinkeepers, 251, 267
in late life gender identity, 108
in non-normative transition personality
trait development, 185, 187
in normative transition personality trait
development, 179–181
in occupational status inheritance, 291
schizophrenic caregiving and, 85
in sibling relationships, 228, 232, 233,
234, 235, 244
Gender identity
acknowledgements regarding, 119–120
comments regarding, 122–123
definition and measurement of
androgyny and, 100, 102, 105, 107,
117–118, 122, 123
cognitive theories of, 100, 117–118
conceptualizations and, 99–100
diminished identity, 106
facade identity, 106
gender expansion and, 105, 106,
117–118, 122–123
gender incongruence and, 105, 106
gender vs. sex and, 99
gender transcendence and, 108
masculinity and femininity scales,
102
object relations theory and, 99–100
Parkville research project and,
100–107, 122–123
self-descriptions in gender terms,
105–107
early experiences and, 115–116, 119
generation gap and
father-son dyads and, 109, 111–112,
123

mother-daughter dyads and,
108–111, 122
implications of
clinical implications and, 118–119
for future research, 119
gender expansion vs. androgyny
and, 117–118, 122, 123
from research, 116
in later life
gender transcendence in, 108
measurement of, 107
normal androgyny of, 108
parental responsibility and
absence of children from home and,
112–115
marriage relationship and, 113–115
self-assertion of mothers and, 113
self-concept of fathers and, 114–115
political activism effects on, 289, 297
significance of, 98
General Social Survey, 276
Generation concept, of life course
perspective, 72–73
Generation-X, 74, 75–76, 290
Generativity, 216–217
Genetic factors
personality change and, 13, 15
schizophrenic "outside of time"
concept and, 80–81
Gough Adjective Checklist, 178
Grief. *see* Adult life crises

Hardiness, stress invulnerability and, 23
Havighurst, Robert, 36, 350–351, 352,
354, 355, 356, 357, 358, 368
Health promotion
of Alzheimer's caregivers, 191–194
coping component of, 26
illness stress reduction by, 28
medical model of, 41–42
proactive preventive adaptation of, 30,
32–33
Health Security Act, 319
Hearing. *see* Sensory function
Helping others, proactive preventive
adaptation of, 30

Historical context. *see* Life course and
psychiatric illness
Holmes and Rahe Social Readjustment
Scale, 13
Hopefulness, 26, 28–29, 34, 36
Hopkins Symptoms Checklist, 191, 192
Hospitals, maternal transference in, 9
Hostility
non-normative transition study of:
divorce, 183, 184, 186, 187, 188
normative transition study of, 179, 181

Identity. *see* Adult life crises
Illness, stress factor of, 28, 31, 35
Immune system. *see* Psycho-immune
system
Impulsivity
non-normative transition study of:
divorce, 183, 184, 186, 187
normative transition study of,
179–180, 181
Instrumental activities of daily living
(IADL), oldest-old study of, 51, 54,
56, 59, 60
Intergenerational caregiving
to Alzheimer's patients, 190–191
analyses of measures of, 191–192
predicting change over time and,
192–194
to schizophrenic patients, 82–86
older caregivers of older patients, 83
parental disappointment and, 82–83,
84
sibling caregiving and, 83–84
Intergenerational equity
children against elderly in, 329–331
concept development of, 328–329
economic downturn affecting, 327–328
social policy issue of, 311–312, 343,
361–362
Intergenerational stake hypothesis,
281–285, 286, 297, 305
Interventions. *see* Life course and psychiatric illness: *specific disorder*
Italian families, sibling relationships in,
244

Jung, Carl, 14–15

Late onset disorder. *see* Psychopathology
Life course
political activism and, 289, 297
sibling relationship changes during,
235–236
middle age events and, 237–239
old age events and, 239–240, 244
parental death and, 237, 238–239,
244
retirement and, 239–240, 244
sibling illness and death and,
240–241
spousal illness and widowhood and,
241–242
young adulthood events and, 237,
245
*see also* Life course and psychiatric
illness; Time continuities and
discontinuities: *specific subject*
Life course and psychiatric illness
comments regarding, 96–97
conclusions regarding, 86–88
introduction to
cohort differences and, 70–71
episodic illness and, 70
social and historical context and,
69–70
schizophrenic patients and
aging and life course and, 77–81
cohort changes and, 79–80
community residence effects and,
78–80
vs. developmentally disabled, 85
episodic character of, 70
ethnicity factors and, 84
expressed emotion and, 81–82
family caregiving to, 81–86
gender factors and, 85
genetic loading factor and, 80–81
lack of control factor and, 85–86
life finitude awareness and, 78
living "outside of time" by, 76–77
older caregivers of older patients,
83–84, 87–88

Life course and psychiatric illness
  *(continued)*
  schizophrenic patients and *(continued)*
    parental disappointment and, 82–83,
      84, 87
    sibling caregiving and, 83–84, 88
    treatment regimen changes and,
      77–78
    vulnerability concept and, 80
  social change and
    cohort concept and, 70–71, 73,
      75–76, 86
    forward vs. backward socialization
      and, 76, 86
    generation concept and, 72–73
    life span or cycle vs. life course
      perspective and, 72, 86
    significance of, 71–72
    time and expectable transitions,
      72–74, 86–87
    *see also* Non-normative old age:
      parents of mentally retarded
      offspring
Life crises. *see* Adult life crises
*Life Cycle Completed, The* (Erikson),
  126
Life expectancy
  intergenerational relationships and,
    292
  trends in, 358
  uncertainty and, 208
Life satisfaction
  bereavement grief and, 153, 156,
    163–166
  internal resource of, 26, 27, 29, 35
  model of aging, 20
  of perpetual parents, 140
  planning and, 30, 33
  project completion and, 218
  rating scale of, 138
  role transition timing and, 74
Life-course social science, 15–16
Limited grievers, 153, 154, 155
Long-Term Care Campaign, 315
Longitudinal Study of Generations, 247,
  248, 304

conceptual framework issue of,
    306–307
  data complexity of, 304, 305
  dyad and family units of, 306
  intra- vs. inter-unit stability and, 306
  research stimulated by, 304–305
  variability issue of, 305–306
  *see also* Time continuities and
    discontinuities: intergenerational
    relationships study
Loss, stress factor of, 1–2, 28, 31, 36

Magical mastery, 128
Marshalling support, proactive corrective
    adaptation of, 31, 33
Marx, Karl, 226
Mastery
  bereavement grief and, 153, 156
  of environment, 127–129, 134–135
  late life gender transcendence and, 108
  oldest-old study of, 53, 58, 59, 61, 67
MCCA (Medicare Catastrophic Coverage
    Act), 314–315, 317
Meaning in life, successful aging
    outcome of, 27
Medicaid
  Congressional support of, 338, 339,
    340
  cuts in, 311
  public support of, 334–337
Medicare
  Catastrophic Coverage Act of,
    314–315, 317
  Congressional support of, 338, 339,
    340
  cuts in, 311
  of Great Society, 308
  public support of, 334, 335, 336, 340
Memory-in-reality, oldest-old study of,
    52
Mental retardation, 132–134
  *see also* Non-normative old age:
    parents of mentally retarded
    offspring
Mexican American study, of depression
    over time, 188–190

*Middle Age and Aging* (Neugarten and Moore), 352, 353, 356
Mini-Mental State Examination (MMSE), 51, 52, 57
MMSE (Mini-Mental State Examination), 51, 52, 57
Mobility, in oldest-old study, 50, 54, 55, 59, 60
Modified families. *see* Time continuities and discontinuities: modified-extended families study
Morbidity compression, 46–47
*Mourning and Melancholia* (Freud), 148
Myers-Briggs inventory of psychological types, 15

NAMI (National Alliance for the Mentally Ill), 83
National Alliance for the Mentally Ill (NAMI), 83
National Council on Senior Citizens (NCSC), 318, 338
National Election Surveys, 341
National Institute on Aging, 67
National Opinion Research Center, 341, 342
National Survey of Families and Households (NSFH), 276
NCSC (National Council on Senior Citizens), 318, 338
Neugarten, Bernice
  1970s work of, 355–361
  1980s work of, 361–363
  on aging society, 327
  on backlash against the old, 327–328, 342–343, 361–363
  biographical information on, 350–352, 371–375
  comments regarding, 368–370
  interdisciplinary work of, 354, 365, 368
  on life events and adaptations, 19, 71, 73, 363, 374
  life satisfaction model of, 20, 27, 374
  *Middle Age and Aging* (with Moore), 352, 353, 356
  on morbidity compression, 47
  *Our Future Selves,* 355, 360–361
  on personality development over time, 174, 180, 195, 363, 374
  on public policy issues, 47, 48, 62, 355–360, 364
  old-age vs. need based approach, 308, 309–310, 315, 361–363
  on purposive aspects of adaptation, 21
  social forecasting by, 352–354, 356–357
  *Social Policy, Social Ethics, and the Aging Society* (with Havighurst), 355, 358
  social policy, social ethics work of, 355–360, 369, 374, 375
  on social time, 205, 210, 219
  summary regarding, 363–365
  "young-old" vs. "old-old" distinction, 46, 61, 62, 66, 67, 126, 309, 325, 351, 359, 374
New Deal. *see* Medicare; Older Americans Act; Social Security
New Federalism, 308, 359
Niche
  of alloplastic extroverts, 7–8
  of autoplastic introverts, 8–9
  loss of, 9–10
Nixon administration, New Federalism of, 308, 359
Non-normative old age: parents of mentally retarded offspring
  acceptance of death
    fear of nonbeing vs. dying process, 131
    of non-normative aging, 134, 136–138, 144
    of normative aging, 131
  case example of, 133–134
  comments regarding, 143–144
  conclusions regarding, 139–140
  demographics of sample, 132–133
  environmental mastery by
    assertiveness and, 128–129, 139
    control and, 127–128
    functional paranoia and, 129, 139

Non-normative old age: parents of
  mentally retarded offspring
  *(continued)*
  environmental mastery by *(continued)*
    magical mastery and, 128, 139
    of non-normative aging, 134–135,
      139
    of normative aging, 127–129
  normative old age vs., 124–127,
    132–134
    integrity vs. integrality, 126, 144
    self-concept and, 125, 139
    self-consistency concept and, 126,
      144
    young-old vs. old-old concept and,
      125–126
  religiosity used by
    cross-bearing and, 135
    death acceptance and, 136–137,
      140
    God's blessings and, 131
    non-normative aging and, 134, 135,
      136–138, 140
    normative aging and, 130–131, 140
    prayer and, 137
    relief of suffering and, 131, 138,
      140
    reunion with loved ones and, 131,
      134
    reward for service and, 131, 134,
      137–138
  reminiscence of
    dramatization and, 130, 144
    non-normative aging and, 134, 135,
      139, 144
    normative aging and, 129–130, 139,
      144
    parental mythicizing and, 130, 144
    past and present interchangeability
      and, 129–130
    self-preservation and, 129–130, 135
  subjective well-being and, 134,
    138–139
Normative old age. *see* Non-normative
  old age
Normative solidarity, 280, 285, 297

NSFH (National Survey of Families and
  Households), 276

Object relations psychic processes
  model, 99
OBRA (Omnibus Budget Reconciliation
  Act), 315
Occupational status, long-term family
  effects of, 289–291, 297
Octogenarian (OCTO) study, 48, 61,
  63
Old-old
  Neugarten's distinction of, 46, 61, 62,
    66, 67, 126, 309, 351, 359, 374
  *see also* Very late life
Older Americans Act, 314
  Congressional support of, 341
  of Great Society, 308
Oldest-old, 47
  NIA research of, 309–310
  social networks of, 47–48
  young-old of, 61, 66–67
Omega generation, 238, 247, 278
Omnibus Budget Reconciliation Act
  (OBRA), 315
Optimism. *see* Hopefulness
Orderly change model, of personality
  development, 176
*Our Future Selves* (Neugarten), 355,
  360–361

PADL. *see* Personal activities of daily
  living (PADL)
Paraphrenia, 11n. 1
Parental death
  family time discontinuities and,
    214–215
  sibling relationship changes and, 237,
    238–239, 244
Parkville gender identity research
  project, 100–107
PCP. *see* Preventive and corrective
  proactivity (PCP)
Perceived health and memory, oldest-old
  study of, 49, 53, 58
Perpetual parents. *see* Non-normative old

age: parents of mentally retarded offspring
Personal activities of daily living (PADL), oldest-old study of, 50–51, 54, 55, 59, 60
Personality development. *see* Time continuities and discontinuities: personality development
Planning for the future, proactive preventive adaptation of, 30, 33
Point or period concept, of life course perspective, 72
Political activism, long-term family effects of, 288–289, 297
Population Association of America, 329
Positive affective states, successful aging outcome of, 27
Preventive and corrective proactivity (PCP) model of aging
  development of
    biopsychosocial models of aging, 20
    conceptual underpinnings of, 21–24
    dependency models and, 18, 24
    person-environment congruence and, 23
    personal characteristics and, 21, 23, 26
    proactive reaction to stress and, 21
    selective optimization with compensation and, 23
    self-initiated environment change and, 19
    successful aging definition and, 19–21
  elements of successful aging and, 24–25
    challenges to, 20, 22, 24, 28
    external resources of, 20–21, 22, 24, 32
    internal resources of, 22, 24–25, 28–30
    interrelationships of, 26–27
    outcomes of, 22, 27–28, 35
    proactive corrective adaptations of, 22, 24, 31–32
    proactive preventive adaptations of, 22, 24, 30

evaluation of
    age specificity and, 35
    continuities vs. discontinuities and, 34–35
    contributions and limitations of, 33–35
    cultural and socioeconomic variables and, 35
    dispositions vs. outcomes, 35
    empirical evidence relative to, 32–33
    outcomes vs. process variables, 34
  historical perspective on, 36, 42–43
  prevention complexities and, 43–44
  principles of, 25–26
  vs. traditional model, 41–42
  in very late life, 61
Proactive adaptation. *see* Preventive and corrective proactivity (PCP) model of aging
Prolonged grievers, 153, 154, 155
Prose recall, oldest-old study of, 52
Psycho-immune system
    depressive illness and T-cell attrition, 3, 11n. 1
    paraphrenia and, 11n. 1
    physical immune system and, 3–4
    roots of disorder and, 10
    self-esteem and trust and, 4, 29, 35
    transitional space and, 5
    *see also* Psychopathology
Psychological disorders. *see* Psychopathology
Psychological functioning, oldest-old study of, 53, 57–58, 59
Psychopathology
    comments regarding, 13–16
    development and transitional space and, 5
    psycho-immune system and, 3–5, 10
      alloplastic extroverts and, 6–8, 9, 14
      autoplastic introverts and, 8–9, 10, 14
      losing the niche and, 9–10
      transitional space and, 6–7
    qualitative stress model of, 2–3, 13
    quantitative stress model of, 1–2

Psychopathology *(continued)*
  *see also* Life course and psychiatric
    illness; Non-normative old age:
    parents of mentally retarded
    offspring; *specific disorder*
Psychosomatic disorder
  bereavement grief and, 153, 156
  late life gender transcendence and, 108
  transference breakdown and, 9
Public policy continuities and
    discontinuities
  comments regarding, 325–326
  discontinuities in, 319–321
  distribution of resources, 47, 62
  facilitating mastery and, 67
  new approach issues and
    benefits reduction and, 317–318
    disability advocacy and, 318–319,
      362–363
    new age markers and, 320
    political viability and, 316–318
    retirement age minimums and, 320
    taxes on benefits and, 316–317
    welfare approach and, 318, 320
  old-age approach erosion and,
    308–309
    Bernice Neugarten impact, 308,
      309–310, 325, 326, 361–363,
      374–375
    economic status criteria and, 308,
      314–315
    long-term care and, 309, 315–316
  oldest-old services and, 62
  political context changes and, 310–311
    apocalyptic demography and,
      312–314
    economic status of elderly and, 312
    federal budgetary limitations and,
      311–312, 362
    intergenerational equity and,
      311–312, 361–362
Public policy continuities and
    discontinuities: public support
  comments regarding, 347–348
  conclusions regarding, 342–344
  continuity of, 341–342

historical perspective on
    Congress: viewpoint of, 338–341,
      347–348
    Congress: the public and, 338–341
    economic downturn effect and,
      327–328, 348
    intergenerational equality concept
      and, 329–331, 343
    during late 1970s, 331–333
    during late 1980s, 334–337, 343

Qualified Medicare Beneficiary program,
    314–315
Quality of life
  intergenerational family relationships
    and, 292
  as model of aging, 20
  successful aging outcome of, 27

Random change model, of personality
    development, 176–177
*Rational Public* (Page and Shapiro),
    342
Reagan administration, social policy of,
    325, 359
Reasonableness
  non-normative transition study of:
    divorce, 185, 186, 187
  normative transition study of, 180–181
Reframing
  coping mechanism of, 29
  dispositional quality of, 26
Relocation, voluntary, 19, 28, 32
Reminiscence
  dramatization and, 130, 144
  by non-normative aged, 134, 135, 139,
    144
  by normative aged, 129–130, 139, 144
  parental mythicizing and, 130, 144
  past and present interchangeability in,
    129–130
  self-preservation and, 129–130, 135
Role functioning
  bereavement grief and, 153, 156
  political activism long-term effects on,
    289, 297

Role substitution, proactive corrective
adaptation of, 31
Rudman, Warren, 312

Sandwich generation, 147
Schizophrenia. *See* Life course and psychiatric illness
Self-actualization, 29
Self-concept. *see* Self-identity; Time
continuities and discontinuities:
personality development
Self-consistency concept, 126
Self-esteem
bereavement grief and, 153, 156
dispositional quality of, 26, 29, 35
late life gender transcendence and, 108
of psycho-immune system, 4
Self-identity
development of over time, 180–181,
185, 186–187, 194–195
in very old age, 125, 139
widowhood and, 154
growth through liberation case
study, 160–163
no pain, no growth case study,
163–166
Self-image. *see* Self-identity
Self-preservation
environmental mastery and, 127–129,
134–135
integrality and, 126
reminiscence and, 129–130, 135
use of religiosity and, 130–131, 135,
136–138
in very late life, 47
in youngest years, 124
*see also* Non-normative old age:
parents of mentally retarded
offspring
Self-sufficiency
by autoplastic introverts, 8–9
control and, 127–128, 139
Sensory function, oldest-old study of, 51,
56
Sibling caregiving
for schizophrenic patients, 83–84, 88

*see also* Time continuities and
discontinuities: intergenerational
relationships study; Time
continuities and discontinuities:
sibling relationships study
Sociability
non-normative transition study of:
divorce, 183, 184, 186, 187
normative transition study of, 179,
181
Social change and context. *see* Life
course and psychiatric illness
*Social Policy, Social Ethics, and the
Aging Society* (Neugarten and
Havighurst), 355, 358
Social relationships
external resource of, 32
loss of and role substitution, 31
maintenance of, 27–28
marshalling support and, 31, 33
Social Security
Congressional support of, 338, 339,
340, 341, 347
cost of living adjustments for, 338,
341, 347
cuts in, 311
of New Deal, 308
Omnibus Budget Reconciliation Act
and, 315
public support of, 334–337, 340, 341,
342, 343
Reform Act of 1983 and, 314
retirement age minimums and, 320
Tax Reform Act of 1986 and, 314
Social time
of perpetual parents, 139, 140
of schizophrenic patients, 72–74,
76–77, 86–87
*see also* Time continuities and
discontinuities: illness process
Socioeconomic status, intergenerational
transmission of, 289–291
Sociological imagination, 223
SSI (Supplemental Security Income)
Congressional support of, 339, 341
public support of, 334, 335, 341

Stability model, of adult personality
    development, 175–176
Stress
    of Alzheimer's caregivers, 191–194
    as discontinuities, 34–35
    illness as, 28, 31, 35
    increased rate of loss and, 1–2, 28, 31,
        35
    of person-environment incongruence,
        23, 28, 31, 35
    proactive reaction to, 21, 31–32
    *see also* Time continuities and discon-
        tinuities: personality development
Structural solidarity, 280
Subjective well-being
    of gender identity, 105–107
    health and memory ratings, 53
    of non-normative aged, 138–139
Substance abuse, bereavement grief and,
    153, 156
Successful aging. *see* Preventive and cor-
    rective proactivity (PCP) model of
    aging
Supplemental Security Income (SSI)
    Congressional support of, 339, 341
    public support of, 334, 335, 340

T-cell attrition, depression and, 3, 11n. 1
Time continuities and discontinuities:
    illness process
    comments regarding
        conclusions, 226–227
        reference groups and, 225–226
        social norms and, 223–224
        social roles and, 224–225
        social stratification and, 226
    conclusions regarding, 219
    family interconnectedness and,
        206–207
        developmental tasks and, 215–216
        ego integrity and, 216–217
        filial maturity and, 215
        generativity and, 216–217
        key informant loss and, 214
        parental death and, 214–215
        parents' longevity and, 215

    reference groups and, 225–226
    social norms and, 214–215
    project completion importance and,
        207, 217–219
        self continuity and, 218
        sense of control and, 217–218
        social roles and, 224–225
    schedule importance and, 206
        being off schedule, 211–213,
            223–224
        calendar time and, 209
        daily routine and, 209, 213
        functions of, 210–211
        institution microcosms and,
            211–212
        life course timetables and, 209
        life's seasons and, 209
        peership cohorts and, 210
        time structure dimensions and,
            208–209, 223–224
        treatment protocols and, 212–213
    social structure of time and, 204–206,
        223–224
    uncertainty and, 206
        life expectancy changes and, 208
        past vs. present vs. future and, 207
Time continuities and discontinuities:
    intergenerational relationships study
    comments regarding
        conceptual framework development
            and, 306–307
        data complexity, 304, 305
        dyad and family units and, 306
        intra- vs. inter-unit stability, 306
        research stimulated by, 304–305
        variability issue and, 305–306
    individual attributes and
        1960s political activism effects on,
            288–289, 297
        occupational achievement transmis-
            sion and, 289–291, 297
    literature review on, 271–272
    methods and procedures of
        attrition bias and generalizability,
            276
        data collection design, 273, 274

population and sample, 273–276
qualitative analyses, 278–279
survey measurement, 277
solidarity and individual well-being,
291
change effect on individuals,
292–297
social support of older parents, 292
solidarity stability or change and
affectual solidarity and intergenerational stake hypothesis and,
281–285, 286, 297, 305
components of, 279–281, 297
dimensions of, 279–281, 297
dimensions of, relationship among,
285, 287, 297
gender differences and, 285, 287,
297
summary and conclusions regarding,
297–298
Time continuities and discontinuities:
modified-extended families study
attachment vs. solidarity and, 269
continuities
"Army" family and, 259–260, 267
"Beachboys" family and, 263–265
"Bergers" family and, 260–261, 267
"Carrs" family and, 257–259, 267
ethnic families and, 264–266
"Expatriates" family and, 262–263,
267
family themes and values and, 267
"Firemen" family and, 261–262
geographic enclaves and, 261–263
integrated: least, 259–260
integrated: most, 257–59
"Italians" family and, 265, 267
kinkeepers and, 257, 259, 260, 261,
262, 263, 264, 267
parent-child linkage and, 257
"Resenters" family and, 263
"Separators" family and, 265–266,
267
discontinuities
"Army" family and, 253–255
"Carr" family and, 255–256

divorce and remarriages and, 251
dyadic relationships and, 252–53
household composition and,
253–256
kinkeeping and, 251
historic perspective on, 246–247
kinship bonds and, 269–270
sample demographics of, 248–250
variables selection and, 247–248
Time continuities and discontinuities:
personality development
assessment approaches to, 194–195
caregiver study and, 178, 190–191
analyses of measures of, 191–194
comments regarding
gerontology research methods and,
201
measurements used variable and,
200
multimethod approaches needed
and, 201, 202–203
self-report inventories and, 201
stability vs. change delimiters and,
202–203
timing of assessments and, 201–202
discussion regarding, 195–197
introduction to
developmental stability model of,
175–176, 196
historical perspective on, 173,
195–196
neo-trait perspective on, 174–175
orderly change model of, 176
random change model of, 176–177
theoretical guidelines regarding,
174–175
metatrait development model of,
194–195, 196
Mexican American study and, 178,
188–189
measures analyses of, 189–190
non-normative study of divorce and,
177, 182, 184
measures analyses of, 184–186
predicting change over time and,
186–188

Time continuities and discontinuities:
   personality development *(continued)*
   normative study of transitions and,
      177, 178–179
   measures of, 179–181
   predicting change over time and,
      182
Time continuities and discontinuities:
   sibling relationships study
   closeness bond and, 228
   comments regarding, 244–245
   findings of
      chronological age and demographic
         factors, 233
      closeness, 231, 233, 244
      life events, 235–242, 244–245
      patterns of change, 234–235
      sample demographics, 231, 232
   implications of, 242–243
   methods used
      interviews, 230
      variables, 230–231
   purpose of study, 229
   sample used, 229–230
Transference
   by alloplastic extroverts, 7
   by autoplastic introverts, 8
   failure of, 9–10
   primary relationships and, 7
   transitional space and, 7
Transitional space, 5
   objective social space and, 7
   psycho-immune system disorders and,
      6
Trust
   of alloplastic extroverts, 6–8
   of autoplastic introverts, 8–9
   psycho-immune system and, 4
   transitional space and, 5
Tsongas, Paul, 312
Typical grief, 153, 154, 155

Unemployment insurance
   Congressional support of, 339
   public support of, 334–335
Unhappiness

non-normative transition study of:
   divorce, 183, 184, 187
normative transition study of
   development and, 179, 181
Unitary adulthood public policy model,
   310

Very late life: study of
   acknowledgements, 62–63
   analyses, 53–54
   cognitive functioning measures used
      clock test, 52, 57
      count money, 52, 57
      *DSM-III-R* diagnosis, 51, 52–53, 57
      memory-in-reality, 52
      MMSE, 51, 52
      prose recall, 52
   comments on, 66–67
   discussion of, 46–48, 60–62
   functional health measures used
      IADLs, 51
      mobility, 50, 54, 55, 59
      PADLs, 50–51
      sensory functioning, 51
   methods used
      measures, 49–53
      procedures, 49–53
      sample and design, 48–49
   preservation of self in, 47, 124
   psychological functioning measures
      used
      depression, 53
      mastery, 53, 58, 59, 61, 67
      subjective ratings of health and
         memory, 53
   results of
      birth year significance, 58, 60
      cognitive functioning, 57
      dementia, 57–58
      IADLs, 54, 56
      mobility tasks, 55, 59
      PADLs, 55
      psychological functioning, 58–59
      sensory functioning, 56–57
   *see also* Non-normative old age: par-
      ents of mentally retarded offspring

Vision. *see* Sensory function
Voluntary relocation, 19, 28, 32,
  127–128
Vulnerability
  intergenerational support and, 292
  of schizophrenic patients, 80
  to stress, 23

Warmth
  non-normative transition study of:
    divorce, 183, 184, 186, 187
  normative transition study of, 179,
    180, 181
Ways of Coping Inventory, 191, 192
Weber, Max, 226
Well-being
  bereavement grief and, 153, 156
  family solidarity and, 291

family change and, 292–297
intergenerational social support and,
  292, 297
*see also* Intergenerational equity
*Why Survive? Being Old in America*
  (Butler), 332
Widows, widowers. *see* Adult life crises
World Health Organization, health
  defined by, 42

Young-old
  definition of, 46
  Neugarten's distinction of, 46, 61, 62,
    66, 67, 126, 309, 351, 359, 374
  of oldest-old, 61, 66–67
  *see also* Very late life

Zarit Burden Scale, 192

# Springer Publishing Company

# GENDER, IDENTITY, AND SELF-ESTEEM
## A New Look at Adult Development

### Deborah Y. Anderson, PhD
### Christopher L. Hayes, PhD

Based on findings from their original research, Drs. Anderson and Hayes explore how men and women shape, form, and integrate their identities and self-worth within the framework of the influential life-ties of family, work, friends, and education, among others.

Gender-balanced personal stories bring the text to life and help illustrate the major findings of their research. This text will be of special interest to professors and students of courses in adult development, life-span development, gender studies, and family studies.

*Contents:*

- Prologue
- Reexamination of Adult Development
- Family of Origin
- Education
- Friends and Mentors
- Intimate Relationships
- Children
- Work
- Conclusion
- Appendices

*1996   320pp (est)   0-8261-9410-9   hardcover*

536 Broadway, New York, NY 10012-3955 • (212) 431-4370 • Fax (212) 941-7842

*Springer Publishing Company*

# THE AGING INDIVIDUAL NEW
## Physical and Psychological Perspectives
**Susan Krauss Whitbourne**, PhD

In this text, Dr. Whitbourne forges a new understanding of the psychological aspects of physiological change in aging persons. This volume integrates theoretical perspectives that are needed for teaching courses in the psychology of aging. Complex biological concepts are illustrated in a clear and accessible style throughout. The book describes physical and cognitive changes as a result of the aging process and the

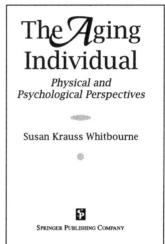

various ways that individuals age and think about their own aging. The benefits of this unique perspective will allow the reader to gain a new understanding of how biology and psychology interact in the aging individual.

*Contents:*

- Models of Identity and the Aging Process
- How Aging is Studied
- Aging of Appearance and Mobility
- Cardiovascular and Respiratory System
- Physiological Control System
- The Nervous System
- Sensation and Perception
- Cognitive Processes
- Intelligence
- Identity and Personality

*1996   328pp   0-8261-9360-9   hard   $42.95 (outside US $47.80)*

536 Broadway, New York, NY 10012-3955 • (212) 431-4370 • Fax (212) 941-7842

# 🕏 *Springer Publishing Company*

# *JOURNAL OF MENTAL HEALTH AND AGING*

**Donna Cohen**, PhD, Editor

Contributing Editor: **Carl Eisdorfer**, PhD, MD

The *Journal of Mental Health and Aging* is for the broad spectrum of mental health practitioners and researchers who work with the elderly. Professionals who are engaged in research, education and training, clinical care, social services, as well as law and policy professionals will find the journal an important source of timely and state-of-the-art information.

Dedicated to the dissemination of current research on mental health and aging studies, this peer-reviewed journal aims to bring the findings of that research to practitioners. The *Journal of Mental Health and Aging* focuses on complex issues and provides options in care delivery by applying advances in research to real-world problems. The journal offers vital and practical information that is essential to professionals, as well as provocative analyses of issues that affect the disciplines and groups that work together.

## Sample Articles

- Contemporary Issues in Mental Health and Aging  *C. Eisdorfer*
- Social Support and Compliance with Hypertensive Regimens Among the Elderly  *G. B. Fosu*
- Living Arrangements, Social Integration, and Personal Control: Correlates of Life Satisfaction Among Older People  *J. Kasper*
- An Analysis of the Global Deterioration Scale in Older Persons Applying for Community Care Services *G. Paveza, L. Jankowski, D. Cohen, S. Freels*
- Staging Functional Impairment in Dementia Using Performance-Based Measures: A Preliminary Analysis  *D.A. Loewenstein and M. P. Rubert*
- Predicting Memory Performance in Optimally Healthy Very Old Adults  *R. D. Hill, M. Grut, A. Wahlin, A. Herlitz, B. Winblad, and L. Backman*
- Ethical Issues in Long-Term Care  *Essayist: L. Polivka*
- Women as They Age: Challenge, Opportunity, Triumph  *Essayist: C. Westerhof*
- Subjective Evaluation of Self and Spousal Marital Satisfaction in Depressed and Nondepressed Couples  *Pamela Hill Epps*

*Volume 2, 1996 • 3 issues annually • ISSN 1078-4470*

536 Broadway, New York, NY 10012-3955 • (212) 431-4370 • Fax (212) 941-7842

# Springer Publishing Company

# SOCIETAL IMPACT ON AGING
## Historical Perspectives

**K. Warner Schaie,** PhD
**W. Andrew Achenbaum,** PhD, Editors

A cutting-edge exploration of the mechanisms through which society influences adult development.

### Contents:

I. **Inventing Pensions: The Origins of the Company-Provided Pension in the United States, 1900-1940.** Commentary: Pensions and Poverty: Comments on Declining Pensions

II. **The Creation of Retirement: Families, Individuals and the Social Security Movement.** Commentary: The Supply and Demand for Retirement: Sorting out the Arguments • Commentary: Family Structure, Family Income, and Incentives to Retire

III. **Over the Hill to the Poorhouse: Rhetoric and Reality in the Institutional History of the Aged.** Commentary: The Elderly and the Almshouses: Some Further Reflections • Commentary: Symbols of the Old Age Pension Movement: The Poorhouse, the Family, and the "Childlike" Elderly

IV. **The State, the Elderly, and the Intergenerational Contract: Toward a New Political Economy of Aging.** • Commentary: Intergenerational Equity and Academic Discourse • Commentary: Elderly Persons and the State: Distribution Across and Within Generations

V. **The Prophecy of *Senescence:* G. Stanley Hall and the Reconstruction of Old Age in Twentieth-Century America.** Commentary: What Became of the Prophecy of Senescence: A View from Life-Span Psychology Commentary: Aging and Prophecy: The Uses of G. Stanley Hall's *Senescence*

VI. **(When) Did the Papacy Become a Gerontocracy?** Commentary: Institutional Gerontocracies Structural or Demographic: The Case of the Papacy • Commentary on (When) Did the Papacy Become a Gerontocracy

**Afterword • Index**

*1993    280pp    0-8261-8200-3    hardcover*

536 Broadway, New York, NY 10012-3955 • (212) 431-4370 • Fax (212) 941-7842